MERRILL SCHNEIDERMAN 65 -

THE CONTEMPORARY KLEINIANS
OF LONDON

Books by Roy Schafer

Aspects of Internalization

A New Language for Psychoanalysis

Language and Insight: The Sigmund Freud Memorial
Lectures, 1975–1976, University College, London

Narrative Actions in Psychoanalysis: Narratives of Space
and Narratives of Time

The Analytic Attitude

Retelling a Life: Narration and Dialogue in Psychoanalysis

Tradition and Change in Psychoanalysis

The Contemporary Kleinians of London

Edited by

ROY SCHAFER

INTERNATIONAL UNIVERSITIES PRESS, INC.
Madison   Connecticut

INTERNATIONAL UNIVERSITIES PRESS and International Universities Press, Inc. (& design) ® are registered trademarks of International Universities Press, Inc.

Library of Congress Cataloging-in-Publication Data

The contemporary Kleinians of London / edited by Roy Schafer.
    p.   cm.
    Includes bibliographical references and index.
    ISBN 0-8236-1055-1
    1. Psychoanalysis. 2. Klein, Melanie. I. Schafer, Roy.
RC509.C624 1997
616.89'17—dc21   96-39138
                                          CIP

Manufactured in the United States of America

*Dedicated to the psychoanalysts
whose work is represented herein
for their enriching and enlivening
contributions to psychoanalysis.*

CONTENTS

PREFACE

This is a book about the contributions of a select group of contemporary London analysts. These analysts work and write within the general psychoanalytic framework established by Melanie Klein. Their contributions have been arousing worldwide interest. Psychoanalysts and psychotherapists in the United States too have begun to respond to them with curiosity, excitement, and a desire for dialogue. Although analysts elsewhere in the world have already been busily assimilating these contributions, they too may find the present collection of essays a source of further inspiration and guidance.

The British group is not hidebound. It has been introducing significant refinements into the adaptations of Freudian theory and technique first proposed by Melanie Klein and then, around midcentury, by her students and followers, among whom it is perhaps Bion and Rosenfeld who continue to stand out most. It is my hope that this volume of innovative writings by the contemporary Kleinian group will raise the level of interest in what they have to say.

I also hope to counter what I see as a growing tendency, in the United States at least, to include the work of the Kleinian group under the broad rubric "object relations analysis." That label is being used to subsume the contributions of Winnicott, along with those of his followers and modifiers, and in certain respects the contributions of interpersonal analysts and self psychologists as well. Much of this latter work has departed far from

Freud's guidelines. The contemporary Kleinians refuse to identify themselves with this loosely assembled aggregate of approaches. They emphasize that they are loyal Freudians. They
consistently focus on manifestations of transference and countertransference in conscious and unconscious phantasy. They
rely on interpretation and scrupulously attempt to avoid other
types of intervention—perhaps even more so than many more
tradition-bound Freudian ego psychologists.

The clinical examples in the papers that follow will also show
that, contrary to stereotype, these analysts remain keenly attentive to "real" circumstances and events in their patients' past,
present, and future lives, including the treatment relationship
itself; however, they systematically explore and emphasize the
unconscious meanings of these "real" details. Thus, when reporting analytic data, they generally avoid speaking decisively about
"what the case really is," "what really happened," or anything
along that line. Their eye is fixed on psychic reality, and they
approach it as being constantly in flux, so much so that they do
not allow many definitive reconstructions. For analytic purposes,
they believe that it is the unconscious phantasies about past,
present, and future relationships that matter most, and they
expect these phantasies to be played out in the transference
and countertransference. On this basis these contemporary
Kleinians rightly view themselves as much closer to Freud's psychoanalysis in its maturity than the other, clearly revisionist approaches.

A somewhat different version of Freud's mature contributions
has dominated Freudian psychoanalysis in the United States
particularly. The great postwar contributions of Hartmann, Kris,
and Loewenstein were most influential in this regard. Like them,
the modern Kleinians retain Freud's dual instinct theory, his
basic emphasis on conflict, repetition, unconscious phantasy,
defense, and countertransference, and his conviction that the
chief instrument of psychoanalysis is interpretation. Their works

differ from other current Freudian approaches by the prominence they give to the interpretation of destructive aggression
and predominantly pregenital emotional experience. They
also approach defense differently in that they highlight the
operation of such primitive defenses as splitting, projection,
introjection, and idealization. Additionally, they construe transference broadly: transference as omnipresent and always potentially accessible and usable in the analytic situation. Similarly,
they construe countertransference broadly, using it to provide
essential information about the clinical relationship. Finally,
they focus in a sustained way on pathological narcissistic phenomena associated with primitive feelings of envy, loss, and
depression.

I review all of this in greater detail in my introduction, after
which I present the set of eighteen contemporary Kleinian papers, two of which have never been published and one of which
is a substantial revision of a published work. Although each of
the essays is heavily clinical, there is a relative shift of emphasis
toward problems of technique beginning with chapter 13. Unfortunately, many other worthy contributions by other authors
as well as by those represented in these pages could not be included in this book owing both to its plan, which is to cover a
variety of central issues, and necessary limitations of length. To
those whose work I have omitted, I express my sincere regrets.

Additionally, I have prepared a short introduction to each of
the essays. I have also included a brief Epilogue. None of my introductions comes close to capturing the complexity of the issues addressed by each essay, especially those issues that will be
encountered in the many clinical examples. In these introductions I have tried to capture some of the freshness of a reader's
first encounter with the essays; to this end I do not always follow
the same course in each. Sometimes my introductions simply
highlight what I see as the chief contribution being made, sometimes I call attention to some problems or limitations that require

further thought, and sometimes I attempt to head off misunderstanding of difficult concepts. Some cross-referencing of chapters and other of my comments are designed to add continuity and coherence to the whole. The aggregate of these essays and my comments should provide the reader with a broad overview of the best modern Kleinian thinking and clinical work.

I particularly recommend careful reading of the clinical material in the essays that make up this book. Kleinian expositions have always relied heavily on examples of analytic work in progress to clarify the meaning and demonstrate the usefulness of their principal concepts and the value of their technical practices. Implicitly, they write as if inviting their readers to enter into provisional imaginative apprenticeships to their way of thinking and analyzing. That apprenticeship in the Kleinian version of psychic reality and its exploration in depth cannot fail to be rewarding.

Those readers who wish to seek further acquaintance with this valuable contemporary body of work should consult the excellent two-volume work by Spillius, *Melanie Klein Today* (1988). Other notable works are Betty Joseph's selected papers, *Psychic Equilibrium and Psychic Change* (1989); Hanna Segal's recent book of essays, *Dream, Phantasy, and Art* (1990); *Clinical Lectures on Klein and Bion* (1992); *The Oedipus Complex Today* (1988); and John Steiner's *Psychic Retreats* (1993). In all of these works, the authors' and editors' references will steer the deeply interested reader to basic sources and other significant contemporary works. Additionally, that reader can always expect to find among the articles in the *International Journal of Psycho-Analysis* worthy additions to this literature.

REFERENCES

Anderson, R., Ed. (1992), *Clinical Lectures on Klein and Bion.* London: Routledge.
Britton, R., Feldman, M., & O'Shaughnessy, E. B. (1988), *The Oedipus Complex Today. Clinical Implications.* London: Karnac.

Joseph, B. (1989), *Psychic Equilibrium and Psychic Change*. London: Routledge.

Segal, H. (1990), *Dream, Phantasy, and Art*. London: Routledge.

Spillius, E. B. (1988), *Melanie Klein Today: Developments in Theory and Practice*, Vols. 1 & 2. London: Routledge.

Steiner, J. (1993), *Psychic Retreats*. London: Routledge.

ACKNOWLEDGMENTS

I am grateful to my wife, Dr. Rita Frankiel, and to Miss Betty Joseph for encouraging me to undertake this challenging work and for their unfailingly helpful suggestions. Both personally and on behalf of The Melanie Klein Trust, Mrs. Elizabeth Bott Spillius gave generously of time and effort in gathering the necessary material and the permissions to reprint it. For their fine secretarial help I thank particularly Mrs. Barbara B. Frank and also Mrs. Victoria Wright. Dr. Margaret Emery, Editor-in-Chief of International Universities Press was most helpful in getting this book to press.

CREDITS

The author gratefully acknowledges the following publishers for their kind permission to reprint the following papers.
The Introduction was originally published in *Psychoanalytic Quarterly* 63 (1994):409–432. Copyright © 1994 The Psychoanalytic Quarterly, Inc. Reprinted by permission.
Chapter 1 was originally published in the *International Journal of Psycho-Analysis* 75 (1994):939–947. Copyright © Institute of Psycho-Analysis, London, 1994. Reprinted by permission.
Chapter 2 was originally published in the *International Journal of Psycho-Analysis* 75 (1994):1031–1040. Copyright © Institute of Psycho-Analysis, London, 1994. Reprinted by permission.
Chapter 3 is a revised version of a paper originally published in the *International Journal of Psycho-Analysis* 75 (1994):359–401. Copyright © Institute of Psycho-Analysis, London, 1994. Reprinted by permission.
Chapter 4 was originally published in *Projection, Identification, Projective Identification*, ed. J. Sandler. Madison, CT: International Universities Press, 1987, pp. 65–76. Copyright © 1987 International Universities Press. Reprinted by permission.
Chapter 5 was originally published in *Clinical Lectures on Klein and Bion*, ed. R. Anderson. London: Routledge, 1992, pp. 74–88. Copyright © 1992 Routledge. Reprinted by permission.
Chapter 6 was originally published in the *International Journal of Psycho-Analysis* 74 (1993):1199–1212. Copyright © Institute of Psycho-Analysis, London, 1993. Reprinted by permission.

Chapter 7 was originally published in the *International Journal of Psycho-Analysis* 66 (1985):273–281. Copyright © 1985 Eric Brenman. Reprinted by permission.

Chapter 8 was originally published in the *International Journal of Psycho-Analysis* 68 (1987):69–80. Copyright © Institute of Psycho-Analysis, London, 1987. Reprinted by permission.

Chapter 10 was originally published in *The Oedipus Complex Today: Clinical Implications.* London: Karnac, 1988, pp. 83–101. Copyright © 1988 H. Karnac Books Ltd. Reprinted by permission.

Chapter 11 was originally published in *Psychoanalytic Inquiry* 14 (1994):379–392. Copyright © 1994 Psychoanalytic Inquiry. Reprinted by permission.

Chapter 12 was originally published in *The Work of Hanna Segal.* London: Free Association Books, 1986, pp. 147–158. Copyright © 1986 Free Association Books Ltd. Reprinted by permission.

Chapter 13 was originally published in the *International Journal of Psycho-Analysis* 64 (1983):291–298. Copyright © 1983 Betty Joseph. Reprinted by permission.

Chapter 14 was originally published in the *International Journal of Psycho-Analysis* 74 (1993):275–285. Copyright © Institute of Psycho-Analysis, London, 1993. Reprinted by permission.

Chapter 15 was originally published in *Melanie Klein Today: Developments in Theory and Practice*, Vol. 2, *Mainly Practice*, ed. E. Bott Spillius. London: Routledge, 1988. Copyright © 1988 Routledge. Reprinted by permission.

Chapter 16 was originally published in J. Steiner, *Psychic Retreats: Pathological Organization in Psychotic, Neurotic and Borderline Patients.* London: Routledge, 1993, pp. 131–146. Copyright © 1993 Routledge. Reprinted by permission.

Chapter 17 was originally published in *Psychic Equilibrium and Psychic Change: Selected Papers of Betty Joseph*, ed. E. Bott Spillius & M. Feldman. London: Routledge, 1989, pp. 192–202. Copyright © 1989 Routledge. Reprinted by permission.

INTRODUCTION:
THE CONTEMPORARY KLEINIANS
OF LONDON

ROY SCHAFER, PH.D.

Psychoanalytic technique has developed to a remarkable extent since the time when Freud devised it. The last great wave of development was initiated by Freud when he set forth his structural theory in the 1920s in two extraordinary monographs, *The Ego and the Id* (1923) and *Inhibitions, Symptoms and Anxiety* (1926). This is not the place to review in detail all that followed under the banner of structural theory or, in its popular name, *ego psychology*, but certainly that review would feature the analysis of anxiety in connection with the infantile danger situations, guilt and the need for punishment, defense against the expression of those drive derivatives that would occasion anxiety and guilt, and negative therapeutic reactions.

In the seventy years since Freud wrote *The Ego and the Id* (1923), other notable advances have taken place in technique, unfortunately often in a fashion that can only be described as schismatic. I have in mind the various forms of object relational thinking and technique, under which heading I would include the developments initiated by Sullivan, Klein, Winnicott, and Kohut. Of this group, I have selected for discussion here those developments

1

initiated by Melanie Klein that I believe have been further developed in contemporary London to a point where they can be of value to every clinical analyst. Just as ego psychological technique is radically different from, but still continuous with, Freud's first technical efforts, so this modern Kleinian work is radically different from Melanie Klein's first work though still continuous with it.

This present phase of Kleinian analysis is represented especially well by Betty Joseph and Hanna Segal and the group working more or less in association with them. This group includes, among others, Michael Feldman, John Steiner, Edna O'Shaughnessy, Irma Brenman Pick, Elizabeth Spillius, Ruth Malcolm, Priscilla Roth, and Ronald Britton. My sketchy summary of their work should be supplemented by a reading of the thorough and lucid summary provided by Spillius in her editorial essays in the two-volume work, *Melanie Klein Today* (1988), if not a careful reading of that two-volume collection of Kleinian papers itself.[1] Summarizing this mode of work is hampered by the fact that, characteristically, this group presents their ideas mainly by way of clinical examples, and to benefit from these examples, one must study them in full. I shall present one of these examples later on and follow it up with some comments of my own on the theoretical and methodological implications of this mode of analytic work. These comments bear particularly on ego psychology, oedipal sexuality, and reconstruction. If nothing else, I hope to counteract a widespread but by now especially ill-fitting stereotype of Kleinian work that deters many analysts in this country from studying that work carefully. We must keep in mind, however, that, as in all groups, there is considerable variation in formulation and practice among contemporary Kleinians and some variation even within the cutting-edge subgroup I shall be dwelling on.

---

[1]This two-volume work contains an excellent bibliography of works through which are dispersed the contributions of the numerous Kleinian authors referred to throughout this discussion.

For the sake of brevity, I shall be referring mostly to "these Kleinians" or, for reasons I shall present later, "the Kleinian Freudians." My purpose is to distinguish this group from the Kleinians of South America and other parts of the world whose technical work and thinking is, on my understanding, different enough to warrant a different presentation.

THE PARANOID–SCHIZOID AND DEPRESSIVE
POSITIONS IN THE INTERNAL WORLD

The overall framework within which these Kleinians work is constituted by two fundamental psychological positions. Implicitly or explicitly, individual instances of clinical phenomena are always characterized within this framework. These two positions are the paranoid–schizoid and the depressive. They are positions in the internal world; they do not point to observable clinical syndromes. They are prototypes in the clinician's mind of the types and degrees of adaptive object relatedness and madness that characterize the analysand's internal world at any moment. These Kleinians do recognize problems stemming from the external world, but they take them up almost entirely in terms of what they imply about current, influential unconscious fantasies. Far from assuming that this internal world is all there is to human existence, they pay close attention to what is selectively emphasized about the external world, and they use that observation to understand the analysand better and to derive effective interventions from that understanding. Thus, the external world is treated in the consulting room rather like the manifest content of a dream: as an arena in which the problems of the internal world are represented and played out.

These Kleinians usually view their analysands either as lodged somewhere between these two basic positions or as fluctuating desperately between the two. In the most general sense, they understand this "stuckness" or flux as the analysand's being confronted in his or her internal world by two painful possibilities, the first being the persecutory anxiety that is outstanding in the paranoid–schizoid position, and the second, the guilt and feelings of devastation in the depressive position. In the paranoid–schizoid position the focus is very much on aggression or self and other directed destructiveness, much of it in the form of envy and fear of envy, and on grandiosity, while in the depressive position the focus is on love, understanding, concern, reparation, desire, and various other forms of regard for the object as well as on destructiveness and guilt.

The paranoid–schizoid position is also characterized by typical defenses such as splitting and projective identification; the depressive position, by regression (to the paranoid–schizoid), flight to a manic position featuring denial and idealization of self and other, or bondage to a reparative position relative to the imagined damaged objects. Mature functioning rests on one's having attained an advanced phase of the depressive position in which object love and sublimatory activity are relatively stable; however, regressive pulls are never absent.

In these general respects, contemporary Kleinians follow the story line laid down by Melanie Klein and elaborated by her contemporaries and later followers, especially Joan Riviere, Susan Isaacs, Paula Heimann, Wilfred Bion, Herbert Rosenfeld, and Hanna Segal. They differ from Klein in their deemphasizing and deferring detailed reconstruction of early developmental history. They prefer instead to stay, for as long as possible, close to, almost fixed to, the shifts of unconscious fantasy in the here-and-now clinical situation and most of all in the transference. Early developmental experiences with parents are usually taken up in a general way and even then mostly in terms of how they were experienced. These Kleinians further differ from Melanie Klein in their emphasis on induced countertransference as an invaluable form of communication or at least as a source of information. Specifically, they try as far as possible to understand countertransference in terms of projective identification, that is, the analysand's unconsciously allocating to the analyst negative or positive aspects of his or her own self or other internal objects in order to get rid of them, use them for control of others, or protect them from internal destructiveness; however, these analysts do not then blind themselves to the analyst's own irrational, disturbing, and self-initiated countertransferences. They take that aspect of analytic work as requiring no special emphasis by them.

In connection with these shifts away from Klein in particular, these Kleinians no longer consistently or prominently emphasize bodily organs as primitively conceived part objects representing total relationships (e.g., the devouring breast). They focus much more on what might be called organ modes such as taking in or emptying out, and also on functions such as thinking, understanding, connecting, remembering. In general, they use terms that correspond closely to conventional experience in human relationships, such as *hope, despair, dependency, denial,* and *idealization.* Additionally, they no longer engage in rapid-fire, symbol-laden interpretations of whatever manifest content comes their way, being rather measured in the speed and quantity of their interpretations, as well as oriented toward gathering immediate evidence on which to base each aspect of their interventions. They favor "showing" over "telling" what's what.

Because these Kleinians seem to find signs of transference in everything, I shall discuss next this way of looking at events in the analytic session. In order to do so, it will be necessary to take up as well countertransference, projective identification, containment, and enactment, for these concepts are intertwined with here-and-now transference analysis.

TRANSFERENCE, COUNTERTRANSFERENCE, PROJECTIVE
IDENTIFICATION, CONTAINMENT, ENACTMENT

Transference

Transference is approached as ubiquitous in the clinical situation. The term is used to refer to the totality of the relationship.

Everything the analysand says is scrutinized for what it indicates about the momentary state of the transference. Pretty consistently, though not necessarily in a steady stream, interpretations are addressed to this transference. This technical practice is based on several assumptions that, although they are somewhat different from the standard Freudian ones, are not alien either.

It is assumed, first, that whatever the analysand says or does rests on a substructure of unconscious fantasies, and analysis proceeds by interpreting these fantasies at propitious moments and appropriate levels. For example, a reference to a calamitous political situation might point to a calamity in the internal world. It is also assumed that the analysand's saying or doing anything in the analytic situation implies something about her or his experience of the relationship with the analyst. For example, that internal world calamity might well refer to some profound disruption of rapport in which the analyst is now suddenly experienced as a loved object damaged by hostile feelings, whereupon the patient begins to feel devastated. That calamitous state of world affairs may have been alluded to in order to make the point that the analyst's absence has caused things to change between them; alternatively, it may be a seductive invitation to the analyst to do something restorative, a positive provocation of guilt, or an expression of despair. Thus, this second assumption about implied transference covers the analysand's ideas about the analyst's attitudes and how these attitudes have been or should be modified in order to fit better into unconscious fantasy.

Third, it is assumed that rather than highlighting what is conventionally realistic, adaptive, and role-appropriate, the analyst's interventions should more or less subordinate these details to interpretation of the unconscious transference fantasies by showing how these "realistic" factors are being used seductively, offensively, or defensively as vehicles or props. For example, an analyst's devastating act may have been a seemingly matter-of-fact observation of some detachment in the analysand's position which was, however, experienced by the analysand as a harsh criticism and intolerant demand. Here, a so-called real event did take place; what matters, however, is how it was experienced in unconscious fantasy or psychic reality, and it is that experience that should be the focus of the interpretation.

All three of these assumptions often figure in standard Freudian interventions, too; however, the standard Freudians prefer to use the term *transference* more narrowly to refer to a somewhat more organized, complex, more or less stable, and fairly repetitive pattern of relationship based on experienced relationships with significant figures from earlier life. To these Freudians, the Kleinian usage often seems indiscriminate, wild, or so diffuse as to lose value or meaning. On their part, the Kleinian Freudians postulate that all relationships involve unconscious fantasy and so may be considered to be mediated through the internal world, which, for them, is made up of more or less primitive object relations. Consequently, the interplay with the analyst amounts to a second step, the first being *projection* from the internal world. In contrast, the standard Freudians often or usually interpret transference as a direct *displacement* from an object representation to the analyst—perhaps a representation distorted by projection but not, to begin with, itself a projection (see Arlow's [1993] recent discussion of transference.)

Countertransference

The Kleinian Freudians assume that unconscious fantasies regularly figure in the thinking of the analyst; however, these fantasies and the feelings associated with them need not be treated as neurotic or psychotic invasions of the analytic process. Rather, unless the analyst is profoundly thrown off, they are to be taken as indications that, unconsciously, the analyst has received certain communications from the analysand about his or her experience of the analytic relationship. Even if these are not intended as communications, then at least they are actions that, unconsciously, are freighted with transference meaning. Thus, in the example I just gave of an unconscious transference of a calamity, the analyst's cue might be an impulse to be reassuring or a sense of impatience with the analysand's seeming hypersensitivity. In contrast, the standard Freudians tend to regard these phenomena as affect signals so that they can reserve the term *countertransference* for personally disturbed responses on the analyst's part. On the whole, however, it is my impression that the standard Freudians, too, would use "affect signal" or perhaps "role responsiveness" as a cue to what the analysand is experiencing or intending in the transference, and perhaps as well a cue as to how the analyst is being provocative actually or in fantasy. In my view, therefore, they would be functioning much as the Kleinians do in this respect.

Projective Identification

The mechanism of these countertransference-inducing communications is generally understood to be a defensive use of projective identification. Projective identification is projection, as usually understood by standard Freudians, but with this big difference: it is conceived in terms of unconscious fantasy content of an object-related nature. That is to say, it centers on an aspect of the self or an internal object that is ascribed to another person in fantasy, in behavior, and in other subtle forms of communication. In the clinical situation, for example, the analyst may be experienced as a critical figure after an internal critic has been projected "into" the analyst. In projective identifications, there are often implications of imagined control of the object through locking it into this role, perhaps with the support of fantasies of omnipotence. In response, the analyst may begin to feel controlled or even *be* controlled, as though possessed by an introject.

Kleinian interpretations of projective identification do not necessarily include explicit attempts to develop connections between, on the one hand, the part object or partial self projected from the internal world, and on the other, past experience with a specific person in "real life"; instead, the emphasis on the moment may be sustained and developed at length. The analytic work proceeds by close scrutiny of such revealing moments. Also to be noted is protective projection, an essential constituent of empathy. Usually, defensive splitting precedes the projective identification so that the term implies fragmentation into good and bad parts of the self or the object or both.

In cases of nonempathic or "pathological" projective identification, the person is likely to experience blurring of the lines between self and object, perhaps with some confusion, and additionally some feeling of the self emptying out or perhaps being imprisoned within the object. Hinshelwood (1989, pp. 178–208) has provided a relatively up-to-date extensive abstract of the literature on projective identification.

Containment

Containment is commonly implied in projective identification. In the transference, the analyst is now unconsciously the container of some concretized aspect of the analysand's internal world; for example, it may be that critical, personified aspect of the self that I mentioned. For a time, the analyst may accept this containing function and defer interpreting it. She or he may do so in recognition of the patient's feeling too fragile to reintroject the self-criticism, which would be the consequence or at least the threat were the projective identification to be interpreted just then. In such an instance, the analysand might experience the interpretation as a passing of abusive judgment and as the analyst's really acting sadomasochistically. In contrast, tactful and timely interpretation may serve to ease the analysand's burden by tempering what has been projected; interpretation shows that the content has been processed by the analyst on a higher level and found not to be devastatingly exciting, painful, or destructive. It is recognized that this is not invariably the result at the moment; it is, however, thought that analytic progress depends on this kind of result. Containing is not used in the sense of setting limits; on the contrary, it has more to do with being patient, tolerant, and steadfast.

On their part, analysands may fantasize being the containers of their analysts. We hear or infer this incorporative phenomenon before or after separations from the analyst, the analysands having continued to feel their analyst's presence, for better or for worse. (Bion's work has been especially important in this area, as it has been in the area of projective identification.) When the analyst's countertransference gets out of hand, he or she is very likely to use the patient as a container for projective identifications of desire, coldness, cruelty, or whatever, just as parents often do in relation to their children.

Enactment

Enactment is another necessary concept in this context of close-up transference–countertransference analysis. Enactments need not be gross. They may be as simple as the analyst's getting too absorbed in analyzing a particular content of communication while losing sight of the indications that, for example, the analysand is putting that content forward to induce the analyst to speak. In this case, the analyst may be being made to speak as a way of eliciting a reassuring show of interest, a sign of having survived damaging attacks, or a proof of still being on the attack in her or his assigned sadistic role. In other instances, to cite only two of them, the enactment may take the form of the analysand's pseudostupidity as a seduction of the analyst to do all the thinking in the room, or the form of the analyst's becoming actively and directively supportive when only containment and deeper understanding are called for.

Because enactments are inevitable and, when analyzed, highly informative of currents in the transference and countertransference, constant vigilance is required both to detect the pertinent signs and to put them to good use. It is impressive how these Kleinian analysts listen to all possible aspects of their analysands' associations *and* their own responses *and* their analysands' responses to their interventions: the where, how, when, and why as well as the what of these communications. Their sense of dialogue is developed to a very high point.

Consider the example of a male patient who presents a tale of having been helplessly victimized, and does so in a way that involves groping for words and struggling to remember related incidents. In this case, the Kleinian Freudian might understand it as an enactment of helplessness in the transference designed to induce in the analyst the countertransference of wanting to step in helpfully or reassuringly by filling in, tying up, and explaining. In this case, this analysand will have been trying to effect a projective identification of his more capable or thinking self—his mind—into the analyst. The analyst might decide, perhaps only after having started down that road before realizing it, to show the analysand that, through projective identification, he is trying to bring about that achievement of personal mindlessness. The interpretation might go on to emphasize the temporal aspect of this interaction, for example, that the analysand is telling this tale in this helpless way after having proudly reported a special achievement and then having begun to fear that this report constituted too much of a damaging attack on the analyst, whereupon he was compelled to enact some restorative helplessness in order to make up for the damage or to get some guilt-relieving reassurance in the form of an unimpaired interpretation. In the continuation of this interchange, the analysand may fail to understand this very intervention by the analyst, or may experience a sense of being deeply understood and freer to make manifest his assets.

Now, in a general way this kind of intervention, too, is not alien to the work of standard Freudians; pertinent examples may be found in many places in our literature. What is important for us to note here is how steadily and acutely these Kleinians emphasize this aspect of the total situation. In this respect the standard Freudians can try to fault them only for overdoing it or overreacting. But in this day and age of multiple approaches, who, I would ask, can still claim absolute analytic authority to pass such a judgment? Differing worlds of analytic work develop their own criteria of validity and thereby defend and assert their own identities. Sweeping rejections are usually exercises of political power rather than demonstrations of analytic sagacity.

Before turning to the clinical example, a word should be said about the place of affect theory in the writings of these Freudian Kleinians. My brief remarks on this topic will continue to be cast in a comparative mode. Freud and those who have developed further his metapsychological enterprise proceeded on the assumption that affect is one of the two "presentations" of the instinctual drives, the other being ideation (Freud, 1915b). Affect corresponded to the energic or quantitative aspect of drives and was a direct or indirect discharge phenomenon. Especially after Freud presented his developmental scheme for anxiety in *Inhibitions, Symptoms and Anxiety* (1926), the way was open for developmental approaches to affective life (Rapaport, 1953; Jacobson, 1971). In recent years ego psychological analysts have increasingly recognized that affects must be conceptualized as having cognitive components, which is to say that they express reactions to experienced situations and so always imply ideational content.

My understanding of the current approach to affect by the Kleinian Freudians is that they deal with affect always in terms of experienced situations. In particular, they focus on experienced vicissitudes of self and objects primarily in the internal world of unconscious fantasy. They continue to give anxiety and guilt central places in developmental theory, but adding depression and envy as factors of equal importance. As well as these, they use the familiar list of love, hate, grief, rage, jealousy, and so on, typically in settings of ambivalence and defense against painful and destabilizing emotional experience. Their conception of envy starts with the first stages of psychic development; depression, a fundamental reference point, is conceived as having significant loving and reparative implications.

Clinical Example

I have chosen my extended example from Betty Joseph's paper on projective identification (1987). I quote from her:

> A patient, N., who had been in analysis many years, had recently married and, after a few weeks, was becoming anxious about his sexual interest and potency, particularly in view of the fact that his wife was considerably younger. He came on a Monday, saying that he felt that "the thing" was never really going to get right, "the sexual thing," yes, they did have sex on Sunday, but somehow he had to force himself and he knew it wasn't quite all right, and his wife noticed this and commented. It was an all right kind of weekend, just about. He spoke about this a bit more and explained that they went to a place outside London, to a party, they had meant to stay the night in a hotel nearby, but couldn't find anywhere nice enough and came home and so were late.
>
> What was being conveyed to me was quiet, sad discomfort, leading to despair, and I pointed out to N. how he was conveying an awful long-term hopelessness and despair, with no hope for the future. He replied to the effect that he supposed that he was feeling left out, and linked this with what had been a rather helpful and vivid session on the Friday, but now, as he made the remark, it was quite dead and flat. When I tried to look at this with him, he agreed, commenting that he supposed he was starting to attack the analysis, and so on. The feeling in the session now was awful; N. was making a kind of sense and saying analytic things himself, which could have been right—for example, about the

Friday—and which one could have picked up, but, since they seemed flat and quite unhelpful to him, what he seemed to me to be doing was putting despair into me, not only about the reality of his marriage and potency, but also about his analysis, as was indicated, for example, by the useless, and by now somewhat irrelevant, comment about being left out. N. denied my interpretation about his despair about the progress of the analysis, but in such a way, it seemed to me, as to be encouraging me to make false interpretations and to pick up his pseudo-interpretations as if I believed in them, while knowing that they and we were getting nowhere. He vaguely talked about this, went quiet, and said: "I was listening to your voice, the timbre changes in different voices. W. (his wife), being younger, makes more sounds per second, older voices are deeper because they make less sounds per second, etc." I showed N. his great fear that I showed with my voice, rather than through my actual words, that I could not stand the extent of his hopelessness and his doubts about myself, about what we could achieve in the analysis and, therefore, in his life, and that I would cheat and in some way try to encourage. I queried whether he had perhaps felt that, in that session, my voice had changed in order to sound more encouraging and encouraged, rather than contain the despair he was expressing. By this part of the session my patient had got into contact and said with some relief that, if I did this kind of encouraging, the whole bottom would fall out of the analysis [pp. 175–176].

In this paper Joseph returns to this material several times in order to integrate and further develop her analysis. She discusses how, instead of asking her to understand, this man was trying to invade her with despair while at the same time to get her to try to reassure herself that meaningful work was going on rather than empty interaction. Thus, he was also projecting into her his defenses of false reassurance and denial, defenses probably modeled on a weak maternal figure in his internal world. Her responding differently then gave him a basis to identify with a stronger object so that he could be firmer himself, and also concerned for her and somewhat guilty as part of a shift ahead toward the depressive position. In the next session, however, he brought a dream, the analysis of which led to the interpretation that he was reacting against this progressive shift and preferring to drown in despair and reject the goodness that had been offered by her understanding. At this point she was supposed to feel hopeless and impotent to help him, and he could restore his identification with that defeated figure.

In view of her impression that the patient made such liberal use of projective identification, Joseph tries to leave open just how weak the maternal figure really was. At the base of that projective emphasis, she surmises, was a wish to get back into the object in an undifferentiated state where he would be mindless and free of pain. She infers this by observing his having become so absorbed in his own words and ideas as well as in the sound of her voice that he rendered meaning itself unimportant. Along the way, she refers also to other aspects of this material pertaining to hostility, sexual arousal, masochism, and omnipotent strivings. In the end she presents an extremely complex analysis that gets well beyond any routine understanding of a negative therapeutic reaction.

Ego Psychology

With this introductory survey and these examples behind us, I go on now to argue my view that this mode of Kleinian work implies and implements an ego psychology of a kind that differs from the one that standard Freudians (especially in the United States) habitually call by that name. It is ego psychological in the following ways. First, it constantly emphasizes the status and use of ego functions in reality relations and intrapsychic operations as well as the invasion of these functions and relations by unconscious fantasy—what we might otherwise call instinctualization and regression. Thus, levels of cognitive function figure prominently in this contemporary Kleinian work;

one sees this focus perhaps most of all in the distinction drawn between the concreteness of primitive mental processes and what, following Bion, is called thinking, which is to say, cognition that features understanding use of verbal signs and symbols. In concrete mental processes, words, sentences, and entire communications function rather as objects so that they may be shattered or be regarded as poisonous, excremental, or nourishing.

There is an ego psychology in the kind of intersubjective and situational focus maintained on transference and countertransference. Here, formulations are, as I mentioned earlier, usually cast in the terms of familiar and conventional conscious discourse about human relations (envy, anxiety, grief, dependency, etc.). Instinct theory remains very much in the background and surfaces only occasionally, typically in introductory and summarizing discussions of cases. Although these Kleinians still pay homage to the overarching concept of a death instinct, they do not do so in any emphatic way, and it is clear that they are talking about rage and destructiveness when they say "death instinct," whatever else those words might mean to them. This aspect of their approach is not so different from that of today's standard Freudians; their presentations, too, no longer center explicitly on the disposition of libidinal and aggressive drive energies, though they would not disavow the concepts of libido and aggression.

Further on ego psychology: I've already mentioned that there is now little emphasis on "part object" references to bodily organs. Also mentioned earlier is that we find few detailed, elaborate reconstructions of early infantile events of the preverbal past. In this present mode of work, the past is not usually emphasized as the "place" where all mysteries will be solved. In the consulting room, it hardly seems that there is a past; instead, the past is customarily part of present discourse, references to it by the analysand always being examined for the function they serve in inner-world unconscious fantasy concerning the here-and-now transference and countertransference. Sometimes these unconscious fantasies get to be successfully actualized through some successful manipulation of the analyst or through the analyst's own poor understanding or narcissistically motivated blunders; more often they are taken up as the analysand's constructions of the present in psychic reality and enactment.

Furthermore, these Kleinians are centrally oriented to the analysis of defense. Among the defenses, they put special emphasis on splitting, denial, projection, introjection, idealization, identification used as a defense, and repression. Although in many instances the dynamic content dealt with defensively is not that usually emphasized in traditional Freudian writings, neither is it utterly alien, as any broad survey of our literature will show. Also to be noted in this regard is that the Kleinian analysis of defense usually takes up both defense and the motivation for defense; that is, the danger situations. These dangers are, however, conceived in somewhat different but not utterly alien terms. Specifically, the Kleinians emphasize a variety of dangers associated with experiences of destructiveness, persecution, or depression, and the annihilation of the self or ego looms large as an ultimate catastrophe.

Next, I would emphasize something I pointed out in an earlier communication (Schafer, 1968).[2] These Kleinians do not exclude fantasy content from their conception of defense mechanisms, seeing splitting, for instance, as also a destructive act; in this respect they make clear that their ego psychology, unlike the conventional structural–functional one, is also a dynamic theory of the ego. We should remember that, already in 1926 and as part of his introduction of structural theory, Freud had

---

[2]See also my "Commentary" on a group of new Kleinian papers (1994), for related comments, both appreciative and critical, on this branch of analytic work.

ascribed dynamic, unconscious fantasy content to the mechanisms of defense (e.g., isolation as a prevention of dangerous touching).

Further, just as superego factors are regularly part of traditional Freudian ego psychology, they are also that in contemporary Kleinian work. There, however, we find not so much reliance on the terms *atonement* and *undoing* as on *reparation*. The emphasis on reparation underscores the love or concern for the object that these Kleinians see as a vital and potentially constructive setting for guilt reactions in the depressive position; by contrast, the traditional Freudians present guilt in a more narcissistic and simply self-punitive light. For these Kleinians, therefore, superego action is always personified, never the abstract code that Freud conceptualized as the endpoint of superego development.

Finally to be emphasized in this ego psychological connection is that, when presenting case material, these Kleinians typically rely on, but do not make a point of, commonsense understanding. Consequently, they are puzzled and sometimes even bridle when critics suggest that they are ignoring certain patent realities of the patient's past and present life or of the clinical situation, or that they bypass the idea that countertransference may have prominent neurotic or psychotic features. "Don't you think we know that?!" they seem to say, "We are talking about work not warped by these factors, that is, we are talking about the psychoanalytic process when it can be considered to be going on as it should." Thus, in this respect, too, these analysts are not so different from traditional Freudians, for they also take many commonsense considerations for granted unless something is very much out of line. Unlike the traditional Freudians, however, these Kleinians just do not seem to see a need to theorize, or to theorize at any length, all these homespun issues, for they do not aim toward a general psychology. This narrower attitude toward theorizing has its problematic side, which I shall take up later on.

By now it may be clearer why I have used the designation "Kleinian Freudians." It is because I see the Kleinian work in the way that the Kleinians themselves see it, that is, as a development out of the heart of Freud's thinking. Although some of their basic theoretical references go back particularly to what Freud wrote in "Instincts and Their Vicissitudes" (1915a) and *Beyond the Pleasure Principle* (1920), their theory is on the whole better grounded in Freud than is commonly recognized. It is, I think, correct to say that we are considering here another branch of Freudian thought. It is not an artificial graft on the Freudian tree, and it is not a cluster of destructive vines on it.

CRITICAL REMARKS

I come now to some concluding observations, suggestions, and criticisms of the work I have been sketching. Like what has come before, however, these concluding remarks are hardly more than signposts of important problems to be confronted in relation to these Kleinian advances in clinical work.

1. These Kleinians remain objectivist or realist in their phenomenology. They consistently present their material as though they are in the position of purely independent observers—even of their own countertransferences. To my mind, this is contrary to what one might expect from the object relational point of view, which would seem inherently to favor a dialogic rather than objectivist idea of the material being analyzed. By "dialogic" I mean put into words and developed jointly by analysand and analyst in their interchanges (Schafer, 1992). They, however, maintain a steadily factual or realist tone throughout their writings; they "discover" rather than "coauthor." In this respect, they do not differ from standard Freudians. Neither group does much to acknowledge divergent points of view, that is, to practice what I call comparative analysis (Schafer, 1985).

2. As I see it, these Kleinians have not adequately developed a position on matters of importance in standard Freudian

structural and functional theory. For example, beyond some dynamic propositions, they do not concern themselves sufficiently with such key questions as what enables their analysands to answer with more or less stable understanding to interpretations. I have tried to show that they do put a lot of emphasis on the motives, mechanisms, and fantasies that interfere with the reception and understanding of what the analyst imparts to them. But because their paranoid–schizoid and depressive positions are presented as all-encompassing, even if with adaptive potential, there is no well-developed theoretical provision for what standard Freudians call the observing ego and the ego's synthesizing function; that is, the analyst's structurally and functionally stable and intact collaborator and dialogical partner in the process. In this connection, the Kleinians do not draw systematic distinctions between self concepts and ego concepts; using them rather interchangeably, they speak comfortably about attacks on the ego, the self, even the mind, in a way that refers in part to actual functional disturbances and in part to unconscious fantasies of the ego, self, or mind being a substance that can be ejected, spoiled, or broken into pieces. The concretistic fantasy of mind is not foreign to any analyst who works on primitive levels of function, but fantasy is not systematic theory, and primitive dynamics cannot account adequately for secondary process communication and organization.

Although it can therefore be argued that significant aspects of their work is undertheorized, it is not at all clear that at this stage of creative endeavor comprehensive systematization should be emphasized; the model set by Heinz Hartmann (1964) is, in general, no longer a major influence in psychoanalysis. Also, variations of function can be taken up in terms of fantasy, too.

3. More and more, these Kleinian Freudians deemphasize reconstruction. Going further, I would say that they seem to deemphasize causal explanations of any sort. Not that they scrupulously avoid these formulations or condemn them, but

primarily they remain intent on developing explicitly the phenomenology of the internal world and the way it is played out in relations with the external world. They fear that otherwise they might interpret before they truly understand, and this, I would say, is a well-taken caution. One sign of this shift of emphasis away from explanation is that, in their case presentations, they do not develop accounts that warrant the designation "life histories." Typically, the examples of work they present are in midstream, and we do not get much of an account of the preceding analytic process and its place in overall history. Thus, they seem to follow the guidelines laid down by Bion (1967): to approach each session so far as possible "without memory or desire." I believe that this restricted emphasis on the present, technically and interpretively, pushes other aspects of the analytic context out of sight and leaves their readers with too many unanswered questions.

Further to this point, I believe that Bion's advice makes a good deal of sense so long as it is not examined too closely; in his own way, Freud had already recommended the same basic approach when encouraging bending one's own unconscious to the patient's. More closely examined, however, the advice clearly misrepresents the mind of any analyst working with an analysand about whom a good deal has already been formulated and in relation to whom a good deal has already been experienced. And this is not yet to speak of theoretical orientation and therapeutic aims, however well regulated they may be. Nor is it to speak of all those benign and malignant countertransferential aims that require constant monitoring. Finally, thinking causally and retrospectively is probably impossible to suspend altogether; certainly, this is so for the short term, and probably it is indispensable in organizing any significant intervention, however phenomenologically cast it may be.

4. Characteristically, these Kleinians view their analysands, including those who diagnostically would not be put in any

seriously disturbed group, as struggling with many unresolved primitive issues associated with the paranoid–schizoid and early depressive positions. By implication, then, it is as if the analysands are struggling with problems that date from their earliest years. Consequently, the prototypical objects they refer to in their interpretations tend to be the mother of unconscious fantasy with her baby or toddler though sometimes also an undifferentiated parental couple. Similarly, the prototypical issues and modes of relationship tend to center around primitive experiences of pain, goodness and badness, anxiety, dependency, loss, abandonment, and the like.

In the current life details in their published process notes, however, their analysands often come across much like those presented in papers written by members of other schools of psychoanalytic thought. That is to say, the analysands are often preoccupied with their sexual relationships, usually heterosexual desire, love and its frustrations, and sometimes with similar homosexual issues. Triangulations, ambitions, and feelings of inadequacy, damagedness, and undesirability are also common. But the Kleinian analyst's interventions tend to reduce this material rather quickly to what the standard Freudians would call the pregenital or preoedipal levels of experience and organization. Consequently, there is precious little development of the analysis of conventionally oedipal sexual conflict in and of itself. Although, in working through problems of the paranoid–schizoid and depressive positions, the analyst may take note of the analysand's developing a reliable capacity for love and concern and a readiness for sexual gratification, and although he or she may refer to an early form of the oedipus complex, that analyst may still treat genital matters much as the manifest content of a dream should be treated, that is, primarily as a pathway to unconsciously dyadic issues.

On their part, however, contemporary Freudians have been paying much more attention to the preoedipal or pregenital, dyadic foundations of the Oedipus complex and its disturbances. They also keep a sharp eye out for signs of early oedipal developments as well as disruptions of early ego and superego development and the stable and constant object relations that should be beginning to evolve. In this, they move closer to the Kleinians. Rather characteristically, however, they seem to me to try to work with *both* dynamic levels, that is, to maintain an optimally flexible position with regard to the dynamic level most appropriate to take up at any given time. In any event, they would not be so quickly reductive as the Kleinians, which is to say that they would not be so quick to view conventional sexuality with suspicion as probably being emphasized for defensive purposes in order to avoid the larger issues appropriate to the paranoid–schizoid and depressive positions. Consequently, in my view, the standard Freudian phenomenology and patterning of sexual experience is more developed even if not always appropriately applied and even if still, and far too often, quite limited in its departure from a narrow oedipal approach.

How does this Kleinian focus on the primitive tie in with these Kleinians' deemphasis of reconstruction? Much of their argument seems to depend on the idea that accounts of the past or of events outside the consulting room, even those in the immediate present, are unreliable. These accounts are not necessarily false; rather, patients are probably presenting them as props in order to develop an emotional position vis-à-vis the analyst. Consequently, one cannot be sure of having a rounded or balanced or comprehensive picture or what, in ordinary terms, would be accepted as the actual life history or the actual present life situation or even a specific other person. I believe that there is much to recommend this policy of suspicion or suspended judgment. Remaining with this moment-to-moment work is essential in the opening up of significant themes and the establishment of communication that resonates with the deep emotional experiences of hitherto inaccessible analysands. I believe that standard Freudians in general take a similar view of the unreliability or undecidability of "case history" material, and yet in their published reports they often seem to forget their appropriate reservations in this regard.

5. Finally, taken in its entirety, we can see that this Kleinian approach is so centered on the dynamic present, and on issues of relatedness and the many forms of dialogue, that it allows these Kleinians much narrative freedom in writing up their cases for publication. We can tell that this is so from the titles of many of their papers. In Betty Joseph's work, for example, we find such titles as "The Patient Who Is Difficult To Reach," "Addiction to Near-Death," "On Understanding and Not Understanding." Other titles from this group of workers emphasize resonance, reassurance, retreats, enclaves, and so on. This narrative freedom becomes most evident within the bodies of Kleinian Freudian papers where the theme announced in the title becomes and remains an organizing principle. On their part, standard Freudians no longer systematically avoid colorful experiential titles, but usually they practice more reserve in the body of their papers, as though to demonstrate that they are scientifically sound and safely neutral. Consequently, and as an extra bonus, these Kleinian Freudians are, I think, usually more engaging writers, and, in this stage of the evolution of psychoanalysis, they can have a liberating and invigorating effect on the reader as well as helping him or her work with patients with greater acuity and depth.

REFERENCES

Arlow, J. A. (1993), Transference as a compromise defense. Presented to the meeting of the Psychoanalytic Association of New York, January.

Bion, W. R. (1967), Notes on memory and desire. *Psychoanal. Forum,* 2:272–275, 279–280. Also in *Melanie Klein Today,* Vol. 2, ed. E. B. Spillius. London: Routledge, 1988, pp. 17–21.

Freud, S. (1915a), Instincts and their vicissitudes. *Standard Edition*, 14:109–140. London: Hogarth Press, 1957.

——— (1915b), Repression. *Standard Edition*, 14:141–158. London: Hogarth Press, 1957.

——— (1920), Beyond the pleasure principle. *Standard Edition*, 18:7–64. London: Hogarth Press, 1955.

——— (1923), The ego and the id. *Standard Edition*, 19:19–27. London: Hogarth Press, 1961.

——— (1926), Inhibitions, symptoms and anxiety. *Standard Edition*, 20:74–174. London: Hogarth Press, 1959.

Hartmann, H. (1964), *Essays on Ego Psychology: Selected Problems in Psychoanalytic Theory*. New York: International Universities Press.

Hinshelwood, R. D. (1989), *A Dictionary of Kleinian Thought*. London: Free Association Books.

Jacobson, E. (1971), *Depression. Comparative Studies of Normal, Neurotic, and Psychotic Conditions*, Chapters 1 and 2. New York: International Universities Press.

Joseph, B. (1987), Projective identification: clinical aspects. In: *Projection, Identification, Projective Identification*, ed. J. Sandler. Madison, CT: International Universities Press, pp. 65–76. Also in *Psychic Equilibrium and Psychic Change: Selected Papers of Betty Joseph*, ed. E. B. Spillius & M. Feldman. London: Tavistock/Routledge, 1989, pp. 168–180.

Rapaport, D. (1953), On the psycho-analytic theory of affects. *Internat. J. Psychoanal.*, 34:177–198.

Schafer, R. (1968), The mechanisms of defense. *Internat. J. Psychoanal.*, 49:49–62.

——— (1985), Wild analysis. *J. Amer. Psychoanal. Assn.*, 33:275–299.

——— (1992), *Retelling a Life: Narration and Dialogue in Psychoanalysis*. New York: Basic Books.

——— (1994), Commentary. *Psychoanal. Inq.*, 14:462–475.

Spillius, E. B., Ed. (1988), *Melanie Klein Today*, Vols. 1, 2. London: Routledge.

EDITOR'S INTRODUCTION TO
WHAT IS A CLINICAL FACT?

Edna O'Shaughnessy makes a strong case for the proposition that a scientifically acceptable model of objectivity is inherent in the psychoanalytic way of working. Her argument applies to all analysis, not just the Kleinian version. Facing the fact that today's world of psychoanalytic theory and technique is pluralistic, she shows how analysts in general may justifiably claim that, when they are working well, they are working with clinical facts and not with inadequate data, wild theories, and untestable phantasies. Those readers who do not share her position on theory, method, and facticity may nevertheless go on to appreciate her distinctive and instructive Kleinian exegesis of three consecutive psychoanalytic sessions.

These three sessions portray analytic work with a profoundly disturbed adolescent boy. That he is adolescent adds extra interest to this discussion, because adolescence is an unusual clinical subject in the Kleinian literature. The context of the sessions was the emotionally intense, self-initiated termination of the treatment of a terribly troubled boy who had already been greatly helped but still had a long way to go toward integration. O'Shaughnessy shows how heavily this boy continued to rely on nonverbal communication. In the face of his oblique mode of participation, she remained steadfast in interpreting the unconscious phantasies that shaped his moment-to-moment experience of her, the setting, and his realization that the time of treatment was running out. It is noteworthy that she recounts this work without insisting that hers were the only interpretations that could be made with validity.

27

To accomplish her goal of getting to understand something of the inner-world turmoil this boy was expressing through his various nonverbal gestures and uses of props, she relied heavily on the broad conception of transference I have described and also on her good grasp of the concreteness of unconscious phantasy. In this way she was able to detect continuity within his fragmentary, apparently chaotic actions, and she could develop some sense of the flux of anxiety and defense in the sessions. Against great odds she was able to shape helpful interventions.

Also, using the Kleinians' broad conception of countertransference and the key role played in it by the patient's projective identifications, she was able to turn to good use material that was all too conducive to her feeling confused, helpless, wounded, and even destructive toward her patient. In the process of demonstrating this aspect of her work, she remains faithful to the point she makes early in this essay concerning the inevitable place in clinical work of fallibility and the anxiety of not knowing—an always useful antidote to analysts' narcissistic needs for omniscience as well as to their being defensively idealized by their patients. Specifically, she shows how she identifies and deals with error in her own work.

Later in this essay, when she makes her second go at her clinical material, she demonstrates that, so far as possible, she seeks to understand error not as an all-or-none misunderstanding but rather as an instance of the analyst's not being sufficiently attuned to what a patient can tolerate at the moment. Her patient's panic and his resort to massive defense alerted her to the fact that something in her work was amiss, and upon review she concluded that she was wrong in this special sense of wrong. She had not addressed what Bion called the "selective fact," that is, that fact pertaining to the relationship of the moment that the patient could grasp, use, and integrate mutatively then and there. Her error lay in her having neglected to track his fear that she would undermine his hard-won defenses and then had not realized that he had begun to destroy from within his positive image of her as the one person who could accept his differentness.

Sensing the disruption, O'Shaughnessy analyzed the role that her destructive countertransference was playing in bringing on her lapse of awareness; that countertransference contributed to her not getting the point of his oblique communications about his inner state. Subsequently, she did go on to convey to him her recognition that he had felt threatened by one of her interventions. This interpretation succeeded in restoring his equilibrium, a result that could be taken to offer some support for her belief that her revised understanding was now on the mark. This part of her report indicates the processive aspect of facticity in clinical work; that is to say, facticity develops over time and with trial and error.

In later chapters, the concepts O'Shaughnessy relied on—such as concreteness of phantasy, projective identification, counter-transference as communication—will be examined more closely and illustrated clinically in further detail.

In the chapters that follow the British spelling has been changed to American usage. On occasion the wording has also been changed for clarity and consistency of style.

1
WHAT IS A CLINICAL FACT?

EDNA O'SHAUGHNESSY

Clinical facts, materially transient, are unexpectedly durable—think how the clinical facts about Dora, the Wolf Man, and the Rat Man have lasted. Yet important current critiques dispute their nature and even their existence (G. S. Klein, 1976; Spence, 1982; and, for a masterly review, Schafer, 1983; Eagle, 1984; Wallerstein, 1992). Such critiques reflect the present tension in psychoanalysis between the conviction that psychoanalysis discovers facts about the mind and the unease generated by the variety of existing clinical and theoretical views. Furthermore, issues of subjectivity, and the overall difference between physical science and human studies, also lead many to question whether it is *facts* that analysts find in an analytic hour.

At the outset allow me to state that there are scientific clinical facts. To support this view I shall offer, first, three sessions in which I claim clinical facts stand revealed; second, something of a philosophical inquiry into what a fact is; and, finally, a discussion of the contribution that clinical facts make to the scientific study of the mind.

This paper was presented at the *International Journal of Psycho-Analysis* 75th Anniversary Celebration Conference, London, October 14–16, 1994.

The Clinical Facts

My patient, whom I call Leon, will soon be 14 years old. At his request, his analysis is ending. Only fifteen sessions remain.

Session 1

Leon puts the large box containing his drawings, paper, pens, etc., up on the table so that it forms a barrier between him and me when he sits down. He looks tense and fearful. He has brought with him a carton of Ribena, a children's drink, on which, in big print, is printed "FIFTEEN FREE EXTRA." Through a straw he starts sucking the drink. He looks no more a schoolboy, but every bit a baby as he empties the carton, which is collapsing in a grotesque shape. Desperately, he sucks for the last drops. Then he hurls the carton violently away into the rubbish bin. I speak to Leon about being near the end of his analysis, of how he feels like a baby whose drinking causes such collapse and ugliness that he must get free—and free of me he will be in fifteen days. I also speak about how he is not satisfied, and desperately still needs and hopes for something more, "extra." There is a long silence. Then, very anxiously, he peers round the box to look at me, retreating instantly. I speak of his terror that I am like the collapsed Ribena carton, and of his being so afraid that he cannot see how I really am. His breathing becomes distressed and he starts to wheeze. It is most distressing to hear. He transmits to me absolutely rending pain and anxiety. And suddenly he falls asleep—it is so unendurable.

Session 2

The next day Leon was different—every inch a schoolboy, a highly defended one. He again made a barrier with his box, and then pulled out a pile of books from his schoolbag and spread them out ostentatiously. He read out his homework assignments loudly. For a brief moment he began to wheeze as if his lungs were again collapsing in agony, but he threw it off, and went on reading continuously in a loud voice bits from various school-books. There seemed no way to make contact with him. I found myself feeling hopeless; I could do nothing but endure his loud blocking reading. I spoke of his need to free himself of a help-less baby who has to endure fear and pain by getting rid of it into me. Leon's response was to print his name on a sheet of paper in big letters and tear it in half, and continue even more loudly with his blocking talk. However, when I later interpreted his terror that I would make his schoolboy self disappear and be lost to him, a striking change came about. Leon was quiet and he put away his schoolbooks.

Hidden by his box, he stayed silent for a long time. I asked him what was happening. He was about to answer, then did not. I spoke of his fear that I would use what he might tell me to say something that would disturb him too much. He then started pushing his chair into view so he and I could see each other and then moving it away so he was again hidden by the box, doing so several times. I was reminded of something he had told me two years before—how he felt half-human and half-bird, that is, half like a human who stays in touch with humans and half like a bird who flies away. When I spoke to him in these terms he was visibly moved. He agreed it was so and then took down the box barrier.

Session 3

He made no box barrier this time. He sat down, openly hard and nasty. He took off his watch and started to draw it. In an exaggerated, mocking way he measured everything with a ruler. I first spoke about the watch being time of which he was so aware in these last days. His nasty performance continued and I then spoke about how he was giving a caricature of me as a cruelly measuring watcher. I went on to say that I thought he knew it was a false picture. Leon continued in the same spoiling way. Suddenly he announced with sarcastic emphasis "I was going to draw it *exactly*, but I have decided not to," and he stopped. He drew the watch now in a straightforward way, and he started to bring his lips gently near to his hand several times as if to touch it with a kiss. I understood him to be showing the affection he feels when he thinks I know he needs me both to be gentle and not force him and also not to be weak and let him take bad advantage and make a mockery of me. He said "Yip." Then, with an effort, he said a clear "Yes," going very pink.

This is my record of the clinical facts as I saw them.

But Are They Facts?

The claim of fact causes disquiet on a number of grounds. There is the nature of the entities themselves, insubstantial and unrepeatable, "immaterial" facts as Caper (1988) aptly calls them. Moreover, a different analyst might see different facts in these three sessions. Is not a claim of fact incompatible with diverse clinical views about entities like these? I shall argue that, once we understand what a fact is, the special features of plurality, subjectivity, and the immateriality of psychological phenomena, though they pose unusual and difficult problems, are not barriers to empirical fact. Indeed, in other forms, these problems are not entirely alien to other sciences, as Wallerstein shows in his important paper "One Psychoanalysis or Many?" (1992).

We tend to think of a fact as stark, out there, independent of theory, language, and person. But investigations have shown such ideas to be naive. By the eighteenth century the great philosopher Kant had already demonstrated that objective reality is known only through the structure of the knowing mind. Kant was speaking of physical nature as known through the mind's categories of space, time, and causality. In the nineteenth century, the remarkable hermeneutic thinker Dilthey added to Kant's categories others for human studies: categories of inner and outer; part and whole; the category of power between people, which helps or frustrates desires; and, overarching all, the category of development, which has a meaning for human beings that needs interpretation. Dilthey surely speaks to all of us and, as is well known, several psychoanalytic thinkers have applied his and other hermeneutic ideas with illumination to psychoanalysis (e.g., G. S. Klein, 1976; Schafer, 1976; Gill, 1983; for good discussions see Strenger, 1991; Duncan, 1992; Steiner, 1992).

With this illumination, however, has come the temptation to adopt a relativism in which interpretations, readings, and narratives are said to exist, each valid within its own nearly closed scheme, but no facts, including clinical facts, can ever be known. Such a view, I think, is flawed. That reality is known through the mind's categories is no ground for lamenting that we can never know the facts. This lament is for nonexistent entities. Rather, that facts are bound up with the nature of persons brings us a better understanding of what a fact is. And, indeed, psychoanalysis itself has discovered further categories that structure our perception and experience of reality; for example, a psychically aware breast, a potent penis, an oedipal situation. (The full set of the mind's categories through which reality is known has yet to be found by philosophical, cognitive, psychoanalytic, or other studies.)

In our own time landmark work in the philosophy of science by Kuhn (1962) has shown further that scientific facts are not research method or theory free; and since facts are stated in language, whether folk or scientific, neither are they language free. This means that the same fact can fall under many different descriptions, and that no one statement of fact ever completely encompasses a fact. As the philosopher Thomas Nagel (1986) expresses it: a view of the facts is always *a partial view from somewhere*. With these regrettably cursory preliminaries, I now come to the nub of the matter.

What is it to make, as I wish to, a claim of fact? A claim of fact has two essentials. When I make a claim of fact, I make a truth claim, and I imply a readiness to submit my claim to verification. As others are speaking on the topic of verification I shall focus here on the truth claim; though, as truth and verification seem sometimes inextricable, I shall occasionally look at both.

First of all, when I make a truth claim, I do not claim to know *the* truth, or *all* the truth, but only *a* truth. Other true formulations are always possible. In a variety of vocabularies analysts make different, similar, or even the same statements about the clinical facts. Sometimes formulations seem complementary; for example, Leon in the third session certainly gives what can be called "a narrative performance" when he draws his watch in a nasty, measuring way. I wonder if Roy Schafer would agree to link his theory of narratives to the theory of internal objects, by letting it be said that Leon's nasty narrative performance is an attack on the better state of his internal objects? Variety of vocabulary aside, there remain nevertheless in our plural psychoanalytic scene real and complex differences of both theory and perceptions of clinical fact that are guided by theory. In my view, all psychoanalytic schools make a claim for truth—which is why, I think, our debates are so impassioned.

And second, when I make a truth claim, I do not make an infallibility claim. I might be mistaken. Here is where anxiety enters. Anxiety starts with the patient when I offer him my understanding of the clinical facts. Along with numerous other anxieties intrinsic to clinical work, there is always the anxiety that the clinical facts are not as I see them; yet, if I am to work, I must risk that I might be wrong. The patient is the first person to check an analyst's statement. Our patients say "No" for many reasons, but the "No" that tells the analyst that he is wrong is of immeasurable help. It may be said in words, or shown in other ways. You will remember how, after being overcome by an infantile state, by the second session Leon regained his schoolboy self. When I interpreted his need to free himself from a helpless baby and project it into me, he renewed his splitting—he tore his name on a paper in half—and his school talk became even louder. Leon showed I was wrong by an immediate increase in anxiety and defensiveness. Mistakes are an everyday risk for the analyst, hence the need for constant inquiry in the session into the patient's response to interpretations, explored in the present series of papers by Britton and Steiner (1994), as well as for what Gardner (1983) has called "Self Inquiry," and Bion (1963) calls "a meditative review of analytic work." Now, writing this paper, I see my hopelessness when faced by Leon's defended, split state, and feeling of just having to endure it, as very likely coming from my sense of failure as an analyst with Leon—so limited was my therapeutic result.

In recent years much attention has rightly been paid to the strain of bearing the state of not knowing, and the analyst's impulse to clutch at certainty out of the anxiety of not knowing. Here I put the emphasis the other way—on the anxiety of *knowing* with its inbuilt risk of being wrong. I wish to emphasize how interpretations may be delayed or vaguely framed by the analyst as a defense against the exposure of his fallibility. Our ego's old wish for omnipotence, the omnipotence with which our patients also endow us, the severe demands of our superego, our concern for our patients for whom we carry clinical responsibility, all of these make us reluctant to expose ourselves to public view, when just as we think we know the clinical facts we may turn out to be wrong. Such anxiety, which starts with our patient, continues before our colleagues when we give clinical presentations, and involves, I think, anxiety both about the standard of our work and about our theoretical orientation. We may not have seen what a more gifted or experienced colleague may see, and we may not have seen what a colleague with a better theory might sec. The question is always lurking: could I be analyzing my patient better from a different theoretical perspective?

Such reflections on our fallibility and our limitations bring again the unease, which I referred to at the start of the paper, over claiming there are clinical facts. When so many individual and theoretical views are possible, may not the psychoanalytic field be more subjective than factual? *Subjectivity* is a word with many meanings. For a start, psychoanalysis studies psychic reality, which, in one sense, is subjective reality. And then, all human studies depend more on the knowing mind than the study of physical nature; in a psychoanalysis the analyst's mind is *the* instrument investigating the mind of the patient. This raises the alarming idea of psychoanalysis being doubly subjective, from the analyst's as well as the patient's side. The further fact that analysts are not standardized, that analysts have "an individual idiom" as Bollas (1987) calls it, plays into the common presumption that the psychoanalytic enterprise is subjective in the pejorative sense of lacking all objectivity. However, the presumption of "no objectivity" needs investigation (for an extensive inquiry see Nagel [1986]). In our age the objective achievements of machines dazzle us and can make us see them as everywhere superior—even in questionable areas. Some philosophers are writing as though, without question, it would be fortunate for us all were the mind to be reduced to the brain, and the brain to be equated with "Artificial Intelligence." In the same vein, a tape recording is presumed to be a more objective record of a session than an analyst's written and mental notes. However, there are other views in contemporary thinking about the mind, brain, and machines, in which the mind is not the loser, among them those of the philosophers Nagel (1986), McGinn (1991), and Searle (1992), and for an exploration of consciousness as nature's "empowerment" to know objective reality, see Brian O'Shaughnessy (1991).

That said, we must now return to the topic of subjectivity—taken in the pejorative sense of "lacking objectivity." We are not all the ablest, nor are we always or with every patient at our individual best. Among analysts of all schools there are variations in the capacity to know the clinical facts of an analytic hour. In this sense one person may be more subjective, or less objective, than another, or than himself at another time. Leon illustrates this when in the first session he cannot see the analyst objectively at all after the carton collapses as he drinks. In great distress, he is then anxious about the analyst's condition. He looks at me to see how I am, but his vision is so clouded by his inner state at that moment that he cannot see how the external analyst is. This small example of the impairment of objectivity comes from a large area, to which psychoanalysis itself has contributed not a little understanding, by showing how out of flooding fantasy, as in the case of Leon, or anxiety, pain, narcissism, envy, the mind may block perceptions or the sense organs become psychogenetically impaired. Psychoanalysis has shown also how projective identifications distort reality, how one mind may be invaded and controlled by another and unable to think freely and objectively. In despair over these troubling problems of subjectivity in the practice of psychoanalysis we may be tempted to clutch at "objectivity" through methods such as tape recordings, or the "pronoun counting" advised by Spence (1994): methods which I believe to be misguided. Better, in my opinion, for the analyst to struggle with these problems by analysis, and by supervision and discussions with colleagues; remembering that because there are impediments to attaining objectivity, this does not mean we have none: it means it is hard to attain.

In sum, I have tried to show that facts are not stark: they are bound up with the species we are, with the language in which they are couched, the method of their investigation, and the theories we hold about them—all of which implies that a fact may be described in many different ways. Plurality and science are compatible, though it must be admitted that there are too many theories in the psychoanalytic field. Any claim of clinical fact is, in my view, a truth claim; but, as with any empirical enterprise, not a unique or an infallible claim. An analyst may be wrong about the clinical facts because of the insufficiencies of his theory, or because of his personal limitations—including impairments to his objectivity.

THE CLINICAL FACTS AGAIN

In the first session we can see some distinctive features of the facts discovered in the analytic hour. The ending of Leon's analysis drew forth from his unconscious inner world his early object relations. In plain view are his primary object, represented by the Ribena carton collapsing from his drinking, and himself, looking and feeling like a terrified unsatisfied baby. We see how psychic reality is formed from a blending of internal and outer reality: his inner world is the source of the subjective meaning of the external event of ending analysis in fifteen days. To Leon in this session (there were other meanings in subsequent sessions) it means weaning after a feeding that leaves him desperate and unsatisfied and his object grotesque and ruined in his mind.

The past is in the present in the way that is familiar to psychoanalysts, which yet is still so very striking. And how individual the relation to the past is! Another patient might experience the infant in himself without being overwhelmed, might wonder about his early history, or be able to discriminate the analyst's condition from that of his archaic internal object, but Leon cannot. His ego collapses under the psychic weight of contact with his unconscious internalized early past, and it terrifies him, all the more because his primary object is also collapsed, useless for modifying the situation. The coming out of these unconscious fantasies in concrete form so dominates Leon that he cannot relate to the analyst as a figure in the present different from his archaic object, and inner and outer reality persecute him. In an attempt to escape he hurls away the empty misshapen carton, but he does not succeed in freeing himself of his damaged and useless object; instead somatization takes place (how should we understand this clinical fact?) and he wheezes painfully with feelings of collapsing lungs. At this point Leon projects into the analyst overwhelming feelings of anxiety and pain, and for respite he resorts to sleep.

It can be seen that Leon's unconscious inner world came into impressive prominence during the analytic hour; and that there was an interaction between inner and outer reality as an entire constellation of object relations, anxieties, needs, and feelings, emerged into view. Leon could also project into the analyst and so communicate unbearable feelings of pain and anxiety. That is to say, under the unusual conditions of an analytic hour an analyst gains privileged access to a patient's *interiority*. Inner life emerges with a detail and depth not elsewhere accessible.

These facts of Leon's mental life, his personality, the internalized history of his object relations, have, at the same time another aspect: they are also clinical facts, living instances of the facts; that is, they are the clinical relations between patient and analyst, part of a therapeutic or not therapeutic process. In the first session this process brought a welling-up of infantile feelings; the following day was different. The extremity of Leon's state had impelled him to use massive defenses and split off the infantile object relations threatening to overwhelm his ego. In the second session he is a schoolboy again, without emotional depth, with surface feelings, and above all, with a functioning ego once more. This, in fact, was an achievement of his analysis. He began treatment in a state of inertia, absorbed in secret psychotic preoccupations.

This second session seems to me to show the difference between a fact and a clinical fact. I mentioned earlier how I mistakenly interpreted that Leon needed to project the helpless baby into me. This was a fact; but it was not a clinical fact, not the immediate emotional reality of the session. When I mistook the emotional reality, the clinical facts of Leon's relations to me changed for the worse. I think he experienced me as very dangerous, as trying to undo his security and to force the overwhelming baby back into him. I drove him to a renewed splitting of himself (as shown by his tearing his name in half) and to louder defensive school talk. When I recognized Leon's anxiety that I would undo his defenses, and interpreted his terror that I would cause him to lose his schoolboy self, his fears diminished and another change, this time for the better, occurred between us in the session.

At that moment I think I found what Bion has singled out as "the selected fact," namely, that fact which gives coherence and meaning to facts already known; in this instance Leon's recovery of his schoolboy self, his loud reading of bits from schoolbooks to block out the analyst and to stop his chest from wheezing, his increased anxiety and defensiveness at the mention of a helpless baby. When the "selected fact" was interpreted the interpretation is mutative and new possibilities then exist for patient and analyst. Leon became communicative and was able to show me, by moving into view and then hiding again behind his box, his need to be half in contact and half out of touch. I then remembered what he had told me in the first months of the analysis when, very unusually (he mostly sat passive and silent), he was eager to speak. Intensely, he told me there had been a biology lesson at school about evolution and Darwin. "There could be new species," he said, "like," he added, "half-humans, half-birds." When I spoke to him in these images, they were alive in the session. At that point I am no longer a figure watching him and threatening to breach his defenses, but a figure who knows him and accepts how he is, and by the end of the session his defenses, box and emotional, come down.

It is clear, I think, that my clinical facts are selected on the following basis: they are the lived facts of the shifting object relations between myself and my patient—as I saw them. In every session observations would have been made and not been included because, though they were facts, I did not see them as clinical facts. Moreover, it is evident that as analyst I both observe and, through fallibility or understanding, contribute to making the clinical facts what they are. It is a further clinical fact that a selected fact, the ground of a mutative interpretation, is highly time-sensitive: it must come from the immediate emotional reality between patient and analyst. And lastly, it can be seen that not all sessions are therapeutic. Leon's first session was an acutely painful emergence, a repetition in the presence of the analyst, without therapeutic benefit. By contrast, in the second session some working through took place between patient and analyst, as it did in the third session.

In the third session Leon continued to communicate. He openly showed me that he is making a mocking caricature as he draws his watch, exaggeratedly measuring everything "exactly." Unlike the previous session, when the external analyst was experienced as a threat to his security, in this session he was showing me an inner danger to his security. His own destructiveness was stripping the internalized image of his analyst of the very quality most important to him the day before, namely, being seen in a way that does not measure him but accepts his being "different," his feeling of being half-bird, half-human. When Leon began analysis he was paralyzed by a superego that watched and measured him cruelly against father, brother, or other ideals. When I interpreted the caricature he was making of his internalized analyst, Leon responded and himself took a decision to stop it. By the end of the hour he could acknowledge his gratitude for an analyst who both saw his destructive mockery, and comprehended also his need for emotional distance—as expressed by his lips going near to, yet not quite, kissing his hand.

These clinical facts are not "stark" facts. Items are not sorted and labeled "observed data," "inference," "psychoanalytic context," "analyst's emotional experiences," "analyst's memory of patient," "hypothesis or theory invoked," and so on. Mostly, the clinical facts are an amalgam of some of these items, some being simpler than others, such as the way Leon looks. In the first session he arrives with his Ribena carton, looking tense and fearful; in the second he comes looking like a much-defended schoolboy; in the third he looks nasty and hard when he arrives, and warmly tender by the end. There are also his actions: he makes the box barrier, he drinks, he reads loudly from schoolbooks, he draws, and there are his words and my own. (I have not included the details of how I spoke to him, since "formulations to the patient" is a topic for other papers.)

However, even such apparently simple data is often complex. Consider descriptions of his appearance, such as, "He looks like a much-defended schoolboy"; or, in session 1, as he sucks the juice from the Ribena carton, my record has it that he, "Looks no more a schoolboy but every bit a baby." Or, even more complex, consider my perception of Leon drawing his watch in the third session. As he draws, measuring everything in an exaggerated way with the ruler, I see him in the context of the analytic process to be destroying the analyst internalized from the day before, who did not criticize or measure him, but accepted his being "half-bird, half-human." I see him as undoing the analytic work and reverting to an old identification with a superego who used to paralyze him by always watching him and measuring him unfavorably against father, brother, or other ideal: a cruel figure dominating hours of analytic endeavor. That is, my perception of Leon's action is informed by the history of the analysis, and by my knowledge of the patient's internal figures. Moreover, my perception is also infused with a particular psychoanalytic hypothesis, first stated by Melanie Klein in an early paper on tics (1925), that unconscious object relations and identifications will be found to underlie all mental and somatic phenomena; and with her general theory (1940 onwards) that in the mind are continual unconscious fantasies of an inner world of objects which, by identification, projection, and introjection, are constantly interacting with outer reality. My clinical observations were not made by observing "basic data" and then making inferences or invoking an hypothesis or a theory, but by experiencing phenomena in a certain way. It is an individual way of seeing, hindered by my limitations, using what capacities I have, infused with theory, or with knowledge of my patient, or with memories of our psychoanalytic endeavors, sometimes devoid of theory or even contrary to theory, and so on. It is very much—and considerably more so than in the case of other scientific methods—"my view from somewhere."

The gap between clinical fact and relevant theory is not, in my opinion, in the consulting room. It is to be found elsewhere: in the imaginative extrapolation, the scientific leap from the clinical facts from one or more pairs of patients and analysts to hypotheses about the psyche, its structure, its development, its treatment by analysis, and so on, which form part of a psychoanalytic theory of mind. At work with my patient, when aspects of theory are relevant they seem "experience-near"; sometimes, however, by contrast, the clinical facts may upset a theory—a different and important possibility for the analyst.

So far, rather than defining the essence of a clinical fact, I have been trying to gather from the three sessions some distinctive features (others might be chosen—see Caper [1994], "What Is a Clinical Fact?") of what psychoanalysis discovers. Given that the method of discovery is in the seclusion of an analytic hour, unrepeatable by another analyst, how then is an alternate view possible? In his paper "What Is a Clinical Fact," given at West Point, Spence says: "We need to find a mode of presentation that will honor the clinical fact . . . [and give] . . . the opportunity to take an alternate stand" (1994). With facts like clinical facts, this looks, and is, not easy to do. Yet I think it is not impossible.

Several things help. First of all, though I have an individual style and a Kleinian orientation, these are of less moment than the vast area of training, practice, and theory, which is common to all psychoanalysts and which underlies my work. There is, for example, the analytic attitude and setting, the recognition of an unconscious, of psychic reality, of the ego's need for defenses against intense anxieties, the assumption of a repetition of the past in the transference situation with the analyst, symbolism, and so on. In Kuhn's (1962) terminology, these form the "shared paradigm" of psychoanalysts, the common ground from which all analysts can assess my work. And we should note that the clinical record itself may communicate to colleagues more than I consciously know, both about the patient and my relations with him, and about my awareness and objectivity or lack thereof. Moreover, colleagues may make inquiries of me, for a fuller clinical record, for further facts which, if they are taking a different view, they suspect might be there. As I see it, an alternate view is not so much the building of a different understanding on the grounds of the same clinical facts—though it can be that—but is more often akin to a shift of perspective that brings about a change of perception, which in turn redescribes and reorders the facts. Naturally, a new view of the clinical facts must, like the first one, be subject to validation, as being a truth about the immediate emotional reality between patient and analyst.

Whichever our school of psychoanalysis, clinical facts have increased the understanding of the human mind enormously. Until Freud invented the unusual conditions of the analytic hour, the mind's inferiority was waiting for the light of a scientific day—even one such as ours, which yields clinical facts with some unusually troublesome problems.

References

Bion, W. R. (1963), *Elements of Psychoanalysis*. London: Heinemann.

Bollas, C. (1987), *The Shadow of the Object. Psychoanalysis of the Unthought Known*. London: Free Association Books.

Britton, R., & Steiner, J. (1994), Selected fact or overvalued idea? *Internat. J. Psycho-Anal.*, 75:1069–1078.

Caper, R. (1988), *Immaterial Facts*. Northvale, NJ: Jason Aronson.

——— (1994), What is a clinical fact? *Internat. J. Psycho-Anal.*, 75: 903–914.

Duncan, D. (1992), Hermeneutics and psychoanalysis. Typescript.

Eagle, M. N. (1984), *Recent Developments in Psychoanalysis*. New York: McGraw-Hill.

Gardner, M. R. (1983), *Self Inquiry*. Hillsdale, NJ: The Analytic Press.

Gill, M. M. (1983), The point of view of psychoanalysis. *Psychoanal. Contemp. Thought*, 6: 523–552.

Klein, G. S. (1976), *Psychoanalytic Theory*. New York: International Universities Press.

Klein, M. (1925), A contribution to the psychogenesis of tics. In: *Writings*, Vol. 1. London: Hogarth Press, 1975, pp. 106–127.

——— (1940), Mourning and its relation to manic-depressive states. In: *Writings*, Vol. 1. London: Hogarth Press, 1975, pp. 344–369.

Kuhn, T. S. (1962), *The Structure of Scientific Revolutions*. Chicago: University of Chicago Press.

McGinn, C. (1991), *The Problem of Consciousness*. Oxford: Blackwell.

Nagel, T. (1986), *The View from Nowhere*. Oxford: Oxford University Press.

O'Shaughnessy, B. (1991), The anatomy of consciousness. In: *Consciousness*, Proceedings of a Conference Sociedad Filosofiica Ibero-American. ed. D. Neubach. Philadelphia: Ridgeway.

Schafer, R. (1976), *A New Language for Psychoanalysis*. New Haven: Yale University Press.

——— (1983), *The Analytic Attitude*. New York: Basic Books.

Searle, J. R. (1992), *The Rediscovery of the Mind*. Cambridge, MA: M.I.T. Press.

Spence, D. (1982), Narrative truth and theoretical truth. *Psychoanal. Quart.*, 51: 43–69.

——— (1994), What is a clinical fact? *Internat. J. Psycho-Anal.*, 75: 915–926.

Steiner, R. (1992), Some historical and critical notes on the relationship between hermeneutics and psychoanalysis. Typescript.

Strenger, C. (1991), *Between Hermeneutics and Science*. Madison, CT: International Universities Press.

Wallerstein, R., Ed. (1992), One psychoanalysis or many? In: *The Common Ground of Psychoanalysis*. Northvale, NJ: Jason Aronson, pp. 25–60.

EDITOR'S INTRODUCTION TO
CONCEPTUALIZATION OF CLINICAL FACTS

Although Ruth Riesenberg-Malcolm's clearly stated approach to conceptualizing clinical facts follows along pretty much the same lines as Edna O'Shaughnessy's in chapter 1, it does include illuminating comments along other lines as well. For example, she clarifies the interplay of theory and observation during the clinical session and also afterward when one reflects on the day's sessions. Additionally she emphasizes how it is an abuse of theory to overwork it; the result can only be pseudounderstanding as a way of dealing with the stress of not understanding at all. Not least she takes up the subtle intrusions of eclecticism in the course of systematic clinical work.

Riesenberg-Malcolm's one extended clinical example invites comment in several respects. First, her intensive discussion of an initial analytic session is easily and usefully generalizable to typical problems all analysts face when beginning an analytic treatment. In this case, she does not hesitate to interpret the patient's transference-based initial anxiety, and she does so in a simple, empathic way. Attentive to the consequences of this intervention, that is, viewing it as always being part of an ongoing dialogue and not as an instrument of closure, she notes that her interpretation both stimulates some hopefulness in her despairing patient, and in so doing, provokes conflict in her about feeling at all hopeful.

My second comment concerns the presentation of analytic material from two points in the same analysis, the second of which is several years after the first. Instructively, this later material illuminates a number of signs of significant progress toward greater depth and breadth of understanding. This progress seemed to depend in large part on Riesenberg-Malcolm's use of the concept of pathological organization as a way of dealing with painful flux between the paranoid–schizoid and depressive positions, a topic most fully elaborated in chapter 8, below. This aspect of the analysis required heavy concentration on defensive operations.

Third, this extended example explicitly acknowledges and applies such basic tenets of Freud's as the centrality of conflict, the power of the compulsion to repeat, and the potential influence of external relationships on unconscious phantasy in pathological states. She shows, for example, how maintaining the more mature depressive position may be facilitated by the support provided by others in the environment. These emphases on ego organization, defense, and the role of external relationships show that in many respects the distance of contemporary Kleinian work from standard ego psychological analysis is often not great at all. Perhaps her readiness to interpret anxiety from the very start manifests a significant difference between the two approaches.

Fourth and last is the author's candid presentation of what she herself did think and say in the course of her work. While recognizing, as Edna O'Shaughnessy had, that she could not rule out alternatives, she too remained in the context that she believed was the useful one of the moment. Remaining in context is, I would add, the preferred position of any analyst in these times when multiple theoretical and clinical psychoanalytic contexts are available for use, and, as the author notes, steadily tempt one toward eclecticism.

Because plural possibilities has been the theme of these first two chapters, and because the concept of pluralism applies within systems as well as between them, I should like here to consider two alternative Kleinian interpretations of Riesenberg-Malcolm's clinical material, following which, for reasons I shall get to, I shall discuss issues involved in reading published accounts of the clinical work done by others.

First of all, one might wonder at the absence of reference to envy in the transference, even in the context of the patient's reporting her response to having encountered the well put together woman. Also, the author does not refer to countertransference enactment, even though it might be thought that she had been caught up in an enactment at one point. That point was when she expressed implicitly some countertransferential enthusiasm by commenting quickly on signs of hopefulness. Enactment is in question here because, from her years of experience with this difficult patient and her earlier comment to the reader on the unusualness of hearing the patient give any positive weekend report, it could be anticipated that the patient would experience prompt recognition of progress as somehow impatient and demanding. Certainly, the intensely regressive material that followed Riesenberg-Malcolm's intervention could have suggested that more was involved here than only the patient's own splitting off and projecting her hopefulness; at least, the possibility of provocation by the analyst might need to be considered.

One might make this point about countertransference enactment without in any way suggesting that the analyst limit interpretation only to what the patient did seem to have projected into the analyst's enthusiastic comment; for rarely are we in an either-or situation in this connection. In this Kleinian approach, however, interpretation might well center on the patient's inner world of object relations once the countertransference has been integrated into the analyst's understanding rather than acted on.

From Riesenberg-Malcolm's condensed published clinical report we cannot know whether she considered these two alternative interpretations and perhaps even acted on them. Nor can we know precisely what her own sense of the momentary context required her to focus on. Here as elsewhere one considers alternatives in order to join the author in thinking through the material as presented. One uses the author's illustrative material to grasp his or her specific contribution as securely as possible and not to engage in second guessing. Therefore, adopting a corrective supervisory attitude toward any clinical report of this type is certainly risky and very likely presumptuous as well. It would be unnecessary to make this point about supervisory attempts were it not that critics of contemporary Kleinian work have often misused published clinical illustrations in ways that seem rather more doctrinaire and polemical than one might expect from their otherwise judicious authors (e.g., Tyson, 1991).

REFERENCES

Tyson, R. L. (1991), The emergence of oedipal centrality, comments on Michael Feldman's "Common ground: The centrality of the oedipus complex." *Internat. J. Psycho-Anal.*, 72:39–46.

2
CONCEPTUALIZATION
OF CLINICAL FACTS

RUTH RIESENBERG-MALCOLM

The conceptualization of clinical facts is a description of the way in which psychoanalytic theories operate in clinical practice. In the process of conceptualizing the fact, the analyst is defining it. In my opinion, a clinical fact happens in the session and is expressed in the relationship between patient and analyst. It is the analyst's theoretical understanding of aspects of this relationship at any given moment, when the analyst believes it to be reasonably correct, that is for me a clinical fact. In this paper I shall describe what I think are the elements that converge to make clinical facts and the way I conceptualize a fact.

My first point, that something is a clinical fact only within a session, is self-evident, since I have already stated that for me a clinical fact occurs in the relationship between patient and analyst. Many things happen in the patient's life and mind outside the session, but they only become available for analytic work, that is, become "clinical facts," when they appear in the session alive in the patient–analyst relationship. Outside the analysis the

This paper was presented at the *International Journal of Psycho-Analysis* 75th Anniversary Celebration Conference, São Paulo, March 31– April 2, 1995.

patient, in his mind, is or could be heavily involved with his analyst, but this involvement can only be analytically sensed and addressed in the interaction between them. The patient's fantasies about the analyst not only become more alive, but are directly or indirectly expressed, experienced, and enacted with the analyst in the session. The analyst's intuition about the patient takes place in the session in the interrelationship between the two. All this can only be perceived and understood through the analyst's theoretical beliefs.

From my theoretical position, I see the patient's way of relating to his analyst in the analysis as an expression of his inner world, that is, of his experiences with his internal objects. These experiences are of old object relationships, which for certain reasons could not develop in a mature way and which contain and maintain within them active infantile conflicts that tend to repeat themselves in all the patient's relationships and behavior. In the analysis, the patient relives these old conflicts in the relationship with the analyst, and the analyst can understand them in a living way and interpret them to the patient. I think this corresponds to what the Sandlers (1987) call the "present unconscious": present as accessible and expressed in the here-and-now of the session. I wish to emphasize that this here-and-now is for me always an expression of the relationship between analyst and patient as representing internal object relationships. These are internal structures, expressed in the analysis bit by bit, following their own dynamics, which become affected by the interventions of the analyst in the moment to moment of the analysis.

I have described how I work from a central theoretical point, that is, the importance of the transference, but the fact that one has a central theory does not mean that other lines of thought do not color the analyst's way of thinking. Ideas from other theoretical systems do influence our own theories, though obviously they do so to a greater extent if they are closer to the body of beliefs we hold true. We are also influenced by ideas belonging to other bodies of thought, possibly to a lesser degree, with more resistance on our part, and more often than not unconsciously rather than consciously.

This last point brings me to an important issue: our theoretical frame—on the one hand, how wide and flexible it is, or should be, and on the other, how firmly defined. The way we feel about this point will strongly influence how we view our clinical work and especially the technique we use in the analysis of it. In my opinion, our theory should encompass both of the above characteristics. To understand what one is doing in one's clinical practice one has to have a solid central core of ideas, a theory (since our theory is the base from which we perceive analytically); from this central theory it is possible to pursue many often apparently unrelated experiences so as to be able eventually to make sense of them in the light of our central ideas. In doing so we must be continuously shaping and reshaping our central body of ideas, and occasionally we may even have to add something new to it.

In analytic work we use theory mainly in two ways. First, when we are with our patients, theory operates on our perceptions mainly, but not exclusively, unconsciously. This central unconscious work is interspersed by quicker, more conscious thinking aimed at making sense of what we observe in the patient, in ourselves, and especially of the interaction between the patient and ourselves. It is this rapid conscious awareness of what is going on which permits us to judge these events so as to select what we make explicit to the patient.

Second, when away from our patients, and we think about what has actually happened, our theoretical notions become central to our thinking. They show us what we understood and what we failed to understand; they impel us to think again or to look at the material in a different way. To do this we detach ourselves from the emotional involvement of the session and try to understand *this involvement* as a crucial aspect of the session. We examine what we see by using the main concepts we believe provide us with the understanding of the workings of the patient's mind. That is, we operate from our own psychoanalytic theory of mind. It is important to keep in mind the differentiation I have just described about how we use theory in analytic work, to prevent both intellectualization during the session and the loss of the necessary level of abstraction when we do our homework away from the patient.

When we conceive our theories clearly, we can attain the security to tolerate the frequent lack of or difficulty in understanding what is going on, to extend our (analytic) senses in all possible directions, without superimposing our theory on to the material because we cannot understand it.

Holding on to a partial, and often unclear, understanding of the new phenomena which emerge in the analysis is often as difficult as tolerating not knowing, and both carry the danger of overreliance on theoretical constructs. The imposition of theory can result in the creation of pseudofacts, instead of the observation of clinical facts, and these pseudofacts are fabrications of the analyst, rather than an evolution of analytic facts in the process of the analysis.

I shall now present some sessions from a patient to show how I actually conceptualized her material. I shall start with her first session, and then continue with material from some years later. I have singled out the experience of hope as the linking point between both pieces of material.

Ms. A

I saw this patient twice prior to the analysis. She was in her midthirties, had a degree in economics, and had worked for some time as a financial consultant in family companies. I formed the impression that she was a very ill patient. She comes from a landed family, is single, and runs a farm which belongs to them, close to

London, where she spends a lot of time devoted to animals: dogs, cats, birds, and some horses and ponies. Her animals are not kept for profit. From what she said I deduced that her training in economics allowed her to manage her farm very well, but her description of her work made me think that she was probably living out obsessional defenses, which appeared most strikingly when she spoke about her animals. The family was often abroad and sometimes as a child she had been separated from her parents. She had been sent to boarding school from an early age. She was knowledgeable about analysis and seemed to have read extensively; a relative of hers is an analyst in another country.

She was not forthcoming about her reasons for seeking analysis, but said she had been advised to come by a friend of the family. Her principal complaints were a total lack of friends and an intense involvement with her animals. When speaking about her animals, though she gave details about her riding, there was something evasive and secretive in her speech. I remember thinking about a possible perversion, though I inferred it more from her tone and nuances than from facts explicitly narrated. She expressed a strong desire to be "like other people," and she repeated this several times in a way that conveyed considerable despair.

First session: On entering the room, Ms. A impressed me with her elegance and gracefulness. She was two minutes late, saying immediately that she was late because "she was not like those *eager* people," making it sound as though she much despised those whom she called "eager" people. She knew about using the couch and lay down on it with what appeared to be great difficulty and discomfort, moving continuously, sitting up, lying back again, putting one and then the other foot down on the floor, and so it went on.

She started speaking with a tense, hoarse voice that made me think of intense anxiety. She said (in brief) that she was very frightened that I would not understand her need for her "routine": if she did not follow her routine she would collapse. Vaguely, she described her routine as having to do with her work on the farm and especially the animals there, and more precisely and with considerable detail she described her need to ride an exact amount of hours a day. She repeated several times, with what I felt to be considerable urgency, her need for her routine and especially her fear that I would not understand this. She said emphatically more than once that without her routine she would collapse. While she was speaking or soon after she stopped, I coughed.

Intensely, as if frightened, she said "she is ill," remarking that she had noticed cough pastilles and a glass of water on my table. In a rather mixed way, in which intense worry seemed to predominate, she said that I was weak like her grandmother. With what seemed some effort, she told me that the grandmother was weak and old. She said emphatically that her grandmother was extremely dictatorial and very critical of Ms. A's way of life. She sounded rather bitter and resentful; immediately she went on to say that her father was also weak, and expanded a bit on this, in a mixed tone of voice, containing both pain and superiority. After a while she went back to emphasize the importance of her routine.

Briefly, my interpretation referred to her fear that on top of being weak, I would be very critical and domineering, wanting to impose my views, without taking into consideration her own ways of dealing with her problems, that is, her routine. I reminded her of the difficulties we had in fixing the timetable (in fact, I had very little flexibility). Then she said, "I had a dream." She had taken some of her animals to Austria because one of them, a horse, "her Jon" was unwell and fresh air would be good for him. She bedded him down and went skiing. She saw a man riding her horse. She stopped to tell me that under certain conditions, when a horse is not well, it is bad to ride it. She then returned to the dream, saying that the horse was being ridden into a half-frozen lake, where he was about to be hit by an ice-berg. She finished narrating the dream there, and was silent.

After a pause I asked her if she had any thoughts about the dream. With a voice that sounded strangled by what felt like anxiety, she said firmly that she did not think the horse was herself. After this she fell silent.

Looking at this part of the session, I first observed an elegant and graceful young woman who expressed with some haughti-ness her superiority to other people while at the same time con-veying an intense level of anxiety. I noted how proper and careful she was in her speech, while simultaneously her playing with her feet seemed to express something very different. Though she was careful in telling me about the importance of her routine and her doubts about me, she took the risk of doing so. But my coughing had frightened her, reminded her of what she had already noticed, and I became a transference object whom she felt to be bad, critical, and dictatorial, an analyst who would not understand the importance of her symptom (who was possibly too weak to take it on board). In other words, a negative trans-ference came to predominate over what at the beginning had seemed a more mixed or oscillating one.

After my interpretation two very important feelings came to the fore: hopefulness and fear of coldness. In the dream, and by bringing it, she was expressing hope. My first interpretation made her feel me less dictatorial, which in turn felt a bit more hopeful, but she had already expressed first her doubts and then her bad feelings about me. These feelings linked in my mind with her fears of coldness, the iceberg in the dream. Already her hopes were shown by her bringing herself to the analysis, and taking the horse in the dream to Austria. Yet the way she pro-nounced part of my name on the telephone (R*ice*nberg) indi-cated her fear of encountering here not just a cold person, but someone possibly even more dangerous than that, a dictatorial me. Also shown in the dream, the horse was in danger of being hit by the iceberg. To express this in more theoretical terms, what I am describing are rather rapid movements of states of mind, resulting from splitting between objects and her relationships with these objects. Thus, through her projective identifications, I became for her one or the other side of the split.

I have reported her reactions to me and how she seemed to feel me. I will now turn to observations that impinged on my mind, such as the disparity between her appearance and language on the one hand, and what I would call her "feet language," a disparity that at that time made me feel or sense that though externally she tried to look very well behaved, she was probably rebellious, provocative, or something else quite different from that which was shown in her genteel behavior. While subconsciously aware of all this, I was also aware of the intensity of her feelings about what she called her routine. With the routine on one side and her responsiveness to my intervention on the other, I thought of another type of splitting operating as well. A splitting between her as a functioning woman (the competent economist) and something much less integrated, probably held together by her routine. Without much evidence other than my intuition, I also kept thinking of something perverse, linked to her animals. As can be seen in what I am saying I have been treating dream and behavior as interrelated, and thinking about this first dream in the analysis as a scenario of her internal world. It should be noted that I could get no associations to the dream, and I felt that she was depositing it on my lap (I will come to this later).

I will now return to the session. My interpretation mainly referred to her hope in coming to analysis (Austria in the dream) and her fear of encountering someone cold (the iceberg). After my intervention she was silent, and then said: "I can deal with what you said, but my animals, especially my horses, are most important to me, I call them 'my boys.'" At this point I felt quite puzzled. After a pause she said that probably I knew that Austria was the home of the Vienna Riding School. Again after a pause, and appearing very uncomfortable she said that when she was a child at boarding school where she felt lost and lonely, she had had an imaginary horse she called Lucifer, whom she would summon into her mind at any time (especially at night in bed), and this gave her immediate relief. I will stop here, for we were near the end of the session.

I think that three main things emerged from this material. My interpretation seemed to bring a shift and she felt hopeful, but very quickly seemed to get disappointed, as if feeling that the other aspect of herself had been neglected. She said "she could deal with what I said," that is, she appeared to understand it, and that I had understood part of her dream, but she seemed rapidly to put it aside and to feel that I neglected something else, represented by her beloved horses. My conjecture was that she seemed to feel that my so-called "neglect" was so important and intensely disappointing that it turned me again into someone different, this time not cold and dictatorial, but an object not really interested in her and her feelings, more concerned with imposing norms of good behavior and achievement: "the prancing horses of the Vienna Riding School." Thus, another aspect of her internal objects emerged.

Third, I thought that Lucifer was important, for he expressed a need or belief in someone magical and exciting who would provide immediate gratification. Of course, Lucifer could be thought of in different ways, but at this point it linked in my mind with her having done what I felt as "depositing the dream on my lap." My theory made me think of her desire for an object that could provide, on its own and at once, what she needed as linked with the issue of frustration. I wondered about her capacity to tolerate frustration, as I knew from her account of the history she had given me that she had probably suffered much of it. In this context I thought about impatience, and whether it would prove to be a problem. I thought that she felt the dream should be dealt with at once by me, in the same way as Lucifer had made her feel well at once.

A first session is a unique situation, which in itself could be thought of as a special "clinical fact." It is a new situation for both participants, each of whom brings a different set of expectations, both conscious and unconscious. An important aspect is that in the first session a decision has been taken, and the decision implies that a commitment had been made by both patient and analyst (even if the analysis does not last more than one session). This commitment precipitates, especially in borderline patients, an intense involvement with the analyst from the very beginning.

In the first session with the kind of patient I am speaking about (and to a lesser extent in all patients) this commitment often telescopes into something like a picture (a kind of tableau and/or moving picture), where much of the patient's internal world appears at once or in quick succession, thus providing vivid information about the patient's way of relating and functioning. I think this can be seen in the material I have presented: there was in her responses to me a quick movement, which seemed to indicate a continuous oscillation in the way she experienced her objects. She felt me to be someone that could listen, and in spite of her doubts she felt hopeful that eventually I might understand her and her routine. But almost immediately, she felt me as a bad and critical object. When I spoke, this experience of me seemed to change again and she could bring the dream. In interpreting it, I was felt as understanding by her and she could "deal with" (take in?) what I said, but very rapidly she was assailed by doubts about me being a bad object, who acts superficially and ignores important feelings. She seemed to wish to encounter in me an omnipotent object, able to deal quickly with what she had reported as one of her main problems, loneliness. Hope and disappointment seemed to move in quick succession; she desired a good object, but no sooner had she allowed herself this feeling than she felt disappointed, and the object became bad; in this same way she was also showing different parts of herself in action in the session.

The theory I am using relates mainly (but not exclusively, of course) to Klein's (1935, 1940, 1946) concepts about the phenomena of the depressive and paranoid–schizoid position, Bion's (1963) movements between PS↔D, and Joseph's (1989) work in bringing together theory and technique in following these movements in detail. An example of this can be seen in how quickly Ms. A moved from depressive feelings, of hope and optimism, to suspicion, and how in these movements I, as the emerging transference object, kept changing. Following the theory and concepts I have referred to, I interpreted the transference from the moment I began to understand it.

To return to clinical material, this time from the fourth year of Ms. A's analysis. During these years the analysis had been stormy and difficult. Soon after the beginning the patient stopped lying down; she would sit on the couch, mainly facing the wall. There were intense swings between mania and depression in the sessions; she was histrionic and communicated a great deal by action. At the time of the sessions I will present, she had decided to delegate the running of the farm and to give up her activities as a financial consultant to go back to university to take a further degree in a specialized branch of economics. About her life I had learned that there were considerable difficulties in her relationship with her family, and that she felt very lonely. She suffered from severe insomnia, and was in a constant panic of not sleeping. She was addicted to all kind of devices, some very bizarre, to make herself sleep (but would not take prescribed medication). It also emerged that she had a perverse kind of masturbation, which took place in relation to her animals, and she felt very ashamed and abnormal because of it. The masturbation occurred mainly when she was very anxious and afraid that her mind was fragmenting, which she described as her brain being "mashed." One other important characteristic during these three years were her intense problems in separation; weekends were especially difficult for her and holidays a major problem. She tended to break down shortly before the holiday period, but during the holiday time itself she more or less coped, albeit precariously.

I will now present three successive sessions in which the patient's intense reaction to hope was at the center of our work. Then I shall go on to conceptualize what I thought was going on, drawing upon the theoretical ideas I use.

In a Monday session, unusually for her, Ms. A spoke about *the weekend not having been bad at all,* she had some guests at the farm, and she mentioned her wish to be friends with them. She had also gone to a dinner party, where she met someone with whom she had been at boarding school. This woman, also an economist, was studying for a Ph.D., and Ms. A spoke in some detail about these events. (While she was speaking, a fragment of a session from some time before came into my mind: vaguely, I remembered something to do with a dream about a shattered glass, and her response to my interpretation, when, with intensity, she had said, *"does this mean that I can get better?"*) Now I interpreted mainly her feeling pleased with these events, and that she seemed hopeful about the analysis helping her. She responded optimistically about her plans and expectations. This soon changed. First in a patronizing, sharp way she said that "not everything was solved for her," and then added, in a bitter tone, that the woman seemed to be all sorted out, she was married, had children, looked happy, and had no problems.

The way I see this material is that she seemed to have kept a good relationship with me through the weekend, and this allowed her to think about friendship and be hopeful on her return. In other words, her life and internal world could be repaired. But these feelings also seemed to bring to the fore a sense of impatience, and mockery of the "her" that was feeling like that. She then split herself; the hopeful her was projected into me while she sided with the her who mocked hope (she had spoken to me as if I had gone over the top) and was rivalrous with the woman with whom she compared herself. In other words, by projecting into me the more constructive aspect of herself she could temporarily avoid the awareness of the conflict, which had been intensified by a mixture of hope and impatience. Because of these schizoid defenses her arrogance increased and she felt internally impoverished (the other woman had everything, not she). My interpretation was mainly about her conflict and her perception of me, because of the projections (of course, in speaking to her I did not use these terms).

The following day she came looking agitated, and was very explosive. She started the session humming to herself, and, almost shouting, she said that *she had a virus; she did not like her life, she did not like her family, and did not like her house.* Any attempt of mine to say something was met with a barrage of scorn. I tried to speak to her about her reaction to having felt somehow hopeful the previous session, but she interrupted before I could end the sentence and mocked me bitingly, mimicking an imaginary analyst speaking about "a typical negative therapeutic reaction." She got very abusive, bombarding me, and I found it difficult to think. After a while, she stormed out, leaving before the end of the session. It was only after she had left the session, when I could think more clearly, that I realized that I had missed a crucial point. This was that the virus she had was *hope,* and no sooner was hope felt than it triggered intense impatience and a wish for an instantaneous solution: house, family, life should already have changed.

The following day, Ms. A telephoned exactly at her usual two minutes late into the session to tell me she was unwell and therefore could not come.

On Thursday she came, and sat down, looking serious and rather sad. Then with a fleeting smile she said, "I don't want you to think that I am pensive and gloomy." After this she remained silent for some time. I said that I thought that she did want me to know that she might be thinking about what had happened between us on Tuesday. She looked alert and expectant, but said nothing. After a pause I went on saying that it seemed to me that on Tuesday she had spoken about a virus which seemed to me to have been hope, but the hope-virus made her ill with burning impatience, expecting everything to be changed at a stroke. I added that when I had spoken about hope she felt that *it was I* who had the hope, and then it was I who had felt disappointed because she had said to me that not everything was solved; following my disappointment she believed that I had started to accuse her and so she responded with her tirade about negative therapeutic reaction. Further, she seemed not to have heard that I had not been talking about the bombardment, but about her hopefulness.

After this interpretation, she mumbled something about it having been her fault. After a brief interchange, she went on to tell me what had happened since the previous session. She spoke about the amount of "substances" she had taken, which had made her ill and caused her to vomit. She had woken from a dream in which her nanny, with a voice that was not her nanny's, was saying that she had to die, better to die or that she was going to die (her nanny is an important person in her life, more like a governess than a nanny, and she remains a close family friend). After waking up, she had vomited. In the morning, though she tried, she could not stay in bed, got up, and kept pacing up and down. She then spoke about the rest of the morning. I asked her what voice the nanny had in the dream and she replied "*the voice of a horse,*" adding after a short pause, "*but you know that horses do not talk.*"

After the events of the previous session and the day she missed, it seemed to me that something had changed in her, but she expected me to speak. This could be thought as perverse, but I felt it was not. Whatever had happened, I had become a better object, but not securely so. Once I reminded her of the previous session, she was more able to listen to my interpreting her conflict and her projections. She could then bring further material about her difficulties related to holding onto a better experience: it made her feel guilty (it was her fault) and this guilt felt so intolerable that I drove her to intensify her attacks (I will come back to this). The dream seemed to indicate the kind of object I had become in her mind (represented by the nanny). It was a mixed object: it was mercilessly accusing and condemning, a persecuting cruel object; it was also the voice of someone she loves (the horse, and the nanny), but it was "voiceless" as well; that is, the object had lost its capacity to help. By becoming such a persecuting object I had lost my analytic capacity, represented by the voice.

My interpretation was directed to the facts of the previous session, which had made her feel that I had lost my understanding voice and had become totally condemning, thus leaving her hopeless. After my interpretation she went back to talk about the previous day, how frightened she had been by all the substances she had ingested. She continued describing how agitated she had been and how finally in the afternoon she had gone riding in an attempt to feel better. But this time her riding did not help and she felt terribly anxious. After a while she started feeling "sexed" in relation to the horse. She tried desperately to stop herself from feeling like that by trying to think about what was going on, but her attempts did not work and she ended up having sex with the animals. She was very upset while telling me this, and ended by saying, "disgusting, is it not?," sounding very harsh with herself and very pained.

I now want to describe how I conceptualized this material while away from the patient during the process I have called "homework." The thinking is predominantly conscious, and this brings together conceptualizations formed during sessions and more systematic theoretical thinking. Usually, one's ideas in this process are even more tentative than when in the presence of the patient.

The experience of hope belongs to the depressive position, that is, to the experience with objects felt to be whole, for whom the patient cares and by whom he feels protected. Here Klein's ideas (1935, 1940) about the depressive position are central to my thinking, and help me to understand my patient's difficulties with hope. Hope is an affect that depends on the patient's capacity to maintain relationships with good internal objects. He recognizes his dependence on these objects and accepts the fact that they can provide for him. The more secure the relationship, the more capable of hope the person is. If the patient is well established in the depressive position and for some reason or other this relationship is disturbed by hostile feelings, which result in attacks on his good objects, the patient will tend to feel guilty. The capacity to sustain hope will depend on the degree of his destructiveness and on his capacity to tolerate guilt and carry out reparation. It will also depend on the extent of help available from his external object. If this fails, the patient feels that he has lost his good objects and may feel that he has lost hope as well. This leads to despair.

The patient I am speaking about had reached the depressive position, but would quickly retreat again. She was not yet able to reestablish and maintain a more integrated level of mental functioning. She had in the past managed to cope by developing a pathological organization. Her obsessional defenses (her routine) and her perverse masturbatory activity contained a more troubled and damaged part of herself in which fragmentation served as a means of attack and as a defense. The organization confined the fragmentation and permitted her to split, and thus to protect a more capable and functioning self. But her functioning was very limited, and she could not tolerate guilt, waiting, or dependency: the impact of any of these feelings drove her to resort to massive schizoid maneuvers, which left her persecuted and threatened by the precarious functioning of her organization. Three years of analysis had also affected her way of reacting and weakened her defenses, but I cannot go into that here.

In the first session on the Monday it was clear that she had kept a better relationship with her internal object, which allowed her to feel hopeful. At first she was friendly in the transference, but then she became impatient, probably stimulated by my presence. Fear of being invaded by it may have led her to project her impatience into me as her internal object, who was then felt to be unrealistically impatient and in possession of everything. How is the Tuesday session to be understood? I think her projections into me had partially failed, so she was left feeling persecuted, and her behavior in the session aimed to evacuate these feelings. I had failed to take them in a more containing way; my thinking had not been clear enough, probably affected by the intensity of the bombardment. One possibility is that she perceived my attempts—particularly when I was unclear about what was going on—as my trying to push her projections back into her. I also think that when she felt so powerful in her bombardment she experienced my attempts to say something as false, as those of a pretend analyst.

The material in Thursday's session permits speculation about what had happened on Wednesday, when Ms. A had missed her session and acted out. The pressure in her mind must have felt unbearable. She woke up from a nightmare, the content of which greatly upset and frightened her, and she felt compelled to expel whatever she had in her mind (concretely, she vomited). This did not seem to relieve her sufficiently and she remained agitated. She tried to use her habitual obsessional defenses, the routine riding. She also tried to regain some contact with a thinking object (we had been familiar in the analysis with her feeling that she experienced me as thinking and wanting her to think and her often declaring that she would not do so). This defense also failed. The masturbatory activity probably served partly as a discharge, and partly as a means of encapsulating her sense of disintegration. This seemed to have been more efficacious.

The object that appeared in the dream was a very mixed one. Its most immediate characteristic is of someone who threatens her with death, or *recommends* death to her. In the first instance it is a hostile condemning object, because guilt about her behavior has turned into horrible persecution. Despite this persecution she managed to maintain contact with feelings of guilt, as seen in the Thursday session when she responded to my interpretation saying, "so it was my fault." This object is also a loved object, she loves the nanny, and she loves her horses, and remembered in the session that she sometimes had complained that her nanny was not very effective. The horses, too, are often elements in her masturbation. So possibly the object in the dream is also a perverse object, since it invites her to a false solution—death or mindlessness—which she acts out instead of coming to the session. I think it is possible that when I could not get through to her on Tuesday she might also have felt me to be pretending. On that Wednesday, when her riding was not helping her, she tried to think, but could not. In desperation she turns to a perverted masturbation in a final attempt to arrest the fragmentation which she felt to be so threatening. Considering the masturbatory activity, I am reminded of Freud's (1911, 1937) descriptions of delusions as an attempt at cure. For this patient it was felt to be the only thing she could do at that moment. In the session on Thursday she was more accessible, and I think this was partly due to the success of her masturbatory activity. She could then tell me what had happened and could work with me on trying to understand the meaning of the masturbation, which always distressed her so much.

It is difficult to demonstrate unconscious conceptualizations bit by bit. I think that these occur at the point where a meaning starts to emerge in the analyst's mind from many disparate elements. For instance, pieces of observation, aspects of the patient's history, emotional responses of the analyst, thoughts that come into his mind, be they directly connected with what the patient is saying or apparently unconnected to his actual discourse but referring to it. An example of the latter was the memory I suddenly had in that Monday session of her saying some time back, "so I can get better"; that is, aspects of the patient's history that at moments emerge in one's mind. Eventually these bits cohere into a configuration which derives from and is made sense of by one's theory. At times, of course, we simply sense something, our intuition (informed by theory) tells us that it is important, but it might take a long time before we can get some understanding of it.

In this paper I have described and illustrated what I understand to be a clinical fact and tried to conceptualize this. It is through our theory that we perceive and understand in analysis, and through our conceptualizing that we can contribute further to our theories.

REFERENCES

Bion, W. R. (1963), *Elements of Psycho-Analysis*. London: Heinemann.
Freud, S. (1911), Psycho-analytic notes on an autobiographical account of a case of paranoia (dementia paranoides). *Standard Edition*, 12:1–82. London: Hogarth Press, 1958.
———— (1937), Constructions in analysis. *Standard Edition*, 23:255–269. London: Hogarth Press, 1964.
Joseph, B. (1989), *Psychic Equilibrium and Psychic Change*. London & New York: Routledge.
Klein, M. (1935), A contribution to the psychogenesis of manic-depressive states. In: *Contributions to Psycho-Analysis*. London: Hogarth Press, 1948, pp. 282–310.
———— (1940), Mourning and its relation to manic-depressive states. In: *Contributions to Psycho-Analysis*. London: Hogarth Press, 1948, pp. 311–338.

———— (1946), Notes on some schizoid mechanisms. In: *Writings*, Vol. 3. London: Hogarth Press, 1975, pp. 1–24.

Sandler, J., & Sandler, A.-M. (1987), The past unconscious, the present unconscious and the vicissitudes of guilt. *Internat. J. Psycho-Anal.*, 68:331–341.

Tyson, R. L. (1991), The emergence of oedipal centrality, comments on Michael Feldman's "Common ground: The centrality of the Oedipus complex." *Internat. J. Psycho-Anal.*, 72:39–46.

EDITOR'S INTRODUCTION TO
PHANTASY AND REALITY

Hanna Segal's original contributions have played a central role in the evolution of contemporary British psychoanalysis. In addition to her contributions on creativity, psychoses, symbolism, and many other topics, references to which will be found throughout this essay, she has published masterful, scholarly distillations and overviews of Melanie Klein's life and works and the evolution of Kleinian theory and practice. Additionally, her many years of organizational leadership and influential teaching in the British Psycho-Analytic Institute have brought her wide recognition and praise throughout the world.

In this chapter she makes a new contribution to the basic concept of phantasy. She has written on phantasy before; on my reading, she enriches the understanding and appreciation of phantasy further. She does this first by showing how integrated it is with her other basic contributions to the major concepts of Kleinian thought. Second, she includes a large number of examples of clinical practice, examples that are up to her very high standard of deep, careful understanding, and reflective integrations of theory and practice.

As to this essay itself, Hanna Segal centers it on the complex, difficult evolution of adequate, stable reality testing out of the primitive morass of early mental functioning. In this respect, she works in the tradition of Freud's discussions of the two principles of mental functioning (1911), Karl Abraham's discussion of stages in the development of the libido (1924), and Sandor Ferenczi's essay on stages in the development of the sense of reality (1911).

She shows how this development is impeded in neuroses and severely damaged as well as blocked in the psychoses. In her clinical examples, she demonstrates how these limitations may be reduced through the psychoanalysis of transference, especially the use of projective identification in the patient's construction of the transference. This construction must be rigid, distorted, and a repetition of the patient's disturbed approach to the ascendancy of the reality principle. Later in the essay she moves on to analysis of how our attitudes toward loss, mourning, and our own death are controlled by the extent to which the pleasure principle has been integrated into the dominant reality principle and the death instinct has come under the domination of the life instinct.

Here, as elsewhere in this essay, Dr. Segal demonstrates how her theoretical propositions, like those of Melanie Klein and other outstanding Kleinians, are rooted in the basic writings of psychoanalysis and how consistent her clinical examples are with careful psychoanalytic practice. Skeptical ego psychological Freudians analysts may balk at her use of Freud's ideas about the life and death instincts; however, I suggest that to get the full benefit of Segal's thinking, they would do best to concentrate their attention on how these controversial ideas are actually used in clinical work and in reflections on the psychoanalytic process and its results.

I would take the same position about the central place accorded to omnipotence and projective identification in the author's discussion of phantasy, for these ideas correspond closely to what Freud wrote about the infant in "On Narcissism" (1914a) and "Instincts and Their Vicissitudes" (1914b), and what Abraham wrote in his "A Short History of the Development of the Libido" (1924). In these essays, omnipotence, the use of projection to create the purified pleasure ego and the resulting primary enmity to reality, and the prominence of part objects and sadism are all laid out in a compelling manner.

Readers unfamiliar with Kleinian discourse might be puzzled by several other features of Segal's discussion. For one thing, there is the use of *ph* instead of the familiar *f* to spell phantasy. This spelling has been adopted to emphasize the fundamental role of phantasy in the Kleinian adaptation of Freud's work on *unconscious* mental processes; this adaptation requires a sharp distinction between it and *f*antasy, which is used to refer to conscious and preconscious daydreaming. Segal makes it plain that it is in phantasy that unconscious desire, belief, and defense meet up with the experience of internal and external reality, before finding expression in actions that inevitably bear traces of their complex origins. In psychoses and extremes of violent action, she argues, these actions show little regulation by reality testing, whereas in neurotic and normal functioning, although phantasy is by no means eliminated, it is integrated under the aegis of the reality principle.

Second, the reader must always bear in mind that in Kleinian thought defensive operations are viewed both as expressions of unconscious phantasies and as mechanisms. That is to say, "defense mechanism" is a concept that belongs to two realms of their discourse, not just one—the structural one of Freud's metapsychology. Thus, it is to be understood as content as well as form, and one may speak of the phantasy aspect of defense as defending against that of another defense just as one may speak of one structural defense being used to defend against another. For example, projective identification is a mechanism that is also an unconscious phantasy of expulsion of parts of the self or internal objects. I believe that this two-pronged approach to defenses greatly facilitates their analysis in clinical work. The difficulty resides in the fact that the Kleinians tend to mix the two types of discourse freely, this practice being a reflection of the general theory they work with.

As for the rest, it is likely to be a matter of the reader's encountering some concepts and usages that have not yet been

taken up in this book in sufficient depth. The chapters following this one will define, amplify, and illustrate these possibly
confusing early references; for example, chapters 4 and 5 on
projective identification and splitting and chapter 8 on the
paranoid–schizoid and depressive positions. I believe that the
full extent of Hanna Segal's new contribution in this chapter
can be appreciated only after the reader has gone much further
into this book. On the other hand, this chapter belongs where
it is because the discussions of later chapters, as indeed the discussions of the first two chapters, depend on a clear understanding of the Kleinian use of phantasy.

REFERENCES

Abraham, K. (1924), A short study of the development of the libido
   viewed in the light of mental disorders. In: *Selected Papers of Karl
   Abraham*. New York: Basic Books.
Ferenczi, S. (1911), Stages in the development of the sense of reality.
   In: *The Selected Papers of Sandor Ferenczi*, Vol. 1. New York: Basic
   Books, pp. 213–239.
Freud, S. (1911), Formulations on the two principles of mental functioning. *Standard Edition*, 12:213–226. London: Hogarth Press,
   1958.
————— (1914a), On narcissism: An introduction. *Standard Edition*,
   14:67–102. London: Hogarth Press, 1957.
————— (1914b), Instincts and their vicissitudes. *Standard Edition*,
   14:109–140. London: Hogarth Press, 1957.

3

PHANTASY AND REALITY

HANNA SEGAL

In this chapter I shall address myself to the interplay between phantasy and reality which I believe molds our view of the world. It profoundly affects our personalities, it influences our perceptions, and it plays a large part in determining our actions. According to Freud (1911), the basic function of phantasy is to fill the gap between desire and satisfaction. Initially this gap is filled by omnipotent phantasy, sometimes by hallucination, but Freud argued that, at some point, the infant discovers that omnipotence does not satisfy his needs, and that a picture of reality has to be formed. At this point the pleasure–pain principle gives way to the reality principle. But at what point, and by what mechanisms, is this transition achieved? Why does it sometimes fail? And what form does the struggle take?

This struggle between omnipotent phantasy on the one hand and the acceptance of reality on the other exists from birth. It reaches its culmination in the depressive position in which, in Klein's definition, the infant recognizes his or her mother as a real, whole, and external object, and simultaneously recognizes

This discussion is based on the paper "Phantasy and Reality," originally written for the weekend Conference of the British Psycho-Analytical Society for English-Speaking Members of European Societies, October 1992.

75

the reality of his own ambivalent feelings. Phantasy is thus modified by experience and becoming less omnipotent is more able
to guide actions without distorting perception of reality. Nevertheless regression to omnipotence constantly threatens the perception of reality and leads to misconceptions and misperceptions
which underlie much of clinical pathology (Money-Kyrle, 1968).

Such misconceptions become manifest in the perception of
the analyst, and their study has been recognized as the crucial
task of analysis ever since Freud discovered transference. In the
transference relationship an image is formed of the analyst, and
the analysis of this image helps the patient gradually to differentiate between realistic perceptions and misperceptions. For
instance reacting to the analyst as though he were a figure of
the past is a misperception of the current relationship; when this
is corrected, the past is also revised. In this way the misperceptions in relation to the original figures can also be corrected,
because, as we have discovered, transference is not a simple
phenomenon of projecting the figures of the parents onto the
analyst. It is internal figures, sometimes part objects, which are
projected, and these internal objects have themselves a history
in which the conflict between phantasy and reality has led to
distortions. In fact the internal models on which we base our
attitudes to one another not only fail to correspond to current
reality, they are also, to a varying extent, a misrepresentation of
past reality.

Recent psychoanalytic work has led to a better understanding
of perception and misperception. I think this may partly be
because perception is particularly subject to distortion through
excessive and pathological projective identification, and, through
work over the past thirty years (Bion, 1962; Money-Kyrle, 1968;
Rosenfeld, 1971), projective identification itself has been much
better understood. When omnipotent phantasy dominates, the
desired state of affairs in accordance with the pleasure principle,
predominates over the realistic. Reality testing has failed as

omnipotent projective identification comes to distort the object and the subject's relationship with it.[1]

The important reality for the infant is the reality of his needs, desires, and fears in relation to his primary objects, and it is in the struggle to satisfy these needs that the conflict between the two principles takes place. Money-Kyrle (1968) suggests that the child has an innate predisposition to relate to objects in a realistic way which is based on inborn mental structures which become active at various stages of maturation. In my view these structures, which Bion refers to as preconceptions (1963), are associated with phantasies of the self and its basic relation to primary objects. Freud had postulated inborn phantasies of this kind which arise out of our common prehistoric past, and Klein (Isaacs, 1948) related them to the operation of instincts. I believe that a biologically based inner perception of our instinctual needs, both physical and emotional, leads to an unconscious phantasy of a need-satisfying object. Money-Kyrle also assumes, and I agree with him, that there is, in addition, an innate phantasy of a satisfying relationship between two other objects, which serves as the basis of the Oedipus complex.

What I am saying here parallels Chomsky's view of the development of language (1968), which always struck me as very close to a psychoanalytical viewpoint. For instance, he emphasizes that language is not a habit or a skill to be taught and learned, but that it is always a creative act. He assumes, and indeed demonstrates, that there is an inborn grammatical structure which does not need to be learned, but which, meeting the external world which provides a vocabulary and grammatical forms, interacts with them to create a language. Having an inborn grammatical

---

[1] This is related to the point made by Wollheim (1984), who described how desire can become confused with belief. When this happens, belief becomes incorrigible and irrational. It is not only distorted by desire but takes on a rigidity which makes it resistant to contradiction.

structure, and yet being able to acquire the different grammars of different languages, is like our view that the Oedipus complex is an inborn structure but that its actual realization will vary in different cultures, and in different individuals within a culture.

Sometimes it is possible to observe the way individual patients can recognize basic mental structures, and are also aware of their hatred and prejudice against the recognition of the reality which this structure represents. Mrs. A's material illustrates my point. She started the session by telling me that she had two very tiny fragments of a dream. In one, she saw me surrounded by middle-aged, stupid, altogether despicable men. Of the second fragment she could remember only that it had something to do with African land and African people. The first dream seemed pretty obvious to both of us, and connected to an impending long weekend. But the other, hardly remembered fragment brought surprisingly rich associations. To begin with, she expressed her horror of racial prejudice from which she cannot free herself, and yet detests. That seemed to provide a link between the first dream of the men with whom I may be spending my weekend and the second about the Africans.

The patient, who was a teacher in charge of a class of young children, started to speak about a child's difficulty in learning any grammar, particularly foreign grammar. She thought that Africa might represent this child's feeling that grammar was totally exotic and incomprehensible. This girl, she said, was quite clever, but very disjointed. She seemed unable to make certain connections, something which was particularly obvious in her total inability to grasp the rules of grammar After all, grammar, with the sort of patterns it describes, should come more naturally. Then she laughed and said, "Maybe to her grammar is as foreign and exotic as parents in intercourse must appear to a child—beyond reach, incomprehensible, exotic, foreign." This patient was often preoccupied and disturbed by very primitive fantasies of the primal scene. In this session she seems to feel that there are certain natural patterns of interrelationship, as in grammar, and that this included an intuitive awareness of parental intercourse. In the first dream that intercourse is attacked and derided. She had a prejudice against it, like a prejudice against Africans, and her associations to it suggested that she was aware how her thinking is dislocated by her attack on those natural patterns of relationships. She made an intuitive link between grammar and object relationships and she felt that there was a natural pattern in both.

Both the object relations structures studied by us and the deep grammar of language have the same source in what Chomsky calls "human functions." Indeed it seems likely that the development of language springs from the grammar of object relations rather than the other way round. An example might be the grammar which governs the relationship between subject, object, and action.

How then is it that despite such preconceptions which connect the subject with reality there are so many distortions and misperceptions which tilt perception in the direction of the pleasure principle? I believe this partly results from the fact that we have learned to recognize that perception is an active process in which phantasy and the perception of reality interact (Segal, 1964). Preconceptions or primitive phantasies are tested in perception, just as hypotheses are tested against reality. This matching of inner phantasies against external reality takes place throughout life but is interfered with if the phantasy omnipotently distorts the object and interferes with reality testing. Reality testing then fails and the wish-fulfilling phantasy is preferred to and dominates reality; but the dominance is always only partial.

Freud recognized this when he wrote as follows in the famous footnote to his 1911 paper, "Formulations on Two Principles of Mental Functioning":

> It will rightly be objected that an organization which was a slave
> to the pleasure principle and neglected the reality of the exter-
> nal world could not maintain itself alive for the shortest time, so
> that it could not have come into existence at all. The employ-
> ment of a fiction like this is, however, justified when one consid-
> ers that the infant—provided one includes with it the care it
> receives from its mother—does *almost* realise a psychical system
> of this kind [p. 220, emphasis added].

The battle between perception of reality and the omnipotent
imposition of phantasy onto reality is a long battle which proceeds in small stages. In part this battle is a constant attack on
perception by the omnipotent self, and it is not only an attack
on external perception but also an attack on perception of one's
own inner states, and on the inborn phantasies such as those of
parental intercourse, which interfere with omnipotence.

Money-Kyrle (1968) remarks that it is striking how children
have every conceivable theory about parental intercourse except the right one. Both the perception of reality and the underlying preconception are attacked in order to produce such
misperceptions. Clinically what we see are objects which are
based neither on pure perception of external reality, nor on the
perseverance of primary internal phantasies, but are the result
of the interaction between the inborn patterns and experience.

Perception is also distorted by the excessive use of projective
identification, and here its effect is twofold. First the object is
distorted because it is not seen as it really is but has properties
attributed to it, and second it has a concrete existence which is
rigidly held onto so that it cannot function as a normal symbol
(Segal, 1957; chapter 7). An infant under the sway of omnipotent phantasies creates a world based on his projections in which
objects in the external world are always perceived in the same
way, since they reflect and embody the subject's own primitive
phantasies and parts of his projected self and internal objects.
They are rigid and repetitive because they are not modulated

by the interaction with reality, hence the repetition compulsion described by Freud (1920).

I will illustrate such a rigid pattern in a repetitive dream from Mr. B, a patient who suffered from gastric ulcer. He had had this dream, which was close to a nightmare, on and off ever since he could remember, and as a very small child he remembered waking up in a panic from it. In the dream he is tied immovably to a chair in a half-lying position. He is threatened from all sides by several elongated animals with crocodile mouths.

The first occurrence of the dream in the course of his analysis was in the context of castration anxiety, the fear of having his penis bitten off or chopped off as a punishment for masturbating. It appeared again in the context of a phantasy of myself being pregnant, and anxiety about attacking the inside of my body and the babies there. The unformed elongated shapes with crocodile mouths represented the vengeful dangerous babies inside the mother. The dream kept recurring in various contexts.

In one session something struck me about his posture on the couch as he was telling me that the dream had recurred, and I asked him whether he had ever been swaddled as a baby. He said he had been, for four months, and he had also been told that he used to scream with pain almost constantly. The cause of the pain had been diagnosed as colic. I thought that the elongated body and the enormous, dangerous mouth was his experience of himself at that time projected outside into his object and coloring his perception. Since that session the dream stopped recurring, and eventually the psychosomatic symptom disappeared as well.

It seems to me that at the core of his personality this patient had a perception of an object endowed with his own characteristics as a swaddled infant, an immobilized body, and a hungry, angry, enormous, biting mouth. The perception of this object is deeply repressed and split off from the rest of his personality. At the most primitive level it was contained in the psychosomatic symptom, his gastric ulcer. But it is also transferred onto other objects; women, children, men. The projections imbued the perception of those other objects with characteristics which were monotonously the same. He felt very persecuted by his wife, and sexual intercourse was disturbed by a phantasy of a vagina dentata. He perceived children as demanding and damaging and was persecuted by men, particularly in his professional life. There was a monotonous rigidity to his object relationships because of the constant projection into them of this basic persecutory object.

Such rigidity, however, is sometimes amenable to analysis, and to illustrate this I shall bring a session from another patient who does show a shift, to a more realistic view of the analyst as an internal object. Mr. C swung between states of schizoid withdrawal and manic overactivity, very monotonously. Each of these states was accompanied by persecution which drove him into the other state. The patient was not overtly psychotic, and on a superficial level he functioned adequately, but his human relations were superficial and unsatisfactory. He first went into analysis in late adolescence because of a fear that he was schizophrenic. He came to me in middle age because of a general dissatisfaction with himself and his life. He came from Scotland and enormously idealized the land he owned there. For weeks before and after a holiday he would withdraw, in his mind, to Scotland.

The session I will report occurred a few weeks before a holiday which he was proposing to take in Scotland. For some time before, the patient had been concerned with his lapses of memory. He admitted something that I had noticed for a long time, but which he denied, namely that if I made a reference to a previous session or past situations he often had no memory of them at all. The same was true within the session. I could refer to what he had said five or ten minutes before, and he would realize that it was a complete blank in his mind. He would cover up by overtalking, which he now admitted was often quite a conscious device to hide his lapses from me. Connected with this overtalking was his tendency to dispose of my interpretations by vague associations, abstractions, and generalizations, stripping the experience of any emotional meaning, and often getting confused at the end. I sometimes experienced listening to him as like walking in a mist, unable to find one's way.

He started the session by telling me three dreams, the first of which he found very moving.

> You were in Scotland and I was thrilled to see you. It was marvelous having you there. But it was not like the last occasion you were in Scotland. I had nothing to do with it. I did not even know what your lecture was to be about. It was a strange experience because I was so pleased to see you, and yet I felt so excluded. It was so awful not even knowing what you planned or what was on your mind.

This was in marked contrast to a previous occasion when I had actually gone to lecture in Scotland and the patient had been greatly pleased but had experienced it as though he had arranged the whole thing and could exhibit me, his marvelous analyst, to the Scottish audience.

In the second dream the analyst disappeared and the patient himself gave the lecture to a very big audience. However, he was given a theme that was much too vague and general, such as how to apply analysis to one's work and he was dissatisfied with it. The lecture itself did not appear in the dream, but afterwards there was a social gathering and a girl shows him a family watch, which he had given her but which did not work, and which he promised to fix. The watch was very big with transparent stripes alternating with black, opaque ones. In the third dream he was trying to mend a crumbling wall.

His first associations were to my previous trip to Scotland, and how different it had been from the dream. On that occasion he

had not felt excluded; he had felt enlarged. The painful exclusion in the dream was much closer to the way he often felt in
England. But he found the dream very moving: it was so good
to have me in Scotland, even though it was very painful. He
thought he had the dream because of the relief he felt after the
Friday session in which we discussed his lapses of memory and
thought that the transparent and black opaque stripes were like
lapses of memory: "Now I remember; now I don't." He also connected the watch with feeling very shocked when I ended the
session on Friday. He usually withdrew and prepared for the end
of the session, but this time it had taken him quite unawares.
The crumbling wall he associated to a neighbor who built a wall
on a crumbling cliff and made a much too heavy superstructure
on something that did not have a proper foundation. He said
he had had a very good weekend in Scotland and he put this
down to the effect of the Friday session.

I kept an open mind. He always has a marvelous time in Scotland, and was invariably manic during holidays. We were a few
weeks from the holiday. I wondered if the good weekend was
because of clear patches in his head or because of the black
patches, having got rid of the memory of the experience. However, it was significant that he did think a lot about the Friday
session, and in contrast to the usual lack of memory he could
immediately connect the dream with it. I took up his associations and linked them with the generalization and vagueness,
which we had also discussed on Friday.

The first dream seemed to represent a shift. Keeping me in
his mind as I really was, meant he also had to admit the perception of me as a very separate object. He was not in control, and
not only was he not omnipotent but could not make me come to
Scotland as he had felt on the previous occasion. He was also not
omniscient and did not know what was on my mind. Hence, to
accept me as this more realistic internal object was a situation of
both gratification and pain. The next dream was an attack on this

perception. I disappeared; he was me; he gave the lecture. In reality he often behaved and felt as though he were me. But the lecture had no substance. The people in the audience were not real perceived objects but projected parts of his child-self. The tubular watch represented what he felt about his patchy memory. The wall with its too heavy superstructure which collapses because it has no foundation is exactly what happened when he gave his empty lecture. Somewhere in the background the crumbling foundations represented the analyst destroyed in his memory.

What I want to illustrate by this material is the shift in his perception of the object. The second and third dreams represent his more usual state of mind, with narcissistic object relationships achieved by projective identification by which the true perception of the object is annihilated. The first dream however, represents a move to an internal object which is a combination of wishful phantasy: to have me in Scotland and also to have me as a part of himself in his mind, but it is also a perception: an object experienced as having given gratification, hence desired but not omnipotently possessed.

I want to emphasize the patient's recognition that *he does not know what is on my mind.* I have always been struck by the way some schizophrenics look into your eyes and say, "I know what you are thinking." This is not surprising if we realize that they believe this because the analyst's mind has been filled with thoughts they have projected there. In this way the objects are felt to be known through and through. In the schizophrenic this is a conscious delusion while in the neurotic it is an unconscious phantasy which nevertheless colors the perception of external objects. By contrast, in his dream the patient does *not* know what is on my mind. One could say I am not a saturated object, therefore I am open to variation. When he reprojects such an object into the external world the patient can recognize what in the object does correspond to his internal phantasies, to aspects of his primary objects or of himself, and yet he recognizes too that he does not know everything about his object. It was therefore open to exploration and allows him to differentiate between external objects and his internal projected phantasy. In the re-internalization he also acquires a variety of objects with different characteristics. The move is from rigidity to flexibility in the perception of external and internal objects.

The nature of identifications also changed. In subsequent sessions the patient commented on the improvements in his memory. He also told me that in the past he did not bother to remember. He left it to me; it was my job; that was how analysis worked. Now he began to feel that he too could, and should, exercise this function.

But the ascendance of the reality principle does not mean that phantasy is abandoned. It continues in the unconscious and it is expressed symbolically. Even our most primitive desires find symbolic forms of expression. But how they express themselves is crucial. Freud has said that every man marries his mother; yet he expressed shook and horror at a colleague marrying a woman old enough, he said, to be his mother. Why is it that it is true that all men marry their mothers, and yet this universal phantasy can also be at the root of disastrous marriages and deep pathology? I have previously suggested (Segal, 1957) that it hinges on the nature of symbolism. I made a distinction between concrete symbolism, in which the symbol is equated with what is symbolized (the symbolic equation), and a more evolved form in which the symbol represents the object but is not confused and identified with it, and does not lose its own characteristics.

This view was later refined by others and developed in my later paper on the subject (Segal, 1978; chapter 7) in which the failure of the symbolic process was linked to failures in the containing function of the object. This is clearly seen in the case of pathological mourning. In normal mourning the lost object is retained in the mind in an alive way while the mourner is also aware of its real absence. But if the loss leads to the feeling of a concrete presence of a corpse inside one's body then the mourning processes cannot proceed. You cannot bring a real corpse to life, any more than you can change feces back into milk. Such an object can only bring you down into melancholia or be expelled in mania, as described by Abraham (1924).

This is illustrated by a patient in the second year of her analysis. Mrs. D came for difficulties in her relationships, but it soon became apparent that she was very severely obsessional. She was a painter, but because of endless procrastinations her work was always extremely slow, and for the last few years it had almost come to a complete halt. She spent hours collecting potentially useful objects, tidying, cleaning, attending to her clothes, makeup, and so on, and her days became completely consumed by these activities.

The material I want to present comes from a period about a month after a holiday when I had taken two weeks off and she had responded by taking an extra week. In that extra week she had nightmares about ruined houses, explosions, and the resulting rubble. Some time after the break, she eventually got her studio ready and was going to start work. She often worked from photographs, and during the holiday in Italy she had taken pictures of various interesting cemeteries, and had by now assembled sufficient pencils, paint, and other material so that she was ready to start.

One day, for the first time in a long time, she actually started drawing. She had told me that she planned a series of sketches and drawings of various cemeteries which could make a complete enough work for an exhibition. Her associations to the cemeteries were that she liked the ceremonial of burial and that her mother, who had lived in another country, had never had a burial in the way my patient would have wished. Her mother was buried like rubbish. That association was crucial and enabled me to show her how her endless clearing of rubble and rubbish was connected with the thought that her mother was buried like rubbish, and that the endless task of clearing, organizing, and tidying the rubbish was her way of trying to reverse the process. It was also possible to make connections with the extra week's holiday she had taken and her guilt at that point of turning her analytical house into rubble. In her drawing she seemed to have found another way of dealing with the situation, by giving her mother a proper burial, letting her die, and keeping her alive in her mind. This had a parallel in the way she used to hang onto my words during my absences, when mostly they felt like meaningless fragments, but sometimes she was able to keep alive the meaning of what I had said.

She was very moved by the session, getting a glimpse of another kind of reparation possible to her, but she showed a typical negative therapeutic reaction the next day. Having complained for years that her husband does not sufficiently care for her work and does not encourage her enough, she realized in the evening that she was furious because he had been so helpful in arranging her studio, and she felt that both he and I were too pleased at her having started to work. We just wanted to lock her up in the studio, so that she would not give us any trouble. It also meant that we did not want her to have a real child, and wanted her to be satisfied with work. She seemed to experience the session as an attack on her way of doing reparation, which had to be concrete, like having a child. In fact it is not her husband and I who had stopped her having a child, but her own procrastination since she was then nearly 50.

This patient was consumed by repetitive, compulsive actions and her sessions were filled with endless repetitions of detail. She was the most overtalkative patient I ever had, and often the barrage of words was like dead rubble between us. The concreteness of her experience that her mother became rubbish inside her seemed to be connected with the compulsion to act as a means of projecting the rubbish outwards and in that way trying to clear it up. We can see how processes which interfere with perception have a decisive influence on the way we act.[2]

Why is it that living in accordance with the pleasure–pain principle in a hallucinated world should lead to compulsive action? It is obvious that acting on delusion is irrational. But why does it compel action? I think this results from the fact that in the delusional world where perception is dominated by projective identification there is an irrevocable tie between the self and the object. The disowned parts of the self which have been evacuated by projective identification are concretized outside, and have to be dealt with by concrete action.

The compulsion to act is particularly devastating in those psychotic patients driven to violence, as in the case of a prisoner who described how he carried out the murder of two children.[3] He took the children to a wood to play with them because he thought they were lonely, and feeling lonely too he thought he would make them happy playing and he would be less lonely himself. However, as he kept them for a long time they were not amused any more, and as it was getting dark the little boy began

_____

[2]Wollheim's distinction between *acting on desire*, which is rational and *acting on phantasy*, which is irrational, has many similarities to the link I am trying to demonstrate between phantasy and action (Wollheim, 1984). He also makes the point that acting on phantasy is compulsive, whilst desire, although a powerful incentive, does not lead to compulsive action. I agree with Wollheim's distinction, except in one respect. I think that acting on desire is also acting on phantasy. What he calls "acting on phantasy" I would call "acting on delusion." Rational action also involves phantasy. But the difference is in the way phantasy functions. Or, to put in another way, the difference is in the level of phantasy. Acting on delusion is characterized by certain conjoint phenomena; a misperception of external reality, a misperception of internal reality, including the reality of one's desire, and a compulsion to act, rather than a choice of action.

[3]This man who was in prison on another charge was undergoing intensive psychoanalytic psychotherapy with an analyst, who consulted me about the case.

to get frightened and started crying that he wanted to go home. The man took a stone and crushed his skull with it. He did not know why, and as the little girl was a witness he had to kill her too. That man, as a very small child, had been evacuated during World War II. In his foster home he was ill-treated, terrified, and lonely. He was so miserable that at the age of 3 or 4 he tried to kill himself by drinking cleaning fluid and eating shoe polish.

In his psychotherapy his material led the analyst to construe that the little boy was perceived by the man as though he was himself as a small child, and when he became frightened, lonely, and started to cry it was as intolerable to the man as was the memory of himself in the same state of mind as a little boy. His suicidal impulse as a little boy became the compulsive murder of the little boy, seen as the child himself, who had to be killed. In my experience, a similar mechanism underlies the dreaded compulsion to kill the baby in severe postpuerperal depression. The baby may represent a hated sibling, but more powerfully it is the baby part of oneself.

Not only parts of the self but internal objects may compel action when projected outward into objects, and such seems to be the case in some cases where prostitutes are murdered. The compulsion to kill may come from a delusional source such as the voice of God, and the prostitutes are confused with a sexual mother and treated in the delusional state as if they *were* the sexual mother. Such hatred of a sexual mother is also linked with a delusional picture of the mother herself. All her other characteristics are split off and she is seen as nothing but a vehicle of obscene sexuality. We know from our clinical practice that in such a situation the child's own sexuality is also projected into the mother. Therefore killing a prostitute would be killing both his sexual mother and his own projected sexuality.

These are gross examples, but this kind of concrete thinking also underlies the irrational behavior of a neurotic, as was illustrated in the tidying up and procrastination of my obsessional patient discussed above. In the case of another borderline obsessional patient who used to deal with hunger by defecating, the underlying unconscious phantasy was that the perception of hunger was a bad thing inside him that he could get rid of by defecating. He had many conscious rationalizations of this behavior, and he dealt with mental pain in a similar way. When his mother, to whom he was extremely attached, died, he experienced no mourning, but had numerous dreams about her which he would write down in a notebook and then forget all about. This was a mental equivalent of defecation and he would evacuate his pain into the notebook and in that way get rid of it.

There are, of course, differences between psychotic and criminal acts and symptoms in neurosis, two major ones being that in the neurotic and the borderline patient ambivalence is more in evidence and the delusion does not invade the whole of the personality but is encapsulated in a symptom.

It is also important to recognize that phantasy exercises a lure which lures one into action (Wollheim, 1984). As a result of projective identification desire is vested in the object and the object which contains the desire exercises the lure. If the object is felt to be possessed by a part of the self the self is then felt to be tied to the object and pulled by the object into compulsive actions.

Delusional actions also tend to be endlessly repeated and this compulsion to repeat has many sources. It is related to Bion's description of concrete beta elements which are not suitable for thinking or experiencing in dreams or phantasy and can only be dealt with by expulsion through action (Bion, 1963). It also arises because the action never accomplishes its objectives. It is a delusion to think that we can get rid of impulses or parts of the self by projecting them into an object.

Thus, acting on misperception is both compulsive and repetitive, since it always misses its objective. But what about acting on desire? How is this reconciled with the reality principle?

Freud suggests that the reality principle is nothing more than the pleasure–pain principle tested in reality. Since a desire always give rise to a phantasy of its fulfillment the reality testing of a phantasy is like a wishful hypothesis which is constantly matched with reality (Segal, 1964, 1991). If the phantasy is omnipotent the desire is replaced by a delusion, while in the more normal infant there is a capacity to perceive a reality which is differentiated from the wished for phantasy and in this way the phantasy is tested.

Reality testing also profoundly affects actions since a realistic picture of the object can lead to the search for an appropriate action in order to obtain optimal satisfaction from the object. A rational action must be based on recognition of realities, including the reality of one's own phantasies.

Freud emphasizes the importance of the recognition of external reality and we now recognize that external reality is inextricably linked with the recognition of the internal reality of one's own desires and phantasies. This recognition necessitates toleration of gaps in satisfaction, and therefore of one's own ambivalence toward the desired object. As I suggested earlier, Freud (1911) speaks of two ways of dealing with this gap. One is through omnipotent hallucinatory phantasy according to the pleasure principle, while the other, under the influence of the reality principle, leads to the development of thought. He describes thought as "experimental action," which I believe is already present in a primitive form in preverbal phantasy. Phantasies can be tested by perception, and through action: for example, crying when hungry, biting in anger, attracting attention and love with a smile. But there is also an experimental testing of the phantasy without an action. If phantasy is, as I suggest, a set of primitive hypotheses about the nature of the object and the world, one can experiment in phantasy by comparing different imagined outcomes. "What would happen if . . ." is very different from the delusional phantasy which creates an "as-if" world. A consideration of probabilities based on "What would happen if . . . ?" is a function of imagination as distinct from delusion and is the basis of flexible thought and rational action, since rational action takes into consideration the consequences of the action. Rationality necessitates imagination, and the infant experimenting in preverbal phantasy, which he tests in external reality, is like a budding scientist, and a highly successful one at that, often amazing us with the speed with which he learns about the nature of the world.

In the course of development, and also in the course of a successful analysis, a shift must be achieved from an archaic phantasy organization, which distorts perception and leads to compulsive action, to one allowing a greater capacity for reality testing. This shift is then reflected in the nature and function of the phantasies which reflect the shift from a basically paranoid–schizoid to a depressive position organization. The gradual withdrawal of projective identifications, the lessening of compulsive and repetitive actions, and the change in the nature of symbolism, are all conjoint phenomena characterizing evolution toward the depressive position.

In many of my papers I contend that the basic internal conflict is between the life and the death instincts, and that development and maturation are linked with the gradual ascendance of the life instinct, and an integration of the death instinct under the aegis of the life instinct. In this chapter I argue that there is a basic conflict between the omnipotence of phantasy and the acceptance of reality, and that development and maturation reflect the gradual ascendance of the reality principle over the pleasure–pain principle. These views are linked to Freud's final theory of the conflict between life and death instincts by virtue of the fact that a major manifestation of the death instinct is the attack on reality.

This becomes abundantly clear in the depressive position where it is the love for the object, and the love for one's life, as well as the love of life itself, which promotes the withdrawal of projections in order to preserve the object, and through the recognition of one's dependency to enable the self to survive in reality. The love of life leads to the preservation of one's object and oneself, which requires a respect for reality, while the death instinct includes the wish to disintegrate or annihilate the reality of life. Its ultimate aim is death.

Yet, paradoxically, the acceptance of reality includes also the acceptance of the inevitability not only of death but also of the existence of the death instinct within us. Denial and projection of this reality also leads to misperception and impulsive action. The life instinct, according to Freud, promotes integration, and that integration includes the recognition of the death instinct itself. What Freud called the fusion of the two I think is an integration, in which the death instinct is recognized and included into our mental lives without dominating and destroying them.

REFEFENCES

Abraham, K. (1924), A short study of the development of libido viewed in the light of mental disorders. In: *Selected Papers on Psychoanalysis*. New York: Basic Books.

Bion, W. R. (1962), *Learning from Experience.* London: Heinemann.

———— (1963), *Elements of Psychoanalysis.* London: Karnac.

Chomsky, N. (1968), *Language and Mind.* New York: Harcourt, Brace, & World.

Freud, S. (1911), Formulations on the two principles of mental functioning. *Standard Edition*, 12:213–226. London: Hogarth, 1958.

———— (1920), Beyond the pleasure principle. *Standard Edition*, 18:3–64. London: Hogarth, 1955.

Isaacs, S. (1948), The nature and function of phantasy. *Internat. J. Psycho-Anal.*, 29:73–97.

Money-Kyrle (1968), Cognitive development. *Internat. Psycho-Anal.*, 44:691–698.

Rosenfeld, H. (1971), Contribution to the psychopathology of psychotic states. The importance of projective identification in the ego structure and object relations of psychotic patients. In: *Melanie Klein Today*, Vol. 1, *Mainly Theory*, ed. E. Bott Spillius. London: Routledge, p. 117–137.

Segal, H. (1957), Notes on symbol formation. *Internat. J. Psycho-Anal.*, 30:391–397.

——— (1964), *An Introduction to the Work of Melanie Klein.* New York: Basic Books.

——— (1978), On symbolism. *Internat. J. Psycho-Anal.*, 59:315–319.

——— (1991), Imagination, play, and art. In: *Dream, Phantasy, and Art.* London: Routledge.

Wollheim, R. (1984), *The Thread of Life.* Cambridge: Cambridge University Press.

EDITOR'S INTRODUCTION TO
PROJECTIVE IDENTIFICATION:
SOME CLINICAL ASPECTS

Along with Hanna Segal, it is Betty Joseph who is recognized as the leading figure in the contemporary British Kleinian group. She has written many influential articles on a great variety of psychoanalytic subjects, among the best of which, in my opinion, are those that have focused on complex and difficult technical problems. In this chapter, she both expounds the concept of projective identification and illustrates its clinical uses subtly and elegantly.

Following the lead of Melanie Klein, today's Kleinian analysts usually speak of projective identification in preference to projection. To set the stage for Miss Joseph's contribution to this topic, I shall provide a brief account of the Kleinians' preference. Freud used projection in the context of the metaphor on which he based his model of mental activity. He likened the mind to an energy-driven mechanical apparatus, the energy being supplied by instinctual drives. He proposed that the instinctual drives may be inferred from their "presentations": affects, drive-cathected ideas, or both. Affects themselves are forms of drive discharge. Projection is defined as the attribution of an affect or cathected idea of one's own to another person or a thing (animism). That person or thing appears mentally as a "representation." The projection is then said to be *on* or *onto* that representation. This usage follows the model of distribution of psychic energies or cathexes. The language employed is dictated by the cathectic model of drive.

Although the Kleinians retain the concepts of libido and death instinct as the sources of motivational energy, they finesse the complex issues of cathectic distributions. Their context is always the internal object relations that prevail in unconscious phantasy. They see the infant as prepared for object-related experience from the first. The infant experiences instinctual impulses, affects, and ideas in concrete relational terms, that is, as parts of the self or the object, each in relation to the other. The materiality or corporeality of these mental experiences requires language that describes the movement of substances in space and not the attachment or discharge of cathectic energies.

In their context, the Kleinians therefore speak of projection *into* the object, as when they speak of forcing something into it or invading it; the same language appears in another form in the ideas of expelling substances (objects) *out of* the self and taking them *into* it. In the unconscious phantasy version of projective identification, some part of the self is portrayed as now being in the object; then the self is not entirely distinct from the object, it may be merged with it, and that part of the self may be imagined as controlling the object. Instead of a part of the self, it may be another mental content that is projected (more exactly, reprojected), namely, an internal object or introject.

The term *projective identification* seems well suited to cover the phenomena of projection in Kleinian thought where the object-relational phantasy is applicable to all mental operations. The Kleinian type of object-relational phantasy applies to defenses, to ego functions, such as the ability to reason, remember, or set standards, and to moral imperatives.

In this framework, Betty Joseph identifies a variety of functions and consequences of a person's using projective identification. This she does especially in her account of transference, the uses of countertransference, and the analysis of impaired ego functioning. She also points out that the person who is targeted as the one to receive the projective identification may begin to experience induced feelings and act on them without being able to explain how these feelings have been transmitted to him or her. The skeptical reader might recall in this regard that, in daily life, it is not unusual for people to comment on how they get to feel or act a certain way around someone else and not quite know why they do so. Technically, the concept of projective identification focuses attention on the frequency of this type of occurrence in countertransferences. Betty Joseph's clinical examples demonstrate how this can be so.

4
PROJECTIVE IDENTIFICATION: SOME CLINICAL ASPECTS

BETTY JOSEPH

The concept of projective identification was introduced into analytic thinking by Melanie Klein in 1946. Since then it has been welcomed, argued about, the name disputed, the links with projection pointed out, and so on; but one aspect seems to stand out above the firing line, and that is its considerable clinical value. It is this aspect that I shall mainly concentrate on here, and mainly in relation to the more neurotic patient.

Melanie Klein became aware of projective identification when exploring what she called the paranoid–schizoid position, that is, a constellation of a particular type of object relations, anxieties, and defenses against them, typical for the earliest period of the individual's life, and in certain disturbed people, continuing throughout life. This particular position she saw dominated by the infant's need to ward off anxieties and impulses by splitting both the object, originally the mother, and the self, and

This paper was first given at a conference on Projection, Identification, and Projective Identification held at the Sigmund Freud Centre of the Hebrew University of Jerusalem in May 1984.

projecting these split-off parts into an object, which will then be felt to be like, or identified with, these split-off parts, so coloring the infant's perception of the object and its subsequent introjection.

She discussed the manifold aims of different types of projective identification; for example, splitting off and getting rid of unwanted parts of the self that cause anxiety or pain; projecting the self or parts of the self into an object to dominate and control it and thus avoid any feelings of being separate; getting into an object to take over its capacities and make them its own; invading in order to damage or destroy the object. Thus the infant, or the adult who goes on using such mechanisms powerfully, can avoid any awareness of separateness, dependence, admiration, or its concomitant sense of loss, anger, or envy. But it sets up anxieties of a persecutory type, claustrophobia, panics, and the like.

We could say that, from the point of view of the individual who uses such mechanisms strongly, projective identification is a phantasy and yet it can have a powerful effect on the recipient. It does not always do so, and when it does we cannot always tell how the effect is brought about, but we cannot doubt its importance. We can see, however, that the concept of projective identification, used in this way, is more object related, more concrete, and covers more aspects than the term *projection* would ordinarily imply, and it has opened up a whole area of analytic understanding. These various aspects I am going to discuss later, as we see them operating in our clinical work. Here I want only to stress two points: first, the omnipotent power of these mechanisms and phantasies; second, how, insofar as they originate in a particular constellation, deeply interlocked, we cannot in our thinking isolate projective identification from the omnipotence, the splitting, and the resultant anxieties that go along with it. Indeed, we shall see that they are all part of a balance, rigidly or precariously maintained by the individual, in his own individual way.

As the individual develops, either in normal development or through analytic treatment, these projections lessen, he becomes more able to tolerate his ambivalence, his love and hate, and dependence on objects; in other words, he moves toward what Melanie Klein described as the depressive position. This process can be helped in infancy if the child has a supportive environment, if the mother is able to tolerate and contain the child's projections, intuitively to understand and stand its feelings. Bion elaborated and extended this aspect of Melanie Klein's work, suggesting the importance of the mother being able to be used as a container by the infant, and linking this with the process of communication in childhood and with the positive use of the countertransference in analysis. Once the child is better integrated and able to recognize its impulses and feelings as its own, there will be a lessening in the pressure to project, accompanied by an increased concern for the object. In its earliest forms projective identification has no concern for the object, indeed it is often anticoncern, aimed at dominating, irrespective of the cost to the object. As the child moves toward the depressive position, this necessarily alters. Although projective identification is probably never entirely given up, it will no longer involve the complete splitting off and disowning of parts of the self. It will be less absolute, more temporary, and more able to be drawn back into the individual's personality, and thus be the basis of empathy.

To begin with, let us consider some of the implications, clinical and technical, of the massive use of projective identification as we see it in our work. Sometimes it is used so massively that we get the impression that the patient is, in phantasy, projecting his whole self into his object and may feel trapped or claustrophobic. It is, in any case, a very powerful and effective way of ridding the individual of contact with his own mind. At times the mind can be so weakened or so fragmented by splitting processes or so evacuated by projective identification that the individual appears empty or quasi-psychotic. This I shall show with C, the case of a child. It also has important technical implications; for example, bearing in mind that projective identification is only one aspect of an omnipotent balance established by each individual in his own way, any interpretative attempt on the part of the analyst to locate and give back to the patient missing parts of the self must of necessity be resisted by the total personality, since it is felt to threaten the whole balance and lead to more disturbance. I shall discuss this in case T. Projective identification cannot be seen in isolation.

A further clinical implication that I should like to touch on is about communication. Bion demonstrated how projective identification can be used as a method of communication by the individual putting, as it were, undigested parts of his experience and inner world into the object, originally the mother, now the analyst, as a way of getting them understood and returned in a more manageable form. But we might add to this that projective identification is, by its very nature, a kind of communication, even in cases where this is not its aim or its intention. By definition projective identification means the putting of parts of the self into an object. If the analyst on the receiving end is really open to what is going on and able to be aware of what he is experiencing, this can be a powerful method of gaining understanding. Indeed, much of our current appreciation of the richness of the notion of countertransference stems from it. I shall later try to indicate some of the problems this raises, in terms of acting in, in my discussion of the third case, N.

I want now to give a brief example of a case to illustrate the concreteness of projective identification in the analytic situation, its effectiveness as a method of ridding the child of a whole area of experience, and thus keeping some kind of balance, and the effect of such massive projective mechanisms on her state of mind. This is a little girl aged 4, in analytic treatment with Rocha Barros, who was discussing the case with me.

The child, C, was a deeply disturbed and neglected child, who had only very recently begun treatment.

A few minutes before the end of a Friday session C said that she was going to make a candle; the analyst explained her wish to take a warm Mrs. Barros with her that day at the end of the session and her fear that there would not be enough time, as there were only three minutes left. C started to scream, saying that she would have some spare candles; she then stared through the window with a vacant, lost expression. The analyst interpreted that the child needed to make the analyst realize how awful it was to end the session, as well as expressing a wish to take home some warmth from the analyst's words for the weekend. The child screamed: "Bastard! Take off your clothes and jump outside." Again the analyst tried to interpret C's feelings about being dropped and sent into the cold. C replied: "Stop your talking, take off your clothes. You are cold. I'm not cold." The feeling in the session was extremely moving. Here the words carry the concrete meaning, to the child, of the separation of the weekend—the awful coldness. This she tries to force into the analyst. "You are cold, I am not cold." I think that here it is not just an attempt to rid herself of the experience by projective identification, but also a kind of retaliatory attack.

The moments when C looked completely lost and vacant, as in this fragment, were very frequent and were, I think, indicative not only of her serious loss of contact with reality, but of the emptiness, vacantness of her mind and personality when projective identification was operating so powerfully. I think that much of her screaming is also in the nature of her emptying out. The effectiveness of such emptying is striking, as the whole experience of loss and its concomitant emotions is cut out. One can again see here how the term *projective identification* describes more vividly and fully the processes involved than the more general and frequently used terms, such as *reversal* or, as I said, *projection.*

In this example, then, the child's balance is primarily maintained by the projecting out of parts of the self. I want now to give an example of a familiar kind of case to discuss various kinds of projective identification working together to hold a particular narcissistic omnipotent balance. This kind of balance is very firmly structured, extremely difficult to influence analytically, and leads to striking persecutory anxieties. It also raises some points about different identificatory processes and problems about the term *projective identification* itself.

A young teacher, T, came into analysis with difficulties in relationships, but actually with the hope of changing careers and becoming an analyst. His daily material consisted very largely of descriptions of work he had done in helping his students, how his colleagues had praised his work, asked him to discuss their work with him, and so on. Little else came into the sessions. He frequently described how one or other of his colleagues felt threatened by him, threatened in the sense of feeling minimized or put in an inferior position by his greater insight and understanding. He was, therefore, uneasy that they felt unfriendly to him at any given moment. (Any idea that his personality might actually put people off did not enter his mind.) It was not difficult to show him certain ideas about myself; for example, that when I did not seem to be encouraging him to give up his career and apply for training as an analyst, he felt that I, being old, felt threatened by this intelligent young person coming forward, and, therefore, would not want him in my professional area.

Clearly, simply to suggest, or interpret, that T was projecting his envy into his objects and then feeling them as identified with this part of himself, might be theoretically accurate, but clinically inept and useless, indeed it would just be absorbed into his psychoanalytic armory. We can see that the projective identification of the envious parts of the self was, as it were, only the end result of one aspect of a highly complex balance which he was keeping. To clarify something of the nature of this balance, it is important to see how T was relating to me in the transference. Usually he spoke of me as a very fine analyst and I was flattered in such ways. Actually he could not take in interpretations meaningfully, he appeared not to listen properly; he would, for example, hear the words partially and then reinterpret them unconsciously, according to some previous theoretical psychoanalytical knowledge, then give them to himself with this slightly altered and generalized meaning. Frequently, when I interpreted more firmly, he would respond very quickly and argumentatively, as if there were a minor explosion which seemed destined, not only to expel from his mind what I might be going to say, but enter my mind and break up my thinking at that moment.

In this example we have projective identification operating with various different motives and leading to different identificatory processes, but all aimed at maintaining his narcissistic omnipotent balance. First we see the splitting of his objects: I am flattered and kept in his mind as idealized; at such moments the bad or unhelpful aspect of myself is quite split off, even though I don't seem to be achieving much with him; but this latter has to be denied. He projects part of himself into my mind and takes over; he "knows" what I am going to say and says it himself. At this point, a part of the self is identified with an idealized aspect of myself, which is talking to, interpreting to, an idealized patient part himself; idealized because it listens to the analyst part of him. We can see what this movement achieves in terms of his balance. It cuts out any real relationship between the patient and myself, between analyst and patient, as mother and child, as a feeding couple. It obviates any separate existence, any relating to me as myself; any relationship in which he takes in directly from me. T was, in fact, earlier in his life slightly anorexic. If I manage for a moment to get through this T explodes, so that his mental digestive system is fragmented, and by this verbal explosion, as I said, T unconsciously tries to enter my mind and break up my thinking, my capacity to feed him. It

is important here, as always with projective identification, to distinguish this kind of unconscious entering, invading, and breaking up from a conscious aggressive attack. What I am discussing
here is how these patients, using projective identification so
omnipotently, actually avoid any such feelings as dependence,
envy, or jealousy.

Once T has in phantasy entered my mind and taken over my
interpretations, and my role at that moment, I notice that he
has "added to," "improved on," "enriched" my interpretations,
and I become the onlooker, who should realize that my interpretations of a few moments ago were not as rich as his are now—
and surely I should feel threatened by this young man in my
room! Thus the two types of projective identification are working in harmony, the invading of my mind and taking over its
contents and the projecting of the potentially dependent, threatened, and envious part of the self into me. This is, of course,
mirrored in what we hear is going on in his outside world—the
colleagues who ask for help and feel threatened by his bril-
liance—but then he feels persecuted by their potential unfriend-
liness. So long as the balance holds so effectively, we cannot see
what more subtle, sensitive, and important aspects of the personality are being kept split off, or why, although we can see that
any relationship to a truly separate object is obviated, with all
that this may imply.

A great difficulty is, of course, that all insight tends to get
drawn into this process. To give a minute example: One Monday, T really seemed to become aware of exactly how he was
subtly taking the meaning out of what I was saying and not letting real understanding develop. For a moment he felt relief and
then a brief, deep feeling of hatred toward me emerged into
consciousness. A second later he added quietly that he was thinking how the way that he had been feeling just then toward me,
that is, the hatred, must have been how his colleagues had felt
toward him on the previous day when he had been talking and

explaining things to them! So as soon as T has a real experience of hating me because I have said something useful, he uses
the momentary awareness to speak about the colleagues, and
distances himself from the emerging envy and hostility, and the
direct receptive contact between the two of us is again lost. What
looks like insight is no longer insight but has become a complex projective maneuver.

At a period when these problems were very much in the fore-
front of the analysis, T brought a dream, right at the end of a
session. The dream was simply this: T was with the analyst or with
a woman, J, or it might have been both, he was excitedly pushing his hand up her knickers into her vagina, thinking that if he
could get right in there would be no stopping him. Here, I think
under the pressure of the analytic work going on, T's great need
and great excitement was to get totally inside the object, with
all its implications, including, of course, the annihilation of the
analytic situation.

To return to the concept of projective identification. With this
patient I have indicated three or four different aspects: attacking
the analyst's mind; a kind of total invasion, as in the dream fragment I have just quoted; a more partial invasion and taking over
of aspects or capacities of the analyst; and finally, putting part
of the self, particularly inferior parts, into the analyst. The latter two are mutually dependent, but lead to different types of
identification. In the one, the patient, in taking over, becomes
identified with the analyst's idealized capacities; in the other, it
is the analyst who becomes identified with the lost, projected,
here inferior or envious parts of the patient. I think it is partly
because the term is broad and covers many aspects that there
has been some unease about the name itself.

I have so far discussed projective identification in two cases
caught up in the paranoid–schizoid position, a borderline child
and a man in a rigid omnipotent narcissistic state. Now I want
to discuss aspects of projective identification as one sees it in a

patient moving toward the depressive position. I shall illustrate some points from the case of a man as he was becoming less rigid, more integrated, better able to tolerate what was previously projected, but constantly also pulling back, returning to the use of the earlier projective mechanisms. Then I want to show the effect of this on subsequent identifications and the light that it throws on previous identifications. I also want to attempt to forge a link between the nature of the patient's residual use of projective identification and its early infantile counterpart, and the relation of this to phobia formation. I bring this material also to discuss briefly the communicative nature of projective identification.

To start with this latter point, as I said earlier, since projective identification by its very nature means the putting of parts of the self into the object, in the transference we are of necessity on the receiving end of the projections, and, therefore, providing we can tune in to them, we have an opportunity par excellence to understand them and what is going on. In this sense, it acts as a communication, whatever its motivation, and is the basis for the positive use of countertransference. As I want to describe with this patient, N, it is frequently difficult to clarify whether, at any given moment, projective identification is primarily aimed at communicating a state of mind that cannot be verbalized by the patient or whether it is aimed more at entering and controlling or attacking the analyst, or whether all these elements are active and need consideration.

A patient, N, who had been in analysis many years, had recently married and, after a few weeks, was becoming anxious about his sexual interest and his potency, particularly in view of the fact that his wife was considerably younger. He came on a Monday, saying that he felt that "the thing" was never really going to get right, "the sexual thing," yes, they did have sex on Sunday, but somehow he had to force himself and he knew it wasn't quite all right, and his wife noticed this and commented.

It was an all right kind of weekend, just about. He spoke about this a bit more and explained that they went to a place outside London, to a party, they had meant to stay the night in an hotel nearby, but couldn't find anywhere nice enough and came home and so were late.

What was being conveyed to me was a quiet, sad discomfort, leading to despair, and I pointed out to N how he was conveying an awful long-term hopelessness and despair, with no hope for the future. He replied to the effect that he supposed that he was feeling left out, and linked this with what had been a rather helpful and vivid session on the Friday; only now, as he made the remark, it was quite dead and flat. When I tried to look at this with him, he agreed, commenting that he supposed he was starting to attack the analysis. The feeling in the session now was awful; N was making a kind of sense and saying analytic things himself, which could have been right, for example about the Friday, and which one could have picked up. But since they seemed flat and quite unhelpful to him, what he seemed to me to be doing was putting despair into me, not only about the reality of his marriage and potency, but also about his analysis. This was indicated, for example, by the useless, and by now somewhat irrelevant, comment about being left out. N denied my interpretation about his despair about the progress of the analysis, but in such a way, it seemed to me, as to be encouraging me to make false interpretations and to pick up his pseudointerpretations as if I believed in them, while knowing that they and we were getting nowhere. He vaguely talked about this, went quiet, and said; "I was listening to your voice, the timbre changes in different voices. W (his wife), being younger, makes more sounds per second, older voices are deeper because they make less sounds per second, etc." I showed N his great fear that I showed with my voice, rather than through my actual words, that I could not stand the extent of his hopelessness and his doubts about myself, about what we could achieve in the analysis and, therefore, in his life, and that I would cheat and in some way try to encourage. I queried whether he had perhaps felt that, in that session, my voice had changed in order to sound more encouraging and encouraged, rather than contain the despair he was expressing. By this part of the session my patient had got into contact and said with some relief that, if I did do this kind of encouraging, the whole bottom would fall out of the analysis.

First, I want to discuss the nature of the communication, which I could understand primarily through my countertransference, through the way in which I was being pushed and pulled to feel and to react. We see here the concrete quality of projective identification structuring the countertransference. It seems that the way N was speaking was not asking me to try to understand the sexual difficulties or unhappiness, but to invade me with despair, while at the same time unconsciously trying to force me to reassure myself that it was all right, that interpretations, now empty of meaning and hollow, were meaningful, and that the analysis at that moment was going ahead satisfactorily. Thus it was not only the despair that N was projecting into me, but his defenses against it, a false reassurance and denial, which it was intended I should act out with him. I think that this also suggests a projective identification of an internal figure, probably primarily mother, who was felt to be weak, kind, but unable to stand up to emotion. In the transference (to oversimplify the picture) this figure is projected into me, and I find myself pushed to live it out.

We have here the important issue of teasing out the motivation for this projective identification. Was it aimed primarily at communicating something to me; was there a depth of despair that we had not previously sufficiently understood; or was the forcing of despair into me motivated by something different? At this stage, at the end of the session, I did not know and left it open.

I have so much condensed the material here that I cannot convey adequately the atmosphere and to-and-fro of the session.

But toward the end, as I have tried to show, my patient experienced and expressed relief and appreciation of what had been going on. There was a shift in mood and behavior as my patient started to accept understanding and face the nature of his forcing into me, and he could then experience me as an object that could stand up to his acting in, not get caught into it, but able to contain it. He could then identify temporarily with a stronger object, and he himself became firmer. I also sensed some feeling of concern about what he had been doing to me and my work—it was not openly acknowledged and expressed—but there is some movement toward the depressive position with its real concern and guilt.

To clarify the motivation as well as the effect of this kind of projective identification on subsequent introjective identification, we need to go briefly into the beginning of the next session, when N brought a dream, in which he was on a boat like a ferry boat, on a gray-green sea surrounded by mist; he did not know where they were going. Then nearby there was another boat which was clearly going down under the water and drowning. He stepped onto this boat as it went down, he did not feel wet or afraid, which was puzzling. Amongst his associations we heard of his wife being very gentle and affectionate, but he added that he himself was concerned, was she behind this really making more demands on him? She, knowing his fondness for steak and kidney pudding, had made him one the night before. It was excellent, but the taste was too strong, which he told her!

Now the interesting thing, I think, was that, on the previous day I had felt rather at sea, as I said, not knowing exactly where we were going, but I was clear that the understanding about the hopelessness and the defenses against it was right, and, though I had not thought it out in this way, my belief would have been that the mists would clear as we went on. But what does my patient do with this? He gratuitously steps off this boat (this understanding) onto one that is going down, and he is not afraid!

In other words, he prefers to drown in despair rather than clarify it, prefers to see affection as demands, and my decent, well-cooked steak and kidney interpretations as too tasty. At this point, as we worked on it, N could see that the notion of drowning here was actually exciting to him.

Now we can see more about the motivation. It becomes clear that N was not just trying to communicate and get understood something about his despair, important as this element is, but that he was also attacking me and our work, by trying to drag me down by the despair, when there was actually progress. After a session in which he expressed appreciation about my work and capacity to stand up to him, he dreamt of willingly stepping onto a sinking boat, so that either, internally, I collude and go down with him or am forced to watch him go under, my hope is destroyed, and I am kept impotent to help. This activity also leads to an introjective identification with an analyst-parent who is felt to be down, joyless, and impotent, and this identification contributes considerably to his lack of sexual confidence and potency. Following this period of the analysis, there was real improvement in the symptom.

Naturally these considerations lead one to think about the nature of the patient's internal objects; for example, the weak mother, that I described as being projected into me in the transference. How much is this figure based on N's real experience with his mother, how much did he exploit her weaknesses and thus contribute to building in his inner world a mother, weak, inadequate, and on the defensive, as we saw in the transference? In other words, when we talk of an object projected into the analyst in the transference, we are discussing an internal object that has been structured in part from the child's earlier projective identifications, and the whole process can be seen being revived in the transference.

I want now to digress and look at this material from a slightly different angle, related to the patient's very early history and anxieties. I have shown how N pulls back and goes into an object, in the dream, into the sinking boat, as in the first session he goes into despair, which is then projected into me, rather than his thinking about it. This going into an object, acted out in the session, is, I believe, linked with a more total type of projective identification that I indicated in the sexual dream of T and referred to briefly at the beginning of this paper as being connected with phobia formation. At the very primitive end of projective identification is the attempt to get back into an object, to become, as it were, undifferentiated and mindless and thus avoid all pain. Most human beings develop beyond this in early infancy, but some of our patients attempt to use projective identification in this way over many years. N, when he came into analysis, came because he had a fetish, a tremendous pull toward getting inside a rubber object which would totally cover, absorb, and excite him. In his early childhood he had nightmares of falling out of a globe into endless space. In the early period of analysis he would have severe panic states when alone in the house, and would be seriously disturbed or lose contact if he had to be away from London on business. At the same time there are minor indications of anxieties about being trapped in a claustrophobic way; for example, at night he would have to keep blankets on the bed loose or throw them off altogether; in intercourse phantasies emerged of his penis being cut off and lost inside the woman's body. As the analysis went on, the fetishistic activities disappeared, real relationships improved, and the projecting of the self into the object could clearly be seen in the transference. He would get absorbed in his own words or ideas or in the sound of my words and my speaking, and the meaning would be unimportant compared with the concrete nature of the experience. This type of absorption into words and sounds, with the analyst as a person quite disregarded, is not unlike the kind of process that one sometimes sees in child patients, who come into the playroom, onto the couch, and fall so deeply asleep that they are unable to be woken by interpretations. It is, therefore, interesting to see in N how he has always concretely attempted to get into an object, apparently largely in order to escape from being outside, to become absorbed and free from relating and from thought and mental pain. And yet we know that this is only half the story, since the object he mainly got into was a fetish and highly sexualized. And still in the modern dream of getting into the drowning boat there was masochistic excitement that he tried to pull me into and in this sense it needs to be compared with T. I described how, as his constant invading and taking over was being analyzed, we could see T's sexual dream as an attempt totally to get inside me with great excitement. I suspect there is much yet to be teased out about the relation between certain types of massive projective identification of the self and erotization.

Now I want to return to the material that I quoted, and to the question of projective identification in patients who are becoming more integrated and nearer to the depressive position. We can see in the case of N, unlike T, who is still imprisoned in his own omnipotent, narcissistic structure, that there is now a movement, in the transference, toward more genuine whole object relations. At times he can really appreciate the strong containing qualities of his object; true he will then try to draw me in and drag me down again, but there is now potential conflict about this. The object can be valued and loved, at times he can consciously experience hostility about this—and ambivalence is present. As his loving is freed, he is able to introject and identify with a whole valued and potent object, and the effect on his character and potency is striking. This is a very different quality of identification from that based on forcing despairing parts of the self into an object, who then in his phantasy becomes like a despairing part of himself. It is very different from the type of identification we saw in T, where the patient invaded my mind and took over the split and idealized aspects, leaving the object, myself, denuded and inferior. With N, in the example I have just given, he could experience and value me as a whole, a different and properly separate person with my own qualities, and these he could introject and thereby feel strengthened. But we still have a task ahead, to enable N to be truly outside and able to give up the analysis, be aware of its meaning to him and yet be secure.

SUMMARY

I have tried in this paper to discuss projective identification as we see it operating in our clinical work. I have described various types of projective identification, from the more primitive and massive type to the more empathic and mature. I have discussed how we see alterations in its manifestation as progress is made in treatment and the patient moves toward the depressive position, is better integrated, and able to use his objects less omnipotently, relate to them as separate objects, and introject them and their qualities more fully and realistically, and thus also to separate from them.

EDITOR'S INTRODUCTION TO
SPLITTING AND PROJECTIVE IDENTIFICATION

This essay, which Michael Feldman wrote as one of a set of introductory lectures on Klein and Bion (1992), supplements Betty Joseph's account of projective identification by providing further examples, and it also introduces clear formulations and examples of splitting. These two concepts are so central to Kleinian analysis that the reader will encounter heavy use of them in virtually every chapter after this, so that their full range of meaning and usefulness should become ever more apparent.

The point that most needs underlining at this juncture is that splitting and projective identification are defenses that operate on two aspects of mind: mental contents such as ideas, feelings, and criticisms, all having more to do with the self as an experiential entity than with the ego; and functions such as perceiving, organizing, and reasoning, all having more to do with the ego as apparatus than with self as content. Betty Joseph has already exemplified this double aspect in her essay. Here, Feldman points out in his example how his male patient rendered some of his own ego functions unavailable to him by splitting so that his capacity for understanding the work was clearly impaired. Feldman's second example features a split representation of the analyst into good (idealized) and bad (hostile, envious). In the third example, the use of projective identification results in the patient's experiencing both some of her ego functions and some of her mental contents as having become attributes of the analyst. In this case, these changes were more than imagined, for the patient had been able to induce a countertransference that culminated in an enactment, and she then used that enactment to validate her defensively revised conception of the relationship.

The third example also includes analysis of a benign aspect of an otherwise problematic projective identification: the use of this mechanism to communicate to the analyst through his experienced countertransference how she experienced certain crucial aspects of her inner life, such as having been exposed to distracted and shallow parental response. Also mentioned is another benign aspect of projective identification, one that is closely linked to communication: its role in empathy. And yet another: putting some good parts of the self or the ego into the object for safekeeping.

All these examples and others as well shed light on the vicissitudes of transference and countertransference and their important role in repetition or recreation of the past. Feldman also cautions against analysts overusing these concepts defensively by neglecting the requirement that they first sort out their personal tendencies to distort a patient's material.

5

SPLITTING AND PROJECTIVE IDENTIFICATION

MICHAEL FELDMAN

The way in which the concepts of splitting and projective identification have evolved in Melanie Klein's work illustrates very well, I think, the creative interaction between theory and clinical observation, which runs through psychoanalysis. The concepts were developed to help understand some of the clinical phenomena with which she was confronted, and, once incorporated into a more general theoretical framework by Klein and her co-workers, these ideas have significantly expanded the range of clinical material with which we are able to work.

I propose to give a fairly brief outline of the concept of splitting and projective identification, and then to describe three clinical fragments in which I think it is possible to see some of the ways in which they operate, and their consequences for the patient and for the analytic situation.

Klein saw splitting as one of the earliest defensive operations called into play by the immature ego in an attempt to cope with intense anxieties to which it was at times subjected. She believed that, from very early on, the infant was capable of some form of phantasy, and that one of the characteristics of these phantasies was that they were related to objects. Thus the infant's early experiences of pleasure were essentially linked to a notion of

119

an object that was the source of pleasure, and conversely the experience of distress was linked to a notion of an object causing the distress.

The primary function of splitting is to segregate the objects associated with good experience from those associated with bad, in order to protect and preserve the good objects on which the survival of the self depended. This involved both segregating off everything perceived as harmful and dangerous internally, and/or projecting it into the outside world.

Klein recognized, however, that the splitting process was not only something brought to bear on the way objects were perceived and organized, but, since the internal and external objects which inhabit the infant's world are essentially related to aspects of the ego, it follows that splitting also involves the ego itself.

As Klein put it: "I believe that the ego is incapable of splitting the object—internal or external—without a corresponding splitting taking place within the ego. Therefore the phantasies and feelings about the state of the internal object vitally influence the structure of the ego" (Klein, 1946, p. 6).

She goes on to say: "It is in phantasy that the infant splits the object and the self, but the effect of this phantasy is a very real one, because it leads to feelings and relations (and later on, thought processes) being in fact cut off from one another (Klein, p. 6).

Klein saw projection as a way the ego had of dealing with anxiety by ridding itself of danger and badness—the psychic equivalent of expelling dangerous substances from the body. But, as we know from the way an infant or young child uses their excretory functions, these may not only be a way of freeing themselves from uncomfortable contents, but also form an important mode of interacting with someone else. These functions can be used aggressively to control, or to engage the other in a positive fashion. Thus, to recapitulate, if we believe that our perception and experience of objects implies a phantasy of the relationship between the object and a part of the ego, then the splitting of objects (at its simplest into good and bad) is inevitably associated with a corresponding split in the ego. Furthermore, the mechanism of projection, by which the organism strives to rid itself of harmful contents, will also involve the evacuation of part of the ego itself.

Klein came to use the term *projective identification* to describe this process whereby the infant projects (primarily) harmful contents into his object (for example into his mother), and by the same token projects those parts of his mental apparatus with which they are linked. Insofar as the mother then comes to contain the bad parts of the self, she is not only felt to be bad, as a separate individual, but is *identified* with the bad, unwanted parts of the self.

The object may now be felt as threatening and potentially intrusive (containing as it does the infant's aggressive, intrusive qualities, and its propensity to deal with things by projecting them into others). The infant may feel, caught up in this vicious cycle, the need to attack the mother further, or to withdraw in order to protect himself. The experience of the object containing parts of the self may also give rise to unpleasant, even panicky feelings of being trapped inside, and the claustrophobic anxieties we see in some of our patients can often be understood in this light.

Although it is not possible to go into all the ramifications of this process, I would like to mention that the projective identification may also involve good parts of the self—projected in love, or in an attempt to protect something valuable from internal attack. Up to a point, this process is a normal one, necessary for the satisfactory growth of our relationships, and is the basis, for example, for what we term "empathy." If it is excessive, on the other hand, there is an impoverishment of the ego, and an excessive dependence on the other person who contains all the good parts of the self.

This has been an interesting and important area of research and development in psychoanalysis over the past forty years, and many of the ideas which have evolved have been complex and difficult. In addition to the papers of Klein herself, there have been valuable contributions from Segal (1964), Bion (1959), Rosenfeld (1971), and Joseph (1987).

Rather than try to give a more detailed theoretical exposition, I should like to describe, fairly briefly, three clinical situations in which I believe it was possible to follow the operation of some of the mechanisms I have been referring to.

A patient, Mr. A, arrived for the first session after a holiday and I noticed that he was moving and speaking in an unusually clear and businesslike fashion. He said that when he had arrived in the waiting room, he had found another man there already (he knows that I share the premises with colleagues, and had occasionally seen other patients in the waiting room). He had not seen this particular person before, and it had disconcerted him at first. He thought I might have made a mistake, and double-booked two patients. He imagined me suddenly discovering my mistake, feeling terribly embarrassed, and not knowing how to cope with the situation. He speculated that I would probably ask one of my colleagues to go to the waiting room to call one of them out, and explain the situation to him, and then I would see whoever remained.

He portrayed me, in his mind, as confused, embarrassed, and, moreover, unable to face the muddle I had created, sending someone else to deal with it on my behalf. The patient found himself very rapidly in a position where he was calmly observing, without a momentary thought that perhaps *he* might have made a mistake.

Later in the session, it emerged that in the course of the previous week, during my absence, he had found himself getting into a terrible mess; he had lost his watch, he hadn't known what was going on, and he described a variety of other difficulties.

What dynamic mechanisms can be invoked to account for the situation which obtained at the start of the session? It seemed to me that the patient's knowledge and experience of his own state of confusion, his embarrassment about finding himself in a mess during the holiday, and his difficulties over time (expressed in his loss of the watch) became projected, in his phantasy, into me. After a momentary sense of discomfort within himself on encountering an unfamiliar person in the waiting room, he cured himself of the unwelcome and disturbing thoughts and experience, and behaved in an efficient and well-organized way, while (in his phantasy) his analyst had to summon help to rescue himself from a muddle.

As the session proceeded, and the patient found himself once more in a familiar and reassuring setting, I think he felt less driven to project these unwelcome mental states into me, and he began to be able to use his perceptions of me—my voice and manner—to recognize that I was probably *not* in a confused state of mind. This was accompanied by his recovering the knowledge and memory of his own distress and discomfort during the holiday, and also his apprehension about returning.

It was evident that what was projected, in his phantasy, into me, and taken as real properties of my mind at that time, was not the whole of the patient's mental contents. He preserved a way of functioning that was well organized, and could work out how I might set about dealing with the consequences of my mistake or confusion, in quite a complex and logical fashion, and he even seemed sympathetic toward me. We are thus evidently dealing with a split which has taken place in his mind, with part of his mental contents temporarily unavailable to him, but coloring his perceptions and his phantasy concerning me.

I should add that there was something slightly unusual about this example of projective identification with this patient. In the situation I have described, I actually felt confident that I *was* seeing the correct patient, at the correct time, and knew that the other person in the waiting room was a patient of my colleague. What my patient said did not, on this occasion, succeed in discomforting me, although on other occasions he could be more accurate about my state of mind, or choose more effectively what he might say or do to *affect* my state of mind, inducing me into impatience, uncertainty, anxiety, hope, or some other mental frame. In other words in many cases we are not merely dealing with the projection, in phantasy, into an object, so that the object acquires certain properties derived from the patient's mental state (which may "fit" the object to a greater or lesser extent), but we are often dealing with an active and dynamic process whereby the mental state of the object is *affected* by the projection.

This formulation regarding what had happened at the beginning of the session seemed to be confirmed by material later in the same session. One of the events which had taken place during the holiday was that Mr. A had moved to a larger office, on a different floor, within the organization where he works. He had actually moved out while the two people with whom he shared the office were away on leave. When they returned, they complained bitterly that he had left the place in terrible mess— not just the area he had vacated, but the whole office was untidy and dirty.

While reporting this, Mr. A sounded slightly injured. He acknowledged that there had probably been a *bit* of untidiness, but he added in an emphatic way that he had *intended* to clean it all up, he just hadn't found the time. He then went on to describe in a more and more emphatic way how unreasonable and neurotic his colleagues were in making such a fuss, and how intolerant and petty they were.

It became evident as he talked that he was assuming a condescending, even contemptuous attitude toward his colleagues. He had not only actually left a mess in their office, during their absence, but he began to portray them as being in a mess psychologically as well, while he assumed a position of detached moral and psychological superiority, from the security of his more spacious, clean office, on a higher level.

You will perhaps recognize this process as being almost exactly similar to the one he had used to deal with his momentary discomfort and confusion at the beginning of the session, which was subsequently related to the disorder *he* had actually been in during the latter part of the holiday. The story about the office made the situation very concrete—he described the way in which he actually vacated a place, leaving a mess dispersed into the space which belonged to other people, while he became the detached, slightly superior observer, watching the others getting into a stew. When he described the interaction with his colleagues at work, it was also very clear that his response to their complaints inflamed them even more, and may well have driven them into speaking or behaving in unreasonable ways, which then of course confirmed his view of them.

Finally I should like to mention the fact that, with this patient in the situation I have described, the projective identification seemed to have been "flexible" or "fluid." In the session, the patient *was* able to recover, and speak about his own anxieties and confusion, without feeling terribly threatened by them, or attacked by me, when I interpreted what I thought was taking place.

I should now like to discuss a second case, Mrs. B. She was the younger of two sisters, brought up by her mother under difficult circumstances, father having left the family when she was very young. Her mother, who was a highly disturbed woman, seems to have focused her hatred and violence on the patient.

In spite of the considerable internal and external difficulties which she faced, Mrs. B had managed to make a success in various areas of her life. She is married, and has two young daughters. She has not, however, managed to free herself from the constant sense of being threatened by the image of an extremely

hostile and envious mother. What she finds the most disturbing is the recognition of aspects of herself which remind her of
her mother, particularly in her treatment of her own daughters.
When she becomes aware of this, she feels a tremendous pressure to disavow these characteristics, either consciously through
her conduct, or unconsciously through the projection of such
features onto a figure in the outside world.

Mrs. B arrived for a session in the middle of the week, and
said there was something she felt she should have mentioned.
She felt uncomfortable about not having done so—she wasn't
quite sure why, perhaps she was waiting for the matter to be
resolved. She then told me that a relative, with whom Mrs. B has
a complicated and difficult relationship had unexpectedly offered to pay for her older daughter to attend a private school.

Mrs. B was evidently uncomfortable and tense talking about
this, and seemed unable to say much more. She said she supposed that she was worried that people might think the family
was well off, which they weren't, of course. It was evident that
Mrs. B was apprehensive about my reaction both to what she had
told me, and to the fact that she had avoided mentioning it for
several days.

There were many features of the situation she described which
reminded me of issues relating to Mrs. B's own childhood and
schooling, and her relationship with her mother. I was particularly reminded of the way she had lived in constant dread of her
mother's explosive, even violent rages, and tried to propitiate
her by behaving in a compliant, submissive way. Any achievement
on her part, anything which she valued and enjoyed, seemed
particularly likely to arouse her mother's resentment and envy.
She had always assumed that this was because of her mother's
own very deprived, poor background.

With some of this in mind, it was possible in the session I have
referred to, to explore her discomfort about her daughter's
move to a private school in terms of the envy which would be

aroused in others who were less privileged. More immediately, I thought the marked tension and avoidance which she showed in relation to myself could be understood in terms of a phantasy of me as a figure who would react to her news by turning on her in a hostile and violent way, possibly even wanting to get rid of her, as she had often felt her mother did.

The patient could, and frequently did, tell herself that such fears were unreasonable and "silly," and she knew I would not react like that, but such attempts to reassure herself did not mitigate her anxiety, or the harshness and severity of the figure which had been projected into me, and which felt very real. When I was able to interpret this to her, she visibly relaxed, as if this figure receded from the foreground, and she felt herself to be with a more supportive person.

She arrived for her session the next day, and I noticed that her face was red, blotchy, and swollen. She was evidently in some distress, and began by saying she hadn't wanted to come at all; she hadn't felt like telling me about her accident, she wasn't sure how I would react. She had tried to tell herself that it would be all right, I wouldn't mind, and she really ought to come.

There had also been a disturbing dream the previous night, which she felt she ought to talk about. She then told me a little about the accident. She was preparing some hot food in the food mixer which blew up in her face. She rather played down what had clearly been a frightening and painful experience. She went on quickly to tell me about the dream. In it, she thought some of the events of the previous evening were repeated, though she wasn't sure; then there were two figures—one was supposed to be looking after the other, but there was a quarrel, and the one supposed to be doing the looking after just pushed the other away, and probably killed her.

I should like to summarize briefly what evolved in the course of this session. Mrs. B told me that she had felt somewhat relieved after the previous session, but some unease about the private school remained. What had made things much worse was the fact that she had then learned that her daughter would have an interview with the new headmistress the following day. Mrs. B would have to accompany her, and she didn't know how long it would take. She might come late for her session, or might have to miss it altogether. There was probably no way she could let me know what was happening. Mrs. B is always very conscientious about being on time, and will strive to get to her sessions in the most difficult circumstances. On the rare occasions she is delayed or prevented from coming, she is always careful to telephone and explain, and apologize, as if constantly having to propitiate a very touchy, potentially explosive figure.

She thus found herself in an extremely difficult situation. She was just about able to cope with the anxiety that I would react in a hostile and envious fashion to the news about the daughter's school fees, perhaps demanding a higher fee for myself. There was then the additional provocation of the session she might miss or come late for, and in her phantasy, that would be the last straw—I was very likely to explode, like the mother she was so familiar with.

This became real in a dramatic way with the incident of the food mixer which exploded in her face, frightening and hurting her, and adding to her anxiety and reluctance to come, because she indicated that she half expected that I would be further provoked and annoyed by the fact that she came bringing all this trouble, and was unlikely to be sympathetic. The dream also represented the situation in which the figure who is supposed to provide care suddenly turns into a quarrelsome and rejecting person. At one level, of course, Mrs. B doesn't believe this of me. On the contrary, in addition to the recognition of the fact that she has actually been helped a great deal, there also exists a rather idealized version of myself, as someone who can understand things perfectly, without her having to say very much, someone who is infinitely patient and helpful. This is an expression of splitting, where each version of the analyst can exist in an isolated way, without modifying the other to any great extent.

In the session I have been describing, I interpreted some of the patient's very real and concrete phantasies about me, and the way I might react, linked with the knowledge we shared both about her actual experience of her mother, and about the internal phantasy figure with which she lived. This seemed to restore her sense of having an analyst who *was* protective, and she left looking greatly relieved.

This illustrates, I believe, an aspect of what James Strachey put forward in his seminal paper of 1934 concerning the therapeutic action of psychoanalysis. The patient is able, in the transference, to project onto the figure of the analyst some archaic form (in this case that of an alarming, persecuting, and explosive figure), and in the course of the analytic work, through the analyst's understanding and interpretation, and his capacity to avoid getting caught up in a reenactment of the phantasied situation, a modification of this primitive form, or imago, may take place, accompanied by a change in the patient's relation to it. The reintrojection of this modified figure gives the patient relief, and he feels less driven to resort to violent projective procedures, and this allows psychic change to occur.

The most difficult problem for my patient is, of course, that this archaic imago of the explosive, envious, and destructive mother has become incorporated into her own ego, through a process of introjective identification, but she finds it nearly intolerable to acknowledge this as part of herself and, as I have described, generally feels driven to enact the role of a tremendously patient, long-suffering, and "good" figure—an example, perhaps, of Freud's description of the defense of reaction formation. The material I have given illustrates how, by means of projective identification, that part of her ego which is identified with her mother is projected into me, which makes me a fearful and worrying figure, which she is inclined either to avoid, or to try to appease.

It will be evident that the threat is much greater for Mrs. B than for Mr. A, and the need to disavow this aspect of her mental contents is consequently much greater. Thus, for example, when she spoke of the possible envious response of neighbors to her daughter's change of school, or her fears of how *I* might react, she seemed completely out of contact with any envious feelings *she* might have towards her daughter, and her own inclination (which sometimes manifested itself) to attack her daughter.

Returning now to the clinical situation which I have been describing, Mrs. B did in fact miss the Friday session, as she had warned me she might. When she arrived on the following Monday, she explained the circumstances in a careful, polite, and terribly reasonable way. She explained how difficult it had been even to get to a telephone, leaving me in no doubt that she had done everything possible. I noticed she said nothing about the interview, or its outcome. As she went on speaking, I thought there was a rather superficial quality to it; she offered descriptions and explanations which sounded right and true, but somehow empty, and I felt I had heard it all before. There was no indication that she had any recollection of the work which had gone on in the last session, although it seemed relevant to her present predicament.

I found myself becoming frustrated and impatient with her as the session went on, and as she continued speaking in this sensible, considered way, with little emotion, and little sense of conviction. The patient herself commented at one point that it felt as if there was something missing. I began to feel that while, on the surface, we were both being reasonable and sensible, there was, at the same time, a subtle invitation to me to react in an impatient or critical way to what was going on, or what was being avoided.

However disturbing the image of her mother, which we had previously encountered, there was a sense in which the patient felt very bound up with it, in a very alive way, and its absence made her feel there was *something* or *someone* missing. I had often noticed how in her everyday life some figure would assume the role of an angry, hateful, and unreasonable person, leaving Mrs. B feeling hurt, puzzled, and victimized.

On this occasion I was able to recognize what I thought the pressure was, and felt I could see something of what was going on, rather than simply *react* to it, which was what took place on other occasions. I was able to interpret something of this to the patient, and she became much more uneasy, but more alive, and more *present* in the room. She then began to say how resentful she felt when I made these links, and addressed something which *I* thought was around but which she hadn't really been aware of. Suddenly she referred in a sharp attacking way to an apparent inconsistency in my interpretation, which immediately revealed how much of our previous work was now available to her. She said, toward the end of the session, in which she had by then become very involved, that she felt quite *explosive.*

I think we can see here not only the projection into me of this violent and aggressive figure, but also a more subtle process whereby, unconsciously, she sought to recreate the familiar object relationship, in which she is the attacked and abused child of an angry, critical mother. This familiar, repetitive pattern, which is part of what Freud refers to under the heading of the repetition compulsion (Freud, 1920), or Sandler describes as role actualization (Sandler, 1976a,b), serves to protect the patient from having to contain and take responsibility for her own envy, hatred, and violence, even if it leads to her feeling rather flat and empty. When, instead of enacting the role for which I was being cast, I was able to interpret it to her, she suddenly became more alive, though now she had to tolerate the anxiety and pain involved in owning these violent and destructive impulses and phantasies.

The third example is a brief one, which arose in the supervision of a young woman in psychotherapy with a therapist who is proving to be sensitive and gifted, with a real flair for the work he is engaged in. In the session prior to the one which was being reported, material had emerged which had enabled us to understand a stubborn provocative quality which the patient, a young woman, possessed, and which seemed to play a large part in the difficulties she experienced within her family and outside it. She arrived three or four minutes late for the next session, but made no reference to the fact that she had kept the therapist waiting. She began by saying she had been to a chemist's just before the session, trying out some perfume which she liked. She had *deliberately* kept the person behind her waiting a bit, while she tried out different brands.

The therapist was not quite sure what to do, and then alluded to the fact that perhaps she had kept *him* waiting in the same way, but the patient appeared not to know what he was talking about. There was some other material, and the therapist then made an interpretation, partly based on what had emerged in the previous session, about the way the patient sometimes behaved in a stubborn and provocative fashion. She said she hadn't properly heard him, although she thought he had said something very important, and would he please repeat what he had said. Rather than responding immediately to the pressure she put on him, the therapist waited a while, and the patient began to berate and challenge him, saying she supposed he *wouldn't* do what she had asked him, he would just sit there in silence, and make her wait, though she *thought* he had said something important.

It will perhaps be evident how the therapist was now being treated as a stubborn and provocative person, withholding something potentially helpful from the patient. I should like to examine this example in some detail.

Before the session, the patient seemed to have been quite aware of an impulse in herself to keep *someone* waiting deliberately, while she tried different kinds of perfume. She gave no indication of whether she was aware that, while doing this, she was also likely to keep her therapist waiting. When she did actually arrive late, and referred to the episode in the chemist's shop, it is difficult to believe she had *no* awareness of the link. It does seem, however, as if the responsibility for the knowledge both of her lateness and its possible motivation is made over to the therapist, who felt somewhat provoked, and driven to point out that she had kept *him* waiting. The patient apparently did not know what he was referring to.

Later in the session, he addressed directly her stubborn and provocative behavior. It seems to me that something of his interpretation must have touched the patient, as she registered that he had said something important, but then instead of having to tolerate any discomfort, anxiety, or guilt about what he had identified as being located *in her*, she immediately projected into the therapist not only the qualities of stubbornness and provocativeness, but also the capacity to think, understand, and remember. She is thus apparently unaware that she was late, and seems to have lost touch with the recognition that she had deliberately kept someone waiting. She apparently puts pressure on him to behave in a *reasonable* and helpful way, by repeating his interpretation, although she has had enough experience of her therapist and his technique to know that he was unlikely simply to comply. If he had done so, I strongly suspect it would have had little or no effect.

On the other hand, by behaving in a way which she expects and indeed half invites him to, a familiar scenario is created in which the patient is the somewhat unfairly treated victim of a provocative and stubborn therapist. The therapist was able to recognize the pressures on him, and to refrain from simply acting out some role with the patient, but remained relatively well able to observe, think about, and comment on what was taking place. It became clear how she used projective identification to defend herself, but in addition, used a more complex defense in which the therapist is required to play a repetitive role in some internal drama of the patient; for example, to be the person who submits, a little resentfully, to the patient's demands, without believing it will do any good, or alternately, who resists this pressure and engages, instead, in angry recrimination and blame. To the extent that he allowed himself to be forced into acting in a certain way in response to such pressure, or as a reaction against the pressure, rather than maintaining an analytic posture, the therapist would support the patient's defense, where this internal situation is reenacted over and over again. This would allow her to avoid having to think or to understand herself and her object relations better.

One further issue which this material raises relates not simply to her defensive use of splitting and projective identification, but, as I will mention a little later, to the communicative function of such mechanisms. The patient created, in the therapist, a very vivid experience of being made to wait for someone who was busy trying on perfume, who arrives in a somewhat haughty way, and does not know what he is talking about when he "complains," as it were. There are some indications that what she is conveying to him, unconsciously, through this drama, is something of her own infantile experience, of having to wait while a rather provocative and narcissistic mother puts on perfume, while the child became impatient and frustrated. When she objects, her complaints are either not understood, not acknowledged, or not properly heard. When he made an effort to address her, there was something of the quality of a mother saying, "What was that, dear? Tell me again," which leaves the child with no conviction that mother will really take in something, however many times it is repeated.

I should now like to bring together some of the aspects of splitting and projective identification which I believe the material from the three patients illustrates. First, to recapitulate: Melanie Klein used the term *projective identification* to refer to what was essentially an unconscious, omnipotent phantasy, in which unwanted, disturbing mental contents were expelled—projected into an object—as a means of ridding the self of something bad, but also at times in order to attack or to control the object into which the projection occurred. Since a part of the ego is also expelled, the object which receives the projection also contains, and is partially identified with, a part of the self. The paradox is that although the object comes to be partially identified with a part of the self, the link between the self and that which has been projected is disowned, so that the object is not recognized as having anything to do with the self, or what was projected, but is seen, as it were, to contain these qualities, motives, or functions *in its own right.*

The other aspect of this original definition of projective identification as an unconscious phantasy is that because it is an omnipotent phantasy, it takes place irrespective of the properties or responses of the object, which does not need, as it were, to participate in the process. I think there are examples of this in all three patients I have described. Mr. A found the discomfort, anxiety, and confusion of the holiday and his return to the analysis difficult to cope with and made it clear that he had, in phantasy, projected the muddle over time, the embarrassment, and the tendency to avoid the mess he had made, into me—before he had actually encountered me again. That part of himself which then dominated the scene was the part which functioned in an efficient and businesslike way, not being bothered by anything. The contact with me during the initial part of the session, the diminution of his anxiety, and his capacity for reality-testing then altered the situation, and he recovered his contact with the confusion and mess which he had previously projected.

Mrs. B forcefully projected an image of an intolerant, irritable, and envious person into me, and was thus reluctant even to face me with the news about her daughter's school, or subsequently to tell me about her accident, and the prospect of having to come late or miss a session. It became evident that the figure which was projected did not merely correspond to a very fixed imago of her mother, but included a part of the patient herself, identified with her mother, which she feared and hated. As long as this remained projected, there was a shallowness and stilted quality to the very polite, considerate, and sensible person who was talking to me. She feared and resented my interpretations which drew attention to the situation, and she felt quite disturbed at the prospect of having to *own* those aspects of herself, in relation to her own daughter, or her analyst, which she found so threatening and painful. She *could*, however, make use of interpretations which put her in touch with previously disowned parts of herself and she then came more alive, more three-dimensional, and could get relief from discovering that we could both survive, and the analysis could proceed.

Rosenfeld (1971) has made the important distinction between the use of projective identification as a means of evacuation, and as a means of communication. He made the point that if the former motive predominates, then my attempt at interpreting the material to the patient will not succeed, as the patient feels one is trying to push something unwanted back into him.

On the other hand, when projective identification is mainly being used as a means of primitive communication, the understanding of what is projected can be felt by the patient to be helpful—the patient may feel relieved that the analyst has been able to understand, and put him in touch with something which the patient could not, himself, either face or put into words.

I thought there was evidence for *both* with Mrs. B, who first felt threatened and defensive, but as the session proceeded, it was evident that something important *had* been able to be communicated to me, and her paranoid anxiety diminished considerably.

Similarly, as I have suggested, in the case of the third patient, there was both the need to disavow her provocative stubbornness and its effects, which might have given rise to feelings of anxiety and guilt, but also to make the therapist have something of the experience of being a frustrated and tantalized child, confronted with a rather narcissistic, perfuming mother.

There is a further aspect of projective identification which we have come to understand better, as other analysts have built on Klein's original work. This concerns the way in which the projection is not only an internal phantasy, or used to communicate an emotional state or states of mind, but actually functions as a means of *affecting* the object, and influencing his behavior. The subjective experience within the analyst is that he "finds himself" saying or doing something under pressure. He feels forced or impelled, in a way which doesn't feel entirely comfortable or ego-syntonic. It is sometimes possible to recognize the pressure, or the induction of a puzzling state of mind, and to try to understand it, but at other times the pressure is either more subtle or more compelling, and the analyst finds himself responding to it.

In the case of Mr. A, I was not aware that there was much pressure on me—I suspect that, partly because of the holiday break, Mr. A was on this occasion unable to tune in sufficiently to what was going on between us to find an effective method of affecting me, and his need to convey something to me was too strong.

With Mrs. B, as I have described, I found myself at one point becoming impatient and frustrated with her bland, slightly-too-good way of speaking and conducting herself, and it would have been very easy to make remarks which would have sounded critical. When I was able to recognize this, and use this recognition to make some sense of the situation, it seemed to be helpful. If I *had* behaved in a critical and impatient way, we would simply have recreated a familiar scenario in which she is the victim of an impatient and hostile figure.

138   MICHAEL FELDMAN

It was very clear with the third case what pressure the therapist was under—to raise the issue of the patient's lateness, which she was either unaware of, or had ignored, and then to respond to her request that he repeat his interpretation—either compliantly, or engaging with her in some process of mutual complaint.

We must, of course, be careful to avoid the temptation to "blame" our patients for our own failure of understanding or technique, or the conflicts or sensitive areas which we ourselves possess, and it is all too easy to attribute most of the difficulties in an analysis to the patient's use of projective identification. It is always important to try to assess the contribution these other factors, which are to some extent the *analyst's* responsibility, make to the difficulties that arise.

However, the concept of projective identification, which Klein formulated, and the development of the theoretical and clinical understanding of what is involved, by Bion, Rosenfeld, and others, has greatly increased the scope and power of the theoretical model, with important implications for clinical practice, as I hope I have been able to demonstrate.

REFERENCES

Bion, W. R. (1959), Attacks on linking. *Internat. J. Psycho-Anal.*, 40:308–315.

Freud, S. (1920), Beyond the pleasure principle. *Standard Edition*, 18:3–64. London: Hogarth Press, 1955.

Joseph, B. (1987), *Psychic Equilibrium and Psychic Change: Selected Papers of Betty Joseph*, ed. E. Bott Spillius & M. Feldman. London: Routledge.

Klein, M. (1946), Notes on some schizoid mechanisms. In: *Writings*, Vol. 3. London: Hogarth Press, 1–24.

Rosenfeld, H. (1971), Contribution to the psychopathology of psychotic states. The importance of projective identification in the ego structure and object relations of psychotic patients. In: *Melanie Klein Today*, Vol. 1, *Mainly Theory*, ed. E. Bott Spillius. London: Routledge, 117–137.

Sandler, J. (1976a), Dreams, fantasies, and "identity of perception." *Internat. Rev. Psycho-Anal.*, 3:33–42.

———— (1976b), Countertransference and role-responsiveness. *Internat. Rev. Psycho-Anal.*, 43–47.

Segal, H. (1964), *An Introduction to the Work of Melanie Klein.* New York: Basic Books.

Strachey, J. (1934), The nature of the therapeutic action of psycho-analysis. *Internat. J. Psycho-Anal.*, 15:275–293.

EDITOR'S INTRODUCTION TO
VARIETIES OF ENVIOUS EXPERIENCE

Elizabeth Bott Spillius offers here a succinct, evenhanded, extended historical review of the trials, tribulations, and transformations in the interpretation of envy. Her review covers developmental influences, defenses against envy, envy itself as a defense against recognizing and feeling gratitude toward the object's goodness as well as against becoming dependent on that goodness. It also covers envy as a potent factor in transference–countertransference phenomena. She goes on to raise necessary evidential questions about Melanie Klein's (1957) having posited a (partial) constitutional basis for envy and having claimed that consequently envy must play an important role in the child's first and very early object relations.

Going further still, Spillius modifies constructively the narrow, restrictive conception of envy that often seems to be implied when this major dynamic factor is mentioned. For her, the concept of envy embraces differences of degree and kind. Thus she distinguishes what she calls ego dystonic envy on the one hand and ego syntonic or "consciousness" syntonic or "impenitent" envy on the other. Typically, the latter type of envy is closer to consciousness and is expressed more or less self-righteously, often in the form of grievance; in contrast, the classically described envy tends to be rather more unconscious, much of it involving painful loss and guilt over destructiveness. Additionally, Spillius argues that envious responses can be influenced by the patient's attempt to reality test the authenticity or inauthenticity in both the giving and receiving of love or goodness.

Of course, the patient may introduce distortion while attempting to test reality. All of which must be tracked if problems with envy are to be worked through.

By means of these theoretical and clinical refinements, Spillius situates envy within the context of generally well-established developmental theory and observation. This is the context in which maturational and integrational differences in ego functioning are emphasized. In this respect, and also in her inclusion of rather more conscious experiences of envy and her centering on impenitent expressions of envy, she does differ with some of her colleagues, specifically those who adhere to a more traditionalist set of ideas. At the same time, she leaves no room for doubt that she remains fundamentally loyal to the customary Kleinian emphasis on unconscious phantasy in transference–countertransference experience. In the end, therefore, this essay demonstrates nicely how much room has been left for individualistic contributions within the general Kleinian guidelines.

One of Spillius' summary-type statements concerning impenitent envy deserves special mention. I regard it as a valuable guide to clinical interpretation in general: "Feeling perpetual grievance and blame, however miserable, is less painful than mourning the loss of relationships one wishes one had had" (p. 154). So many patients in analysis present a virtually intransigent, implicitly envious position of being filled with grievance.

6
VARIETIES OF ENVIOUS EXPERIENCE

ELIZABETH BOTT SPILLIUS

Envy is disturbing—both as a feeling and as a concept in psychoanalysis. Freud's idea of penis envy has aroused anger in many women, especially feminists; and Klein's idea that envy has a constitutional basis evoked a storm of protest from many analysts. Envy has the special distinction of being listed as one of the seven deadly sins, but at the same time it is not frequently the subject of philosophical or social debate. It is as if it were recognized on the one hand, while being rapidly dismissed on the other.

Freud, of course, was the first analyst to use the concept of envy, both in the idea of penis envy and in the idea that the members of a group can forgo their envious rivalry with one another in a common idealization of the group leader (Freud, 1921). Abraham (1919) uses the idea of envy to explain a destructive attack that certain patients make on psychoanalytic work. Eisler (1922) notes that envy derives from the oral instinct. In her 1932 paper, "Jealousy as a Mechanism of Defence," Joan Riviere regards pathological jealousy as a defense against unconscious oral envy of the parents in intercourse. Karen Horney (1936) points to the role of envy in the negative therapeutic

143

reaction. Melanie Klein, however, was the first analyst to make the concept of envy central to her psychoanalytic theory.

Klein used the idea of envy in much of her earlier work (Klein, 1929, 1932, 1945, 1952, 1955), but toward the end of her life she wrote about it much more systematically, in *Envy and Gratitude* (1957). "I consider," she writes, "that envy is an oral–sadistic and anal–sadistic expression of destructive impulses, operative from the beginning of life, and that it has a constitutional basis" (1957, p. 176). A little later she describes it as "the angry feeling that another person possesses and enjoys something desirable—the envious impulse being to take it away or to spoil it" (p. 181). In her view, it is a manifestation of the death instinct, which she thinks of as an instinctual internal destructive force felt as fear of annihilation.

Klein distinguishes with care between envy, greed, and jealousy. *Greed* she defines as "an impetuous and insatiable craving, exceeding what the subject needs and what the object is able and willing to give . . . its aim is destructive introjection; whereas envy [aims] . . . also to put badness . . . into the mother . . . in order to spoil and destroy her" (p. 181). *Jealousy* she describes as a three-person situation in which "the love that the subject feels is his due . . . has been taken away, or is in danger of being taken away, from him by his rival" (p. 181).

These three states of mind are frequently found in close association. Greedy acquisition can be a defense against being aware of envy of those who have or who are what one wishes one had or were oneself. Analysts are familiar with the sort of patient who makes insatiable demands on the analyst but trashes whatever he is given—a mixture of greed and envy. The jealous lover is often driven less by love than by envious hatred of his lover's capacity to arouse the love of another. In everyday English the words *jealousy* and, more rarely, *envy* are often used where *admiration* would be appropriate, for example, in statements such as: "I am jealous [or envious] of your lovely garden." Even

Shakespeare has Iago describe the crucial element of jealousy in terms that are an excellent description of the core of envy:

> O! Beware, my Lord, of jealousy;
> It is the green-eyed monster which doth mock
> The meat it feeds on
>   [*Othello*, Act III, Scene iii, lines 165–167].

Thus, in literary and everyday usage, the terms overlap, vary in meaning, and have a large penumbra of associations. These varying and overlapping usages are enshrined in the *Oxford English Dictionary*. Klein's definition of envy is well within the dominant traditional usage, though it emphasizes the malignant aspects. There are difficulties, however, in treating much used words like *envy* and *jealousy* as technical terms, as Klein does, for people are sure to add their version of the various associated and overlapping meanings.

According to Segal (personal communication), Klein developed her ideas about envy in the course of analyzing three particularly difficult patients. Elliot Jaques (1969) adds that some of Klein's evidence for envy and for its early nature derived from her work with "Richard," a 10-year-old patient who, after acknowledging a helpful bit of the analytic work, often used to attack and belittle it. These attacks appeared particularly often in the context of Richard's feeling that Klein and his mother possessed the feeding "breast," which was giving mental nourishment not only to him but also to others (Klein, 1961). More generally, Klein thought that envy was a major motive for the sort of negative therapeutic reaction that sometimes sets in after helpful work has been acknowledged by the patient (see also Rosenfeld, 1975). She was impressed, too, by the intense pain and depression that many patients experienced when attempting to integrate their increasing awareness of making envious attacks on the analyst's goodness with their conscious positive feeling toward the analyst;

she gives several moving examples of such struggles in *Envy and Gratitude* (1957).

Klein lays especial emphasis on the fact that envy leads to psychic attacks on the goodness of the object, which, if unchecked, leads to great difficulty in taking in and in learning. As envy leads to attacks on the goodness of the object, it is likely to result in confusion between the object's goodness and badness, which impairs processes of differentiation and of the development of rational thought (see Rosenfeld, 1947, 1950). Because of the attacks on goodness, which are much more difficult to acknowledge than attacks on badness, envy leads to premature development of guilt before the individual is able to stand the pain of it, leading to confusion between depressive guilt and paranoid—schizoid persecution, and sometimes to confusional states. It is important to remember that the "good" object of these discussions is not so much a good object as perceived by an outside observer, but as perceived by the subject, whose perception is deeply influenced by his conscious or unconscious fantasy. Frequently, the object is not good but idealized, that is, endowed with all resources and all power (Menzies Lyth, personal communication). It is Klein's view that in satisfactory development, a deep-rooted relation with a good object (here meant as good, not idealized) is built up and internalized, and then the child can withstand temporary states of envy, hatred, and grievance, which arise even in children who are loved and well mothered.

Klein does not assert, as is sometimes thought, that envy is entirely constitutional. As she puts it: "In speaking of an innate conflict between love and hate, I am implying that the capacity both for love and for destructive impulses is, to some extent, constitutional, though varying individually in strength and *interacting from the beginning with external conditions*" (Klein, 1957, p. 180; emphasis added). Or again: "Furthermore, whether or not the child is adequately fed and mothered, whether the mother fully enjoys the care of the child or is anxious and has psychological difficulties over feeding—all these factors influence the infant's capacity to accept the milk with enjoyment and to internalize the good breast" (1957, p. 179).

It is my view, which I think is consistent with Klein's approach, that the experience and expression of envy, and indeed of love and hate in general, occur and develop in relationship with objects, so that one can never meet the constitutional component unmodified by experience. Nor can one tell, from the perspective of the consulting room, how much of a patient's envy is constitutional, how much has developed because of his or her experiences with objects, or how much is the result of the process of interaction between the two. What one *can* tell from the way the patient behaves in the consulting room is what his envy is like in his internal world now, how severe it is, how it expresses itself in relation to the analyst, and what defenses are used.

Klein's book on envy provoked a storm of disagreement in the British Psycho-Analytical Society, chiefly on the grounds that it was preposterous to regard such pernicious attacks on goodness as inherent in human nature; that the death instinct, of which envy was one expression, was not a viable concept; that envy is a complex feeling, not immediately derived from instinct; that Klein ignored the environment; that what she described as envy in infants could better be described as "eagerness"; that she was attributing to infants thoughts of which they were not capable; that her theory of envy was a theory of despair, scientifically unproved; and that the Kleinians' preconceived theoretical expectations of envy were leading them to find confirmation of intractable, vicious, and destructive envy in all their clinical material.

These criticisms were voiced in a symposium on envy and jealousy held by the British Psycho-Analytical Society in 1969, and the main critical paper, by Walter Joffe, was published in the same year. Other, unpublished criticisms were made by Winnicott, Khan, Gillespie, King, Bonnard, Heimann, and

Limentani. Much of the discussion focused on whether or not envy was constitutional, and there was little examination of the clinical material Klein described or her particular use of the concept of envy in elucidating it. The discussion was complicated further by the fact that many speakers were tacitly emphasizing other aspects of the traditional usages of the term *envy*, and by the presence of other complex theoretical issues which have still not been fully clarified or agreed upon: the mutual relationships between the concepts of instinct, mental state, affect, character trait, and object relationship.

Joffe and other British colleagues have not been the only critics of Klein's use of the concept of envy. In 1958, Elizabeth Zetzel wrote that "[t]he hypothesis developed in *Envy and Gratitude* suggests that Melanie Klein is moving further away from, rather than toward, the mainstream of contemporary psychoanalysis" (1958, p. 412). In 1961, Guntrip expressed dismay at Klein's treatment of envy as "unmotivated and ultimate, and as a basic manifestation of death instinct" (1961, p. 344). More recently, Earl Hopper has written that "The critique [in the Envy Symposium of 1969] was telling—if not devastating, and remains so" (1992). Feldman and de Paola (1994) stress the importance of distinguishing between envy as impulse (instinct) and envy as feeling. In their conjectures about the mental development of the infant, they suggest that "precursors of envy" are felt when the infant experiences the catastrophic loss of his belief that he *is* the idealized breast-self; fuller development of the feeling of envy occurs with the greater awareness of object and self characteristic of the depressive position.

In spite of criticisms of the concept of envy, most Kleinian analysts have continued to treat the concept as a cornerstone of their theory and their clinical approach, although few papers have been specifically written about it (Segal, 1964; Joseph, 1986; Etchegoyen, Lopez, and Rabih, 1987; Brenman, 1990; Lussana, 1992). One important difference between Klein's presentation and those of current Kleinian analysts, especially in Britain, is that the latter speculate less than she did about the development of envy in infancy and focus more on the expression of envy in the clinical situation. One of the hard-won clinical understandings arising from the insight of Klein is that in some patients envy can be extremely destructive, both to the individual and to his or her objects, including the analyst. In severe cases it is as if envy held the patient in thrall; the patient feels that his or her convictions and defensive system are infinitely preferable to the tentative relationship with the analyst as a good object, and the patient attacks this relationship remorselessly, especially when he or she feels the analyst has been helpful (e.g., Rosenfeld, 1971; Joseph, 1982).

Although the use of the concept of envy has deepened clinical understanding, there has been a gradual assimilation of some of the criticisms of Kleinian usage, such that there is now a greater acceptance of the inevitable ubiquity of envy, more understanding of the need for defenses against it, and a somewhat less confrontational interpretation of it. It is now generally accepted that it is not usually helpful to interpret envy directly to patients who are locked into the psychopathology of the paranoid–schizoid position (Klein, 1946) and have very little insight or interest in understanding their motives. The analyst may think the patient is envious; the patient has no such idea.

Klein assumes that a propensity for envy is present from birth, a view that is consistent with her idea that some form of selfobject differentiation and some rudimentary form of object relationship is present from the beginning. We cannot, of course, know what preverbal infants think—nor, for that matter, what anyone thinks except by inference—but her assumption is consistent with some observations of babies. For example, a very young baby characteristically did not take hold of the nipple readily; his father, watching him, said: "He only takes hold of it if he thinks he has come across it by accident. I don't think he likes to feel he really needs it." It was clear, too, that the father did not think his baby's behavior was bad, only that he was precociously independent and did not like acknowledging his need for help. Both parents were sympathetic to their baby and his expressions of envy or proto-envy—an important attitude for analysts as well as parents.

When the individual approaches the depressive position, Klein and her colleagues assume that the object's existence is experienced in a much more fully developed way (Klein, 1935, 1940). The object is known to be needed by the individual, but is also known to have an independent existence, to be both good and bad, loved and hated, to have relationships with others. The stage is set for greater awareness of envy and jealousy, and, in the case of our patients' fluctuations between the depressive and the paranoid–schizoid positions in the analytic situation, it is when they approach the depressive position mode of thinking, with its tendency toward integration and its awareness of the object's separateness, that envy is likely to be experienced most acutely, sometimes consciously, and retreat to the defenses of the paranoid–schizoid position may ensue.

Klein, as I have briefly described above, uses a restricted definition of envy and regards it as an expression of death instinct. Some Kleinian analysts now define death instinct in more abstract and biological terms than Klein herself used. Such analysts think of death instinct and envy as forces whose aim is to reduce differentiation and diminish structure, especially structure that involves differences between subject and object. Any difference may be attacked by envy, but goodness is its special target. In this view, much stress is placed on the "malignant destructiveness of envy, which is anti-life, anti-creativity, and anti-growth and development" (Steiner, 1992, and personal communications). To those who hold this view, degrees of envy are recognized, but the idea that there might be qualitatively different sorts of envy or different subjective experiences of envy is not really a meaningful idea; envy, if consciously experienced at all, is thought to be experienced by the individual as a bad, destructive attack on an object recognized to be good. Analysts who subscribe to this definition of envy do not, for example, regard as true envy the case of an apparently envious and deprived individual who ceases to feel envious if the deprivation is removed. And the case of an individual who easily says that he envies a more skilled colleague (or musician, or skier, or whomever) would be regarded as "admiration" rather than envy, or perhaps as admiration used as a defense against real envy.

I believe that this narrow definition of envy is in keeping with the clinical experiences that Klein was trying to delineate and understand, though the definition that is used nowadays is probably even more restricted than Klein's own usage. This restricted definition has become a hallmark of the current Kleinian approach. Like my colleagues, I use the idea of envy in this restricted sense, but I think it is important to note that this idea of envy is *envy as defined by the analyst*; envy as experienced by the patient, consciously or tacitly, may not fit this definition, and the relation between the two definitions, that of the analyst and that of the patient, is clinically significant.

I used to think that envy was only destructive to the individual and to those around him or her when it was unconscious and split off, and that in analysis it would become conscious, arouse guilt, and gradually become integrated with more positive dispositions. I soon found, however, that this notion was too simple. In some patients envy appears to be very obvious, certainly to outside observers, and sometimes it appears to be conscious in some form or other to the envious individual, but without arousing his or her guilt or remorse.

In all the clinical examples given by Klein in *Envy and Gratitude*, in one of Segal's (1964), and in most of Joseph's (1986), the examples of envious reactions are of the first type described above: envy was mainly unconscious and usually well contained.

It rarely expressed itself directly, though its unconscious operation led to inhibition, sometimes severe inhibition, of the patient's creativity in work and in personal relationships. In the case of these patients, conscious envy emerged late in the analysis, at moments when the patient was feeling the analytic work to be deeply helpful, and the patient experienced acute mental pain and a sort of circumscribed depression as he integrated the awareness of his envy into his picture of himself. In this sort of patient the experience of envy is ego dystonic, or, perhaps more accurately, consciousness dystonic; his envy is usually unconscious, and intense guilt is aroused if the individual becomes fully aware of it. In such cases, both analyst and patient are using the same definition of envy.

But in some of my patients, and in a few reported cases—including some of Joffe's (1969), one of Segal's (1964), and in many of the "social" examples described by Schoeck (1969) and Berke (1988), envy is much more obvious to the outside observer and sometimes to the person expressing it. I suggest the term *impenitent* for this way of experiencing envy. I assumed at first that this impenitent way of experiencing envy, which seemed to be virtually conscious, would be much less severe than the ego dystonic way of experiencing envy as described by Klein and others. In fact, I have found that this is not necessarily so. In my experience, there is considerable range in the severity and destructiveness in both ways of experiencing envy. Furthermore, there may well be other ways of experiencing envy; several colleagues have suggested that severely manic and schizophrenic patients use other modes than the two I have described. Nevertheless, it is the ego dystonic and impenitent modes that I have chiefly encountered in my practice and that I want to discuss in this paper.

Envy may be felt, according to the *Oxford English Dictionary*, when the individual compares himself with someone superior in happiness, reputation, or in the possession of anything desirable.

In my view, envy is especially likely to be felt when the individual has to *depend* on someone who is felt to be this sort of superior person, and all envious patients defend themselves to some extent against being aware of such dependence. The person whose envy is ego dystonic directs defenses against becoming aware that envy may be the basis of his behavior, especially his various forms of attack on good objects. In the analysis of this sort of patient and this sort of envy, both analyst and patient have the same, or potentially the same, definition of envy: it is a destructive attack on a good object. The person whose envy is impenitent, however, does not suffer from conscious guilt and a sense of responsibility for his envy; he thinks it is the envied person's fault that he, the envier, feels so wretched. His defenses are used to maintain and enhance what he regards as a legitimate grievance. In the analytic situation, such a patient's definition of envy is different from that of the analyst. The analyst, if he is using the Kleinian definition I have described above, thinks the patient is making a destructive attack on a good object; the patient thinks he is making a legitimate attack on an object who deserves to be hated. The patient may not jib at being told he is envious—should his analyst be so unwise as to tell him so directly—because the impenitently envious patient does not define envy in the same way as his Kleinian analyst does.

This experiencing envy without guilt, which I am calling impenitent, is also described by Kernberg, who says it is typically found in the narcissistic personality disorder, especially when this disorder takes the form of pathological narcissism or antisocial personality disorder (Kernberg, 1984, pp. 193, 197, 303; 1989, p. 559). It is described particularly clearly by Dennis Carpy (n.d.) in a paper called "Fantasy versus Reality in Childhood Trauma: Who's to Blame?"

A frequent aspect of the defensive arrangements of the person who suffers from impenitent envy is that he feels unconsciously that he is profoundly unlovable and inferior, qualities which he projects onto those toward whom he feels superior. Thus the person with impenitent envy and a persistent sense of grievance tends to find himself in a world in which some people are unfairly superior to him while others are justifiably inferior. In such a person character perversion is likely to play an important role—sadism and masochism are sometimes pronounced, and frequently there is a preoccupation with the issue of power. Such a person reminds one of Milton's Satan, with his abandoning of hope, good, and remorse, and his welcoming of evil and power:

> So farewell hope, and with hope farewell fear,
> Farewell remorse: all good to me is lost;
> Evil be thou my good;
> [*Paradise Lost*, Bk. IV, 1, lines 108–110].

Like Carpy, however, I have found that in cases of grievance and impenitent experiencing of envy, defenses are used not only to maintain and enhance the sense of grievance, but also to evade acknowledging the acute pain and sense of loss, sometimes fear of psychic collapse, that would come from realizing that one wants a good object but really feels that one does not or has not had it. Feeling perpetual grievance and blame, however miserable, is less painful than mourning the loss of the relationships one wishes one had had. Grievance is thus a form of narcissistic defense. "Envy and narcissism," as Segal said at the Symposium on Envy and Jealousy in 1969, "can be seen as two sides of the same coin."

Defenses against envy are multiple, and frequently reinforce one another to form what John Steiner (1985) has called a "pathological organization." This is especially likely in cases of impenitent envy, but is also found in severe cases of ego dystonic envy. The main defenses against envy are described by Klein and have been slightly elaborated by her colleagues. They are:

1. Denigration of the good qualities of the object, which will then provoke less admiration and dependency (Klein, 1957; Segal, 1964; Joseph, 1986);
2. Projection of envy so that the individual sees himself as a non-envious person surrounded by envious destructive people (Klein, 1957; Joseph, 1986);
3. Idealization of the envied object, so that comparisons with oneself become irrelevant (Klein, 1957; Joseph, 1986); or it may take the form of denigration of the envied object and idealization of some other object; or some aspects of the envied object may be denigrated and others idealized;
4. Identification with the idealized object or idealized aspects of the object through projection and introjection so that the individual feels that he is the possessor of the admired attributes of the envied object (Klein, 1952, pp. 68–69; Rosenfeld, 1964, p. 71; Sohn, 1985);
5. A stifling of feelings of love and, correspondingly, an intensifying of hate, sometimes expressing itself as indifference or emotional withdrawal (Klein, 1957; Rosenfeld, 1969);
6. A form of masochistic defense in which the individual feels himself to be omnipotently hopeless, so that the envied object, who cannot cure the individual's despair, is proved to be worthless (Joseph, 1982, 1986).

I want now to describe sessions with two patients that illustrate the ego dystonic and impenitent ways of experiencing envy. In the sessions I shall describe, both patients somewhat resented the fact that recent analytic sessions had been helpful, and both expressed some degree of negative therapeutic reaction. To Mrs. A, envy is ego dystonic, and although she was considerably upset when she became aware of it, as in the sessions that I report, her envy is not pervasive or deeply destructive. Mrs. B has a sense of grievance, and although she would not be described as deeply disturbed or fragmented, she is considerably more troubled by envy than Mrs. A, whose tacit definition of envy is close to mine. Mrs. B's impenitent experiencing of envy is virtually conscious, but her definition of envy is different from mine; what I regard as envy she regards as justified grievance.

Mrs. A

Mrs. A mistakenly came to her session fifteen minutes early. While waiting to start the session I was puzzled, for Mrs. A was generally punctual. Was she in an unusual state of eagerness? In a panic? Was it connected with the previous day's apparently "good" session? Once the session had begun, she explained that she hadn't realized at first that she had come early, and she had felt angry with me for keeping her waiting. Then she realized what had happened and felt very embarrassed, as if she had been caught in the act of spying on me. She had found it reassuring while she was waiting to hear me talking to the woman who cleans my house. It meant that I was involved in all the sounds of domesticity.

"Because you too make pretty much the same sort of sound," I said, "so it means you and I are alike." She agreed, and went on to tell me that she had found yesterday's session particularly helpful, that she had understood many things that she hadn't thought of before. I said she was very grateful for this, but it also seemed possible that it had made her feel that she couldn't provide for herself the sort of understanding that I had, so she had regained her balance by arranging to hear me in my domestic role, in which I was reassuringly similar to her.

She thought briefly, agreed, saying that it wasn't very nice. Then she talked about one of her colleagues, with whom she was having a lot of difficulty because he had said that one of his bosses is "past it" and hardly worth bothering about. "Oh dear," she said.

"You seem to have started listening to what you were saying and translating it," I said. "Yes, and it seems to be that I'm saying you're 'past it.' Even worse." She paused, and then went on to tell me that a close friend of her brother had rung last night, and how important it was because they had been somewhat estranged. Then she told me a long, harrowing, and exceedingly interesting story about the heroism of this brother's friend during the recent revolutions in Eastern Europe.

For some time I was completely caught up in listening to the story, then I began to think about why I had got so involved in it, and whether it was possible that her telling of the story had something to do with the situation we had been talking about earlier. Eventually I said I thought she was worried I might think she was past it, and she was again regaining her balance, this time by telling me a very interesting and dramatic story that she thought I would find utterly absorbing. It was a way of arranging things so that she felt she was the one who had the valuable stuff and I was the one who was being enriched by it—she was the giver, I the receiver, reversing the roles she felt we had been in the previous day.

"I've suddenly remembered a dream," she said. "It was pretty dreadful:

> I was with my sister. All my crowns fell off my teeth. I was trying to push them back on but even the stumps were falling out. I was a wreck. Then I saw an old friend walking past with her back very straight. She looked very regal, wearing a kaftan. Father used to tell me off for not walking with my back straight."

I said that she had remembered the dream almost at the end of the session so that if I talked about it I would be pronouncing on it in the sort of regal manner that she felt was characteristic of her sister. I thought she felt that in the dream the repair work we had been doing had fallen to pieces, that there wasn't even a foundation for it. It wasn't clear whether she felt my supposed repair work was attacking her teeth, or she was attacking the work we had been doing together, but it did seem that I was queening it over her and she was a wreck.

Reflecting on the session, after she had left, it seemed to me that as the session proceeded she had gradually moved closer to a more explicit recognition of making an envious attack.

The Next Session

She went back to the dream at once. She agreed, with some discomfort, that her self-attack was really an attack on the work we had been doing. The straight-backed old friend, it emerged, was her view of me, in which I was made out to be haughty and regal rather than helpful. Furthermore, she thought she had wanted to be like this sort of person herself, hardly a compliment to the analytic enterprise. She then talked in detail and with pain and seriousness about the difficulty she has in getting hold of things in herself that she really doesn't like.

As time went on in successive sessions, she realized that her envious attacks on me and on her own progress were not as deeply spoiling as she had feared. She became more objective about my vices and virtues and more forgiving toward herself for her periodic impulses of envious attack. Very gradually, she also became less inclined to blame herself endlessly for what she felt to be her mother's defects.

Mrs. B

Before the sessions that I shall report, Mrs. B had had several "good" sessions in which she felt I had understood something particularly painful that she had undergone.

Session 1

She seemed to be in a bad mood. She said her students hadn't turned up, so she'd canceled her seminar. Then she had had a piano lesson and felt it had gone well; it made her furious that she was dependent on something external like that. Furious also, I said, that she had felt better during yesterday's session, another external something she perhaps felt dependent on.

She said I could add her mother's visit. It had gone well and that had made her disgruntled too. Silence. Then she said she had had a dream, but didn't propose to tell me. The atmosphere was heavy with resentment.

I waited for quite a long time and then said I thought she didn't want me to have the pleasure of working with her to understand the dream. "I suppose not," she said. A long silence, then she said, "Having said I won't tell you, here it is: I'm with my grandmother. She was dancing with me in a lively fashion. I was half enjoying it but half afraid she would have a heart attack and die."

She said she couldn't make much sense of it, then spent quite a long time explaining that her grandmother had a weak constitution, a constitutional defect. After a pause, she talked about a woman colleague whose marriage looked very trendy and successful, but she thought it was all a great strain on the couple and their children. She herself and her husband are the same—everything looks fine on the surface but things aren't really right.

As in the dream, I said, in which your grandmother looked full of life, but seems to have been unaware of the fact that she might have a heart attack and die at any moment. I went on to say that I thought she had similar mixed feelings about me. I looked all right on the surface—she'd been told I was a respected training analyst, and so on—but what sort of strain was going on under that supposedly trendy exterior? What sort of strain was the dance between us putting on us? Would I be overwhelmed and she be blamed?

Silence. "You mean because of my telling you about feeling troubled yesterday." "Yes, perhaps."

I waited some time, then said that, like her grandmother in the dream, I thought that she felt I was unaware of the danger I was in. She thought I was idealizing my energy and my dancing partnership with her, just as her colleague at work idealized her trendy marriage. So there was a constitutional weakness in me that she knew about and I did not.

There was a longish pause. Then she said that there was something ridiculous about her grandmother in the dream.

"You're right. I've just realized there is something I've been feeling about you that is ridiculous. It's about your garden. It makes me think you're silly. Why did you choose a house that is overlooked? At first I thought it must be some American custom—you're so urbanized you don't care about being overlooked. Anyway, so long as you only had a mess out there it didn't matter, there was nothing to see. But now you've put in grass and plants. Surely you must realize there is no point in doing that when you're overlooked. It's silly."

Normally I would have explored her choice of my garden a bit further, but it was getting near the end of the session. I said the garden was her analysis—so long as it was barren and a mess, she could overlook it and it didn't matter. But now I was aspiring to grow things in her analysis with her, and it made her furious. It made her feel overlooked, resentful, shut out, and she dealt with it by thinking she was the one overlooking me, superior. I was unaware of this and silly.

"Yes," she said, "and *you* overlook that there is something in me that is going to spoil everything—my inheritance, my bad constitution." (This was said with a mixture of grievance and contempt, as if she did not have to carry any responsibility for spoiling everything because it was her bad constitution that was to blame, and I was too stupid to have seen this.)

I said she put it cogently, triumphantly; she felt I deserved to be put down. And, as in the dream, she felt I was a slightly absurd, vulnerable granny, oblivious of the dance of death she was enacting with me, and oblivious too, perhaps, of her fear that she would get blamed for the terrible outcome it might have. (In addition to the three meanings of "overlook" in this interchange, namely, [1] to see into or over; [2] to ignore; and [3] to look down upon, there is another meaning, according to the *Oxford English Dictionary*, which is "to look with the evil eye," a concept very close to envy. I doubt very much, however, whether my patient knew this; certainly, I did not know it at the time.)

Next Session

She felt marvelous and sounded absolutely triumphant. Three good students had appeared and she had assigned them all to her own seminar; she didn't see why her colleagues should expect to share in her decision. After all, their work wasn't any better than hers just because they had Ph.D.s. I said she felt she was not only the equal of her colleagues with Ph.D.s, but also the equal of the me who had a Ph.D. She had become me, or, rather, the impressive Ph.D. aspects of me.

Gradually, in the course of the session, it became clear that her image of me was increasingly split. The incompetent granny me was being denigrated more and more, and was arousing in my patient not a sense of responsibility, but the persecutory guilt that Klein describes (1957, pp. 194–195). The Ph.D. me was exalted, idealized; she had taken it over and become identified with it to the extent that she was almost talking as if she had a Ph.D. herself. Certainly she was as good as me.

Eventually, though not in this session, her spell of narcissistic self-sufficiency collapsed into futility and hopelessness, which she felt I could do nothing to help. It became clearer that she found it very difficult indeed to bear the intense pain of the loss of all the good experience that she wished she had had, good experience that had in part been denied her by others, but that she herself had also spoiled.

Looking back now on these sessions of Mrs. B's, I think there was something that had been particularly provoking to her in the sessions before the ones I have reported. In those earlier sessions she had felt very troubled and felt I had understood this, not only in the sense of interpreting her pain in a way that made sense to her, but also in the sense of registering her pain empathically. But my patient is very threatened by this sort of empathic understanding, which, I think, is too close to the love she longs for but must not let herself know she wants. She deals with such emotions by denigration; empathy is a sign of weakness, even lack of insight. To her, goodness is weak, inferior, unsafe, even persecuting. Strength is cruel, superior, safe. Something that is good cannot be strong and vice versa.

Kernberg (1984, p. 299) describes the same sort of belief, but in much more pathological types of character than Mrs. B. Mrs. B has a sense of grievance against her parents for being weak, and in the session she had a sense of grievance against me for being a weak granny. Perhaps my capacity to see that she felt I was a weak granny provoked an even greater sense of grievance. Certainly she did not see my capacity to see this as a strength that could help her. Only my (irrelevant) Ph.D. was impressive and desirable.

The differences between Mrs. A and Mrs. B are partly of degree. Both were provoked by "good" sessions, which made them feel dependent, although Mrs. B was more humiliated than Mrs. A. Both picked on something to idealize and identify with, but Mrs. A's identification (with the old friend in the kaftan) was transitory, whereas Mrs. B's (taking over my Ph.D.) was more insistent. Mrs. A's denigration of me was slight, Mrs. B's was more intense. But in this respect there was a difference of kind as well as degree. To Mrs. A I remained a basically good figure, whom she discovered, to her chagrin, she was attacking for base reasons; Mrs. B felt that when I was attacked by her "constitutional defect" I was damaged and became a bad persecuting figure, and she would be blamed for my damaged state. The splitting between the good me and the bad me was more profound in Mrs. B than in Mrs. A. But the main difference was that, whereas Mrs. A's defenses worked tentatively and singly, Mrs. B's worked together to make a strong system that maintained her view of herself as someone with a legitimate grievance.

It is of some interest that these two patients described their childhoods in similar terms. Both felt they had overbusy and very preoccupied parents who were basically unhappy, and both patients thought they had missed out on the love and attention they wished they had had. If anything, Mrs. A felt even more left out than Mrs. B because she felt that her mother had greatly preferred some of the other children to her. But Mrs. A had a profound feeling of concern and responsibility about both parents, particularly her mother; she worried about her and wished more than anything that analysis would show that her mother had really loved her after all. Mrs. B respected those members of her family whom she felt were strong and successful, and felt rather ashamed of those whom she thought were weak. As I have described above, she closely associated weakness with goodness and ineffectualness, and all three were unsafe and contemptible. I believe that she despised weakness in others because she believed unconsciously that she herself was weak, inferior, and unlovable. Perhaps her greatest difficulty was in mourning not only the loss of the ideal parents she would like to have had, but also the loss of the ideal self that she would like to have been.

I do not, of course, know what the parents of Mrs. A and Mrs. B were actually like, and the very different outcome in my two patients' expectations of life makes one aware of the enormous complexity of the interplay of psychic and material reality, and aware too of how cautious one needs to be in assuming that in analysis one can discover historical as distinct from remembered truth. I do not think it would be right to assume that Mrs. B's parents were "worse" than Mrs. A's—I simply do not know. Nor would it be correct even to say that Mrs. B *thought* they were worse. What *is* clear is that, in analysis, Mrs. A was better able than Mrs. B to mourn the loss of the good parents (and the good analyst) that she would like to have had.

We could describe the way Mrs. A expressed envy in the session I report, as envy in the depressive position, whereas the way Mrs. B expressed envy, at least on this occasion, could be characterized as envy largely in the paranoid–schizoid mode, a retreat to paranoia as a defense against depressive anxiety. I do not mean that Mrs. A's sort of envy is the only type that is found in the depressive position. It can often be more severe, as shown in the cases described by Klein and others, and it may be different at different periods in an analysis. Nor do I think it would be right to assert that impenitent envy is the only form of envy that one encounters in patients who are enmeshed in the pathology of the paranoid–schizoid position.

Rather than characterize the comparison between ego dystonic and impenitent envy solely in terms of the paranoid–schizoid and depressive positions, however, I want to describe in greater detail a model that I have gradually constructed of the factors that I think mitigate or exacerbate envy. My model centers on the *perceived relation between giver and receiver*, partly because it is this relation that we see especially clearly in analysis, as in infancy, but also because it is the relation in which envy is particularly likely to be aroused.

One crucial factor seems to me to be the conscious and unconscious feelings of the giver about giving, and the way these feelings are perceived or misperceived, consciously and unconsciously, by the receiver. It must already be apparent that my model is potentially exceedingly complex. Presumably there is some "factual" reality about the nature of the giving and receiving, but this reality is complicated enormously by the conscious and unconscious feelings and perceptions of both giver and receiver, and it is these psychic realities that are especially important in the experience of envy.

Let us suppose that the giver takes pleasure in giving, and, further, that he is not, for example, giving in order to establish superiority over the receiver. Let us suppose, too, that the receiver is able to perceive this accurately and also to realize that the giver knows that he, the receiver, might resent being given to—like the father described above observing his baby's approach to the breast. In this type of giving and this type of perception by the receiver, it is likely to be relatively easy for the receiver to acknowledge envy and to feel positive feelings as well. In particular, the receiver may feel able to give something back to the giver in the form of feeling pleasure as well as some resentment about being given to. If the giver can recognize and accept this return gift, this gratitude, a benign circle may be set up in which both parties give something of value to each other. The receiver's capacity to be given to is a return gift to the original giver. Goodness in the other becomes bearable, even enjoyable. The receiver introjects and identifies with an object who enjoys giving and receiving, and an internal basis for admiration can develop, and hence emulation of the generous giver becomes possible.

Let us suppose, in contrast, that the giver actually takes little pleasure in giving, that he is narcissistic and uninterested in the receiver, or that he is outright hostile or inconsistent toward the receiver, or that he feels, consciously or unconsciously, that the receiver is making unreasonable demands or draining his resources unfairly; or suppose that the giver gives eagerly and with pleasure, but only in order to demonstrate his superiority over the receiver. Or, further, let us suppose that he gives reluctantly and unwillingly because he is trying to conceal the fact that he feels what he gives is bad. And, still further, let us suppose that the giver's lack of genuine pleasure and generosity is accurately perceived by the receiver. In any of these examples, envy is likely to be exacerbated; pleasure in receiving cannot easily develop; and the receiver will not readily feel grateful. The receiver is likely to feel resentful and to give as little as possible back to the original giver. Deprived of gratitude, the original giver gives less, or more aggressively, and the deprivation–envy circle continues. So, somewhat paradoxically, envy is likely to be greatest when the giving object is felt to give little or badly. The receiver takes in and identifies with a giver-object who does not enjoy giving and receiving, and the vicious circle is perpetuated internally. Genuine emulation

becomes very difficult, and is likely to involve splitting, projection, and a takeover of the giver's power, as with Mrs. B's
identification with my Ph.D.

The contrast I have drawn so far is, of course, much too simple.
It takes some account of the giver's motives and mode of giving, but it assumes that the receiver perceives and interprets
these modes correctly. In reality, however, the receiver may make
many types and degrees of misperception and misinterpretation.
For example, the giver may give with pleasure and in good faith,
yet the receiver may misinterpret the gift as an attempt by the
giver to establish superiority. A giver may have a reasonable expectation of gratitude for a gift generously given, but the receiver
may be so resentful that the giver has the capacity to give, whereas
he, the receiver, cannot supply the good thing for himself, that
he reacts with hatred, contempt, conventional politeness, or
simply ignores that the gift has been given—all of these being
forms of spoiling. Or the giver may give diffidently because of a
conviction, conscious or unconscious, that what he has to give
is really bad, and the receiver may misperceive this as stinginess,
superiority, or indifference.

These examples of misperception have concerned cases
where the giver's emotions are basically good, but the receiver
misinterprets them. But there are also cases of "bad" giving which
the receiver misconstrues as good. It took some years of analysis, for example, before Mrs. A was able to realize that I had made
a bad interpretation, or that I should have made a particular interpretation but had failed to do so; it took still longer before
she could tell me immediately that I was wrong instead of waiting until the next session.

I have not tried to exhaust the possible variations, and it is
obvious that there can be very complex interactions of giving,
receiving, further response by the original giver, and yet further
response by the receiver. We have only to think of an hour or
two in the life of a mother and baby, or a session or two in the

course of an analysis, to realize how complex these interchanges can be.

Although my basic model of giving-receiving has become very complicated, I have found it essential to include the conscious and unconscious feelings, perceptions, and misperceptions of both giver and receiver. And, in spite of its complexity, I have found the model and its many variations useful in making a first step toward understanding the connections between giving, receiving, and envy in the inner worlds of my patients and in understanding their expectations of me and my reactions to them. I should like to emphasize, however, that I use my model to achieve more accurate *descriptions* of envious reactions. When it comes to attempts at causal explanations, I think one must be very cautious. I think I have a fairly clear picture of the role of "ordinary" and ego dystonic experiences of envy in Mrs. A's life, and of the role of grievance and impenitent experiences of envy in Mrs. B's life, but if I were asked to explain the ultimate cause of the differences between them I do not think I could answer.

Finally, I think it is important to be constantly aware of the similarities and differences between our own definitions of envy and those of our patients—an awareness that working with my model of giving and receiving has helped me to become aware of.

SUMMARY

This paper discusses Melanie Klein's use of the concept of envy and some of the criticisms of it. Two ways of experiencing envy, ego dystonic and impenitent, are described and illustrated in clinical detail. The paper concludes with a description of a model of the relation of giving and receiving, especially of the conscious and unconscious feelings involved in giving and receiving, for I believe that it is in this relation and its internalization that envy is particularly likely to be aroused, diminished, exacerbated, or perpetuated.

REFERENCES

Abraham, K. (1919), A particular form of neurotic resistance against the psycho-analytic method. In: *Selected Papers on Psycho-Analysis*, tr. D. Bryan & A. Strachey. London: Hogarth Press, 1942, pp. 303–312.

Berke, J. H. (1988), *The Tyranny of Malice, Exploring the Dark Side of Character and Culture.* London: Simon & Schuster, 1989.

Brenman, E. (1990), Envy. Paper presented at a Tavistock Lecture Series on The Seven Deadly Sins.

The British Psycho-Analytical Society (1969), Symposium on envy and jealousy. Typescript.

Carpy, D. (n.d.), Fantasy versus reality in childhood trauma: Who's to blame? Typescript.

Eisler, M. J. (1922), Pleasure in sleep and the disturbed capacity for sleep. *Internat. J. Psycho-Anal.*, 3:30–42.

Etchegoyen, R. H., Lopez, B. M., & Rabih, M. (1987), On envy and how to interpret it. *Internat. J. Psycho-Anal.*, 68:49–61.

Feldman, E., & de Paola, H. (1994), An investigation into the psycho-analytic concept of envy. *Internat. J. Psycho-Anal.*, 75:217–234.

Freud, S. (1921), Group Psychology and the Analysis of the Ego. *Standard Edition*, 18:65–163. London: Hogarth Press, 1955.

Guntrip, H. (1961), *Personality Structure and Human Interaction.* London: Hogarth Press.

Hopper, E. (1992), Discussion. Varieties of envious experience, by E. B. Spillius. British Psycho-Analytical Society, November 18.

Horney, K. (1936), The problem of the negative therapeutic reaction. *Psychoanal. Quart.*, 5:29–44.

Jaques, E. (1969), A discussion of envy. Paper presented to the Symposium of the British Psycho-Analytical Society on envy and jealousy.

Joffe, W. G. (1969), A critical survey of the status of the envy concept. *Internat. J. Psycho-Anal.*, 50:533–545.

Joseph, B. (1982), Addiction to near-death. In: *Psychic Equilibrium and Psychic Change: Selected Papers of Betty Joseph.* London & New York: Routledge, 1989, pp. 127–138.

——— (1986), Envy in everyday life. In: *Psychic Equilibrium and Psychic Change: Selected Papers of Betty Joseph*, ed. M. Feldman & E. Bott Spillius. London & New York: Routledge, 1989, pp. 181–191.

Kernberg, O. (1984), *Severe Personality Disorders*. New Haven: Yale University Press.

——— (1989), The narcissistic personality disorder and the differential diagnosis of antisocial behavior. *Psychiatric Clin. N. Amer.*, 12:553–570.

Klein, M. (1929), Personification in the play of children. In: *Writings*, Vol. 1. London: Hogarth Press, 1975, pp. 199–209.

——— (1932), An obsessional neurosis in a six-year-old girl. In: *Writings*, Vol. 2. London: Hogarth Press, 1975, pp. 35–57.

——— (1935), A contribution to the psychogenesis of manic-depressive states. In: *Writings*, Vol. 1. London: Hogarth Press, 1975, pp. 262–289.

——— (1940), Mourning and its relation to manic-depressive states. In: *Writings*, Vol. 1. London: Hogarth Press, 1975, pp. 344–369.

——— (1945), The Oedipus complex in the light of early anxieties. In: *Writings*, Vol. 1. London: Hogarth Press, 1975, pp. 370–419.

——— (1946), Notes on some schizoid mechanisms. In: *Writings*, Vol. 3. London: Hogarth Press, 1975, pp. 1–24.

——— (1952), Some theoretical conclusions regarding the emotional life of the infant. In: *Writings*, Vol. 3. London: Hogarth Press, 1975, pp. 61–93.

——— (1955), On identification. In: *Writings*, Vol. 3. London: Hogarth Press, 1975, pp. 141–176.

——— (1957), Envy and gratitude. In: *Writings*, Vol. 3. London: Hogarth Press, 1975, pp. 176–235.

——— (1959), Our adult world and its roots in infancy. In: *Writings*, Vol. 3. London: Hogarth Press, 1975, pp. 247–263.

——— (1961), The Narrative of a Child Analysis. The Conduct of the Psycho-Analysis of Children as Seen in the Treatment of a Ten-Year-Old Boy, *Writings*, Vol. 4. London: Hogarth Press, 1975.

Lussana, P. (1992), Envy. *Riv. Psicoanal.*, 38:122–153.

Riviere, J. (1932), Jealousy as a mechanism of defence. In: *The Inner World and Joan Riviere*, ed. A. Hughes. London: Karnac Books, 1991.

Rosenfeld, H. (1947), Analysis of a schizophrenic state with depersonalization. In: *Psychotic States*. London: Hogarth Press, 1965, pp. 13–33.

——— (1950), Notes on the psychopathology of confusional states in chronic schizophrenias. In: *Psychotic States*. London: Hogarth Press, 1965, pp. 52–62.

——— (1964), On the psychopathology of narcissism: A clinical approach. In: *Psychotic States*. London: Hogarth Press, 1965, pp. 169–179.

——— (1969), Discussion. Symposium of the British Psycho-Analytic Society on Envy and Jealousy.

——— (1971), A clinical approach to the psychoanalytical theory of the life and death instincts: An investigation into the aggressive aspects of narcissism. In: *Melanie Klein Today*, Vol. 1, ed. E. Bott Spillius. London & New York: Routledge, 1988, pp. 239–255.

——— (1975), The negative therapeutic reaction. In: *Tactics and Techniques in Psychoanalytic Therapy*, Vol. 2, ed. P. L. Giovacchini. Northvale, NJ: Jason Aronson, pp. 219–228.

Schoeck, H. (1969), *Envy: A Theory of Social Behaviour*, tr. M. Glenny & B. Ross. London: Secker & Warburg.

Segal, H. (1964), *Introduction to the Work of Melanie Klein*. London: Heinemann.

——— (1969), Discussion. Symposium of the British Psycho-Analytical Society on Envy and Jealousy.

Sohn, L. (1985), Narcissistic organization, projective identification, and the formation of the identificate. In: *Melanie Klein Today*, Vol. 1, ed. E. Bott Spillius. London & New York: Routledge, 1988, pp. 271–292.

Steiner, J. (1985), The interplay between pathological organizations and the paranoid-schizoid and depressive positions. In: *Melanie Klein Today*, Vol. 1, ed. E. Bott Spillius. London & New York: Routledge, 1988, pp. 324–342.

——— (1992), Discussion. Varieties of envious experience, by E. Bott Spillius, British Psycho-Analytical Society, November 18.

Zetzel, E. (1958), Review of Klein's *Envy and Gratitude*. *Psychoanal. Quart.*, 27:409–412.

EDITOR'S INTRODUCTION TO
CRUELTY AND NARROW-MINDEDNESS

This essay on the psychology of cruelty centers on the analysis of a Holocaust survivor and is a most useful addition to the analytic literature on Holocaust survivors and their families. Eric Brenman includes a second case that illustrates some of his principal points in another context that speaks for itself.

Brenman presents a moving analytic account of his treatment of a survivor. The climax of his story is defined by the metaphors of homelessness and finding a home in the inner world. In his patient's concretely phantasized inner world there resided a cast of characters often painful to contemplate: the patient as disturbed infant; the patient as exile; the patient as survivor identified with Nazi persecutors; the patient as guilty to an extreme and irremediable degree; also, the analyst in the earlier stages of transference as a terrible persecutor, along with a cruelly rejecting mother and a mother who was a fellow exile. With the patient's progress in analysis this mother both makes a home for the patient in the inner world and finds a home there for herself. An equivalent transformation had taken place in the patient's inner experience of the analyst. In that connection, the patient was able to curtail her cruel attacks on the analyst's goodness and creativity, attacks which were designed to put him through the ordeal that she desperately had to avoid going through within herself, the ordeal of confronting the fact, as she saw it, of "living a lie" and fearing that without that lie she would be left with nothing but unbearably cruel guilt feelings.

The author's analytic material exemplifies many of the central variables emphasized by contemporary Kleinians, a number of which he formulates in his discussion section, but some of which he leaves implicit. I would judge that the following seven major variables played crucial roles in the first case he reports:

1. The excruciating guilt the patient experienced in her shattered internal world in reaction to her own cruelty within the analysis, in her earlier attacks on her mother, and in her having survived while her parents had perished;

2. Projective identification (the construction of the persecuting analyst) and introjective identification (first the patient's identification with the Nazi figure and later with Brenman as "container," the latter taking place once Brenman's forebearing and empathic interpretations finally qualified him to serve as a good "home" for the patient's infant self and exiled self);

3. The stimulation through projective identification of Brenman's countertransferential experiences of hopelessness and uncertainty of his own goodness and creativity;

4. Progression, despite temporary relapse, from the paranoid–schizoid position to the depressive position, the patient's having started out from a narcissistic, omnipotent, envious, persecutory set of phantasies that relied heavily on the defenses of splitting, denial of reality, and projective identification and having slowly moved toward feelings of gratitude, acceptance of responsibility, tolerance of ambivalence and guilt, inclinations toward reparativeness, and a relatively more balanced and integrated sense of reality.

5. The overcoming of massive negative therapeutic reactions;

6. Concurrently, the relative resolution through psychoanalysis of pathological mourning and developmental arrest in adolescence, that being the time in development when she had been separated from her parents; the result of that resolution was a

greater capacity for integration of the self and object and the tempering of cruel superego functioning;

7. The patient's ultimately turning to artistic creativity to help her rebuild her shattered internal world, a development that is an instructive example of the mutual shaping of inner and outer reality in the course of one's making reparative efforts.

7

CRUELTY AND NARROW-MINDEDNESS

ERIC BRENMAN

In normal development love modifies cruelty; in order to perpetuate cruelty, steps have to be taken to prevent human love
from operating. My contention is that in order to maintain the
practice of cruelty, a singular narrow-mindedness of purpose is
put into operation. This has the function of squeezing out humanity and preventing human understanding from modifying
the cruelty. The consequence of this process produces a cruelty
which is "inhuman."

If we consider the Oedipus myth from the angle of the role
played by the gods, we can follow this process. The god Apollo
had ordained that Oedipus would kill his father Laius and marry
his mother Jocasta. No mortal, that is, human, intervention
could be proof against the god's prediction. Here we see the
omnipotent narrow-minded persistence: nothing can stand in
the way of the omnipotent gods' determination.

Laius' only hope was that Oedipus should not survive. Here
we see countercruelty presented as the only solution. Oedipus

This paper is a development of the paper on "Cruelty and Narrow-
mindedness" read at the European Congress in October 1970. It was not
published at that time for reasons of confidentiality.

was delivered to a shepherd with orders to abandon him on a mountain; but human compassion, the antidote to cruelty, intervened, because the shepherd had not the heart to do this and entrusted the child to a Corinthian shepherd. But this humanity was of no avail.

As a result of cruel destiny, Oedipus killed his father on his journey to escape patricide, emphasizing again the impotence of human understanding. After marrying Jocasta, Oedipus had to root out his father's murderer, and pursued this course with persistent vigor, excluding all human counsel. The tragic revelation led to his plucking out his eyes, and his abandonment to cruel exile.

What this myth shows, over and above the accepted interpretation, is that the powerful omnipotent Gods are determined to triumph over human compassion and understanding, and this in itself prompts countercruelty. The revelation of guilt likewise leads to the relentless cruel judgment of loveless exile, with the deprivation of human comfort; equivalent to the cruelty of the superego. Some human comfort was, however, derived from his daughter Antigone.

It seems to me that this myth shows another interesting feature; the omnipotent, cruel, and relentless gods are actually worshipped and revered and given a higher status than human love; I think that it is because they are in fact "loved" (as well as feared) more than humanity that such catastrophes take place.

When love and hate clash, either we feel guilt and make reparation, or we are persecuted by guilt. To avoid either consequence, we can pervert the truth, draw strength from a good object, and feel free to practice cruelty in the name of goodness. It is as though we omnipotently hijack human righteousness and conduct cruelty in the name of justice.

We now take for granted that omnipotent behavior belongs to the nature of man. History affords us many examples of this: the Hitler regime, idealized omnipotent national conquest, revolutions and their subsequent regimes. This perversion is well illustrated by the Spanish Inquisition, which took the Christian ethic of tolerance, understanding, and brotherly love, and tortured ruthlessly in the name of Christianity.

In Greek tragedy the chorus sees the tragedy in a broader spectrum, but only hopelessly observes while the tragic hero is locked in the narrow confines of his destiny. The analyst witnesses, as the chorus does, but hopes that intervention of understanding can modify the process. In my clinical examples I refer to patients who are persistently cruel and who persist with their grievances in a cruel way and, by projection, experience the interpretations of the analyst as having the identical qualities of cruelty. I also wish to show the narrowing of perception (narrow-mindedness) that facilitates this process, and with it the avoidance of psychotic catastrophe.

CLINICAL EXAMPLE

The patient, a Jewish woman of 42, born in Eastern Europe, presented with belligerent complaints of suffering. She had had two previous attempts at analysis. She complained of intolerable suffering. She was in agony of spirit, depressed in a tortured way. She had unbearable backache which was unresponsive to medical treatment, agonizing headaches, stabbing pains in her eyes, with an inability to concentrate, inability to see clearly, and difficulty in focusing her eyes for any long period.

I learned in the course of treatment that she had tormented her husband, humiliated and derided him, left him for long periods, having affairs with his knowledge; she neglected her child, and was cruel and spiteful to her acquaintances. She believed, however, that she was the victim of cruel fate, and she felt cruelly treated by almost everyone.

Her previous analysis, which lasted one year, was spent screaming at her analyst, reproaching her, and complaining of inhuman treatment.

By the time she came to me for treatment, her husband had divorced her. She spent the first period of analysis screaming at me and complaining.

In the analysis I felt trapped in a cruel siege, unable to interpret meaningfully as she went on and on with her grievances, which she documented with the relish of a collector of antiques.

She accused me of being a cold, merciless Anglo-Saxon, and complained that I forced her to yield to my analytic theory, with complete disregard for her human plight.

The combination of cruel attacks on me and, by projection, the guilt of cruelty that was alleged to be mine, showed her particular need to have someone who could both tolerate being the victim of cruelty and who could bear the guilty responsibility for these attacks.

For example, she dreamed that she parked a lorry at a parking meter. The lorry, however, was too big and took up too many spaces. She was approached by a traffic warden who questioned her. She immediately rammed the lorry into a telephone kiosk and smashed it up.

She associated the traffic warden with the small-mindedness of a petty official, later attributed to me. Apart from many other meanings in her dream, the rage which smashed up all forms of communication (the telephone) was her reaction to what she perceived as my small-minded, omnipotent officialdom. Her perception of me was as one who could only moralize, only see where she was doing "wrong" (a harsh superego). She felt I could not see her need to park the lorry; to find a resting place or home. She felt I could have no sympathy with her requirements for more space, more time, more sessions, or with her plight.

Therefore, living in such a cruel and narrow-minded reproachful environment, all she could do was to smash up our means of communication: the analysis.

It is of interest to note that she herself had no conscious knowledge of her need to "park" herself and be given a "home" by me. She saw me as behaving like a tin god, but was not aware of her need for me.

She obtained some relief from my interpretation. I was also able to show her some of her own behavior; that she was acutely "switched on" to my faults, showing the acumen of a specialist. She was "switched off" to any goodness and helpfulness which might be in me, to her own dependent needs, and to the fact that she really behaved in this way.

This patient was uprooted from her home by the Nazis at the age of 14, and her parents were taken to a concentration camp where they subsequently perished. This tragedy played a vital part in her development. However, it did not seem to me that the picture of me as a traffic warden corresponded to the brutality of the Nazis, but rather to the officiousness of the projected child part of herself.

I learned in the course of subsequent sessions that she had uprooted—left her husband and child to go abroad for her artistic pursuits, with little regard for their needs, or indeed, her own.

Gradually I was able to study the dossier she had built up about me. I was depicted as complacent and smug, and she seemed determined to put an end to my peace of mind. She maintained that I practiced analysis solely in order to make money and in order to believe I knew everything about life. She tried to make me feel that my whole belief in psychoanalysis was based on a lie motivated by my greedy omniscience. Above all, she wanted to know if I could face this false life I had built up; face the illusion and the guilt and have to give it up with nothing to fall back on. She even begrudged the fact that I could practice as a doctor if I realized psychoanalysis was a delusion; I was to be left with nothing at all.

These attacks on me were her attempt to destroy my goodness and creativity, but above all, I felt at the time that she conveyed to me an ordeal that she felt I would not have the courage to face. I knew what I was supposed to experience, and that she

had to face this in herself; she wanted the experience of someone who could share such a predicament and give her the
strength to face this in her life. Her cruel fate was to realize that
she had built her life on a lie, and that she had nothing left. The
lie was for her quite specific. She was a woman of talent who had
created works of art depicting deep human qualities, but her
personal life was devoid of these qualities. She felt alone, unloved, and persecuted by a reproachful superego.

The capacity to tolerate these projections, and my sharing her
task in facing the way she had built up her life, gave her some
security. She gradually was able to see this as an internal problem which tormented her whenever she had to make a decision.
For example, when she had to buy kitchen units, she felt that if
she bought a large unit she would be tortured with the thought
that she had spent too much money. On the other hand, if she
bought a small unit, she was tortured with the thought of being
mean and stupid and thereby spoiling the whole character of
the kitchen. Both thoughts were cruel and relentless, and she
felt exhausted.

In actual fact, whatever decision she made would not be all
that bad in reality. However, each "voice" in the argument had
this cruel quality. If she spent extra money she was reproached
for producing a state of utter bankruptcy, and she would regret
it for the rest of her life; she would be excommunicated and
forced to live in guilt. Equally, if she was careful with money her
whole mean character would be exposed and disgraced so that
she would again be derided and reproached for spoiling the
whole house.

The quality in all this cruelty, her behavior to me, her picture
of my behavior to her, and the elements in the internal conflict,
all had the same unbearable consequence—that she would be
excommunicated, left alone, unlovable, with the reproach that
she had ruined everything irreparably, and there would be no
chance of forgiveness or opportunity for reparation. To my mind

it was characterized by another quality; there was no "rest of her life" available to carry on with. The whole of life was narrowed to these elements, and there was nothing else. Every issue was one of life and death. It followed closely the pattern of fanatic puritanism, in which any one sin leads to eternal damnation.

Gradually some elements of a good understanding analyst began to develop, relieving the cruelty. But I wish to show what happened to this understanding.

During a session she experienced feeling understood, and she felt that I empathized with her predicament; she obtained great relief from her physical pain. By the next session (after a weekend break), her memory of the good session was lost.

She did, however, produce a dream: she was a student at the University hostel in Kiev, where there was a special area provided for her to rest and find shelter, and she was nursed by a couple who understood her as an individual.

She associated: that it was odd of her to find comfort in the capital of Ukraine, which she considered was the capital of pogroms against the Jews. She felt it perverse and strange to give such qualities to such people, who did not deserve this.

She came to realize: (1) That she had destroyed the good memory of an understanding session; equated with love. (2) That the good humanity was given to omnipotent racists who practiced cruelty, but whose cruelty was denied; instead they were idealized as so comforting.

In this she reenacted her past history, when she had despised her parents, identified herself with fair-haired, blue-eyed Aryans, and likened herself to them, in spite of their arrogant contempt of her Jewish qualities.

So it could be seen that she identified herself with cruel omnipotent gods, perverting the good aspects of her parents and my analysis. She bestowed the attributes of human understanding and love onto the tormentors with whom the omnipotent part of herself identified.

She did come to realize that in her belief that she was the champion of humanity (that was the way she practiced cruelty) she stole the humanity from her parents and me, and she was the perpetrator of cruelty. It was she who practiced the Inquisition in her analysis, in the name of righteousness, with fanatic persistence, and even contrived to suffer in its cause.

Later on, she dreamed of going to a station with a time-bomb in her belly. This she associated with an explosive outburst with her ex-husband when he was boarding a train, accusing him of infidelity. This she "timed" to justify her outrage and squeeze out of her mind that she had left him for three months for an affair. By narrowing her mind to his possible infidelity she occluded her guilt and could produce the explosion for this isolated incident. This coincided with my approaching holidays.

The same night, she dreamed of an Amazon woman, who was evil but did not know what she had done. This woman's head was cruelly smashed again and again, and the onlookers thought this was just. Among the onlookers was the figure of Justice, but instead of being blindfolded, this figure of Justice had daggers in her eyes.

She associated that she had wanted to paint a picture of Amazon life. If she created a picture of other people's cruelty she could justifiably attack it in a relentless way. But in order to do this, the vision of Justice was not made impartial by blindfolding; instead the eyes were filled with daggers. Here she could both "look daggers" and have her perceptions attacked by daggers. (One is reminded of the fate of Oedipus.)

The daggers in the eyes of the figure of Justice she associated to the stabbing pain in her eyes, and her inability to concentrate and have any breadth of vision. The analysis of this relieved the pains in her eyes but confronted her with guilt, and she could now see the injustice of her attacks that had been so righteously upheld.

The analysis of the guilt is of course essential; the experiencing of it is made difficult by the narrow-minded, unforgiving torture of the superego.

She could defend herself against this by a desire to devote her life to what she believed to be an all-righteous cause, by fighting for Israel.

The rationalization of self-centered omnipotent narrowmindedness, and the defense against guilt, was perpetuated in the name of survival. Consequently all issues were felt as struggles of life and death, and so became unbearable. She thus so narrowed her perception that she was constantly in the position of the baby whose only horizon was the nipple, and it was right and natural to focus her life on satisfying her needs, and to demand that I too focus my mind on the satisfaction of her needs.

The great tragedy of her life was that at the age of 14 she had had to leave her country with her brother and sister to escape extermination by the Nazis and so survive. Her parents stayed behind and were murdered. So her survival was felt to be at the expense of her parents' lives, and she felt she should have shared their fate. The guilt over this never left her, and she felt reparation was impossible. It was not only the burden of guilt that prevented the enjoyment of life, but she began to see there was a "kill-joy" part of herself in operation. (In fact, this was the cause of a good deal of guilt.)

She realized there was a part of herself that behaved in a particularly cruel way. If I did not satisfy her completely and make her feel special and unique, she killed my analysis and my work in a vicious annihilation. When I pointed this out to her she claimed that I condemned her to feeling guilty and tortured as unlovable for the rest of her life.

The fact that I tolerated this, contained it, continued to try to understand and help her, brought her no joy. She could not see that she was killing joy and comfort; only the pain she suffered. She screamed and shouted at the pain that she felt I inflicted on her.

When she saw that it was the good parents in me she destroyed in her self-absorption, she obtained dramatic relief and eventually could appreciate me and feel sorry. She could then experience guilt, together with a more understanding superego, and have more strength and hope to deal with *it*.

This was in contrast to her actual past, where I have reason to believe that her mother submitted to her attacks, with the patient introjecting a hopelessly destroyed and reproachful mother.

DEVELOPMENTS IN THE ANALYSIS

In an earlier account of this patient, I described how she was locked in the narrow confines of cruelty and cut off from a "home." Gradually some concept of a home was built in the analysis, which enabled humanity to counteract cruelty. Following the dream about "Kiev" we saw the beginning of her realization of her need for a home for the needy baby part of herself, and her recognition that she stole from her parents and myself and gave our good attributes to the cruel "ideal Aryans" with whom she identified.

We also discovered that she had her own ways of trying to provide herself with a home. She could establish a comforting home if she was in a blurred state of mind, with no distinction between herself and her object. She got a feeling of "belonging" in intense physical sexual union. She also had a feeling of security in her manic paranoid episodes when all the goodness was felt to be inside her. But none of these experiences could nourish her and assist in growth. All these processes destroyed the really helpful separate breast-mother-analyst.

The analysis of these issues enabled her to recognize the paramount importance of her search for a home for the needy parts of herself. She came to value the psychological home I gave her and the home given to her by friends; she began to admire people who provided homes and those who could admit their need for homes.

She described vividly to me how she met a Russian Jew who managed to leave the Soviet Union and was in transit to Israel. This man had sacrificed an important prestigious position in his field of work. He assumed, for her, heroic proportions and she yearned to be united with such a man, who could keep a concept of home alive in him, risk prison in his country, and finally achieve his home in Israel.

She spoke with genuine admiration about the fact that this Russian Jew had given up his worldly success for more human aspirations. After meeting this man, however, she had a dream in which she was fishing in the River Thames. She caught something at the end of her line but she could not pull in her catch, however hard she tried. Eventually she followed the line and it was attached to a metal box which was embedded in rock. The box had written on it "Bank X" and inside "Café Y." (I use "X" and "Y" to disguise identity.) Bank "X" was associated with her ex-husband's bank and the time when money seemed inexhaustible. Café "Y" was associated with a café where she used to meet her artistic friends who would "run the world" in a superior fashion from their coffee tables. The Thames was associated with the publishers of books on art, which she hoped would publish her art.

She soon realized that in spite of the preface to the dream of the sacrifice of worldly success for a "human home," her yearning for money and success were firmly embedded and rocklike. This dream does contain an element of her search for "omnipotent gods" (Café "Y"), but it did not seem to me sinister and cruel in nature. The overall picture is her search for money and success, which had some realistic basis. She was not nursed in a "cruel perverse home" as she was in the dream about Kiev. She was fishing for money and success and there was a struggle between the different parts of herself. She struggled with her ambivalence, instead of reverting to a perverse solution to obviate this.

But what I consider the most striking development was the way she reacted to the realization of what she was doing in the dream. She did not have to "pluck out her eyes," narrow her perception, justify herself, or feel mercilessly reproached. She could look at this part of herself, give it a home, and realize it was her task to struggle with these elements. I believe this was the result of my having a "home" for these parts of her as well as the needy parts, and the subsequent introjection of my "psychological home." This enabled the analysis to proceed in a way in which insight could be used constructively rather than being regarded as the cruel reproach of a moralizing superego.

On her own reflection, she recognized the power of these forces and thought about the way she behaved with her son, being rejecting if he were not highly successful. She felt genuine guilt and seemed determined to give him a proper home whatever he achieved or did not achieve.

A most significant part of her development was the giving of a home to the memory of her mother. She had described her mother, perhaps not inaccurately, as always anxious, always complaining about father and nagging her if she, the patient, was not "just so," and not at all interested in the patient's work or enjoyment. She stood somewhere between a broken-down mother and a demanding figure. Now she could see her mother as depressed and unhappy but always striving; a woman who gained satisfaction from making a good physical home for the family, who always fed and clothed her well and did what she could in "her way." It was a sad picture in many ways, but there was one feature that left its mark—this was her mother's struggling and carrying on in spite of adversity and depression. It was this quality of her mother that the patient felt sustained her (the patient) in her journey across Europe and Turkey when she left her native land at the age of 14.

It was through the realization of what I endured in giving her a "psychological home" that she gave a home to the memory of her real mother, drew strength from this, and felt free to avail herself of new loving experiences without feeling she abandoned her mother. She could now begin to live in a more generous world which reduced her hatred and helped her to deal with her aggression, and mitigated the vicious circle of her previous cruel and narrow world.

Second Clinical Example

In the first example, I described how the patient narrowed her perception to the picture of a nipple as the means of survival. In the second clinical example the penis took the place of the nipple and was the focal point in the patient's world.

This patient was a homosexual male aged 30. It first seemed that his narrow-mindedness was localized in sensuous satisfaction, but it soon became apparent that the penis stood for very much more. His whole life revolved around worshipping penises. He had sexual adventures in public toilets many times a day, mainly of fellatio or being the passive partner in anal intercourse. He would go into eulogies about these penises—they were straight, upright, noble, and so on. The fact that these penises belonged to men who sometimes robbed him of money or assaulted him did not lead to any modification of his views. Any strength he obtained from me was denied and attributed to these penises.

For example, he would be relieved of some misery in a session, proceed to lose all the understanding I gave him, and turn to these "magnificent" penises for relief, only to be plunged into depression once again. This pattern was repeated again and again. In essence the buggery was always cruel and was used to triumph over the good internal object, linked in the analysis with my understanding.

In the countertransference he produced a feeling of helplessness in me and a feeling that there was nothing I could do against the powerful omnipotence of the religion of phallic worship. He tried to force me to believe in his system and to get me to admit my impotent envy of his exciting exploits.

When this picture of a phallic world began to break down, and he experienced depression, he would eulogize depressive writers and try to make me believe that only those who saw the futility of human life were the true giants of the human mind; and the others, like me, were pathetic cowards. Again, there were persistent, narrow, cruel attacks against life itself. What became clear was the omnipotent cruelty, which made creativity and joy as nothing by comparison with his depression.

When he moved to heterosexuality he mercilessly focused his mind on all the defects of his girl friend and tormented her for her deficiencies with an arrogant belief in his godlike superiority. He was identified with the ideal object and felt entitled to torment the actual woman for her failings.

After laborious analysis he began to come closer to the realization of his cruelty and to approach some feelings of guilt.

His ace card in acting out was to come one day to the session in a distraught state, earlier than his appointment, and go into the waiting room. Soon after arriving, he left my house knowing I could hear him leave, and paraded outside my house, knowing I could see him from my window. He knew I would not call him in, so when he did come to the door, missing about five minutes of his session, he was now armed with righteous reproach. Here was he, the patient, distraught with suffering and I, the analyst, extremely cruel, worshipping my analytic technique and putting it above humanity and suffering. I would never deviate to help him, so he could now establish that the cruelty was mine.

Throughout the whole pattern of this cruelty, the narcissistic preoccupation that he was right, he knew the real truth, he loved the really worthy objects, was persistently maintained. Ultimately he alone walked with "humanity" and I had none.

I have little doubt about his basic envy of humanity and creativity, but the point I wish to emphasize is the way he narrowed
his perception to "his world" and kept out any fuller understanding. His analysis was not like this all the time, of course,
but it is the strength of this feature and its power that I wish to
emphasize. This pattern was resurrected at every crisis.

Whatever the perversion and narrow preoccupation may be,
I think that it is ultimately goodness, humanity, and truth that
are so sorely coveted. It also shows in this case the painfulness
of guilt in realizing what he had done; he had to frame me for
this sin, and was prepared to suffer to vindicate himself.

THEORETICAL CONSIDERATIONS

Freud (1917), in "Mourning and Melancholia" described how
the melancholic would both torture his object and cling to it,
refusing to establish a new object relationship. Abraham (1924)
made the observation that in the cruelty of melancholia these
patients treated the object as if they owned it. Both Freud and
Abraham emphasized the regression to narcissism, with no differentiation between self and object.

As I understand Melanie Klein's concept of the depressive
position (1934), a development takes place in which the infant
begins to realize the separateness of himself and the object. As
I see it, he is therefore confronted with inferiority and envy of
the mother, a realization of the human nonideal mother, whom
he does not own; and therefore has to confront frustration, guilt,
and the anxiety of losing this mother.

In order to remain in the narcissistic position, attacks are
made on this awareness, which include attacks on the internal
object. These attacks destroy the awareness of the human mother
and the patient is therefore left in a cruel, loveless world.

To put this another way: perception develops from the nipple
to the breast, to the body, face, and ultimately the mother's
mind and love, producing a picture of "Mommy." This can be

introjected and be given a "home" inside the infant's mind and feed the infant's capacity to love. It is the obliteration of the concept of the whole human mother that narrows the picture of the world to a cruel loveless place.

Furthermore, the attacks on the real mother for not being the "ideal breast" (which satisfies through narcissistic identification the demand to have the ideal, and be the ideal) leads to the incorporation of a superego which demands that the infant has to satisfy it for the rest of his life. Therefore he lives in a cruel, exacting, narrow world, which feeds his fear and hatred, and he is forced to worship this system, subordinate himself and identify with it, partly out of fear, and partly because it contains his own vengeful omnipotence. This superego ego ideal dominates his life. That which Freud and Abraham described as the patient clinging to his object and treating his object as if he owns it, now becomes, through introjection, a patient possessed by a cruel superego which will not let him be free.

He is therefore confined to his narrow loveless narcissistic demands, governed by narrow loveless narcissistic gods. Added to this, the infant casts out and abandons the real human mother to cruel exile, and introjects a mother that does the same to him, and therefore gives him no home. In addition, the narcissistic part of the personality exiles the needy real baby part of himself. A home is therefore only given to gods and the godlike narcissistic part of the self, leading to a "false self" and living a lie.

This problem is complicated still further as the infant may have been denied a good home in the first place. He may have had a mother who rejected the baby part of him, could not stand his anxieties, and failed in this sense to provide a home for this baby. His anxious needy self may have been psychologically cast out and abandoned in cruel exile. He may have had a mother who could only tolerate an "ideal baby" and rejected the real baby, or he may have had a mother who overindulged him and satisfied his omnipotent cravings. In either case, he lusts for vengeance and the recreation of the "ideal world."

By the time the patient arrives for analysis we are therefore faced with a complex problem. But it seems to me the clinical task is to enable the patient to make use of a fuller, understanding, loving world which is the only experience that can rescue him.

I have attempted to show in this paper how such patients try to confine the analyst's understanding to the justification of their grievances under the guise of moral justice, and squeeze out or prevent any fuller love from modifying this situation. In doing so, they cast themselves into exile, devoid of love, at the mercy of the primitive superego.

The sum total of this narcissistic organization ensures that the patient does not find a good home in which to grow up, enjoy life and have the experience of human sharing.

With a "good home," problems of cruelty are humanized by interaction with parents. I cannot help speculating whether Oedipus would have behaved as he did had he been brought up at home. His tragedy was that he started life in exile and finished in exile.

The converse of the cruel vicious circle is mutual shared concern; the mother giving a home for the baby inside her mind, and the baby giving a home for the real mother inside his mind.

Conclusion

The normal process that leads to seeing the mother as a separate person who feels pain, joy, and gives creatively, is, in cases of cruelty, viciously squeezed out of perception, leading to a narrow mind.

The narrowing of perception restricts the imagery of the whole object to the role of a nipple that the patient owns, and so restricts conscious love and conscious guilt.

Demands are put on this object to be ideal and consider the patient ideal, or be vengefully punished.

Goodness is hijacked and perverted to the side of cruelty to give it strength and avoid catastrophe. This perversion is worshipped as a religion and the analyst is required to convert to this worship, and "God help you if you don't." The introjection of this leads to a cruel superego and establishes a hopeless vicious circle of cruelty and slavish devotion to a cruel perverse moralizing god. The real mother is cast out and abandoned and the real needy "Baby part" is likewise cast into exile.

Unfavorable early and analytic environment may support the omnipotent delusion; enact countercruelty; provide its own omnipotent cruelty as a model for identification; collapse or die. All may have disastrous consequences.

The role of the analyst is to widen the patient's perception against militant attacks designed to keep both his and the patient's minds narrowed, and to supply the right environment by his careful analysis. The fuller understanding of the analyst must be matched against the narrow-mindedness, as this fuller understanding is the means of modifying cruelty and allowing goodness, strength to deal with hatred, and forgiveness to intervene.

By this means a "home" is given to new good experiences; this enables the good aspects of the original "home" to be rehoused inside the patient's mind. An exiled mother comes home, becomes an ally in the work of goodness and the task of mitigating cruelty is strengthened and shared.

SUMMARY

The contention of this paper is that human understanding modifies cruelty, and that in order for cruelty to remain unmodified various mechanisms are employed. The most important processes include the worship of omnipotence, which is felt to be superior to human love and forgiveness, the clinging to omnipotence as a defense against depression, and the sanctification of grievance and revenge. In order to avoid conscious guilt, the perceptions of the mind are narrowed to give ostensible justification to the cruelty, and the obviation of redeeming features in the object.

The paper explores how these processes operate and how by virtue of projection the analyst's interpretations are perceived as cruel, and how the patient arranges to be locked in this vicious circle.

Technical problems of dealing with these forces are explored together with the task of bringing alive the human concern that modifies cruelty.

REFERENCES

Abraham, K. (1924), A short study of the development of the libido, viewed in the light of mental disorders. In: *Selected Papers on Psychoanalysis*. London: Hogarth Press, 1942, pp. 418–501.

Freud, S. (1917), Mourning and melancholia. *Standard Edition*, 14. London: Hogarth Press, 1957.

Klein, M. (1934), A contribution to the psychogenesis of manic-depressive states. In: *Contributions to Psychoanalysis*. London: Hogarth Press, 1948, pp. 282–310.

EDITOR'S INTRODUCTION TO
THE INTERPLAY BETWEEN PATHOLOGICAL
ORGANIZATIONS AND THE PARANOID–SCHIZOID
AND DEPRESSIVE POSITIONS

The clinical examples that fill this book frequently feature one or another version of patients struggling with painful flux in their own psychic positions between the paranoid-schizoid and the depressive. It is not so much that the authors have selected only certain kinds of patients to present, as is often thought to be the case, as it is that this common feature represents an essential aspect of Kleinian understanding of psychic suffering and the analytic process. In this essay, John Steiner takes up another aspect of the struggle with flux, the construction of "pathological organizations." He provides a much fuller treatment of this important variable in his recent monograph, *Psychic Retreats* (1993).

The concept of pathological organization is a significant refinement in contemporary Kleinian thinking. It is one that has already been addressed by some notable Kleinian writers in the past, among them Riviere (1936), Rosenfeld (1971), Segal (1972), and Edna O'Shaughnessy (1981). In these writings a special organization of unconscious phantasies and defenses has been interpolated between the paranoid–schizoid and depressive positions. In Steiner's terms, this special organization serves as a psychic retreat for patients, a retreat they use to defend themselves against the intolerable anxieties of the paranoid–schizoid position and the unbearable guilt, anguish, and other burdens of the depressive position. Steiner offers here some further articulation of both of these positions.

A well set-up pathological organization blocks movement from it in either direction. Clinically, it then presents itself as a kind of pseudointegration and even functional efficiency with a decidedly narcissistic coloring. The clinical manifestations of this suspension of flux can vary considerably, but what they have in common is their presenting major obstacles to any genuinely available relatedness to others and to the development of both a deep sense of reality and a capacity for insight and change. The fear of disintegration is always active, even though it varies in degree.

One highlight of the present chapter, as of Steiner's chapter 16, below, is his careful consideration of technical measures that offer some hope of being effective in these difficult cases. In his interesting clinical example, as well as frankly acknowledging the negative countertransferences and false steps that so often are induced by patients of this sort, he clarifies the significant contributions to treatment that may be derived from these disruptions of the analyst's understanding and functioning.

Pathological organization appears to have become a well-established part of Kleinian discourse. Looked at most broadly, the problems to which it pertains are familiar to analysts of all persuasions; often they are described under the heading of character disorder or character resistance. As one might expect, that problem has been conceptualized and discussed technically in a great number of ways, some eclectic and some in keeping with one school of thought only. Also, some technical approaches are more consistently analytic than others in that they continue to rely essentially on interpretation rather than turning to subtle or obvious forms of manipulation or even collusion. In this example, Steiner's work is consistently analytic along Kleinian lines. It shows how a contemporary Kleinian approach can be applied beneficially to these patients' common struggles against change for the better: their manic "triumphs" over problems, their envious and sadistic negative therapeutic reactions.

8
THE INTERPLAY BETWEEN
PATHOLOGICAL ORGANIZATIONS
AND THE PARANOID–SCHIZOID
AND DEPRESSIVE POSITIONS

JOHN STEINER

In this paper I shall discuss some of the ways defenses may be assembled into pathological organizations which have a profound effect on the personality and can lead to states of mind which become fixed so that the patient in analysis shows a characteristic lack of insight and resistance to change. I will emphasize the clinical importance of these organizations and try to show how they exist in an equilibrium with the paranoid–schizoid and depressive positions. I shall only briefly describe the characteristics of these positions since they are now well known, but I will emphasize transitions within them that are easy to overlook and which I believe are points when the patient is particularly vulnerable to the influence of a pathological organization.

Melanie Klein's differentiation of two major groupings of anxieties and defenses, the paranoid–schizoid and depressive,

This paper was read to a Scientific Meeting of the British Psycho-Analytical Society on February 20, 1985.

has proved to be a major conceptual tool which has made it easier to examine the way mental structures are organized at different levels of development (Klein, 1952; Segal, 1964). This is an important technical aid since it helps us to orient ourselves to clinical material by enabling us to assess the level at which the patient is functioning. We can learn to evaluate whether his anxieties, mental mechanisms, and object relations are primarily depressive or primarily paranoid–schizoid, and this will determine the way we interpret.

A continuous movement between the two positions takes place so that neither dominates with any degree of completeness or permanence. Indeed it is these fluctuations which we try to follow clinically as we observe periods of integration leading to depressive position functioning or disintegration and fragmentation resulting in a paranoid–schizoid state. Such fluctuations can take place over months and years as an analysis develops but can also be seen in the fine grain of a session, as moment-to-moment changes. If the patient makes meaningful progress, a gradual shift toward depressive position function is observed, while if he or she deteriorates we see a reversion to paranoid–schizoid functioning such as occurs in negative therapeutic reactions. These observations led Bion (1963) to suggest that the two positions were in an equilibrium with each other and hence joined schematically with a bi-directional arrow, that is, $P/S \leftrightarrow D$. This way of putting it emphasizes the dynamic quality and focuses attention on the factors which lead to a shift in one direction or another.

As a brief summary, in the paranoid–schizoid position anxieties of a primitive nature threaten the immature ego and lead to the mobilization of primitive defenses. Splitting, idealization, and projective identification operate to create rudimentary structures made up of idealized good objects kept far apart from persecuting bad ones. The individual's own impulses are similarly split and he directs all his love toward the good object and all his hatred against the bad one. As a consequence of the projection, the leading anxiety is paranoid, and the preoccupation is with survival of the self. Thinking is concrete because of the confusion between self and object which is one of the consequences of projective identification (Segal, 1957).

The depressive position represents an important developmental advance in which whole objects begin to be recognized and ambivalent impulses become directed towards the primary object. These changes result from an increased capacity to integrate experiences and lead to a shift in primary concern from the survival of the self to a concern for the object upon which the individual depends. Destructive impulses lead to feelings of loss and guilt which can be more fully experienced and which consequently enable mourning to take place. The consequences include a development of symbolic function and the emergence of reparative capacities which become possible when thinking no longer has to remain concrete.

The distinction between the two positions has an impressive clarity but does sometimes make us forget that, within the positions, mental states with very different qualities exist. In the paranoid–schizoid position the type of splitting described above can be considered as normal and distinguished from states of fragmentation which result from disintegrative splitting. Projective identification of a violent kind may then lead to both the object and the projected part of the ego being splintered into minute fragments creating persecutory states, often with depersonalization and extreme anxiety. Such states may result when hostility predominates and especially if envy stimulates attacks on good objects. When this happens the normal split between good and bad is likely to break down, leading to a confusional state (Rosenfeld, 1950; Klein, 1957) and these states seem to be particularly difficult to bear and may lead to disintegrative splitting. As I will try to show later, the breakdown of normal splitting may make the patient vulnerable to the influence of a pathological organization which offers a kind of pseudostructure to help deal with the confused and chaotic state of mind (Meltzer, 1968).

Another important differentiation exists within the depressive position where it is easy to forget that splitting also plays an important role. Klein (1935) emphasizes how splitting is resorted to again when the good object has been internalized as a whole object and ambivalent impulses toward it lead to depressive states in which the object is felt to be damaged, dying, or dead and "casts its shadow on the ego." Attempts to possess and preserve the good object are part of the depressive position and lead to a renewal of splitting, this time to prevent the loss of the good object and to protect it from attacks. The aim in this phase of the depressive position is to deny the reality of the loss of the object by concretely internalizing it, possessing it, and identifying with it. This is the situation of the bereaved person in the early stages of mourning and appears to be a normal stage which needs to be passed through before the subsequent experience of acknowledgment of the loss can take place.

A critical point in the depressive position arises when the task of relinquishing control over the object has to be faced. The earlier trend, which aims at possessing the object and denying reality, has to be reversed if the depressive position is to be worked through, and the object is to be allowed its independence. In unconscious fantasy this means that the individual has to face his inability to protect the object. His psychic reality includes the realization of the internal disaster created by his sadism and the awareness that his love and reparative wishes are insufficient to preserve his object, which must be allowed to die with the consequent desolation, despair, and guilt. These processes involve intense conflict which we associate with the work of mourning and which seem to result in anxiety and mental pain. A central theme in my paper will be that this is another critical point for the patient, and if these experiences cannot be faced a pathological organization may again be called into play to deal with the conflict.

It is therefore at the transitions which take place within both the paranoid–schizoid and the depressive positions that the individual seems to be most vulnerable to the influence of a pathological organization.

THE CHARACTERISTICS OF PATHOLOGICAL ORGANIZATIONS

These organizations have been described by a number of different authors who stress different aspects. Riviere (1936), Segal (1972), Riesenberg-Malcolm (1981), and O'Shaughnessey (1981) give clinical descriptions which illustrate the defensive nature and the variety of forms of expression, while Rosenfeld (1964, 1971), Meltzer (1968), and Sohn (1985) emphasize the narcissistic nature of the object relations, the organization into a gang or mafia and the perverse nature of the relationships involved.

The nature of the defenses which become organized into a pathological organization varies in different patients and may, for example, be predominantly obsessional, manic, perverse, or even psychotic. The variety of form does, however, conceal common elements which reflect the underlying organization of the defenses. This organization is basically narcissistic in all these conditions and reflects the preponderance of projective identification which creates objects which are controlled by parts of the self projected into them. Splitting tends to create multiple objects which are then assembled into a highly organized structure. Within this common structure the clinical manifestations vary considerably. For example, the organization may be held together by obsessional mechanisms where control is paramount, erotization may play a role, giving a hysterical flavor, or manic mechanisms may result from an identification with a powerful figure, sometimes the leader of the gang, which results in triumph and excitement.

In psychotic states the personality may be taken over by a psychotic structure which imposes a delusional order. What these different conditions have in common is a stability and resistance to change which derives from the common underlying structure. The main features of this are first that objects are controlled and identified with by projective identification, and second that the object is split and projected into a group and that this group is assembled into an organized structure by complex and often perverse means. It is particularly when defenses become organized into such complex systems that they seem to give rise to lasting pathological states, which are extremely damaging to development and which can be very resistant to change.

THE INTERPLAY WITH THE PARANOID–SCHIZOID
AND DEPRESSIVE POSITIONS

To take account of these states and to facilitate their recognition, I have found it conceptually helpful to consider these pathological organizations to have characteristics distinct from both the paranoid–schizoid and the depressive positions and to exist in an equilibrium with them. We can construct a triangular equilibrium diagram as follows:

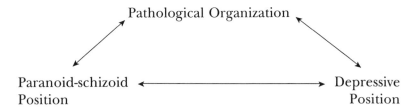

Pathological Organization

Paranoid-schizoid   Depressive
Position   Position

which I believe can help us to orient ourselves more precisely to the patient's material. We can then attempt to assess whether the patient is functioning at a paranoid–schizoid, or a depressive level or whether we are in the presence of a pathological organization; we can also try to follow the shifts between the pathological organization and the other two positions. When we do this it becomes clear that the pathological organization functions as a defense, not only against fragmentation and confusion, but also against the mental pain and anxiety of the depressive position. It acts as a borderline area between the other two positions, where the patient believes he can retreat if either paranoid or depressive anxieties become unbearable. It is common to observe that a patient will make contact with depressive position experiences and then retreat again to the paranoid–schizoid position as if he could not tolerate the mental pain he encountered (Steiner, 1979; Joseph, 1981). He then meets the disintegration, fragmentation, confusion, and persecutory anxiety of the paranoid–schizoid position, and if these too become unbearable the patient has nowhere where he feels safe unless he can find or construct a defense against both positions.

To do this, omnipotent fantasies and primitive mental mechanisms are brought into play, and these have usually been considered as paranoid–schizoid position activities. What I am suggesting is that when these take the form of a complex organization of defenses they have special properties which make it helpful to consider them separately as a pathological organization. They provide a kind of pseudointegration under the dominance of narcissistic structures which can masquerade as the true integration of the depressive position, and which can provide, or give the illusion of providing, a degree of structure and stability for the patient and a relative freedom from anxiety and pain.

The balance between the pathological organization and the other two positions will vary in different patients and in the same patient at different times. All patients, however, seem at times to come under the sway of a pathological organization especially in periods when the analysis is stuck and the patient seems to retreat from contact. This is true even in patients who can function at a relatively mature level in other settings. In other patients the pathological organization seems to dominate a whole analysis and produces formidable obstacles to progress. Even in these patients, however, it is often possible to trace movements between the organization and the other two positions. This may enable the analyst to identify those minute shifts toward the depressive position which can be so important clinically.

CLINICAL MATERIAL

I will try to examine the value of this approach by considering some material from a patient who was often difficult to understand, and who presented problems of technique which seemed to be linked to the difficulty I had of orienting myself to her material by assessing the level correctly.

She was an attractive, recently married woman in her twenties who had dropped out of university, and who tended to develop withdrawn states when she would take to her bed and do nothing except read novels endlessly. When still a baby, her family had escaped from a country where they experienced political persecution. They were occasionally able to return to visit her grandmother, and these visits and the border crossings they entailed were especially anxious times for her.

She sought treatment because of attacks of incapacitating anxiety, at first associated with major decisions such as whether she should stay in England, or whether she should let her future husband move into her flat when, at that time, he didn't intend to marry her. They would also occur when she got involved in long discussions on existential themes which resulted in panic when she realized that she saw no meaning in life. She would find herself trembling, would feel her surroundings recede and become distant, and found that she could not make contact with people because a diffuse barrier came between them. When her husband agreed to marry her the anxiety lessened but would reappear periodically; for example, once when she lost a locket containing a piece of his hair. In addition, she suffered from a specific fear of being poisoned from tinned food which she would become convinced had been contaminated. Even between anxiety attacks she was preoccupied with pollution and poisoning and had terrifying dreams in which, for example, radioactivity produced a kind of living death and people became automata. A fascination with deadness and aridity was linked to a preoccupation with the Sahara Desert which she had visited and to which she planned to return with an expedition when her treatment was over.

A central feature of the analysis was the fact that she was a silent patient, in fact often silent for the greater part of the session for months on end. She would begin with a long silence or a comment such as, "Nothing has happened," or "It is going to be another silent session." Occasionally she would give an explanation and, for example, say, "I sort things out into what I could say and what I couldn't say, and the things I could say are not worth saying." Very often there was a mocking, teasing quality, usually accompanied by a sulky little girl voice. "I felt totally misunderstood yesterday and I am not going to say anything today, so there!" Or she might admit that she said to herself, "Don't show anything to him unless you have thought it all out so he cannot find fault with it," or "Don't say anything to him unless you are sure you can win the argument." The silence might turn into a game in which she would alternate between starting a session herself or making me start, or she might gamble on how long she would have to wait before I spoke. During the silence she often thought of herself as sunbathing on a desert island, and she acknowledged that she enjoyed these games and their accompanying fantasies. The most prominent mood was of a smiling indifference, a kind of nonchalance and a playful lack of concern in which the difficulties of the analysis and indeed the realities of life going on around her were *my* problem.

This sometimes made me feel exploited and put upon as if I had colluded with the notion that I should care more about her analysis than she did. At other times I seemed to be provoked to interpret her lack of concern in a critical way, as if I was trying to persuade her to become more caring because I was unwilling to take on the responsibility.

At the same time there was a deadly seriousness about her analysis, and she was rarely late and almost never missed a session. On one occasion, when I had let a silence go on for longer than usual, she began to weep silently and when I asked her what she was thinking I was told a tragic story about a girl who had taken an overdose and was left to die because nobody came until it was too late.

As she lay on the couch, the patient would move her hands restlessly and incessantly. She would pick at her fingernails in a jerky and irritating way, or pull threads out of a bandage or out of her clothing or play with her sleeve or her buttons. For a time she found it hard to resist picking at the wallpaper next to the couch, where there was a small raised piece at an edge which she longed to pull off. Most often she played with her long hair, pulling down a bunch as if milking it, teasing out individual hairs, making patterns with them, twisting them, and then milking them free again. I was reminded of Freud's statement in the Dora case that, "no mortal can keep a secret. If his lips are silent, he chatters with his finger tips . . ." (1905, p. 78), but for the most part I could not understand the factors behind her silence or the meaning of the hand movements.

She would say that she had a large number of thoughts which she could not string together, and this suggested a fragmentation such as that seen in the paranoid–schizoid position. However, it was clear that something more active, teasing, and pleasurable was going on, which resulted in long periods of deadness and aridity in which no development was discernible. This state seemed to protect her from anxiety, both paranoid–schizoid anxiety represented by her panic attacks and depressive anxiety if she inadvertently allowed herself to acknowledge a capacity to care about herself and the treatment. The evident gratification which her games provided suggested a perverse element.

She began a session some two years into the analysis, by hunting in her bag for her check which she eventually gave me, and which I noticed had been incompletely filled in. She then spoke after only a short silence to tell me a dream.

> *In it she had invited a young couple for a meal and then realized that she had run out of something, probably wine or food. Her husband and the friends went out to get the provisions while she waited at home. When they returned they brought the girl back on a stretcher and explained that she had been cut through at the waist and had no lower half. The girl did not seem upset but smiled and later went off on crutches. The patient asked her husband to take her to show her where it had happened. He did this and explained how a car had hit her from behind and cut her in two.*

It was a relief to have a dream instead of the silence, and I interpreted that the dream itself might represent provisions for the analysis, as if she realized that we had run out of material to work with. The girl in the dream had been violently attacked when she went out for the provisions, and I suggested that she might be afraid that something similar would happen to her if she brought material for analysis. Perhaps, I added, she was less afraid of being attacked now and could express a wish to understand these fears, represented in the dream by the request to find out how the accident had happened.

She was attentive and nodded as if she understood what I meant, and this led me to go a little later and try to link the dream with her experience at the beginning of the session when she was hunting for her check. I suggested that she might be divided in her feelings about paying me, having brought the check and then losing it in her handbag, and also by filling it in incompletely.

There was a sharp change of mood and the patient became flippant saying that if that was the case she could put it right immediately because she had a pen with her, and she didn't want me to have anything I could use in evidence against her. It felt as if the contact with her had been abruptly cut off. She now seemed to feel that I had caught her out and was making a fuss, using her mistake with the check to put pressure on her to admit her ambivalence and to talk about her feelings. A mistake which she hadn't noticed left her feeling dangerously out of control and she had to attack the mood of cooperation and correct the mistake as quickly as possible. The mood in the earlier part of the session had, however, given a feeling of contact, and I think it did represent a move toward the depressive position in which she could show some concern for herself and her objects. This, however, stimulated a violent attack when it seems I went too far or too fast, to link it up with something actual which had happened in the session.

In retrospect I think I got the level of this interpretation wrong and that I did not realize that she was unable to sustain the integration which would enable her to hold on to me as an analyst she could work with, and at the same time admit negative feelings toward me. Instead she reverted to a state of mind in which she was cut off from her feelings just as the girl had been in the dream. The fact that the girl smiled and did not mind being cut in two seemed precisely to reflect the patient's smiling, flippant lack of concern. There was also an innuendo that I was more concerned with my check than with her needs, so that she acted as if she had to satisfy me. Coming from behind, the attack seemed to come from me and to be directed against the relationship with me and against any part of her which had a desire to cooperate with the analytic work by bringing material and to acknowledge her ambivalence and understand it. Subsequently all the desire to understand resided in the analyst and she directed her endeavors to keeping me at bay. I think we can see how I became part of the pathological organization and played an essential role in maintaining it by acting out these attacks for her. In fact I may even have been set up to attack her over the check, and I suspect that I could not avoid being party to a shift in mood which she then dealt with by retreating out of contact.

I think envy played a part in provoking these attacks, and perhaps it was to avoid them that she seldom acknowledged any improvement in our working relationship or indeed in her life in general. It was only in passing that I heard, over the next few months, that she had applied to an art school for which she was preparing a portfolio, and that she was taking driving lessons. She did, however, mention that her husband was installing central heating, and that although she was reluctant to leave her art work, she had somewhat grudgingly agreed to help him. She had become quite involved and interested in this work and had admitted that when she did bring herself to help she found it satisfying. This seemed to correspond to a warmer atmosphere which had begun to develop in her sessions, although she remained somewhat grudging, sulky, and sensitive.

She then failed to turn up for three sessions, and because this was so unusual I telephoned her to inquire what had happened. She explained that while working on the central heating she had dropped a radiator on her toe and that she had tried to ring me at her session time, but I had failed to answer—my telephone bell had inadvertently been turned off. On her return she could admit that not only her toe but her feelings had been hurt by my failure to be available, and she had once more taken to her bed and her novels. She then described a dream in which a girl had died of a mysterious illness and she had been summoned by the girl's parents to talk to them. She did not know what to say, and was told that it did not matter, as if they saw that she was upset and were being careful not to make her cry. She then added, "You can say, 'How nice' when something good happens but . . ." and she trailed off. In the dream the room to which she had been summoned contained bookshelves and a coal stove which she was able to link to bookshelves in a children's home where she had been left as an infant. She idealized her memories of this home; in particular the beautiful dolls there, but in fact said that she had been left there while the family went on holiday with her younger brother and on their return she refused to recognize her mother and became so ill that she was unable to leave the home for a further two weeks.

A further association then emerged to a waiting room on the frontier when the family had been stopped after a visit to her grandmother. Her mother had on this occasion been taken off the train by border guards to have some irregularity in her passport checked, and the family waited for her in a room with bookshelves and a coal stove.

I was able to interpret that elements in the dream reflected her feeling that when I did not answer the telephone, a tragic event like a death from a mysterious illness had occurred, and that when I had telephoned her, it felt as if I had summoned her back to the analysis to ask her to explain her reaction. I think the analytic work represented by the installing of central heating had put her more in touch with her feelings, and the associations to the dream seemed to confirm that horrific memories were revived of times when she feared she might lose her mother.

We can conceptualize the movement in this fragment of the analysis to reflect a shift from a pathological organization toward the depressive position where contact of a meaningful kind took place and analytic work was possible. The patient, however, also shows how narcissistic defenses are redeployed to pull her back into a pathological organization when depressive feelings become intolerable.

The pathological organization seems to offer the patient an idealized haven from the terrifying situations around her. The perverse flavor was connected with the apparent lack of concern on the part of the patient, and the evident pleasure and power she derived from the self-sufficiency of the borderline state. The analyst by contrast feels extremely uncomfortable, being asked to carry the concern and yet knowing from his experience with the patient that whatever he does will be unsatisfactory. If I had not telephoned the patient I had the impression she would not have been able to make the move toward me and we might have had a very long absence or even a breakdown in the analysis. On the other hand, I was also left feeling that telephoning her was a serious error in technique and I had an uneasy sense of doing something improper as if I had been seduced or was seducing *her* to make her feel she was coming back to the analysis for my benefit and at my summons. It is interesting to observe that it is sometimes the analyst's shortcomings which are exploited to justify a return to the pathological organization. Here the patient could argue that my failure to answer her telephone call meant that I had let her down, and this justified a retreat to her bed and her novels, which could again be idealized as safe and warm. This makes the analyst feel that any lapse on his part can become a stimulus for a perverse orgy.

Precisely the same kind of issue seemed to be a factor in her silence which also seemed to be a retreat to an idealized state which she could call her desert island where she could sunbathe. I thought she had some insight into the way she created these states of mind, and that the safety she found there was illusionary while the deadness and aridity she created was real and extremely disabling. She therefore had a true desire to make progress in the analysis and to find creative capacities within her, which could lead to development professionally and to the satisfaction of a long-hidden wish to have a family.

Such developments, however, depended on her capacity to withstand destructive attacks which were regularly mounted whenever she approached the depressive position and got in touch with her need of objects and her reparative impulses toward them. In fact some progress gradually became apparent, and she began her art course and passed her driving test. She also made better contact with her parents whom she was able to invite and even appreciate. Her silence remained a problem throughout the analysis, however, and periods of productive work continued to be interspersed by long periods of deadness and aridity.

I think it is possible to see how the pathological organization protected the patient from both paranoid–schizoid and depressive anxieties. It offered the comforts of withdrawal to a state which was neither fully alive nor quite dead, and yet something close to death, and relatively free of pain and anxiety. This state was idealized, even though the patient knew she was cut off and out of touch with her feelings. I think perverse sources of gratification were prominent and that these helped to keep her addicted to this borderline state of mind. The panic attacks seemed to represent a breakdown of the defensive organization and a consequent return to the persecutory fragmentation of the paranoid–schizoid position. At other times it was possible to observe a change of attitude which seemed to represent a move toward the depressive position, and these could be recognized as constituting analytically meaningful change. She seemed able, at least temporarily, to relinquish her dependence on the pathological organization and establish a relationship with me as her analyst. It was evident, however, how precarious this contact was and how rapidly it could be cut off, as, for example, happened when I interpreted her ambivalence regarding the check.

DISCUSSION

There are several excellent descriptions of pathological organizations (Riviere, 1936; Meltzer, 1968; Rosenfeld, 1971; Segal, 1972;

O'Shaughnessey, 1981; Riesenberg-Malcolm, 1981; Spillius, 1983; Sohn, 1985), and I will here only mention a few features which were prominent in the patient I have described. I will then briefly discuss some of the possible reasons for the tenacious hold which these organizations have on the personality and describe the way they interfere with development. Finally I will emphasize the clinical relevance of recognizing the equilibrium between the organization and the two basic positions.

In fantasy the organization can be represented in a variety of ways, most vividly as a gang or mafia in the manner described by Rosenfeld (1971). He showed how splitting and projective identification lead to the disowning of destructive parts of the self and destructive internal objects which are distributed in the members of the gang. The group is idealized and the cohesion of the defensive system is represented by the cohesion of the gang which depends on perverse methods to ensure dependence and loyalty. The gang or its leader will persuade, seduce, and if necessary threaten, to obtain obedience from its members including the patient, who often seems to be an unwilling member but too weak to escape.

I have previously suggested (Steiner, 1982), that the patient's attitude to the organization is not always as innocent as he pretends, and that a perverse collusion develops involving complex relationships between parts of the self in which good and bad parts become inextricably entangled. This often makes it difficult for the analyst to find a trustworthy patient he can address, and interpretations which imply that the patient is a victim who needs to be rescued by the analyst may be experienced as a collusion.

At other times the organization has a predominantly spatial representation, sometimes in the form of an idealized place such as a desert island, or a cave or building within which the patient can take refuge. In my patient, for example, the room on the border seemed to have become an idealized haven, and the terrifying experiences associated with it were denied. The patient may then find it very difficult to emerge from this haven to face the real world where pain and anxiety threaten.

This spatial aspect of the organization may be why several writers have used the term *position* in connection with it. Melanie Klein herself (1935) spoke of the manic position as a defense against both paranoid–schizoid and depressive anxieties, Segal speaks of a narcissistic position (1983), and I have thought of it in terms of a borderline position (Steiner, 1979). This helps us to visualize the equilibrium diagram in spatial terms, but can be misleading because the organization is actually making use of paranoid–schizoid mechanisms. Unlike the situation in the other positions, I believe these organizations are always pathological and always interfere with development. Indeed I think most analysts see in them an expression of the death instinct and a manifestation of envy as well as a defense against it (Spillius, 1983). It may allow a restricted type of life, and even at times prevent or postpone an acute breakdown, but it must be relinquished for a true contact with reality to be achieved.

The organization consequently seems to offer a solution to what Rey (1979) has called the claustroagoraphobic dilemma. If the patient attempts to emerge from it and move toward his objects he will often retreat and argue that he cannot afford to experience the emotional contact which closer relationships entail. In many cases this is experienced as a claustrophobic anxiety, and the object is felt to threaten the ego by imprisoning it, by suffocating it, or by making too many demands on it. On the other hand there is also a fear that a relinquishing of the defenses will plunge the patient into schizoid anxieties, especially confusion, and fragmentation which are often experienced as agoraphobia. If he moves toward his objects he becomes claustrophobic, while if he moves away from them he is agoraphobic. The pathological organization often appears to be the only way out since in it objects are bound in an organized

structure where the emotional distance to them can be controlled.

At times the anxieties of relinquishing the protection of the
pathological organization seem very real and the patient will
vividly convey the horrors he would have to face if it were to be
abandoned. At other times, however, the need for it is less convincing and the impression develops that the organization is
turned to not so much of necessity but because the dependence
on it has become a kind of addiction. The patient may then show
that he has insight into the essentially self-destructive character
of the organization and that he is at least partly aware that the
equilibrium provides only an illusion of safety. Nevertheless the
organization is adhered to, and this seems partly at least to be
due to the perverse gratification which it provides. Sadomasochistic elements have been described by most of the authors
writing about organizations, and I think were clear in the way
my patient teased and tormented me in her silences.

Sometimes the perverse flavor arises primarily from the way
truth is twisted and distorted, which leads to a peculiar borderline relationship to reality which is similar to that which has been
described in perversions (Chasseguet-Smirgel, 1974). Freud
(1927) first drew attention to these mechanisms in his study of
fetishism in which the female penis is recognized and yet dis-
avowed, often with the help of an ingenious rationalization. I
think they are characteristic of pathological organizations and
are at the root of the perverse atmosphere.

It is these distortions which evade the internal reality of the
depressive position so that the catastrophic state of the inner
world is not faced, and there is consequently no acknowledgment of a need to mourn and no reparation to be done. The
patient seems not so much to destroy his insight but rather *turns
a blind eye to it* and may then become involved in a complex cover
up of the truth (Steiner, 1985). This often misleads the analyst
and provokes interpretations at the wrong level, as in my patient,

for example, where I was often persuaded that she had the capacity to understand, only to find that she was unable or unwilling to sustain it. It is also, I suspect, one of the reasons for the paradoxical impression which the patient conveys of a serious and honest wish to have analysis, combined with a continuing need to distort and misrepresent reality.

The aim of the organization seems to be to retain the status quo, namely the situation where narcissistic object relations persist and projective identification leads to self and object being confounded. The situation bears a similarity to that seen in the early phases of the depressive position, and the object is possessed, controlled, and identified with through projective identification. It is the organized character of the defenses which serves to cement the objects and projected parts of the self together, and consequently to prevent the latter from being withdrawn and returned to the ego.

This means that the next phase of the depressive position in which the object has to be relinquished and mourned, does not proceed, and the patient is stuck with concretely internalized objects each containing parts of the self of which he cannot let go. To do so would involve not only facing the loss of the object but the loss of the self which is contained in it. Mourning, which would normally allow the gradual separation of self from object, does not proceed and the consequent advantages, such as the enrichment of the ego derived from the return of projections and especially the resultant capacity to think symbolically, does not ensue.

Pathological organizations clearly have an important theoretical interest, but it is as a clinical tool that I believe the concept is most helpful. If the triangular equilibrium diagram is kept in mind it helps us to identify the leading anxiety of the session which is often connected with a transition or a threatened transition between two of the three states. For example, the transition:

Paranoid–schizoid Position

Pathological Organization

is often the area of maximum tension in disturbed patients, especially early in an analysis. The patient may in fact have sought analysis as a result of a breakdown in a defensive organization which may lead to the development of symptoms. In analysis he may then try to reestablish the organization in order to get relief, and will often use the analyst as part of the defensive system (Riviere, 1936; Joseph, 1983). The analyst needs to understand that in this phase there is no question of interesting the patient in understanding in the usual analytic sense since his priority is to find his equilibrium. Sometimes, the anxiety quite rapidly improves, only to usher in a long stuck period in which the patient manages reasonably well so long as the analysis is there and so long as no development proceeds. The fear of a return to fragmentation and confusion is such that no development is allowed. For long periods my patient seemed to be afraid of such disintegrative states as were represented by her panic attacks, and the equilibrium she achieved in the analysis kept her relatively free of anxiety, and quite unable to develop.

Sometimes it is possible to observe patients operating in less pathological ways in which defenses operate in isolation without being caught up in an organization, and this can be considered as an expression of the equilibrium:

Paranoid–schizoid
Position

Depressive
Position

Even in relatively well-adjusted patients, however, situations arise when pathological organizations take over, and the patient will become stuck, sometimes only in a restricted area of his mental life, because he is unable to negotiate a particular conflict.

The situation here is a less malignant version of that seen in the patients whose whole analysis is dominated by the organization. If the analysis is trying to deal with the difficult area of conflict, the analytic work in both types of patient takes place in the equilibrium:

Pathological
Organization

Depressive
Position

Even those patients who are very stuck will usually be seen to make occasional movements toward the depressive position, and I believe it is important to recognize and interpret these. It is, of course, common to find that a move toward contact with depressive anxieties is followed by a retreat back to a pathological organization, as if the patient argues that he cannot afford to experience the emotional contact which a closer relationship with objects entails. Sometimes this seems to be connected with an intolerance of experiences such as guilt and despair which characterize the depressive position and sometimes in addition, with the development of an unbearable quality to the psychic pain associated with the relinquishing of the protective organization (Joseph, 1981). Much of an analysis may be occupied with following these shifts to and fro, and in some cases progress and development do occur and the patient manages to emerge from the pathological organization into a more real object relationship (Segal, 1983).

SUMMARY

I have presented clinical material to illustrate how a pathological organization can be considered to exist in an equilibrium with the paranoid–schizoid and depressive positions. While making use of paranoid–schizoid mechanisms such as primitive splitting and projective identification, the defensive structure

is highly organized and held together by narcissistic intrapsychic relationships in which perverse gratification plays an
important role. This organization of defenses seems to be designed to produce a place of real or illusionary safety from the
anxieties experienced in the other two positions. All individuals fluctuate in the defenses they employ, and hence can be
thought of as moving between these organizations and the
other two positions. They consequently demonstrate some
evidence of paranoid–schizoid level function, and also of the
existence of pathological organizations, even if they may function in a relatively mature way at other times and in other settings. In some patients, however, the pathological organization
dominates the personality and leads to analyses which become
fixed and stuck.

It is argued that a recognition of these organizations of defenses enables the analyst to orient himself more accurately to
the clinical material and hence to address himself to the patient
at a level he can understand.

REFERENCES

Bion, W. R. (1963), *Elements of Psycho-Analysis.* London: Heinemann.
Chasseguet-Smirgel, J. (1974), Perversion, idealization and sublima-
    tion. *Internat. J. Psycho-Anal.*, 55:349–357.
Freud, S. (1905), Fragment of an analysis of a case of hysteria. *Stan-
    dard Edition*, 7:1–122. London: Hogarth Press, 1953.
——— (1927), Fetishism. *Standard Edition*, 21:147–157. London: Hogarth
    Press, 1961.
Joseph, B. (1981), Toward the experiencing of psychic pain. In: *Do I
    Dare Disturb the Universe?* ed. J. S. Grotstein. Beverly Hills, CA:
    Caesura Press, pp. 93–102.
——— (1983), On understanding and not understanding: Some tech-
    nical issues. *Internat. J. Psycho-Anal.*, 64:291–298.
Klein, H. (1935), A contribution to the psychogenesis of manic-
    depressive states. In: *Writings*, Vol. 1. London: Hogarth Press, 1975,
    pp. 262–289.

——— (1952), Some theoretical conclusions regarding the emotional life of the infant. In: *Writings*, Vol. 3. London: Hogarth Press, 1975, pp. 61–93.

——— (1957), Envy and gratitude. In: *Writings*, Vol. 3: London: Hogarth Press, 1975, pp. 176–235.

Meltzer, D. (1968), Terror, persecution, dread. In: *Sexual States of Mind*. Perthshire: Clunie Press, 1973.

O'Shaughnessey, E. (1981), A clinical study of a defensive organisation. *Internat. J. Psycho-Anal.*, 62:359–369.

Rey, J. H. (1979), Schizoid phenomena in the borderline. In: *Advances in the Psychotherapy of the Borderline Patient*, ed. J. LeBoit & A. Capponi. New York: Jason Aronson.

Riesenberg-Malcolm, R. (1981), Expiation as a defence. *Internat. J. Psychoanal. Psychother.*, 8:549–570.

Riviere, J. (1936), A contribution to the analysis of the negative therapeutic reaction. *Internat. J. Psycho-Anal.*, 17:304–320.

Rosenfeld, H. A. (1950), Notes on the psychopathology of confusional states in chronic schizophrenia. In: *Psychotic States*. London: Hogarth Press, 1965.

——— (1964), On the psychopathology of narcissism: a clinical approach. In: *Psychotic States*. London: Hogarth Press, 1965.

——— (1971), A clinical approach to the psychoanalytic theory of the life and death instincts: an investigation into the aggressive aspects of narcissism. *Internat. J. Psycho-Anal.*, 52:169–178.

Segal, H. (1957), Notes on symbol formation. In: *The Work of Hanna Segal*. New York: Jason Aronson, 1981, pp. 49–65.

——— (1964), *Introduction to the Work of Melanie Klein*. London: Hogarth Press.

——— (1972), A delusional system as a defence against the re-emergence of a catastrophic situation. *Internat. J. Psycho-Anal.*, 53:393–401.

——— (1983), Some clinical implications of Melanie Klein's work: The emergence from narcissism. *Internat. J. Psycho-Anal.*, 64:269–276.

Sohn, L. (1985), Narcissistic organization, projective identification and the formation of the identificate. *Internat. J. Psycho-Anal.*, 66:201–213.

Spillius, E. (1983), Some developments from the work of Melanie Klein. *Internat. J. Psycho-Anal.*, 64:321–332.

Steiner, J. (1979), The border between the paranoid–schizoid and the depressive positions in the borderline patient. *Brit. J. Med. Psychol.*, 52:385–391.

———— (1982), Perverse relationships between parts of the self: A clinical illustration. *Internat. J. Psycho-Anal.*, 63:241–251.

———— (1985), Turning a blind eye: The cover-up for Oedipus. *Internat. Rev. Psychoanal.*, 12:161–172.

———— (1993), *Psychic Retreats.* London: Routledge.

EDITOR'S INTRODUCTION TO
PUTTING THE BOOT IN:
VIOLENT DEFENSES AGAINST DEPRESSIVE ANXIETY

Robin Anderson builds this essay around an extensive case report that in many ways fits well John Steiner's account in chapter 8 of pathological organizations. More about Anderson's patient will be found in his chapter 18, below.

This clinical narrative concerns a patient in the midst of making the difficult and wavering transition from the paranoid–schizoid position to an early phase of the depressive position. The man had begun analysis lodged in the more primitive position of the two. There he had been engaging in violent sadistic phantasies that focused on tyrannical control and abuse of an object he could not allow to establish any separateness from him. He felt that should he allow that separateness, he would suffer all the pains of entering the depressive position, namely, acute ambivalence, loss, mourning, guilt, and depression, on top of which there would be the crushing burden of having to make reparation to the good internal objects he felt he had damaged.

Consequently, he had been and continued to feel beset by "depressive anxiety," that is, the warning signal that change for the better can only be dangerous. In the past, in order to spare himself this anxiety or at least to dull it, he had, among other things, established a boot fetish and masturbation fantasies in which he was somehow allied with great tyrants and violent men. In the transference, which he constructed along these lines, he made extensive use of projective identification by means of which he stimulated intense countertransference reactions. Along with Anderson's having to cope with induced feelings of irritation, despair, and paralysis, he also became engaged in enactments that he was able to put to good analytic use once he understood what he had got caught up in.

Anderson shows that after he had persevered in his analytic role for some years, his patient had begun to move into the depressive position. Then he could allow himself to feel guilt toward his abused objects, tolerate recognizing their separateness, and not flee from painful experiences of mourning. All these changes were played out and worked out analytically (including some subtle dream analysis) in the transference and countertransference. It was a major sign that this developmental progress was underway when the analyst and patient could feel they shared some live emotional experience instead of remaining collusively trapped in the patient's earlier, sadistically inflicted deadness. Now the patient was revealing the hope for something better that previously he had buried under his massive defenses.

In the process of change, the patient also became less involved in his phantasy of omnipotence, another aspect of his defense against depressive anxiety. Anderson does not develop this point about omnipotence, and at this point the interested reader might want to scan the clinical material for the evidence on which one might base an interpretation of omnipotence as a major factor.

This graceful, graphic, and candid narrative of a patient's making this painful transition illuminates a crucial aspect of the task of helping seriously disturbed patients come psychically alive. There is much suffering to confront and live through before one can begin to overcome serious handicaps and collaborate in developing a forward-moving analysis. Gaining access to true feelings of hope and love seems to depend on this trial by fire.

9
PUTTING THE BOOT IN: VIOLENT DEFENSES AGAINST DEPRESSIVE ANXIETY

ROBIN ANDERSON

The rewards of the depressive position, independence and freedom of thought, the secure possession of an inner world, and a self supported and strengthened by good internal objects, are gained only at the price of facing up to the damage sustained to our good objects by our hatred and destructiveness. The depressive position is not a leap into the light but a period of great pain. The gains must be earned, and not once, but again and again. Melanie Klein described it as a *position*, not a *phase*, because we gain it and then lose it repeatedly throughout our lives.

For many more disturbed patients, particularly those functioning at a more borderline or narcissistic level, the depressive position remains a distant, shadowy, and feared state, threatening to confront the fragile self with pain it cannot endure. Joan Riviere, in her paper on the negative therapeutic reaction, considered such patients' fear that insight will drive them to suicide or madness (Riviere, 1936).

Such patients erect powerful defenses against these anxieties, which are usually nearer to the paranoid–schizoid functioning,

223

often forming pathological organizations which can protect the self against psychic pain, though usually at the terrible price of loneliness and impoverishment of the personality. These defenses are often so effective that there is little trace of depressive anxiety visible. However, I believe that it is possible in the analysis of some of these patients to discern depressive anxiety and to see defenses against it. Once it becomes clear that such patients are defending themselves against knowledge of good objects that have been attacked and damaged, then it may be possible to direct our attention to this area and help them to face what they have always avoided. I would like to describe one such patient in his early and very tentative encounter with depressive anxiety.

The patient was a man in his thirties who had been in analysis some years, having presented with complaints of long-standing depression and unhappiness, difficulties in his relations with others, and in particular a lack of any relationship with a woman.

He came originally from another continent, having moved to Britain with his family as a very young child. The family was not poor; both parents were professionals. So far as I could be sure about his history there were no major traumas; but there was a sense that something was wrong within the family, though it had never been possible to be clear about this. His father had had a mild cerebral hemorrhage when the patient was 8 or 9, and seemed to have remained somewhat depressed after this, with fears that it could recur. The patient had, however, shown signs of disturbance before this. He was the oldest of four children, three boys and a younger girl. It was quite difficult to get a sense of his life as a child. His descriptions of the family were of a harsh, depriving, and cold place, with extreme competition between the brothers for their powerful mother's affection, which the patient felt he always lost out on. But later in his analysis the picture seemed less extreme, and I never felt I could be certain what the true situation had been.

He hated reaching puberty, and was subsequently very sexually inhibited, and when he first presented in analysis he had never had any sexual experience other than masturbation. His masturbation was frequently accompanied by putting on boots and looking at himself in a mirror. He was also often preoccupied with boots, admiring them and acquiring different kinds— army boots, police boots, riding boots, cowboy boots. There were often links between the boots and violent sadistic and very powerful men like Hitler and the Nazis, Stalin, Saddam Hussein; and sometimes less obviously tyrannical figures like police officers, soldiers, people on horseback, or motorcyclists. He maintained that the masturbatory activity made him feel manly, but I did not feel convinced by this. There was little sense that he felt either excited or very satisfied by it. I had more an impression that the perverse activity united him with an object, giving him a protective covering, a kind of rubber or leather skin which dulled his anxiety but gave him little satisfaction. Indeed, when I considered it in relation to its manifestation in the transference it seemed that he was as much imprisoned by it as rescued. Though the activity implied violent and cruel phantasies, in his external life he was not physically violent. However, his feelings toward those he felt had slighted him, his parents, his colleagues at work, and his analyst, were extreme—unforgiving and full of hatred.

He had made some progress during his analysis and this was most apparent in his professional life. Having been almost unable to function at work because of his shyness and awkwardness, resulting in the loss of several jobs, he had become an increasingly successful scientist working in the field of microbiology, where he seemed to be well regarded. He was more successful socially, less isolated, and had a few friends; but he had difficulty with all close relationships and had not had a girl friend for about two years, since he had broken up with the only girl friend he had ever managed to have.

In working with him, I became increasingly aware of an atmosphere created by his way of relating to me which had a powerful effect on me, and on himself too. I would like to illustrate this by bringing some fairly typical material.

He arrived a few minutes late for a Monday session, looking rather gray and unsmiling. He began:

> The weekend was awful. What could anyone expect, as I have no girl friend. Without a girl friend there isn't really any point to anything. I did almost nothing—all the things I had intended to do, like studying, producing food for the party, cleaning my flat—none of them. I haven't seen anyone except my parents . . . how devastating to be in my thirties and only have my parents to go and see. . . . They have so much to answer for—to have been treated so terribly as a child and with such a cold mother. Then my father spoke about the homosexuals at his barbershop and I knew by the way he spoke that he just can't cope with homosexuality. . . . Anyway, what's the point in coming here. You can't deal with my problems. I think you're not up to it. In fact, if it wasn't for the fact that I know you give lectures I would be absolutely convinced that you aren't capable of working with me. I don't know whether I'm too much for you, or my case is just too difficult. . . .

And so it went on, in an all too familiar unfolding of a kind of commentary which I would try to relate to, to work with, and think about the ideas presented. Yet I knew from experience that this did not really arise from someone who wanted the situation to be any different, or indeed had any idea that it could be. And yet the notion that he was feeling hopeless and wanted this to be understood did not seem right either. The sense that he wished to nurse this aggrieved state felt nearer the mark and aroused some counterindignation in me. And yet I knew too that such an interpretation would not change the situation, and would be likely to lead to a sense of two people complaining, an aggrieved patient and analyst.

His way of relating conveyed a sense of lifelessness, a feeling that any goodness was absent and had never been present; but much more importantly, it aroused and created this sense of lifelessness in the room, and this was most disturbing. What was sometimes possible to observe was that what motivated this material was not a wish to convey what was true, but a desire to induce feelings in the object (and, I felt, in himself, too) of despair and paralysis. But this was done with such conviction and forcefulness that they became *the* reality for him, and frequently for me too, despite my attempts to resist the pressure. I was at times aware of a kind of relish which this hold over reality gave him, and this provided some evidence of the underlying sadism and violence taking place.

By this activity he locked himself into the object, creating an inseparable couple united in a kind of loveless sadistic marriage. Listening to his material at these times did not result in a sense of something to address—indeed there was no sense of a patient willing to listen—no sense of two people talking and listening to each other. Instead, the analyst was trapped and able only to endure, with no prospect of escape.

It was this kind of position in which the analyst was held that I think was closely linked to the patient's perverse masturbatory activity which I described earlier, in which he and his object were fused in a grim rubberized togetherness, where cruelty and violence were taking place and yet the distinction between self and object was obliterated. In this way he was "married" permanently to his object which was kept in a subjugated and depressed state.

As I tried to study this whole situation I became aware of a number of factors that affected it. Any improvement or forward movement seemed to increase the intensity of this process of violent constriction of the object; as did anything that led to his noticing the independence of the analyst. I think these two were related, as though anything that opened a gap between us, between his imposed world and one which the analyst was manifestly independent of, produced a violent re-action whose purpose seemed to be to reestablish the old equilibrium. When it was possible to see what was happening; and to interpret it firmly but without any hint of violence or retaliation, he was enormously relieved and the atmosphere of the session changed abruptly and profoundly, in a way that was almost tangible.

This powerful tyranny over the object seemed to obliterate the possibility of any enquiry into the state of the object, or of any interest in it, or even knowledge of it, and in this way operated as a powerful defense against depressive anxiety. But it also produced such additional damage to the object that the resulting guilt induced even greater persecution, so that any real facing of the state of the object and the associated guilt remained an almost insuperable task.

This more overtly violent relation to a damaged object, "putting the boot in," was illustrated in some later material.

It was the first day back after a public holiday, and I had forgotten to unlock the entry door to my office. As a result, the door failed to open when I pressed the lock release, so that he was denied his usual "automatic entry," and had to wait until I unlocked the door. I knew that this was likely to cause a reaction—perhaps for several weeks—and in a slightly flustered way I accidentally set off my watch alarm at the end of the session. He seemed somewhat less upset than I had expected, and the next day he brought a dream in which a bumble-bee had got into his home. He had mixed feelings about this bee: on the one hand he hated it and feared it would sting him and should be killed; on the other, that it was trapped and only wanted to be able to follow its natural instincts to get out and pollinate flowers, collect nectar, and breed.

He began to kill it by hitting it repeatedly, but after five or six blows he was surprised to notice that it was more resilient than he had expected (he described it as "tougher" and therefore less squashable than he had thought) and he wished he had not started to kill it. But now he had started he felt he had to continue, because otherwise it would be left injured and he could not let that happen.

The dream seemed to demonstrate how he could not stop his violent, damaging activity, not only because of his sadistic gratification, but just as importantly because he would have to stop and face what he had done; and so he went on with the killing. It may be that what could initiate this process was some sense of an already damaged object as manifest in this material by my forgetful and bumbling behavior on that day. Equally, the perception of a more resilient and less squashable object enabled him to bring a dream about the incident and to recover from the episode more quickly than usual.

I think the fact that he could bring a dream about the incident was in itself an indication of some development of a more resilient and therefore less persecutory internal object, and this had (to his surprise) survived better over that holiday weekend. At the same time it revealed his despair at what he felt caught up in and unable to stop. He was confronted by his violent defense against depressive anxiety—continuous "putting the boot in," the awareness of which pained him and made him have to engage further in this defense.

Some further understanding of his tendency to exaggerate and overemphasize any slights and setbacks in his life became possible some time after this. He arrived at this session and reported a "disaster." A junior technician where he worked, a woman, played squash with him. On the way to the court she had said, "I hope you don't hit me." He was infuriated that anyone should suggest he ever hit anyone, and was then "outraged" and "devastated" when she hit him in the mouth with her racquet and broke his front tooth. He was furious with her and said he "realized" that this was an "envious attack" by her, and he thought of suing her. He had a conviction that now his looks were permanently spoiled and the small chance he had to be married had now been taken away for ever. Every grievance that he had ever had became more and more exaggerated. He brought a dream in which he was enlarging a photograph. His association was to an art exhibition he had recently visited, in which the artist had produced a vast photo enlargement (30 feet long) of a crater, which he had then altered with dynamite and produced a second vast photograph.

This sense of a vast enlargement of the damage to his tooth seemed to illustrate rather clearly his relationship to damage and defect in himself (and usually, by identification, in his objects). He involved himself in a process of vast enlargement and exaggeration, and then displayed them for all the world (especially his analyst) to see. He made a work of art out of his defects for which the object was to blame—and this was then his main interest in life, which took precedence over, and indeed allowed him to ignore and avoid really facing up to, the state of his world, and of his part in its creation. (In fact his dentist made a "beautiful repair" of his tooth—he reported the next day.) By the same token the enlargement meant that he had far more to face because everything he did, as well as what was done to him, became so exaggerated. I felt too that this process was related to his masturbatory activity, as though the boots made him enormous and eradicated all feelings of smallness and helplessness.

He was quite shaken, but was able to listen when I interpreted this to him. Moreover I found that the knowledge of it strengthened me in my work with him so that I felt more aware, when I was feeling useless and demoralized by him, that this process contributed to it.

I think it was clear from this material that a quite different way of relating to the object was possible. It demonstrated that he was not so completely committed to constricting the object as he had been, and that he could also listen when a quite disturbing interpretation was made which certainly opened a gap between us. How could this be possible for him?

I think that in the world of "locked-in," "rubberized" relationships, where there was no real object, he was deprived even of the awareness of an understanding object, so that when he could discern that he was being understood this did also satisfy a longing in him (a preconception) that he had lost contact with; and when he could allow, and then receive, understanding, I think this was a deeply gratifying experience for him which he had given up ever having again.

Moreover, I think that when he heard the analyst making sense to him of his experience he did feel that there was a "beautiful repair" not only of himself but of his object as well, and this was enormously reassuring to him when he lived in a world populated by objects that were damaged, blaming, and persecutory. For this reason I believe he could tolerate the disturbing aspects of the contact—the narcissistic wound.

I think that this tended to support the view that his difficulties were not only, or even mainly, brought about by his envy, but derived from his absolute intolerance and fear of a perception of damaged objects which he therefore defended himself against so vigorously.

The summer holiday was approaching, and following this work it was possible to discern the emergence of a different kind of depression in him, marked by experiences of loss and accompanying sadness. During this period there was frequently a more openly aggressive quality in the sessions, but at the same time there was also a sense of more freedom of movement in the analysis.

Up to this point he had always arrived a few minutes late; now he was occasionally coming early. This confronted him not only with my separateness from him but also, since he was the first patient of the day and I work at home, with his experience of me upstairs with my family.

On the day prior to a more detailed session, which I shall describe, he had arrived early and spent much of the session complaining that I could not work with him because I obviously did not like him since I had greeted him in such an unfriendly way. I was clearly not pleased to see him despite the fact that he had made the effort to come early. It was possible eventually to discover that what had upset him was that instead of my pressing the lock release immediately, as I would have done if he had been late (since I would have been in the consulting room and near to the button), there had been a slight delay since I was upstairs in my house and engaged in activities which meant it had taken a little longer for me to reach the release button. At the end of that session he had been able to make the unusual acknowledgment that he knew that just because he had felt those things about me it did not mean that they were true.

The following day, a Thursday, he arrived four minutes late again, and wondered if it had to do with the "tiny delay" yesterday (note the lack of exaggeration). He had forgotten his beeper as well, but he said this was not too serious and would certainly not lead to a patient's tests being delayed, but it might lead a doctor who was trying to reach him to wonder what on earth had happened. I pointed out that he had managed to hold onto the fact that it had been a *small delay* yesterday, but he had nonetheless wanted to make a colleague suffer by wondering what had happened, just as he had been left wondering what had happened to me yesterday.

He then spoke of his anger with his boss over his holiday plans. He had been put on a duty rota when he was supposed to be at a conference, and his boss should have remembered that. He did realize that his boss was very busy, but he had told him of his plans. I connected this with an attempt to be more flexible with me over my holiday plans, which did not coincide with his own arrangements. (He had previously made some holiday arrangements which meant he would have to restart his analysis one week late, and he had threatened to leave his analysis unless I altered my holiday dates.) Now he was saying that he realized he had never discussed his own plans with me; so it was not really fair of him to go on at me about it.

He had had a dream in which he was in a room like mine, consulting a woman about a virus infection. She was not taking his infection seriously enough. He had a chicken-pox-like rash, and he noticed he had some vesicles in his eye. He remembered in the dream that he had already had chicken pox. Could it have been shingles? If so, to get it so young could mean that he must have a disturbance in his immune system. Did this mean he had AIDS or leukemia? Should he, therefore, take a modest antiviral agent or a more powerful and dangerous one—he was not sure.

Then he reported a second dream, in which a man drove up in a subcompact yellow car to consult him about a rabies risk. This man was either vacationing in a risky area, or had just returned from one, but he needed this to be properly looked at and resolved.

An association to the yellow car was his neighbor, an old man, who had recently died. He was actually not poor, but drove a small car because he was a very unpretentious man—not the type to drive around in a Rolls Royce, even if he had the money, because he had different values. He would rather have a photograph of his grandchildren or books on world wildlife. (In a session not long before this, he had also spoken of the neighbor as a man who could live on his own; because although he had lost his wife he had loved her and the memory of this could sustain him, even though he was now without her.) At this point the patient paused, and looked at his watch—there were ten more minutes—and said, "I have another association, rather a lengthy one." He then launched into a long and involved account of a rabies call that he had had recently. He reached a point in the story where the specialist had rightly decided that there had been some urgency and had insisted that the vaccine must be sent by Express mail.

I broke in and suggested that there was an infection that needed urgent treatment and that it could not wait till the next day. I suggested that the infection that could flare up was due to my small delay the day before, because I thought he did look at me in his mind's eye. The vesicles meant that he was aware that something had happened in that look, that he had hated me when he "saw" me with my family upstairs. He did not know how seriously he had damaged me, but he struggled to restore me—to remember me as a good man who holds onto a picture of the child/himself; but there were painful things about this good man. He had died, and when he was alive he had been sad because he missed his wife and was old and infirm; so it was hard to hold onto this good but painful picture and he was tempted to go off into his own expertise and silence me in the last minutes of the session instead of allowing a modest treatment that might help him to recover his health. He remained silent but thoughtful for the last few minutes of the session.

I think that following the fluctuations in that session shows something of the struggle this patient was having just on the threshold of the depressive position.

He had arrived at the session in a better state, aware that my "crime," and perhaps his own, was not too serious; it had not become exaggerated in his mind and the delay had remained a "tiny one." I think his association about the forgotten beeper not being "too serious" was also some measure of this. He could allow himself (the "hospital doctor") to wonder what on earth had happened to me, without succumbing to overwhelming guilt and persecution. Indeed he could allow himself to have an object about which he was curious.

I think at this point I did not understand him so well and my interpretation that he had wished to make the hospital doctor suffer was probably not only incorrect but was also aggressive. I assailed him somewhat with this interpretation. He followed my interpretation with a criticism of his boss for "not remembering," though he held onto a sense of proportion about this—"my boss is very busy." Through the dream he attempted to restore a damaged good object and to stay in relation to it, but it was too painful for him, and when he launched off into the "long association" I think he was rapidly losing contact with me as a functioning partner. Had I let him run on I would once again have been trapped, held, and unable to respond; but even in this attempt to erect a defense against depressive anxiety he left open the possibility of being rescued. I was not at this point enduring in a dead and despairing way; I found I wanted to interpret the dream, and he could give me an opening to do this so that between us the session could end with contact once more being reestablished, suggesting that a commitment and wish to have contact with the object had survived.

This emergence of a sense of loss, of mourning even, made further appearances. The following week, at the end of a session, he looked up at some flowers in the consulting room and said they reminded him of the flowers that his girl friend had given him when they had finally parted—he had tried to preserve them, to keep them alive as long as possible, but eventually they had died and he felt he had completely lost her.

DISCUSSION

I think that at that moment he was in touch with an experience of knowing that he had not been able to keep a good object alive and that he had been helpless to prevent this situation. This sense of facing the death of the object is so much at the heart of the depressive position. What seems so striking to me is that when he wards off this experience with his relentless dulling of sensitivity, he and I and the atmosphere feel as dead as the flowers he could not keep alive. But when he is actually facing the loss, and something of the despair, there is an entirely opposite atmosphere—both he and I feel moved, feel sad, and feel alive. There is a sense of empathy, of contact, which transforms the experience of being with him. This, it seems to me, so much captures the paradox of the depressive position, and I think is near to what Melanie Klein describes when she refers to the stage when suffering can become productive: "Thus while grief is experienced to the full and despair is at its height the love for the object wells up and the mourner feels more strongly that life inside and outside will go on after all and that the lost object can be preserved within. At this stage in mourning suffering can become productive" (Klein, 1940, p. 360).

It is only by facing the total loss of the object and the inability ever to repair it that it is then possible for the self to feel alive and not be in projective identification with the dead object from which it is never possible to separate.

Steiner (1990, 1992) has described how the facing of the loss of the object is that part of the depressive position where the awareness dawns that the object is not under the control of the self and cannot be protected from attacks from within, from either destructive parts of the self or internal objects. It is the moment when the self and object are acknowledged to be separate. When the projections of the self into the object are withdrawn the self must face its loss. Steiner (1990) has also pointed out how the very defenses against guilt in certain narcissistic patients are the source of further guilt, which makes them so intractable in analysis.

I think that in my patient the source of the guilt is caused not only by attacks on the object but by the attacks on his own vulnerable self, as in Rosenfeld's (1971) description of destructive narcissism. Rosenfeld described how the destructive self, identified with an omnipotent destructive object, captures the libidinal self, and holds it hostage by a mixture of bullying and seduction. It is thus prevented from forming a dependent and creative, and of course sometimes painful, relationship with a good object. I think what is discernible in my patient's material is the way in which his attacks are not only on his objects but on his own perceptual apparatus. In the dream of the viral infection he described how the virus had attacked his eyes. I think that this is where the kick ultimately lands, and which thus feels so violent. When I represent a perceiving, seeing object for him it is his own/my soft eyes which he must destroy with his hard boots, and he does it with such ferocity that at times I cannot see, or even remember what it was like to see. I think that this is such a source of guilt that he retreats into his perversion to avoid any danger of seeing and suffering.

When he feels that his object's sight can recover from and resist such attacks his sense of guilt lessens and he can then for limited periods allow himself and his object to see more clearly, even though his own capacity to look is still very limited, since unbearable guilt is so easily aroused, from which he would then defend himself again.

I think it is only by attending to, and indeed remaining sympathetic to, such patients' extreme sensitivity to depressive guilt that they can be given a glimmer of hope that using, rather than destroying, their own and their objects' capacities to see and feel will offer them a surer relief from anxiety and persecution than is offered by their ultimately cold and lonely defenses.

REFERENCES

Klein, M. (1940), Mourning and its relation to manic-depressive states. *Internat. J. Psycho-Anal.*, 21:125–153.
Riviere, J. (1936), A contribution to the analysis of the negative therapeutic reaction. *Internat. J. Psycho-Anal.*, 17:304–320.
Rosenfeld, H. A. (1971), A clinical approach to the psychoanalytical theory of the life and death instincts: An investigation into the aggressive aspects of narcissism. *Internat. J. Psycho-Anal.*, 52:169–178.

Steiner, J. (1990), Pathological organisation as obstacles to mourning: The role of unbearable guilt. *Internat. J. Psycho-Anal.*, 71:87–94.

——— (1992), The equilibrium between the paranoid–schizoid and the depressive positions. In: *Clinical Lectures on Klein and Bion*, ed. R. Anderson. London: Routledge.

EDITOR'S INTRODUCTION TO
THE MISSING LINK:
PARENTAL SEXUALITY IN THE OEDIPUS COMPLEX

The contemporary Kleinians do not systematically ignore or fail to work through the mature, triangular forms of the Oedipus complex; however, some misunderstanding persists that in this respect their work is flawed. The fact is that these analysts take up oedipal matters under the aspect of working through the depressive position. Their concentration on difficulties encountered in achieving and maintaining the depressive position may then give a reader the superficial impression that they have pushed oedipal matters altogether to the side. In this essay Dr. Britton shows how working through the Oedipus complex and the depressive position go hand in hand.

Another source of misunderstanding may derive from the fact that Kleinian analysts do a good deal of spadework on more primitive versions of the Oedipus complex, specifically, those that are encountered at the heart of the paranoid–schizoid position. There, the familiar triangularity of the Oedipus complex is obscured by intricate defensive operations, destructive phantasies concerning both the self and one's objects, and movements to and fro within the dyadic relationship that is at the core of unconscious phantasy. Dr. Britton presents an illuminating synopsis of the treatment of a patient with psychotic features in which he highlights both these archaic manifestations of the Oedipus complex and the barriers standing in the way of the patient's moving beyond these barriers. Along with the synopsis he offers some helpful technical suggestions. Much of this analysis is transposable to the more primitive layers of oedipal conflict in neurotic and character disordered patients.

In discussing the mature, triangular Oedipus complex that signifies entry into the depression position, however unstably, Dr. Britton offers a useful concept of his own—the oedipal illusion—and he illustrates it with some clinical material. He shows that, at the center of this illusion, is refusal to acknowledge the sexual union of the parents and one's exclusion from it; one hopes thereby to avoid painful experiences of loss, mourning, and depression. He describes processes very much like those described by Freud when Freud discussed splitting and denial in the analysis of fetishism. The defensive function of the oedipal illusion is to protect the inner-world experience of the patient's being in exclusive dyadic relationship with each parent while hating the other. "The missing link" refers to erasure of the parents' conjugal relation with each other. In this aspect of the analysis, explicit sexual fantasies and desires play prominent roles.

Of particular significance is Dr. Britton's tracking the way in which the maintenance of the oedipal illusion causes blockage of both personal integration and integration of the object in the inner world. Along with these blocked developments come restrictions on a person's capacity to envision and accept reciprocal observations and independence of thought. These mature ego functions require the establishment of "a triangular space," without which there is severe basic impairment of the capacity for reality relations. A significant part of the patient's ambivalent transference to the observing analyst derives from the patient's defense of the oedipal illusion.

Issues pertaining to genital intactness, gender role definition, childbearing, and so on, are to be worked out within the context described by Dr. Britton. In this respect there is a difference from traditional ego psychological Freudian analysis where, usually, genital intactness and associated issues are themselves the context in which the other matters are to be worked out. Even so, the range of variables covered in the two approaches is quite similar, recognizing that phallic–genital–gender issues are best worked through when they are taken to be the foci around which the patient has organized unresolved relational issues of sadism, envy, loss, trust, dependence, and many of the other variables that the Kleinian group tends to focus on as a matter of course.

10

THE MISSING LINK: PARENTAL
SEXUALITY IN THE OEDIPUS COMPLEX

RONALD BRITTON

For Freud the Oedipus complex was the nuclear complex, from its discovery in 1897 to the end of his life (Freud, 1892–1897, 1924a). It remained central in the development of the individual for Melanie Klein. She adopted the term *oedipal situation*, and included in it what Freud had referred to as the primal scene, the sexual relations of the parents both as perceived and as imagined (Klein, 1928).

From the outset of her work with children Melanie Klein was impressed at the ubiquity of the oedipal situation and its unique importance; she also thought that it began much earlier than did Freud and that it began in relation to part objects before evolving into the familiar Oedipus complex, which related to the two parents perceived as whole object; that is, as persons. So for her it began in infancy with phantasies of a relation to breast and penis and phantasies of the relationship between these two part objects, which would be succeeded by ideas about the parents under the influence of these earlier phantasies. She felt that the child's attitude and relationship to this unfolding situation was of profound significance for the urge to learn, which she called the epistemophilic impulse, and for the individual's relationship to reality. In 1926 she wrote that at a very early age children become

242

acquainted with reality through the deprivations it imposes on them. They defend themselves against reality by repudiating it. The fundamental thing, however, and the criterion of all later capacity for adaptation to reality is the degree in which they are able to tolerate the deprivations that result from the oedipal situation (Klein, 1926).

This was written more than a decade before Klein was to describe what she called the "depressive position," that period of integration and recognition which entailed a realization of the nature of the world outside the self, and of the nature of the internal ambivalent feelings toward it; in other words, the beginnings of a sense of external and internal reality and the relationship between them. Since the delineation of this central concept of Kleinian thinking, it has become increasingly evident that the capacity to comprehend and relate to reality is contingent on working through the depressive position. Klein repeatedly emphasized that the Oedipus complex develops hand-in-hand with the developments that make up the depressive position, and I have suggested elsewhere that the working through of one entails the working through of the other (Britton, 1985).

The initial recognition of the parental sexual relationship involves relinquishing the idea of sole and permanent possession of mother and leads to a profound sense of loss, which, if not tolerated, may become a sense of persecution. Later, the oedipal encounter also involves recognition of the difference between the relationship between parents as distinct from the relationship between parent and child: the parents' relationship is genital and procreative; the parent–child relationship is not. This recognition produces a sense of loss and envy, which, if not tolerated, may become a sense of grievance or self-denigration.

The Oedipus situation dawns with the child's recognition of the parents' relationship, in whatever primitive or partial form. It is continued by the child's rivalry with one parent for the other, and it is resolved by the child relinquishing his sexual claim on his parents by his acceptance of the reality of their sexual relationship.

In this chapter I want to suggest that if the encounter with the parental relationship starts to take place at a time when the individual has not established a securely based maternal object, the Oedipus situation appears in analysis only in primitive form and is not immediately recognizable as the classical Oedipus complex. In the first part of the chapter I describe patients who illustrate this situation.

In less severe disorders it is the final relinquishment of the oedipal objects that is evaded. An illusional oedipal configuration is formed as a defensive organization in order to deny the psychic reality of the parental relationship. I emphasize that it is a defense against psychic reality because these defensive phantasies are organized to prevent the emergence of facts already known and phantasies already existent. The parental relationship has been registered but is now denied and defended against by what I call an oedipal illusion. These illusional systems provide what Freud called "a domain . . . separated from the real external world at the time of the introduction of the reality principle . . . free from the demand of the exigencies of life, like a kind of reservation" (Freud, 1924b, p. 187). In the same passage, he describes the person who creates such a domain in his mind as lending a "special importance and secret meaning to a piece of reality" which is different from the reality which is defended against.

In the second part of this chapter I discuss patients who exemplify such oedipal illusions. In contrast to the fixity of these oedipal illusions, the oedipal rivalry both in the positive (heterosexual) form and in the negative (homosexual) form provides a means of working through the depressive position. In each version one parent is the object of desire, and the other is the hated rival. This configuration is retained, but the feeling changes in relation to each parent. Thus good becomes bad and vice versa as positive changes to negative. My contention is that the evasive use of this switch is halted by the full recognition of the parents' sexual relationship, their different anatomy, and the child's own nature. This involves the realization that the same parent who is the object of oedipal desire in one version is the hated rival in the other.

The acknowledgment by the child of the parents' relationship with each other unites his psychic world, limiting it to one world shared with his two parents in which different object relationships can exist. The closure of the oedipal triangle by the recognition of the link joining the parents provides a limiting boundary for the internal world. It creates what I call a "triangular space," one bounded by the three persons of the oedipal situation and all their potential relationships. It includes, therefore, the possibility of being a participant in a relationship and observed by a third person as well as being an observer of a relationship between two people.

To clarify this point it is helpful to remember that observed and imagined events take place in a world conceived of as continuous in space and time (Rey, 1979) and given structure by the oedipal configuration. The capacity to envisage a benign parental relationship influences the development of a space outside the self capable of being observed and thought about, which provides the basis for a belief in a secure and stable world.

The primal family triangle provides the child with two links connecting him separately with each parent and confronts him with the link between them which excludes him. Initially this parental link is conceived in primitive part object terms and in the modes of his own oral, anal, and genital desires, and in terms of his hatred expressed in oral, anal, and genital terms. If the link between the parents perceived in love and hate can be tolerated in the child's mind, it provides him with a prototype for an object relationship of a third kind in which he is a witness

and not a participant. A third position then comes into existence from which object relationships can be observed. Given
this, we can also envisage being observed. This provides us with
a capacity for seeing ourselves in interaction with others and for
entertaining another point of view whilst retaining our own, for
reflecting on ourselves whilst being ourselves. This is a capacity
we hope to find in ourselves and in our patients in analysis. There
are analyses when for some time, or at certain times, this seems
impossible, and it is at those times that one realizes what it means
to lack that third position.

PATIENTS WHO EXEMPLIFY DIFFICULTIES
WITH THE OEDIPAL SITUATION
IN THE FIRST ENCOUNTER

I have been impressed by a number of analyses that exemplify
difficulties with the oedipal situation in the first encounter. This
account is a compound of a few such cases. In my early work with
these patients, I was hardly aware that my difficulties in understanding them had anything to do with the Oedipus complex.
What gradually became evident was that at such times they lacked
the "third position" described above. They could not include
within their most personal version of me my relationships with
others. It was also intolerable for them to feel that I was com-
muning with myself about them independently of them.

I came to learn that they could not allow the notion of parental intercourse to exist because they could only anticipate it
as a disaster. The possibility of my communicating with a third
object was catastrophic and so the third position I refer to was
untenable. During the early years of these analyses I found that
any move of mine toward that which, by another person, would
have been called objectivity could not be tolerated. We were to
move along a single line and meet at a single point. There was
to be no lateral movement. A sense of space could be achieved
only by increasing the distance between us, a process they found

hard to bear unless they initiated it. What I felt I needed desperately was a place in my mind that I could step into sideways
and from which I could look at things. If I tried to force myself
into such a position by asserting a description of them in analytic terms, they would become violent, sometimes physically,
sometimes by screaming. One shouted: "Stop that fucking thinking!" I came to realize that these efforts of mine to consult my
analytic self were detected and experienced as a form of internal intercourse of mine, which corresponded to parental intercourse. This they felt as a threat to their existence. If I turned
to something in my mind later on, when things were not so
primitive, they felt I was eliminating my experience of them in
my mind. The only way I found of finding a place to think that
was helpful and not disruptive was to allow the evolution within
myself of my own experience and *to articulate this to myself*, whilst
communicating to them my *understanding of their point of view*.
This, I found, did enlarge the possibilities, and my patients could
begin to think. It seemed to me that it was a model in which
parental intercourse could take place if the knowledge of it did
not force itself in some intrusive way into the child's mind.
Should it do so, it appeared to be felt to be annihilating the
child's link with her mother both externally and internally.

In an attempt to understand this clinical situation, I have called
on Bion's concept of the "container and contained," in addition
to Melanie Klein's theories of the early Oedipus situation. Bion
(1959) has described the consequences for some individuals of
a failure of maternal containment as the development within
them of a destructive envious superego that prevents them from
learning or pursuing profitable relations with any object. He
makes it clear that the inability of the mother to take in her child's
projections is experienced *by the child* as a destructive attack *by her*
on his link and communication *with her* as his good object.

The idea of a good maternal object can only be regained by
splitting off her impermeability so that now a hostile force is felt

to exist, which attacks his good link with his mother. Mother's goodness is now precarious and depends on him restricting his knowledge of her. Enlargement of knowledge of her as a consequence of development and his curiosity are felt to menace this crucial relationship. Curiosity also discloses the existence of the oedipal situation. This in the development of every child is a challenge to his belief in the goodness of his mother, and a reluctance to admit it into his picture of his mother is normal. In the child already menaced by any enlargement of his knowledge of his mother because of her existing precarious status in his mind, the further threat of acknowledging her relationship with father is felt to spell disaster. The rage and hostility that would be aroused by this discovery is felt to threaten his belief in a world where good objects can exist. The hostile force that was thought to attack his original link with his mother is now equated with the oedipal father, and the link between the parents is felt to reconstitute her as the nonreceptive deadly mother. The child's original link with the good maternal object is felt to be the source of life, and so, when it is threatened, life is felt to be threatened.

In some personalities, therefore, the full recognition of parental sexuality is felt as a danger to life. The emergence in the transference of the full emotional significance for them of an idea of the primal scene is followed by panic attacks and fear of imminent death. Greater knowledge of the oedipal situation is also felt to initiate a mental catastrophe.

Faced with this—as Klein (1946) and Bion (1956) have pointed out—the psychotic mutilates his mind in order not to perceive it. In schizophrenic patients the mental apparatus is splintered, and thinking becomes impossible. The patients I am describing appeared to have preserved a great deal by a violent severance of their minds so that some parts were protected from knowledge and only emerged in a breakdown or in analysis.

There was in them an "infantile" self that appeared ignorant of anything other than an ideal breast and a state of persecution.

The persecutor was a hovering male presence, which they feared might oust the good mother, and they were terrified that they might be left alone with this figure. Interruptions in analysis and any interruptions in the flow of good experience were felt to be the result of violent attacks from this hostile object. At times I was taken to be this hostile object; at other times I was felt to be the victim of it. I was also familiar with it in the form of my patients attacking me. As progress was made and communications between us became more possible, their internal situation became clearer. They contained a hostile object, or part of themselves in fusion with a hostile object, that interfered in their attempts to communicate with me. At times this had the power to control their speech, and they could not articulate. At others times words were whispered and broken phrases were managed. If I could demonstrate that I really wished to know them, which I could only do by demonstrating some minimal understanding, their capacity to communicate would be recovered. The way I came to understand that often repeated sequence was that they needed some experience of my taking them in *before* I could return in their minds as the good maternal object they could talk to. Otherwise I might be what one called the "wrong person."

The "wrong person" looked like the right person but had connections with father, For many years there was the threat of these crucially distinguished figures becoming confused. The thought of the idealized mother becoming united with father was the greatest fear. In the transference it took the form of a fear that the different aspects of my relationship with the patient would not be distinct from each other. Some of my functions were regarded as good; others as bad, such as my going away; they kept them distinct in their minds as if they were different transference figures. From these patients I learnt how essential it was to distinguish between the integration that is sought for as a means of working through the depressive position, and a fusion of elements that are not stabilized and distinguished in their qualities and attributes, and whose union produces a sense of chaos.

If any pressure toward precocious integration was felt to come from me, it provoked great anxiety and either violent refusal or abject masochistic submission. This latter reaction turned out to be based on a phantasy of submission to a sadistic father and was regarded by my patients as profoundly wicked but always tempting. It appeared to serve the purpose of providing both perverse gratification and an avoidance of the phantasy of the parents uniting.

I must not become "one thing," a monstrous amalgamation of the separate maternal and paternal identities attributed to me. The amalgam that would result from this union was an ostensibly loving maternal figure who had inside her a contradiction of her own nature; a presence that made all her apparent good qualities treacherous. I was always reminded of descriptions of demonic possession, in which the devil was felt to have infused all the characteristics of the person with hidden evil. The horror felt about this figure was to do with its contradictory nature. One patient called it "unnatural" and the emergence of this idea of me in the transference was felt to be disastrous because it destroyed not only all good but also all meaning previously established.

This fearful outcome corresponds to Melanie Klein's description of the child's terror of the combined object as a persecutory phantasy of the parents fused in permanent intercourse. I would describe my patients as having an infantile phantasy that father was of such a nature and power that he could penetrate mother's identity in such a way as to corrupt her goodness; and maternal goodness, although precariously idealized, was the only concept of goodness. It always impressed me that for such a patient the very concept of goodness was at stake and not simply its availability or presence.

It is not my intention here to go into the factors in the patient's disposition and life circumstances that contributed to this inability to surmount the earliest stages of the Oedipus situation in any detail. I would simply like to say that in my view it was the initial failure of maternal containment that made the negotiation of the Oedipus complex impossible. The personality and intrusiveness of her father into her mother's mind were very significant, but these were combined with the patient's own considerable difficulty in tolerating frustration. The phantasy of parental intercourse was constructed from a combination of projections of themselves and perceptions of her parents.

My wish is to draw attention to the reality of the belief that catastrophe was associated with the emergence of the oedipal situation and that consequently there was a resort to violent splitting to prevent it from occurring. The result was an internal division within their minds organized around separate parental objects whose conjunction they believed must be prevented.

External reality may provide an opportunity for benign modification of such phantasies, or it may lend substance to fears. It may also provide material for the formation of psychic structures that are meant to prevent the recognition of the Oedipus situation. The gradual reclaiming by the patients of projected parts of themselves, in the course of long and difficult analyses, led to the emergence of the idea of a couple who could unite willingly and pleasurably. New difficulties then arose with the eruption of envy and jealousy; these emotions were felt to be unbearable and seemed to become almost pure psychic pain.

I would like to distinguish the problems of these patients from the others referred to in this chapter. I think etiologically the difference lay in the failure to establish a securely based good maternal object before encountering the vicissitudes of the Oedipus complex.

OEDIPAL ILLUSIONS

As described briefly above, oedipal illusions are a developmentally later phenomenon than the primitive wiping out of the parental relationship with delusional developments that I have described in the previous section. When these illusions are paramount, the parental relationship is known but its full significance is evaded, and its nature, which demonstrates the differences between the parental relationship and the parent—child relationship, is not acknowledged. The illusion is felt to protect the individual from the psychic reality of his or her phantasies of the oedipal situation. These I have found, in such cases, to be expectations of an endlessly humiliating exposure to parental triumphalism or a disastrous version of parental intercourse. This latter is perceived either as horrific, sadomasochistic, or murderous intercourse, or as depressive images of a ruined couple in a ruined world. However, whilst such illusions are perpetuated as evasions of the underlying situation, the Oedipus complex cannot be resolved through the normal processes of rivalry and relinquishment.

I think that in normal development such illusions are frequent and transitory, producing cycles of illusionment and disillusionment that are the familiar features of an analysis. In some people, however, the persistence of an organized oedipal illusion prevents the resolution of the complex and in analysis the full development of its transference counterpart.

These illusions are often conscious or almost conscious versions of actual life situations. For example, I heard about a young woman in supervision: she was a musician who gave to her professional relationship with her music teacher the secret significance of preparation for a love affair. Once she was in analysis, her ideas about her analyst were suffused with the same erotic significance and the belief that it would end in marriage.

These wish-fulfilling ideas are often undisclosed in analysis, where they take the form of the patient's belief in a secret understanding between patient and analyst that transcends that formally acknowledged, as Freud points out in his paper "Observations on Transference-Love" (Freud, 1915). The illusory special relationship may take much less conspicuously sexual forms than the example I have quoted, whilst still having an erotized basis.

The transference illusion is felt to protect the patient from what is imagined to be a calamitous transference situation. As such, it poses considerable technical problems. Whilst it persists, all the analyst's communications are interpreted by the patient in the light of the illusional context.

I would like to illustrate the fears defended against by such an illusional construction from the analysis of a male patient. He had originally been a refugee from a foreign country and now worked as a government scientist. He regarded his parents as having lived separate lives, although they shared the same house. It became clear that the reality of their relationship had given some substance to this idea but also that his fixed mental picture was a caricature. It served as the structure for phantasies involving each parent separately, phantasies that were never integrated, and, though mutually contradictory, they remained adjacent to each other, as it were in parallel.

He transferred his picture to the analytic context in a rigidly literal way. He had a slight acquaintance with my wife in his professional context but never brought any thoughts from that context to his ideas of me as his analyst. He developed pictures in his mind of his analyst and of his analyst's wife in entirely separated contexts. Two wishful outcomes of his analysis lay side by side. One was of a permanent partnership with me in which he and I were alone together; the other was my death coinciding with the end of analysis, when he would marry my widow. This formed the basis of a complex psychic organization in which the patient was able to oscillate between such contradictory beliefs without ever giving them much reality, or ever giving them up. Whilst this mode was operating in the analysis, things were always about to happen but never did; emotional experiences were about to occur but never materialized. The consequence for the patient's own mental operations was profound. Despite his considerable intellectual gifts, he was not able to bring things together in his mind, which resulted in learning difficulties as a child and a lack of clarity in his thinking as an adult, which had limited his originality. The consequences for his emotional life were a pervasive sense of unreality and a constant feeling of unfulfillment. There was a quality of nonconsummation in all his relationships and projects in life.

When change did begin to occur in his analysis, it provoked phantasies of great violence. Initially they were confined to the nighttime. They took the form of murderous intercourse between the primal couple, which filled his dreams in many forms, and when they could not be contained within his dreams, they erupted as transitory nighttime hallucinations of a couple who were killing each other.

In contrast to this, the analysis was for a long time an ocean of calm. Calmness was his aim, not fulfillment, and calm detachment was idealized. For a long time this was thought by him to be the aim of analysis and the aspiration of his analyst. Thus he thought his task was to facilitate this in both of us by forever finding agreement. His dreams were enormously informative but were a vehicle for getting rid of his thoughts into me, so that he could relate to my interpretations instead of to his thoughts, and therefore to himself second hand. What his dreams made clear to me was his belief that bringing his parental objects together in his mind would result in explosion and disintegration. When the relationship between us did begin to feel rather different in the sessions, so that we both made more contact and yet were at greater variance, it led to fears of imminent catastrophe.

One form this took was a fear of sudden death. In particular, he had attacks of panic when he thought his heart was about to stop beating. His fearful expectation of violent collision took a concrete form in the emergence of a new fear of driving. Prior to this I had been hearing a lot about "contraflow systems" in his sessions—both in dreams and in reports of daily life. (At that time, some years ago, contraflow traffic systems were a novelty on British motorways and were in the news.) I took them to be a representation of the way my patient had segregated so carefully two different and contradictory streams of thought. I had wondered if their appearance in the analysis indicated that things were coming closer together in his mind. My patient then developed a panicky conviction when driving that unless there was a central barrier on the road, the streams of traffic would crash into each other. It reached such proportions that for a time it stopped him driving. This heralded changes in the transference relationship, which now did develop within it some conflict and opposition. The fear of finding within himself the violence that previously had only appeared in projected forms as violent parental intercourse became prominent for the first time. It is best conveyed by a dream he brought after a weekend break, at a time when weekends were very difficult and full of anxiety:

> He was about to be left alone in a room with a dangerous, wild man by a couple who are going to the theater. This man has always been locked up and restrained—he should be in a straitjacket. The patient is terrified that the man would destroy everything in the room. On his own he will not be able to reason with him. The man begins to speak. Previously, it seemed, he had been a mute. Help comes in the form of a Senior Negotiator from the Ministry (where the patient worked in reality). The Negotiator can speak to the Man, but if the Man realizes that the Negotiator has connections with the law, this will provoke him to even greater fury. (In reality, the Negotiator was concerned with terrorists in prison.)

The patient had many associations to this dream, and they made it clear that there was a situation in the patient's life involving a sense of betrayal by a woman and sexual jealousy that was connected to the dream. They also made clear that the couple went to the "Theater of the Absurd." This, in turn, was associated with a debate he had participated in once as to whether a theatrical performance in a church could include the word *fuck*. It was clear, I thought, that the man who represented that aspect of himself that had been mute and locked up was wild with jealousy. That was the new element, in my patient, in his analysis. The debate as to whether the idea of a "fucking couple" could be allowed in the "church" of the transference was still taking place in his analysis. My patient's dream suggested that he thought it an "absurdly" dangerous venture to admit into his mind phantasies of his analyst, as one of a sexual couple, provoking a violent emotional reaction inside him. I interpreted myself as represented by the Negotiator as well as by the parental couple. The law that would further inflame the wild man was, I think, the law of the Oedipus complex—the law that distinguishes the sexes and the generations, provoking not only jealousy but also envy of the parental couple for their sexual and procreative capacities. My intention in describing briefly some aspects of the analysis of this patient is to illustrate some of the fears and conflicts from which the oedipal illusion was felt to protect the patient.

Summary

The oedipal situation begins with the child's recognition of the parents' relationship. In severe disorders development founders at this point, and the Oedipus complex does not appear in recognizable classical form in analysis. The failure to internalize a recognizable oedipal triangle results in a failure to integrate observation and experience. This was the case in the first patients I described. I suggest that it is a consequence of a prior failure of maternal containment.

In the second part of the chapter I described what I call oedipal illusions as defensive phantasies against the psychic reality of the Oedipus situation, and suggested that if they persist, they prevent the normal "working through" of the Oedipus complex, which is done through sequences of rivalry and relinquishment.

Finally, I would like to clarify my view of the normal development of the Oedipus complex. It begins with the child's recognition of the nature of the parental relationship and the child's phantasies about it. In the Oedipus myth this would be represented by the story of the infant Oedipus abandoned on the hillside by his mother—a tragic version in the child's phantasy of being left to die whilst the parents sleep together. The complex unfolds further in the development of the child's rivalry with one parent for absolute possession of the other. This we see exemplified in the myth by the meeting at the crossroads where Laius bars the way, as if representing the father's obstruction of the child's wish to reenter mother through her genital. This is what I regard as the psychic reality of the Oedipus complex, as are the fears of personal or parental death as imagined consequences.

What I have called oedipal illusions are defensive phantasies meant to occlude these psychic realities. In the myth I see the oedipal illusion as the state in which Oedipus is on the throne with his wife-mother, surrounded by his court, turning a "blind eye," as John Steiner has put it, as to what they already half know but choose to ignore (Steiner, 1985). In this situation, where illusion reigns supreme, curiosity is felt to spell disaster. In the phantasied tragic version of the Oedipus complex the discovery of the oedipal triangle is felt to be the death of the couple: the nursing couple or the parental couple. In this phantasy the arrival of the notion of a third always murders the dyadic relationship.

I think this idea is entertained by all of us at some time, for some it appears to remain a conviction, and when it does it leads to serious psychopathology. I have suggested that it is through mourning for this lost exclusive relationship that it can be realized that the oedipal triangle does not spell the death of a relationship, but only the death of an idea of a relationship.

REFERENCES

Bion, W. R. (1956), Development of schizophrenic thought. In: *Second Thoughts*. London: Heinemann, 1967.
——— (1959), Attacks on linking. In: *Second Thoughts*. London: Heinemann, 1967, pp. 93–109.
Britton, R. S. (1985), The Oedipus complex and the depressive position. *Sigmund Freud House Bull.*, 9:7–12.
Freud, S. (1892–1897), Extracts from the Fliess papers. *Standard Edition*, 1:173–280. London: Hogarth Press, 1966.
——— (1915), Observations on transference-love (Further recommendations on the technique of psycho-analysis, III). *Standard Edition*, 12:157–171. London: Hogarth Press, 1958.
——— (1924a), The dissolution of the Oedipus complex. *Standard Edition*, 19:171–179. London: Hogarth Press, 1961.
——— (1924b), The loss of reality in neurosis and psychosis. *Standard Edition*, 19:181-187. London: Hogarth Press, 1961.
Klein, M. (1926), The psychological principles of early analysis. In: *Writings*, Vol. 1. London: Hogarth Press, 1975, pp. 128–138.
——— (1928), Early stages of the Oedipus conflict. In: *Writings*, Vol. 1. London: Hogarth Press, 1975, pp. 186–198.
——— (1946), Notes on some schizoid mechanisms. In: *Writings*, Vol. 3. London: Hogarth Press, 1975, pp. 1–24.
Rey, J. H. (1979), Schizoid phenomena in the borderline. In: *Advances in the Psychotherapy of the Borderline Patient*, ed. J. LeBoit & A. Capponi. New York: Jason Aronson, pp. 449–484.
Steiner, J. (1985), Turning a blind eye: The cover up for Oedipus. *Internat. Rev. Psychoanal.*, 12:161–172.

EDITOR'S INTRODUCTION TO
OBSESSIONAL CERTAINTY VERSUS
OBSESSIONAL DOUBT: FROM 2 TO 3

In this essay, Ignês Sodré provides an instructive contemporary Kleinian exposition of how oedipal conflict is central to the obsessional phenomena of controlling compulsiveness (certainty) and tormenting obsessions (doubt). Along with these she considers such obsessional correlates as fear of contamination, word magic, and phantasies of imprisonment. The dynamic context includes two sets of factors. On the one hand, there is ambivalence, anxiety, and guilt over the triangularity of oedipal relationships, accompanied by heavy reliance on the defenses of isolation and undoing. On the other hand, there is a desperate clinging to the dyadic relatedness characteristic of the paranoid–schizoid position. The subtitle "From 2 to 3" refers to the progression from the dyadic to the triangular.

Sodré argues that compulsive certainty is the paramount need when the regressive defenses against triangularity are fully in place. In contrast, painful doubting may ensue upon any decrease in the stability of this defensive organization. At first, the reader is shown how these ideas fit the material Freud (1909) presented in his analysis of the Rat Man's doubting. There follow two contrasting case examples, one of certainty and one of doubting. Her complex discussion of these two cases covers many important factors, and it is particularly helpful in understanding some of the vicissitudes of the analytic process itself. For example, as we have already seen in previous chapters, when

patients begin to progress in analysis, they must make the difficult transition from the paranoid–schizoid to the depressive
position. In effecting this change they find that their familiar
defenses are no longer as effective as they once were, whereupon
those who are so disposed intensify their obsessionality; in chapter 12, we shall see how those with manic inclinations intensify
their manic reparativeness under these same conditions.

   Drawing on Freud's and Bion's analysis of words, thoughts,
and thinking, and their relation to other mental operations,
Sodré makes much use of the obsessive–compulsive concrete
experience of words as things with their own powers and dangerous potential. She also draws extensively on the general
Kleinian expectation that the obsessional patient may experience the analyst's words and interpretations as a third party's
forcible intrusions into the psychoanalytic situation. It has already been pointed out by Dr. Britton in chapter 10 that the third
party in this instance is the analyst's capacity for independent
thought, the implication being that the patient has split off the
analyst's mind from the analyst's person. The analyst's interpretations also demonstrate that he or she is different from the
patient, thereby further disrupting the patient's dyadic phantasy with its subtle or obvious implications of unity through
sameness. Because this third presence is an unwelcome intruder
and as such always a painful reminder of the parents' sexual
union, steps must be taken to get rid of it. For similar reasons,
difference is intolerable so that it too must be eliminated. Consequently the patient may, to give but one example, regularly
modify interpretations in subtle ways that eliminate their significance. This observation throws needed light on the frequent
analytic phenomenon of patients altering interpretations to fit
in with their established psychic organizations. This form of
subversion acts as a powerful defense against change of any sort.

   In its most general aspect, this essay provides illuminating
examples of how mental operations can be impaired when they

get caught up in the complex interplay of destructive and self-protective unconscious phantasies. As we are seeing repeatedly throughout these essays that pay such close attention to the analysis of countertransference, is that impairment of ego functioning can be visited on the analyst by means of certain projective identifications. Sodré's essay can help analysts maintain their equilibrium in the face of assaults not only on their interpretations but on their ego functions; for it helps keep in focus the patient's fright, pain, and heightened defensiveness when they are making their individual transitions toward maturity.

REFERENCES

Freud, S. (1909), Notes upon a case of obsessional neurosis. *Standard Edition*, 10:151–249. London: Hogarth Press, 1955.

11
OBSESSIONAL CERTAINTY VERSUS OBSESSIONAL DOUBT: FROM 2 TO 3

IGNÊS SODRÉ

In all obsessional states of mind there is a predominance of a tormenting, compulsive quality of thinking; but the obsessional need to hold on to certainty, and the torments of obsessional doubt, are extremely different, in fact diametrically opposed, states. One is dominated by inflexibility, rigidity, immobility. It is as if one tyrannical thought is constantly keeping out all other points of view; doubt is forbidden. In the other, dominated by constant oscillations, it is as if the mind is constantly thrown from side to side by opposing thoughts: no certainty can be achieved.

In this paper, I will suggest that obsessional defenses that involve rigid adherence to sameness, with the need for rituals against contamination and disorder, belong to a schizoid way of functioning, in which splitting mechanisms are used not only against the experience of ambivalence, but also for the preservation of an exclusively two-person relationship with the object. Triangularity represents the major threat; new ideas, different points of view, anything that disturbs the equilibrium of this fixed, mutually interdependent couple is experienced as a "third" intruder, that must be immediately got rid of.

When tormenting obsessional doubt predominates, on the other hand, the underlying conflict is not only due to ambivalence and to the difficulty of making a choice between objects, but also to the presence in the patient's mind of the parental couple with whom he is, unconsciously, excessively involved. The triangular situation is not avoided. On the contrary, it is omnipresent, to the extent that it seems impossible to establish a peaceful, undisturbed coupling of any sort. Tormenting doubt, therefore, seems to belong to a state where oedipal conflicts are extremely intense and seemingly unresolvable. (I do not wish to imply that these two states cannot exist in the same individual, at different stages. I am taking for granted that different modes, more or less regressed, more neurotic or predominantly psychotic, can be observed at different points. But, for the sake of clarity, I will illustrate them with clinical material from two very different individuals.)

Freud's discovery of the centrality of the Oedipus complex, further explored by Klein, became a central point in Bion's theory of thinking. Bion (1959) connected disturbances in thought processes to unconscious phantasies of attacking the link between the parents in intercourse.

Like Bion, Money-Kyrle (1968) believed that human beings are innately predisposed to discover the truth about parental sexuality, but that emotional obstacles create "unconscious misconceptions," misrepresentations of the primal scene aiming at evading the full experience of the oedipal situation. Even in individuals who do not suffer from severe disturbances, he says, "while part of the developing personality does learn to understand the facts of life, suffers the pains of an Oedipus complex, discards it from guilt, becomes reconciled to the parental relation, internalizes it and achieves maturity, other parts remain ignorant and retarded" (p. 693).

Britton (1989) has described two types of disturbance in relation to the oedipal situation. In the first one, "the Oedipus situation appears in analysis only in a primitive form and is not immediately recognizable as the classical Oedipus complex." In the second, less severe disorder, "it is the final relinquishment of the Oedipal objects that is evaded." This evasion is made possible by the creation of a defensive, illusory oedipal configuration which denies "the psychic reality of the parental relationship" (p. 85). In my view, the oedipal illusion in obsessional doubt is a defense against the certainty of exclusion from the parental intercourse: the illusion that it is possible to omnipotently intrude, disrupt, and in this way, participate in it.

In obsessional states, thoughts are felt to be concrete and threaten to be out of control. Obsessional thinking masquerades as real thinking, but in fact consists of a series of mental actions, aimed at controlling bad, disturbing, intrusive things, called thoughts or ideas, that occupy the mind.

In "A Theory of Thinking" (1962) Bion states: "Thinking has to be called into existence to cope with thoughts." In psychotic states, "What should be a thought . . . becomes a bad object, indistinguishable from a thing-in-itself, fit only for evacuation" (p. 180). I am suggesting that in severe obsessional states, even though the individual is not psychotic, and maintains some contact with reality, a part of the personality gets involved in such powerful defensive maneuvers that a form of thought disorder occurs, in which *thinking becomes ineffectual in relation to thoughts.*

Freud's famous obsessional neurotic, the Rat Man, presents us with a striking example of obsessional thinking: The Rat Man tells Freud that he heard from "the cruel Captain" a story about a horrible torture: a pot containing rats was inverted onto a criminal's buttocks, and the rats would then burrow their way into the person's anus. The patient's "great obsessional fear" takes over at this point, as he has the horrible thought that the rat torture will happen to his two love objects, his father and "the lady"; he has both thoughts "simultaneously," which I think implies that the rats attack the parents together, that is, in intercourse. This triangularity becomes even more explicit in the episode that precipitates the onset of the full-blown obsessional neurosis.

The cruel captain tells the Rat Man that Lieutenant A paid the post office girl the money he (the patient) owed her for the delivery of his prince nez; and even though the Rat Man knew this to be a mistake (he knew the girl had paid for it herself), he immediately abandons what he knows to be the true version of events, and adopts the captain's version. This new, false version changes a dyadic relationship (Rat Man/girl) into a triadic one (Rat Man/Lieutenant A/girl). Paying A back now becomes the central point of his tormenting situation: the rat torture will happen to his father and "the lady" if he does not pay the money to A.

From this point onwards he is totally in the grip of obsessional thinking. The phantasy is of attacking sadistically, and also of excitedly participating in the parents' intercourse through the omnipotence of his thoughts. On the other hand, the words of the cruel captain (who clearly represents a sadistic father) intrude violently into his mind (against his will, as it were, through the backside of his mind), and become these concrete, ratlike thoughts which torture him. Against rat thoughts, rational thinking is powerless; only obsessional rituals can be used to try to control these torturer thoughts. So, whilst the phantasy is of a sadistic attack that destroys the link between the parents, and corrupts their intercourse, a sadistic attack is being perpetrated by rat thoughts in his mind, attacking his thinking process so that mental links are destroyed. Ultimately, the Rat Man's thinking is the real victim of the rat torture. Thinking is attacked to destroy the knowledge, the absolute certainty, that the parents' intercourse excludes him.

OBSESSIONAL CERTAINTY: MR. A

Mr. A came to analysis suffering from depression and acute anxiety states dominated by fear of contamination along with obsessional rituals to control this. He felt very fragile and sometimes depersonalized or fragmented, and welcomed the psychoanalytic relationship as something to hold him together: a safe place to be in. As a child, Mr. A suffered considerable emotional neglect, which included long periods of separation from his mother, even when he was a small infant.

An immediate idealization of the analyst and of the relationship with her took place, and was very persistent; ambivalence was kept out by the use of splitting mechanisms, with the constant projection of all negative aspects onto the external world. This idealization was a rigid defense to keep the two of us together and exclude any possibility of there being a third. The third was often felt to be not an actual rival, but an intrusive, disturbing, insight-producing thought.

In the sessions, interpretations had to be felt to match the associations perfectly, and new associations to match the interpretations, like in a domino game. This created for the patient a comforting situation in which no further different thinking could exist (disturbing aspects of the interpretation were, unconsciously, subtly modified to become something that could be known).

I will now bring a brief example from the time when things were beginning to change; moments of doubt were appearing, moments when the analytic relationship seemed less than ideal, and the idea of separating could, for an instant, be conceived of.

In a session where I was taking up his tenacious holding on to a "certainty" of being the "favorite," so that nothing and nobody else seemed to be of any importance, he commented that the analytic situation constantly feeds this idea, since his only experience here is that he has my absolute attention. (He had no conscious experience whatsoever of jealousy of other patients.)

In the next session, he started by telling me the following dream:

I was in a flat belonging to an architect or interior designer—he wanted me to stay in the flat, not to go out at all, so the flat wouldn't be burgled. I wanted to go to a meeting somewhere else, but couldn't because I had to guard this flat. The flat was completely empty, completely bare, nothing inside it at all.

I said, "Isn't it interesting that you had to guard the flat from burglars even though there was nothing at all that they could steal?" He said: "*This* flat (my consulting room) was burgled and there was nothing they could steal!" (at the time when the consulting room had been broken into he had joked about the burglar coming in and finding nothing that could possibly interest him).

He said that he didn't remember why I had made such a point of his certainty of being my favorite in the previous session. He explained that although his brother had at some point become his mother's favorite, that when he was small he was definitely her favorite child. It was only much later, when he "started attacking her for her absences" that he became less favored. He was always his nanny's favorite, and when she left she just disappeared—he had no knowledge of her going to work for another family, and therefore he couldn't have been jealous of the little girl she went to look after.

I think he makes it clear that the aspect of the analyst experienced as someone who looks after somebody else "just disappears," is canceled out of his mind. The knowledge of somebody looking after somebody else (a triangular relationship in which he is the left out one), would create the dreaded situation in which he would "attack me for my absences," and the illusion of being the favorite would be destroyed, creating an unbearable state of mind.

I commented on his phantasy of being my guardian, because *I* need him to protect *me* from intruders, like from any thought that might disturb this relationship and rob it of his conviction of perfection. Somewhere in his mind he pictures this as an empty flat; but this must be kept secret.

He reacted immediately by saying that he had been invited to a party, and had wanted to go to it, but now he discovered that the party would take place in a small flat with a small garden; he realized now that it would be very full of people and full of smoke. He was glad he found out that this would be a really horrible party. Now he had decided not to go at all.

In the first instance he was saying, as he said in the dream, that he had wanted to move away from this "guardian" position in which I put him and go to a meeting, but now he realized that this was a mistake: it was much better for him to remain in his usual position in the analytic relationship. I think at this point he was trying to reassure *me* that he had no intention of ever leaving.

What seems to have happened is that the interpretation about the "favorite" position, given in the previous session, was felt as a "burglar" (as insight about this situation threatened to rob him of the illusion of an ideal "two"). This intruder was pushed out by the reestablishment of a preferable version of the past; but, more importantly perhaps, the thought that the analytic situation fostered the maintenance of this phantasy facilitates the projection into the analyst of the wish for him to be the "guardian." In the "empty flat" dream, it was the analyst who now feared insight, and who wished to be idealized.

But I think he was also saying that when I invited him to meet some other version of the analysis—invited him to be in contact with the part of him that knows that he idealizes himself as a guardian of an empty flat—he then presented me with what he feared were the inevitable consequences of giving up this illusion. He would find himself in an absolutely unbearable state of mind, with so many rivals that there would be no place for him; and, more internally, crowded with awful thoughts, confused, chaotic; the state which gave rise to his terror of contamination and disorder.

When I went away he placed himself in the guardian position, which made the unfaithful nanny-with-the-other-child aspect of me disappear forever. When he was firmly ensconced inside, holding onto the illusion that he can be, and that I want him to be, permanently there, everything else was irrelevant. On one level the burglars represented a very real threat as rivals; but, more importantly, they represented a more insightful part of him that knew that the guardian story was an illusion. As such, they would both reveal the emptiness of the idealized relationship, but also destroy any good contact with me as mother (who would then be "attacked for her absences," and turn against him). If he does not see me when I am not with him, it is not because I am away with somebody else, but because he is permanently inside. The "certainty" of the two of us together is a powerful illusion, which almost totally obliterates the reality (internal and external) of a "third."

OBSESSIONAL DOUBT: MR. B

Mr. B came to analysis following the breakdown of his marriage, suffering from depression, quick changes of mood, and, especially, a tremendous difficulty in taking decisions. He had close relationships with his parents and a very rivalrous relationship with his younger brother. I think his mother found it particularly difficult to deal with his very acute jealousy when his brother was born. Mr. B felt that the difficulties in his marriage, which seemed to have increased considerably at the time of the birth of his first child, were partly connected to this childhood situation.

Soon after he started his analysis, he had to make serious decisions about his work situation, which were important in their own right but also in some ways connected to decisions concerning his family life. The sessions at that time were mostly taken up with tormenting obsessional thinking. He would carefully put a case for a particular decision, and then, after succeeding in convincing his analyst that he had finally arrived at a sensible plan, he would suddenly feel this was wrong and proceed to argue convincingly for the other point of view. Mr. B felt tormented by this, and felt it had a crippling effect on his life.

At this time he often dreamed of situations where he was stuck, imprisoned, unable to escape. He dreamed, for instance, of being in an underground system of tunnels, like a maze; or of being stuck in a swamp. Then, one day, he dreamed of being on a horribly muddy, sticky, tortuous road, in a car with his mother; it was very frightening as they seemed to be sliding toward a precipice. Suddenly he said, "I don't have to be here!" and woke up, feeling relieved.

This dream followed a lot of work on the reason why this internal situation had such a hold on him. At its center was the idea that any decision represented a loss, and that this loss was unbearable, bringing with it sadness and rage. Giving up his early relationship with his mother, a situation inevitably bringing with it the need to mourn, was vividly colored by intense jealousy, of mother and father together, and also of mother and baby brother. Jealous attacks on the couple were instantly followed by intensely persecuting guilt. As soon as he felt he had become coupled with his object, he felt compelled to renounce it in favor of whoever in his mind was being excluded, and therefore felt to be dangerously jealous and envious but also to be suffering intense pain. Each time he reached a decision, he felt immediately that, able for a moment to think for himself and to be free from his tormenting conflict, he had now moved away from mother and left her to father or brother. His relief at achieving a sense of mental freedom and space was followed immediately by the idea that the analyst, liberated from the tormenting situation, was also now able to separate, think for herself. He resented the fact that the analyst was now "out of it," and he would then throw himself (and me, of course, too!) into the doubting situation again. Gradually it became clear to me that each time we arrived at a "certainty," this was felt as a "two" that was immediately attacked by a "third" who couldn't bear it.

This process was of course mostly unconscious, and was unraveled very slowly. The conscious experience was that he was a passive victim of his thoughts. But gradually the patient became aware that the obsessional doubt was a "nasty thing," a jealous, envious part of himself that would viciously attack him whenever a good link was made—with the analyst, other people, or within himself.

Following an interpretation which was helpful, Mr. B felt that he could now see more clearly into a situation in which he had been feeling rather stuck. He briefly referred to a useful change of point of view; and after a pause told me that the dinner party he had been so anxious about had in fact worked very well. He and his new girl friend Anna had invited some friends for dinner at his house; she had cooked a very nice meal, he had helped her. He had been anxious about his friends meeting her friends and not liking them, but in fact everybody got on quite well. But there was one very difficult moment. During the meal, Anna's brother asked him, "Was the kitchen like this when you moved in, or did you have to do a lot of work in it?" When he first moved into the house, he and his ex-wife, Tessa, had redecorated the kitchen together; this made him feel it was impossible for him to answer the question. If he answered, "*We* have done the work," Anna would have felt excluded and jealous; whereas if he answered "*I* have done the work" he would have been attacking Tessa in his mind. It was a very uncomfortable moment, and he just remained silent, feeling tortured.

I think it is clear that at that moment Mr. B's thoughts were invaded by a tormenting triangular situation. The word "*We*" became unutterable because it evoked "three" (Tessa and himself together, excluding Anna) as did the word *I* (Anna and him together, excluding Tessa). He felt paralyzed by doubt, as whatever he said would be an attack on someone. In the session, relief at feeling "unstuck," and a sense of greater integration, led to being separate ("I"), forming a new couple ("We"), and then a terribly jealous "third" rushed in; the result was that for a moment he cannot think or speak.

The point I am making is that the passive experience of being caught up in tormenting indecision has as its unconscious motivation a desperate holding onto an archaic situation in which the oedipal conflict is continually being played out in its different versions—the characters taking different positions in relation to each other—and can never be finally worked through. So when he moves out of the excluded position into being in a couple, the primitive superego in all its sadism attacks the self which is felt as triumphing over the rival, now excluded, and persecutory guilt takes over, followed immediately by attempts at reparation in the form of obsessional undoing. (The primitive superego is invested with the hatred of a desperately jealous little child attacking the "cruel" parents for doing this terribly "immoral" thing: having sexual intercourse which excludes him.)

The patient is therefore constantly tying himself to his primitive objects, unable to move in either direction, as if stuck forever under the parents' bed. Consciously he feels imprisoned by his tormenting thoughts; unconsciously he repeats over and over again the same tormenting situation.

I will now report some detailed material to illustrate the conflicts I have described:

Following a Christmas break, the patient arrived for his Monday session in a depressed mood; he was silent a lot of the time, and complained that everything seemed meaningless. In the following sessions it emerged that he had had quite a nice holiday with his new girl friend; he had enjoyed his visit to his parents, though his fear of his brother's envy of his new relationship was a problem. As the work proceeded, it became clear that the mood in the beginning of the week was connected to his hurt and resentment about being left by the analyst, and the "mean-inglessness" of the analysis was a consequence of having (uncon-sciously) felt he had damaged his relationship with her. On the Friday session he brought the following dream:

> He was in Anna's parents' house; the living room had a carpet that looked like crushed wheat. The whole family was there, watching television. He dropped coffee on the carpet, and felt worried about it. Nobody else seemed interested in his problem. This made him anxious; but he cleaned the stain with a tissue and it seemed all right. Then he lifted the carpet and discovered that underneath it there was another one: a very beautiful old white silk Persian rug, which, to his horror, was badly stained. Anna's mother was angry. He felt guilty and sad. A baby boy appeared; he picked him up, started talking and playing with him. Looking after the baby seemed to make the situation better.

I will not discuss the associations to this dream in detail; but one important thing he said was that he had discussed with his girl friend the possibility of their having a baby. He had thought, for the first time, that his mother would be delighted if this happened.

I think the dream illustrates what happened in his mind dur-ing the Christmas break, and during this first week. He felt that when "nobody is interested in his problem," when I was away with my family, looking away from him, he had no help with his an-ger, his jealousy, his wish to make a mess. This led to a more cata-strophic situation in which he felt that the valuable aspect of the analysis was spoiled. Later in the week, contact with depressive pain and sorrow and the understanding of the internal situation made it possible to bring this dream, in which holding a baby symbolizes his regained capacity to hold his baby self, as he felt during the week held by the analyst, and not neglected like in the break. In the session, this appeared very movingly as his wish to have another child, now felt also as reparative to his mother.

He arrived for a session in the following week and started talking immediately, very excitedly, about a strange coincidence that had happened the previous night. He went to a dinner party at the house of his friend Martin and, "You will never believe what happened! Something incredible!" he exclaimed. Martin's parents had lent him a very beautiful Persian carpet, made of cream silk, *just like the one in his dream!* Martin had put it in the entrance hall, which he thought was the safest place; but somebody had dropped a bottle of wine on it, and stained it. It was amazing: what happened in last week's dream had happened, almost identically, at the party. He seemed excited, but also rather alarmed, at the idea that his thoughts were omnipotent—the dream might have produced the accident, or have predicted it; but, of course, he knew this was nonsense.

I commented on his mood, very excited, but also anxious, about this "amazing" event, and said I thought he was very involved with feeling that what he was saying must be having a tremendous impact on me. He then told me that in fact he had been feeling awful since the party, and had hardly slept at all thinking of something terrible he had said. To start with he had not felt at all shy; on the contrary, he felt "bubbly," and talked a lot. Then this terrible thing happened, so embarrassing that he can hardly bring himself to tell me. The conversation was about worms; everybody seemed to be talking very excitedly about worms, about how they get into your inside, what they do inside you. It was *really* horrible, worms are the most disgusting thing in the world. Then the conversation changed; one of the guests, clearly an intellectual, said he worked in a library. He said jokingly, to this man, "So you are a bookworm!" and immediately felt *so* terrible; he had meant it to be a joke but it wasn't at all funny, it sounded aggressive and disgusting. From that moment the party was a nightmare. He kept thinking that everybody now hated and despised him; at night he could not sleep, trying to work out endless plans and tactics of how to change the picture these friends now have of him in their minds.

He had become fully involved again in tormenting obsessional doubt; his shame, his pain at having done something irreparably bad was very present in the session.

The bizarre coincidence of the dream and the event at the party precipitated him into a pathological way of functioning, dominated by a phantasy of having omnipotent thoughts that can "worm" their way into my mind to excite me. The horrible thoughts about the worms indicated that there was a lot of anxiety around in the phantasy of getting inside. (Later in the session he remembered having one of his "old" dreams, about being a prisoner in an underground prison). When he used the word *bookworm*, he suddenly became aware of the spoiling nature of his intrusiveness. I think this was reenacted in the session, as he seemed to have experienced my interpretation both as putting him more in touch with his anxiety but also as "telling him" he was a worm. The supposed "attack" on the man at the party unconsciously represented the moment of change from a state of manic excitement in which, in his phantasy, I joined him, into one of anxiety and shame. He was thrown back into the obsessional torment, trying to find a way of undoing the effect of his "worming his way in." He now felt unloved and deserving only of contempt.

Some discussion followed which led to an understanding of this situation. Mr. B's associations centered again around the loss of something important, and being left out of a "wedding." Near the end of the session, he remembered the following dream:

> The dream took place on something like a map, which was also a real place: something that does not make sense realistically. He was on the extreme north of Norway, climbing a very high mountain. The main feeling was of being horribly cold. (He added that I knew how much he hated being cold.) He could see the whole

map of the world, specially the other side, North America and
South America.

He commented that he knew that I came from the south of
South America: a warm place, and as far as possible from north
Norway. There was a conversation at the dinner party yesterday
where people were discussing the fact that North Americans call
themselves "Americans," very arrogantly, because the others are
left with no names. He remembered that Tessa and her new boy-
friend may move to North America to live; this made him very
jealous. And what about the poor people of South America, what
could they call themselves? At the dinner party he was conscious
of being English and wishing he had been born in a more exotic place, and feeling very critical of the North Americans.

I think, in broad lines, this means: North America and South
America represent the huge parents linked together; in his excitement and fear of the omnipotence of his thoughts (his dream
had come true, and the beautiful carpet belonging to the parents had now really been damaged by a careless messy child),
he felt he could worm his way into their intercourse, as he felt
during the carpet event at the party—that I would be really excited by him telling this to me. In the dream, he invested the
father North America with his own possessiveness and omnipotence, so he was seen as the "arrogant" North American. The
intercourse between the parents was now experienced as an arrogant taking over of mother to the extent that she lost her
identity (what could the poor South Americans call themselves?).
He was afraid that my identity as the analyst who was able to help
him with the carpet dream was undermined by the excited him
who uses the carpet dream coincidence to have a powerful effect on my state of mind. This dream may be seen as a picture
of the world after this had taken place; the parents, and specially
the South America mother, are now terribly far away, like the
friends at the dinner party. They now dislike and look down on

their child, who is consequently out in the cold. Depth and tri-dimensionality have disappeared: a graphic description of the states of meaninglessness and superficiality which result from the aggressive projective identification. The obsessional, how can he undo the past, how can he modify the horrible picture they (the analyst, standing for the disapproving parents) have in their minds, represent attempts at reparation through using the same primitive mechanisms—undoing, controlling, worming his way again into my mind.

At the point in the session where he remembered this dream, his anxieties had been worked through enough so that the pathological methods of dealing with the painful situation could be given up. Realization of the damage done to his internal objects, of the consequent loss of their love, and of the loss of depth, were now possible. The apparently unbridgeable distance between South America and Norway in fact grew shorter as the work in the session proceeded; remembering the two-dimensional dream and experiencing the pain of loss was of course part of the process of recovering real three-dimensionality.

To conclude: When powerful defense mechanisms are used to avoid facing some aspect of the oedipal situation, some disturbance in the thought processes may occur. In this way, the capacity to preserve a free mental space where meaningful thinking can develop depends to some degree on the capacity to bear the pain of separation from the internal parents, thus allowing them, in phantasy, the freedom to relate to each other. I have described two situations in which thinking is impaired by an excessive use of obsessional mechanisms. A differentiation has been made between two modes of obsessional thinking, which I think belong to two different developmental stages; one in which the oedipal situation is avoided at all costs, and thoughts connected to it forbidden; in the second, more at the threshold of the depressive position, the oedipal situation is omnipresent, and thoughts constantly engage in rivalrous battles with each other, as if they were no longer thoughts about objects, or thoughts representing objects, but the objects themselves.

REFERENCES

Bion, W. R. (1959), Attacks on linking. *Internat. J. Psycho-Anal.*, 40:308–315.
———— (1962), A theory of thinking. *Internat. J. Psycho-Anal.*, 43:306–310.
Britton, R. (1989), The missing link: Parental sexuality in the Oedipus complex. In: *The Oedipus Complex Today*, ed. J. Steiner. London: Karnac Books.
Freud, S. (1909), Notes upon a case of obsessional neurosis. *Standard Edition*, 10:151–249. London: Hogarth Press, 1955.
Money-Kyrle, R. (1968), On cognitive development. *Internat. J. Psycho-Anal.*, 49:691–698.

EDITOR'S INTRODUCTION TO
MANIC REPARATION

For the most part Hanna Segal deals in this essay with an especially difficult and not at all rare clinical problem, namely, how
to bring pathological manic reparativeness into the treatment
so that it can be analyzed. She begins with two short discussions
of the phenomenon of reparation: (1) reparation proper, which
is understood to be plainly rational, realistic, and constructive;
and (2) the manic form of reparation that appears when de-
compensation seems to threaten the defenses of men and
women who have developed a more or less manic organization
of the personality. Dr. Segal presents a brief case illustration of
this disturbed state.

She then turns her full and acute attention to the difficult
problem of those patients who resort defensively to manic
reparation at the point of analytically fostered emergence from
embeddedness in the paranoid–schizoid position. This transition into separation, guilt, and responsibility is an exceptionally
difficult one, as we have just seen in a number of the preceding
chapters and as will be plain in a number of those that follow.
The present context is that of a patient who, in order to defend
against the feelings of guilt over having enviously destroyed good
objects in the inner world, adopts a superior, helpful, generous,
enthusiastic, optimistic, imperturbable posture. To succeed in
this attempt the patient relies on intensive use of his projective
defenses. This defensive strategy can only lead to pseudore-
parativeness, as, for example, by giving with an empty hand,
helping in an obstructive way, rescuing others who not only need

no help but who, in the patient's omnipotent phantasies, are being diminished into inferior objects who stand very much in need of rescue. In short, the show of reparativeness is unconvincing, and it is felt by others to be hostile, burdensome, and destructive.

All of which becomes apparent in the transference and countertransference, which the analyst attempts to interpret along the lines of the preceding formulations. At hand for this purpose are revealing dreams, unstable enthusiasms, blatantly projective creation of villains, actings out of various kinds, and sustained verbal attacks on genuine analytic work. As Segal presents material from the analysis of this defensively manic patient, she demonstrates how, in the transference, one may track the transition from the more severe aspects of manic reparativeness toward a workable depressive position. Her astute clinical grasp of implicit references to the transference is a model of interpreting here-and-now material in a way that brings one in touch with the deepest layers of the personality.

12
MANIC REPARATION

HANNA SEGAL

I propose to discuss in this paper some problems connected with the use of manic reparation as a defense against insight.

Reparation proper, in the definition of Melanie Klein, arises out of feelings of loss and guilt experienced in the depressive position. Reparation is based on the love for the object and the wish to restore and regain it. The reparative drives contribute to the development of the ego and the object relationships; they cannot be considered as a defense since reparation does not aim at denying psychic reality but is an endeavor—realistic in psychic terms—to resolve depressive anxiety and guilt.

Manic trends in reparation, on the other hand, aim at denying guilt and responsibility and are based on an omnipotent control of the object. The defense against anxiety and guilt is paramount and love and concern for the object—the hallmark of genuine reparation—are relatively weak.

As I have encountered it, there are two types of patients in whom manic reparation presents a particular problem. To the first type belongs the patient whose whole life structure seems to depend on a manic defense system with manic reparation as its most constant characteristic. Very frequently, breaches in the defense appear in midlife crisis. What follows is a fairly typical example of how a case history may present itself.

The patient was in his late thirties. He had a great deal of drive and ambition and was a successful doctor devoted to his patients. The profession is characteristic (helping the sick). He came to the analysis suffering from a gastric ulcer, feelings of inability to cope, and depression, a depression which was more paranoid than appeared at first sight. The symptom he presented was his wife. According to him, she was withdrawn and cold, partially frigid, and drove him to distraction. It soon became clear that an important aspect of his relationship with his wife had to do with her illness. He was aware of her difficulties when he married her but convinced that his relationship to her, basically his sexuality, would cure her. Gradually, her lack of response undermined his confidence, and he began to hate her and to experience paranoid rages at her, sometimes quite murderous. He felt that she was giving him nothing, exploiting him, frustrating him, and robbing him. The analysis revealed quite clearly that what he felt so robbed of was his phantasy of an imaginary, omnipotent, curative penis. One of his earliest memories of childhood was of a little potato patch on his father's farm; he was convinced that this was the source of food for the whole family. As an adult, he recognized it to be a phantasy, but for quite a few years he maintained in the analysis that he was, as a little boy, the one who helped his mother do all the housework. He believed this to be a reality even in his adult life until, while in analysis, he suddenly realized that at the age at which he supposedly did this, 2½ to about age 4, he could not possibly have done any actual work for her and that, in fact, this was the way in which mother kept him busy and happy.

When the patient was about 7 and a sibling was born, he was sent away for more than a year to an aunt. There he was quite happy and did not seem to miss his home. Far from admitting any feelings of rejection, he felt himself very wanted and needed. His aunt was childless and a widow, and he thought he was sent to her to relieve her loneliness. Here again, he was the provider.

His leading memory of that phase of his life was how he got up at the crack of dawn to collect the milk for his aunt. He presented a lot of material that looked like an idealization of breasts. He saw himself as a great lover of women and particularly of breasts. It was the breast in a woman that attracted him most. He often complained that he vested all his interest in the maternal breast and it let him down. One day, in associating to a dream, he had a phantasy of an empty breast which he was filling with his tongue. The experience was lovely. This phantasy was the basis of all his relationships to women. The ideal breast for him was an empty breast, which he, the baby was feeding with his tongue and later with his penis, urine, and semen. If, in such a position, the idealization of the magic powers of his tongue or his penis failed, he faced the breast as a vengeful abyss. As a young man he could maintain this position up to a point. He was the benevolent physician—father, husband, provider. He was never exposed to envy, jealousy, rage or deprivation. Bad feelings were projected into the objects who depended on him and denied in them, for he felt he could satisfy them all.

Around middle age, his idealization of himself as the provider began to collapse, and persecution made its appearance. Slowly, it dawned on him that his siblings resented him because he got the best of the parental inheritance; the same was true of his colleagues whom he thought envied him because of his rapid promotion. Most of all, his wife did not respond to his ministrations. She was experienced by him as this abyss of the empty breast defying his claims of the magic curative powers of his penis. Another internal abyss was opening right in his very stomach (his ulcer). He was bewildered. Here he was, so good to patients, wife, children—all to no avail.

Patients of this kind do not usually come into analysis unless the defenses are already breaking down. I think this is so even if the apparent reason for starting an analysis is professional, for instance, becoming a candidate. The fact that the defense is breaking down, or on the point of breaking down, makes the task of the analyst easier, even though the patient will battle desperately to reestablish the defense. The patient I have referred to openly longed to be the way he was 10 or 20 years ago. The cry was "But it worked, why doesn't it work now?"

I think a more difficult technical problem arises when the manic reparation emerges in the analysis partly as a result of an improvement which allows the patient to start emerging from the paranoid–schizoid position, and then it is apt to be organized into a formidable defense against any further progress. A central European woman, who started analysis also in her middle thirties, had been suffering for a long time from a state of disintegration, fragmentation of personality, hypochondriasis, and very vague and diffuse paranoia.

Gradually, this stage of diffusion and disorganization lessened; the patient became more coherent. She could go back to work as a nursery teacher (another helping profession, you will notice) and even started working for a higher qualification. She became more aware of her feelings and relationships, and some genuine depressive feelings began to emerge. These were immediately counteracted by a flurry of activities, felt by her as reparative, taking the form of acting out, and interfering with any further development of insight. This had appeared intermittently earlier in her analysis as depressive anxieties were approached, but a new phase of her analysis started when manic reparative activities seemed to bring her analysis to a standstill. This phase was ushered in by a dream. She was very excited because a Mr. X from abroad, who had certain contacts in the psychiatric world, was going to visit her and her husband. The following week, her brother was also visiting them in London. In her dream, she had lots of visitors in her kitchen; men, women, and children. She was feeding them pink cakes and chocolate cakes. She felt very good and very excited. In the corner of the kitchen, there was a paper bag of sugar with very little sugar left and that spilled on the floor. Her associations were first to the exciting visits of Mr. X and her brother. When I drew her attention to the bag of sugar toward the end of the session she remembered that the bag was exactly like the one used by her mother. The meaning of the dream was that she was giving an exciting sexual and anal meal to all, while her mother's breasts, empty and discarded, were pushed into a corner. This expressed very well her feeling toward the analytic breasts at that time. She paid a great deal of lip service to how marvelous her analyst was and how the analysis had helped her, but, in fact, the analyst was completely disregarded and the interpretations were used only to produce her own "food"; and her child, husband, and friends were treated to quite regal helpings of my interpretations intended for the patient herself.

Soon after the kitchen dream, the patient's father died, and his death contributed very much to the manic trend. She came back from his funeral very elated by the marvelous religious service with the hymn singing, etc. Though feeling herself an agnostic, she felt that through these observances the spirit of her father was kept alive. She had a dream of a man and his family under water and she saw in the dream that, though some people might think that they had drowned, they were, in fact, perfectly happy. After some interpretation of her denial and idealization of death, she started associating to a patchwork quilt that was made by her father's mother and which always moved her to tears. She referred to something which she had spoken about in the past, about her idea of her father having a very good internal mother as a source of goodness and strength. She herself noticed that this idealization of her father's mother contrasted very much with her feelings about father's wife, her own mother. In connection with her idealization of the dead objects, that is, the man and the family under the water, I reminded her that her father's mother died when he was very little, and she agreed that the main point was that the *ideal* mother was a dead mother, not her own while she was still alive. Her other associations were to the quilt. It represented the patchwork of her own activities, and it emerged fairly clearly that her activities were concerned with an object mother or father, felt to be dead, but covered up by a quilt of patchy, colorful activities.

This association was followed by a few days of quieter feelings about her father and some reawakened mourning for her mother. She also resisted acting out in a ready-made situation. She was visiting her mother-in-law, old and ailing. The old woman was lighting a fire, slowly and painfully, but lighting the fire was her great pride. The patient was longing to make her sit down while she lit the fire for her; she felt like screaming with impatience. But she resisted the temptation, and she let the old lady get on with it. Two points emerged clearly from this situation: first, her difficulty in sympathizing with or containing a damaged object ("If I had a handicapped child, I would kill it"); and second, her insistence that she must be the giver of light and warmth, that all life must come to the objects from her ("I wanted to treat her as though she were a mummy"). This insight led to some quietening in her acting out, but it did not last long. She was full of ideas about translating a book of her father's into English, neglecting her own work and her own analysis. True to her patchwork quilt tendencies, a day or two later, she was planning to do some research into the battered children syndrome. One Friday, she came a quarter of an hour late, very excited. She thought she had had a very good talk with the mother of a pupil, one of "my evacuated mothers"; maybe she could combine research into battered children and evacuated mothers. I drew her attention to the fact that currently I was being an evacuated mother by her quarter of an hour lateness and interpreted the evacuated mother as the mother, myself, changed into feces and evacuated. The battered babies of the mother were being treated in a similar way. As was typical with her, she reacted to the interpretation with a kind of persecuted collapse and the comment, "I thought I had a good interview." A day or two previously, she had a similar reaction when her husband made a critical remark about her plan for redecorating the kitchen: "When E. said that, it all collapsed, and I had thought it was such a good plan."

The next week ushered in two more great reparative plans. Her father's book, battered babies, and evacuated mothers disappeared from the scene and a threatened park in the country suddenly emerged as the object to be rescued. The patient had read in the papers that the owner of a famous hilly park had died and she decided that it would be wonderful to make it into a national park. She wrote to the paper and to her M.P. Here the paranoid element came more clearly to the fore. The park had to be saved from the "Edwards." This was her name for get-rich-quick exploiters, because Edward is the name of a young businessman relative. Further, at the time of her mother's illness and after her mother's death, the mourning for her mother was quite inaccessible to the patient. All her emotions then were switched into a paranoia about Edward, who was accused of exploiting her parents and making her mother's life and death a misery. Her parents had been, in fact, fond of Edward and she could never bear this blindness in them. The rescue of the park from the "Edwards" represented a situation in which her dead and idealized mother had to be rescued from her brothers, into whom the patient projected all her own exploitation and ruthlessness toward mother.

Simultaneously, the patient was defending the school in which she worked against exploitation by a child psychologist fraudulently representing herself as an analyst. With all these rescuing operations of the good mother (the park) and the good analysis at the school, she regularly forgot all her dreams; she came late and did not retain any links with the previous day's analysis. When this was pointed out to her, she reacted with a violent feeling of being attacked; and she accused the analyst of confusion and of not being able to distinguish between her and the people she was describing, the "Edwards" and the fraudulent child psychologist. The paranoia, however, was of much shorter duration than in the past.

A few days later, the patient was again a quarter of an hour late and in the same excited mood as when she was dealing with the evacuated mothers. An old tree in the school playground was being cut much too short, and she started a tremendous agitation in the school to get a protest to stop this process. In doing this, the patient got into a paranoid quarrel with two of her colleagues. She said that she thought she was at last undoing the damage she had done to me in the past. Indeed, in the past the tree represented a good father's analytic penis, and she was identified with children damaging it. But this rescue operation left her confused. It got her into a new quarrel and, in fact, as I pointed out to her, cut the analytic hour short.

I have given here a long and rather anecdotal account of this phase of the patient's analysis to bring out the feeling of the relentless repetitiveness of her acting out.

As it is, I gave only some examples; I left out many concurrent intermittent activities imbued with the same excitement. Most of those activities included the following elements: a good object has to be preserved or rescued as is the Park from the "Edwards," the school from the fraudulent psychologist, the tree from the school authorities. This threatened good object could be her father (the book), the penis (the tree), or mother (the school or the hilly park).

The villains varied. Her brothers, represented by the "Edwards," were seen as villains. But often, this switched to her father if the object of rescue was her mother; or her mother became the villain if her father or brother were to be rescued. All the patient's own bad impulses were projected into the villains. However, interpretations of projections were lapped up by the patient without making the slightest therapeutic change. She was quite aware that the villains contained projected bad aspects of herself, but she felt that this was all the more reason to stamp them out.

The only approach which made an impact on her was that of constantly pointing out to her how these phantasies and activities were to be a rescue of the good analysis but were, in fact, an unremitting attack on analytic work. The phantasies were both escapes from facing the analysis and her internal world and a positive attack on the analyst's capacities and the analysis. Thus, when the patient was planning to save the evacuated mothers, she was actually evacuating her analyst, in her lateness. And while she was saving the tree from being cut too short, she was actually cutting her session short.

It could be shown to the patient that she felt, in fact, that her internal objects were dead; if the analyst, who represented them, showed any signs of effective functioning, that functioning was immediately cut short and deadened. This, of course, was found to be very persecuting; it was a different kind of persecution from that by the "Edwards" and similar objects. It was far more devastating in two ways: first, it was the persecution by the dead, unrestored internal parents; and second it was experienced as an attack on her goodness, on what she felt was best in her, her love and reparation.

Interpretations on these lines, though rejected by the patient, brought some shift. The internal objects and the analysis showed some life, and dreams reappeared.

The patient dreamed about a broken vase; she was trying to put it together and I was helping her; it was the first time during that phase of the analysis that she had had a dream in which she allowed me to help her. Then, in the dream, she was putting two coats on me, one blue, one brown. Her associations were that the blue coat belonged to her mother, and the other to the maid Maisie, who had looked after her when she was a child. Her mother was admired but felt as unhelpful; the maid was helpful but despised, a borderline mental defective. The patient thought that it was the first time that she had brought these two aspects of mother together.

As dreams reappeared, the acting out continued but with a lessened intensity and she was more aware of its interference with the analysis. Her father, who was an eminent politician in his own country, left some memoirs. She no longer thought of publishing them, but her sister wrote to her asking her for ideas for the foreword to the book. This excited her greatly.

A few days after the dream of the two coats, she came very elated. She started the session by saying that she had been superefficient that morning. She had visited a journalist friend and discussed with him ideas for the foreword. She had even written her reports at school and had put her watch on the table to watch the time and not to be late for the session. But halfway to the consulting room, she realized that she had left the watch in the office. She was very despondent about this because the watch belonged to her father-in-law and was treasured by her husband. It also reminded her that not long ago she had lost her own father's watch. She had to put the watch on the table because the strap of the watch was broken. (The breaking of the strap of the watch was a regular event: even a steel strap she got for her last watch broke on the second day. When the strap was broken, it did not take long for her to lose or mislay the watch.) She had a dream. In the dream, the analyst was present in the background, but it was Maisie, the maid, who was really her companion. She was very surprised because in the dream it seemed that she had written a book about mental deficiency but she had not known that she had written it. She was surprised and disbelieving. In another part of the dream, she was giving a lift to Mrs. X somewhere in the wilderness. Mrs. X was indicating where she wanted to go and what direction the patient should take. She thought it was incredible cheek from a person to whom she was giving a lift, and she stopped the car, deciding to go on strike.

Her associations were mainly to Mrs. X. She thought that Mrs. X was a kind of superior nanny person; in fact, she must have been a nanny or a nursery teacher before her marriage. Nevertheless, the patient had to admit that Mrs. X had published some very good research on deprived children.

I shall not go into the detailed interpretations, but the dream is obviously a continuation of the "two coats" dream. What appeared in the two coats dream as an integration between mother and nanny became more clearly a denigration of myself and mother as an internal object. Her superefficiency is obviously at the expense of the analyst, who is turned into a mentally deficient nanny in the internal world, about whom the patient writes a book. (A very similar thing happens, of course, with her father's book. By virtue of her foreword, the book becomes her book at the expense of her father.) The breaking of the strap and the losing of the watch represented a break in contact with the analyst as mother or father as a helpful figure. In the part of the dream about Mrs. X, some rehabilitation of the analyst occurs. She was a superior kind of nanny, and the patient has to admit her grudging respect; but at the thought of dependence on this internal figure, which told her the direction to take, she revolted and went on strike.

In spite of the rather hectic excitement at the beginning of the session, the patient quieted down a great deal and cooperated much better than in the previous month. Toward the end of the session, however, she was evidently preoccupied with something. In fact, I had a cold that day, though by no means a bad one. Suddenly in the middle of my interpreting her going on strike against Mrs. X, she burst out with the exclamation, "But you should not be working at all now; you should be in bed, being looked after and given hot drinks!" It is very difficult to convey the subtlety and impact of what she did at that moment, but I had no doubt that she was making a mental defective out of me. She was interrupting my adult mental functioning as the parent in relation to her as the child and wanting me to become a help-less baby in bed. But from the connections to the dream and the impact of this sudden interruption on the analytic process, I think it was more making me into an idiot than into a baby. I do not remember how I formulated the interpretation, but, rather surprisingly for her, she did not react with injured inno-cence and saw the point that an adult working person, who would collapse and retire to bed to be looked after because of a touch of cold, would be rather deficient.

It is significant that when this type of pseudoreparative feel-ing is brought directly into the transference, it invariably be-comes an attack on the analyst's functioning and the analysis itself. It never takes the form of actually helping the analyst to function by bringing material or dreams or providing links, but it strips the analyst of his powers of functioning. The direct re-parative thoughts in relation to myself in this patient took usu-ally one of two forms: either I was ill and helpless and being looked after by her, or, particularly early in her analysis, she had phantasies of buying material, making clothes, and dressing me, almost like a doll.

The following day, she again had a dream and quite rich as-sociations, showing further mobilization of her internal world. She came five minutes late and said that she had again been very efficient but something went wrong. She put my fee, which she was going to bring me, and the key of the car into a bag and then mislaid the bag. She added, "It's funny. When I put things in the bag, I feel I have done what I ought to do. I need not concern myself with it anymore; the job is done. I forget I still have to bring it here." She then spoke of how efficient she was in arranging the painting of a room in her house. I was able to interpret to her, using some additional past material, that the bag represented all the external jobs and activities into which she put things from the analysis, breaking links with me and not bringing anything back into the analysis. I connected the analysis with the internal world which remained unreplenished and the internal Maisie/mother. That reminded her of a dream which was in two parts. First, she was clambering, she did not know where, into a clock, or down a clock, but she could not see the clock face. She thought, "I must be able to get in, because there must be an exit." Inside the clock there were some very beautiful objects, like delicate ornaments on a mantlepiece, but then, as she was climbing down, everything seemed to be in the usual muddle, her husband, her child, schoolchildren, all sorts of bits and pieces in confusion. Then, she was again giving a ride to Z, a doctor and the wife of an analysand of mine. She took a violent turn which could have led to a fatal accident. She then tried to reassure herself that they were both not frightened or hurt, but she was not convinced. She noticed that there was a further rehabilitation to the woman to whom she was giving a ride: first to Maisie, then Mrs. X, the superior nanny, now Z, the object of frank admiration and envy as a woman doctor standing for the analyst. I pointed out to her that with the rehabilitation of the object goes increased violence. Maisie is unharmed; with Mrs. X, she goes on strike, but she wants to smash Z in the car. She protested that she only wanted to show off but then admitted that the feeling in the dream was quite murderous and that this murderous feeling was part of the showing off of her superior power and strength. She then came back to the clock and remembered a book she had read as a small child, called *The World Behind the Clock*. She had also had a grandfather clock in her home which intrigued her greatly. She thought of all my interpretations in the past about clocks and watches and her inability to look at a watch and the connections I had made in the past between the watch and the breast. The clock part of the dream showed an important aspect of her relation to the object. The getting inside the breast and the confusion that arose, for instance, between the entrance and the exit, had, at one time, played a much more prominent role in her analysis. In this context, I think it was mainly an indication of how she got possession of the car in which she gave rides. She got inside the breast, partly messing it up, the muddle below in the clock representing her mother's messed up internal objects, and she got control of the nipple as a kind of steering wheel. But she also felt completely cut off from the real world and drove blindly. The superefficiency in her control of the nipple was constantly interrupted either by confusion or by persecution coming to her from the breast inside of which she resides or by identification with the mentally deficient, depleted internal object. The so-called reparative activities—her wild, controlling driving in this dream—appeared more clearly here as an envious attack and taking over from mother.

This theme became still clearer the following week. A new ploy was looking after Jean. Jean was a schizophrenic girl in analysis with Miss B. My patient's sudden excited interest in her was due to the fact that Jean's parents were friends of a friend of the patient's. This friend of the patient was Dr. O, who had died recently. The patient wanted to arrange for Jean to go to her nursery school as a kind of occupational therapy. She was furious when I pointed out her rivalry with Miss B and her cutting Miss B out by never checking whether this kind of occupation was suitable for her patient. The next day, she said that she had had a dream which made her furious because it made her think that my interpretation was right. She was giving a party in what might have been her mother's house, but there were a lot of analysts there, so it might have been mine or Miss B's, but it was *her* party. She was wearing a peculiar floppy hat. She thought the dream confirmed that she was in rivalry with Miss B and me, and was taking over our house and practice. The floppy hat had associations to Dr. O and, she thought, it meant that she had a secret relation to his penis. As usual in this kind of dream, she was very distraught because there was no food and everything was in a muddle. There was no one to help her arrange things.

This dream was like a synthesis of the dream about the clock and the dream about Mrs. Z. Here clearly, she got inside the mother's body, in envy and competition. She took over the nipple and the penis (floppy hat). Jean was the projected mad child, herself, whom she insisted she could look after better than her mother. In fact, the concern for Jean was minimal even in that context, so minimal that, a few days later, when the plans were coming to fruition and everything was arranged, she forgot to take Jean to the school.

It is, of course, characteristic of manic reparation that love for the apparent object of concern is shallow and unreal. The external object is there to distract attention from the internal situation.

In the patient described, the internal situation underwent a certain rehabilitation. At the beginning of the term, her internal objects were felt to be dead. Later, the mother appeared first as a mentally deficient nanny, then as a superior nanny, and finally as the admired and envied Z, and the patient's hostility and envious attacks were more openly acknowledged. She could then see more clearly the functions of her compulsive manic reparation: first, the denial of the deadness of the object through maintaining a flurry of activity; second, a denial of her own hostility and envy by taking over the place of the mother and constantly doing good, and third, the projection of badness into the villains. All this defended her against guilt. At the same time, a continuing attack was being made on the internal objects kept dead or deficient and triumphed over. In the transference, this became a continuous attack on the analyst's functioning, either by keeping the analysis defeated and dead or by demonstrating that every intervention of the analyst was an attack on the patient's reparative capacities.

Only the ceaseless analysis of this process in the transference can lessen the omnipotence of these mechanisms and lead to a gradual restoration of a good internal object.

POSTSCRIPT 1980: MANIC REPARATION

In this paper I try to emphasize two points; one is theoretical, trying to show the links between envy and manic reparation. The patient was in despair because her internal objects were dead or destroyed, largely because of her envious attacks. She was frantic to restore them, but her reparative activities had to be compatible with her envy and because of that they failed in relieving the guilt—the objects remained in subjection.

The other point I make is technical. It is very dangerous to go along with the patient's manic reparation, as it does not solve the vicious circle of despair, but the analysis of the underlying internal situation does bring relief, and I show in the paper the gradual rehabilitation of the patient's internal objects.

EDITOR'S INTRODUCTION TO
ON UNDERSTANDING AND NOT UNDERSTANDING

Among the many difficult-to-treat patients encountered by analysts are those who seem to be entrenched in their masochism, massively resistant, lacking in motivation for treatment, vigorously involved in negative therapeutic reactions, or some combination of these. These patients are deeply rooted in the paranoid–schizoid position. There, as we have already seen repeatedly, thinking is concrete and defensive reliance on omnipotence, splitting, and projective identification has reached an extreme. Joseph emphasizes here that, in one way or another, these patients project their capacity for understanding, sanity, curiosity, or any ordinary sense of connection of ideas, people, or even parts of the self. Consequently, they seem to be essentially unrelated to objects and incapable of experiencing the content of analytic interchange. If they give an inch, they seem to feel, they would have to face the dreaded prospects of understanding or being understood and thereby undermining their precarious equilibrium.

Analysis may show that these patients have arranged an invasion of the analyst's mind, perhaps accompanied by a disassembling of their own; they may behave as though they have gained control of the situation through an omniscient and omnipotent participation in the analyst's understanding. In part, their so believing can provoke the analyst's antagonism, thereby successfully recreating a sadomasochistic environment in which the patient can feel at home; however, behaving in this way may also be designed to communicate to the analyst, via the countertransference induced by projective identification, their own experience of having developed in an uncomprehending sadomasochistic environment and being now confined to that environment in their inner worlds. The case examples, one of which concerns a child, include different forms and degrees of this struggle against understanding and being understood.

Betty Joseph argues that under these circumstances the analyst's burden may well be to refrain from interpreting, perhaps frequently and for extended periods. Rather, he or she may have to be limited to exploring cautiously the various aspects of the patient's paranoid–schizoid orientation to the treatment situation, and his or her defensive blocking of any and all understanding. The analyst may also be called upon to do considerable "containment," not only of the patient's projective identifications but also of the analyst's own difficulties with remaining in the position of not understanding for long periods of time. One of the important cues that this containing approach is called for is the analyst's beginning to feel a distinctive kind of countertransference: that it is "material" that is being understood rather than a person, and that it is "material" one is *talking about* in one's interventions rather than a person who is being *talked to and with*. Associated with these moments may be the analyst's frequent feelings of meaninglessness or even boredom.

This essay is one of those that makes it plain why Betty Joseph has been widely acknowledged to be a superb teacher and supervisor of psychoanalysis. The essay combines frankness, humility, patience, technical finesse, and deep understanding of the sources of the dread of relatedness, personal growth, and insight.

13
ON UNDERSTANDING
AND NOT UNDERSTANDING

BETTY JOSEPH

This paper is about understanding and being understood. It concerns ways and motives our patients have for making themselves understood or not understood, and the problem for the analyst in gaining understanding as well as tolerating not understanding.

We could describe the beginnings of psychoanalysis as the attempt to make the incomprehensible in mental life comprehensible, and the development of such tools as free association and listening. Freud started by listening to his patients, taking everything that they said extremely seriously, and from this building up the unconscious meaning of their communication, using, of course, not only words but also tone, gesture, and the like. Following Freud's discoveries, Melanie Klein explored the very early period of the child's life, of object relationships, anxieties, and defenses, and began to make more comprehensible areas which had previously been beyond our understanding. It is some of the consequences of her findings on our technique that I want to discuss here.

Presented at the Conference celebrating the Centenary of Melanie Klein's birth, at the Tavistock Clinic, London, July 17, 1982.

I think that we, as analysts, need to approach the question of understanding our patients, in a sense, differently, depending on whether they seem to be operating more within the paranoid–schizoid or in the depressive position. Broadly we can include under the latter, patients who are able to relate to themselves as whole people and to feel some responsibility for their own impulses and themselves, as well as relating to the analyst as a whole person. Those who are still caught up in the paranoid–schizoid position are necessarily splitting off and projecting a great deal of themselves and their impulses and are unable to relate at all fully to either themselves or the analyst.

All our patients come to us, we and they hope, to gain understanding, but how they hope to gain it must vary, I am suggesting, according to their position; that is, according to the basic nature of their object relations, anxieties, and defenses. The very nature of the defenses used in the paranoid–schizoid position in itself militates against understanding, which is frequently, but not always, not what these patients want. In fact, many are against understanding despite their protests to the contrary. Of course, there is another aspect of being against understanding, that is the aspect of attacking, destroying, and undermining the patient's understanding of his analyst's understanding aggressively and enviously. But it is not this aspect of understanding that I so much want to discuss, although, with the patients I am going to speak about, there is often a mixture of destructive antiunderstanding and the use of primitive splitting defenses which are working against understanding. It is, to my mind, very important that we tease out with our patients, and clarify, the difference between these two elements, and also that we constantly attempt to tune in to our patients sufficiently accurately to gauge where they are: basically in the paranoid–schizoid or depressive position. Otherwise I think we shall find that we are, as it were, able to understand the material but not the patient. I shall try to exemplify these points.

First I want to clarify what I mean by understanding in the depressive position. I suspect that it is only those patients who are really well into the depressive position who can use understanding in the sense that we tend to think about the term ordinarily, I mean in the sense of discussing, standing aside from a problem, seeking, but even more, considering explanations. Such mental activities probably involve the capacity to take responsibility for one's impulses and, as I have said, to relate to the analyst as a whole person and to introject freely. I want, therefore, to leave aside this slightly hypothetical, more mature group of patients, since they do not present us with our real technical problem, and to concentrate on aspects of gaining and giving understanding to patients who are more tied up in the paranoid–schizoid position.

If we consider briefly Melanie Klein's work on the types of object relationships, anxieties, and defenses mainly used in the paranoid–schizoid position (Klein, 1946), we are thinking of relationships not just with people, but with people or parts of people used as part objects. We are thinking of the kind of anxieties of a very disturbing or persecuting kind that set going and support defenses such as maintaining a highly omnipotent and narcissistic attitude, splitting off various parts of the self or internal objects, and the considerable use of projective identification. Taken at the simplest level it can be seen that constantly to split off and project out parts of the self must necessarily be inimical to understanding. But, as I want to go on to discuss, the problem is not so simple, because even such projective identification can be used as a method of unconscious communication between patient and analyst. Our understanding of this aspect of Melanie Klein's work has been considerably augmented by the work of W. R. Bion (1962, 1963); for example, on container and contained, communication between infant and mother, in other words on aspects of the healthy as opposed to the more pathological use of projective identification. I think it is impossible to overestimate the importance of Melanie Klein's concept of projective identification for the development of our sensitivity and our technique in this generation.

I want to start with an example, to indicate both the difficulties and the importance of locating the main position in which the individual is operating. I shall use a fragment of material from the work of Dr. Mauro Morra, who was discussing this case with me. This comes from the analysis of a 4-year-old boy who had been in treatment for a few months, and as the holidays were approaching the child had been showing behavior in which he wanted to be near to the analyst, as if inside him, or, as he demonstrated with sticking plaster, stuck to him. Then on the following day he came in, called the analyst a stupid idiot, threw a small container in the analyst's face, tied up his ankles with string, stuck him round with Scotch tape, got glue onto his trousers, and stuck a bit of chewed chewing gum onto him. He talked about the analyst being tied up and unable to move, and indeed the analyst felt quite immobilized. Here we can see that there is manifestly an attempt to tie the analyst up, control and hold onto him before the holidays. But I think there is also another communication going on: the child is projecting into the analyst his own infantile self, with its experience of being desperate and a stupid idiot of an infant, unable to move, immobilized, stuck in his gluey, gummy fecal diapers, wet and dirty, while his parents came and went and left him alone in his distress, and this is called "holidays"! (Indeed, there is a story of his having cried ceaselessly for eighteen hours when he was aged only a few months, on being left by his parents.) This is the only way that he can as yet convey something of his experiences, which are outside his verbal range. When the child sticks, attaches, and attacks, his behavior seems a direct, nonverbal communication. But where Melanie Klein's understanding has given us a new technical tool is in the understanding of projective identification—its concreteness in the transference and in the countertransference. The analyst feels immobilized, responding to a projective identification of the child, as I have tried to describe. The awareness of the use of projective identification in this way gives us an additional dimension, it enables the analyst to use his countertransference as a positive tool in his understanding. But the child, by projecting this experiencing part of the self into the analyst, both communicates his distress and temporarily rids himself of it and therefore of his understanding.

If our patients are operating largely with early defense mechanisms, and to some extent every patient is, then we may expect that our technique has to deal with two factors: one, that the patient who believes he comes in order to be understood, actually comes to use the analyst and analytic situation to maintain his current balance in a myriad of complex and unique ways; two, that verbal communication, therefore, has to be listened to, not only or even primarily as to its content, but in terms of what is being acted in the transference. Defenses like projective identification, splitting, or omnipotent denial are not just thought, they are in fantasy lived in the transference. These two points I want to develop as I go on.

Understanding, as such, belongs, I am suggesting, to the depressive position. The patients I am concerned to discuss have hardly reached, and certainly not worked through, the depressive position, and though they believe they come for understanding, immediately other forces in their personality take over, and unconsciously they attempt to engage the analyst in all kinds of activities, drawing the analyst into their defensive structures and so on. These are the things then that need to be understood. All of us, I assume, have had the experience at times of listening to our patients, believing we understood the material and its unconscious meaning, its symbolic content, only to find that our subsequent interpretations seem to fall flat, or that we are getting bored in the middle of an interpretation. If I am bored I stop, assuming I am talking about material but not to the patient.

This highlights a point, which in a sense is only too obvious, that analysis to be useful must be an experience, in contrast, for example, to the giving of understanding or explaining.

It also helps to clarify an issue often raised in discussion on technique—does one interpret only in the transference, or also about other areas of the patient's life? I don't think it is only/or, but rather whether one can focus one's understanding and therefore interpretations on what is being lived and experienced and then fan out or down or back from there. Out, I mean, into the outer or inner world, down or back into history or more unconscious fantasy.

I am going to give a brief example of a patient apparently intellectually trying to understand, though actually negating my attempts at understanding, and yet communicating a very significant part of her early relationships. This is the kind of mixture that I feel we need to tease out. A rather new patient, whom I shall call A, a young professional woman, arrived a few minutes late, explaining that she was very tired and had overslept. Her boss was expecting her to do a great deal of the work which should be shared out to other people as well, she was very angry, she was going to discuss it with him. No, no, no, she was not going to do that work. The reason for anger, if genuine, seemed real enough, but the way that she talked was rather like a self-consciously naughty little girl. I made a rather general interpretation linking what she was saying with what we had been seeing in previous sessions about her actual annoyance being that I don't let her do my work, so she digs in her heels and rejects what I have to say. She replied, "Yes, I always dig in my heels, I can't let people be over me, just as when I was at the university and people tried to bully me. I . . ."

Now that sounds as if my patient is agreeing with my too general remark that she can't let people be over her (but said very, very easily) but if they, I, am over her then apparently I am like her bullying boss—so one would think she would be right to dig in her heels. So she agrees and placates me—because I am said to be right, but insofar as I am bullying one would assume that I must be in the wrong, but she indicates that her behavior is wrong. So I am quietly placated by her statement of guilt. But this ambiguity and twist takes all the meaning out of our communication and leaves it useless. I show her this. She quickly adds that this must be "because . . . ," so that long before anything has been established between us, any understanding, it is explained away—"because. . . ." So here I think she shows that there is no belief or trust in the reality of what we are doing together in the analysis. It seems as if there is nothing genuine and sincere going on. I tried to show this point, which is linked, I think, with her ambiguity. Immediately she responded that the word that really affected her in what I was saying was about there being "no trust"—and she started again to explain about the notion of no trust in the abstract "because. . . ." But again the meaning has gone, there seems to be no feeling about what I was trying to show her but a quick explaining it away "because. . . ."

I have brought this fragment because it raises the particular kind of issue that I am trying to discuss. One could interpret the content of parts of her material, such as how I (and the analysis) am experienced in a persecuting way as her bullying boss, or one could explain something about the fragments of her childhood that are brought up after the "becauses." But I believe that would not help us. I think the experience that is going on, the thing being acted out in the session, is an extraordinary ambiguity constantly followed by a kind of placating and agreeing with me: and my patient always having to know what she means or what I am saying. Actually in this way the meaning of what I am saying disappears. I think this quality in the work needs to be linked with another feeling that I have, almost constantly, with this patient and which seems unique to her. I find I listen to but almost do not believe what she is telling me, as if she were confabulating history, inventing boyfriends, or details about boyfriends, or stories that she tells me that people have told her. Yet I do not think that I think that she is consciously lying, but my countertransference is very uncomfortable. My suspicion is, and only time will or may show whether I am right, that this patient as an infant or young child had no real belief in her world, in her emotional surroundings, as if deep sincerity was lacking between her parents and herself and that there was a lack of belief in, and a phony idealization of, her parents— whom I suspect at depth she felt she saw through. And this mixture of disbelief and pretence in real relationships is what she is living out with me in the transference. I have already alluded to that in the fragment of material I gave, but these interpretations, too, get absorbed into the defensive system and cannot, or dare not, be taken seriously by her.

It is interesting that the picture of her family that I get is of a very unreal mother, who, although quite unconnected with psychology, so far as I yet know, seemed to talk to her daughter and husband in a quasi-interpretive way, a role that I am clearly being invited to play, as if interpretations took the place of emotions and real living. What is also manifested in the session is the way in which defenses are mobilized at the moment of her nearly having to face her psychic reality. Thus, when I interpret her conviction of the emotional falseness and lack of sincerity in her objects, the very words, or some, that I use, like *trust*, will be used defensively to make it meaningless. And she will get power over the meaning of what I say by dislocating the word from its context and then explaining away its nonmeaning with the "because." Thus her anxiety is evaded and her psychic history distorted.

This whole complex system of object relationships, fantasy, anxiety, and defenses against anxiety is brought into the transference and countertransference, as I feel useless and impotent in the face of the pseudolies. The patient is clearly against understanding—though believes she is for it. Understanding, so

far as I know at the present, would mean facing the unsatisfactory nature of her early objects and her complaints and
doubts, as well as their value and maybe the value of her current object—myself. We can also see this patient's omnipotence
and omniscience; she believes that she wants to be understood
but she cannot tolerate not knowing. Her aggression is mobilized when this omniscient balance is disturbed by my interpretations. Then placating is mobilized to deal with this, as she
unconsciously tries to draw me into her defensive organization
and keep us in perpetual agreement. It is also only through my
attempts to tolerate long periods of not understanding at all
what is going on, that I can perhaps begin to clarify a little what
it is about.

In cases such as the one I have just quoted, where primitive
defense mechanisms and omnipotence are so striking, we can
see that aggression apparently arises when interpretations disturb the patient's balance, since the balance aims in one part to
obviate envious aggression. Many patients, as we are only too
aware, will try to destroy their understanding, will develop a
negative therapeutic reaction and annihilate their knowledge,
will enviously beat down and devalue what the analyst has just
shown them. But as I indicated at the beginning of the paper, it
is not these patients who show such manifest and active, or silent but significant, attacks that I am so concerned about here.
I am concerned with those who are more split and stuck and
unavailable. The particular ones that I am going on to describe
are those in whom part of the apparatus that is needed for understanding, part of the ego, seems to be unavailable owing to
early splitting and projective mechanisms. If we do not find the
missing parts of the apparatus we talk, we interpret, in vain.

To take an example from B, who came into analysis worried
about his relationship with his wife—or, to be more accurate,
worried that she was worried that their relationship seemed poor
and unsatisfactory to her; he did not see anything particularly

wrong with it. He seemed a very decent man, basically honest, immature, and terribly lacking in awareness of himself and his feelings. It soon seemed that he unconsciously wanted an analysis in which things would be explained in relation to the outside world, not experienced in the transference, and usually when I interpreted he would go quiet, blank, unable to remember what I said, and shift off untouched onto another topic. Or he would repeat what he had just said. The impression I got was that he became anxious, broke up his mind, stopped being able to listen or hold together what we were discussing. This began to improve. Slowly I gained the feeling that I was supposed to follow him, almost pursue him with interpretations, but he did not seem interested in trying to understand or actively to use the analysis—it was as if it was I who wanted him to use individual interpretations or the analysis in general, just as it was his wife who apparently wanted him to have the analysis and who was worried about the marriage. So we could see that the active, alert, wanting part of the self was split off and apparently projected into me, and he remained passive and inert.

Unless one becomes aware of this and begins to focus on this aspect of the work, one can interpret endlessly and uselessly about what the patient is talking about, and it will not reach him, or he will become harassed, persecuted or even excited. In such patients I think progress will be indicated not only by a broadening and deepening of emotions but by signs of parts of the ego engaging in a new way in the analytic work. For example, B was anxious but also rather relieved as he began to feel himself coming more alive sometimes during the sessions. I have not the space here to give details of such a session with a dream, just before a holiday, when B became very clear about simple feelings of jealousy and anger linked clearly with his early and current family experiences. He was unusually moved by this dream and our work on it and as the session was coming to an end, said in a happier voice: "I must tell you about my grandiose idea. I think that car manufacturers should build a front passenger seat so that it can turn round and the passenger join in with and face the children sitting at the back, or a child could sit in the front and turn to the others. I shall write to the head of B. L."

So I showed him, by his tone and the way that he spoke to me, as well as by what he said, the pleasure in the session of getting into touch with his childhood, the experience of being really able to love and feel jealous. What he had been talking about had brought him into contact with the child in himself, which he was beginning to turn to and face, instead of his usual way of withdrawing, losing contact, and projecting the needing-to-know part of himself into me. Here some part of him wants to have a look at what is going on. Until he can integrate this part more fully and consciously into his personality he will remain passive, which he complains about, and not able to use his mind properly.

Here we are talking about patients who seem to be beyond understanding, because the part that could aim at understanding and making progress is split off and projected into the analyst—in the transference. We see similar interference when sanity and intelligence is projected, and the patient acts and talks as if stupid—unable to hold things together or draw conclusions about what he or she is saying. I am thinking about a particular man, whom I shall call S, who described happenings in such a way that the analyst was bound, and must, I think, be known by the patient to be bound, to draw conclusions. For example, he would give a long description of the behavior of his girl friend, whether accurate or not is not the issue at the moment, but which seemed to convey that any sane person in the room would assume that she, the girl friend, was very sadistic, to the point of being seriously emotionally disturbed.

This raises an interesting technical problem, since the patient would go on talking as if not drawing any conclusion from his own remarks, as if the capacity to understand was split off and projected into the analyst. If the analyst does not deal with this aspect of the transference, but instead acts sane and demonstrates that the patient must realize that he is talking about a girl friend who is deeply disturbed, the patient is likely to react as if the analyst were attacking his girl friend and then be upset, hurt, or offended, and the analyst may find himself or herself urging, almost bullying the patient to see her "point of view"—so a vaguely forcing or near sadomasochistic situation arises, as if the problem has shifted from the home to the consulting room. I think that in this kind of situation one can see both the projection of apparent sanity into the analyst and the appearance in the patient of naiveté bordering on stupidity, which is apparently innocent but, in fact, is splendidly provocative. Real understanding is not the patient's aim at this moment, but nor is the behavior consciously provocative, though I think secondarily it is often used in this way.

I have been describing patients in whom understanding seems to become unavailable because the part of the ego that might want it is projected into the analyst, and the analyst becomes identified with that part of the self and is then warded off, as with B. I have also indicated with the man patient, S, how the resulting naiveté or stupidity can often be felt in the transference as having something vaguely provocative about it. In such cases the patient seems unconsciously to be trying to involve the analyst in acting out with him. If the analyst does not watch what is going on in the transference most carefully he may be tempted to prod, as if to suggest that the patient ought to work harder, or be tempted to push superego-ishly to get the patient moving. If the analyst does act out the role of the active ego or superego with the patient it will simply encourage the patient's passivity or his masochism and perpetuate the problem. In fact, the analyst is fortunate in being given the opportunity to experience his impotence, his desire for change, his desire for the patient to make progress. If he can really contain this and try to understand why the patient needs to split off and project so much that is potentially valuable in his ego into the analyst, then analysis will go on, as opposed to subtle acting out and moralizing by both patient and analyst. Such acting out must lead to a stalemate and most likely to a repetition of what has gone on in the patient's past.

This type of splitting and projective identification of valuable parts of the ego into the analyst is also seen in another group of patients, who are basically very masochistic and more or less perverse in character or behavior, a group whom I cannot discuss in detail here. In them one gets the impression that there is a profound split in which the patient remains almost dominated and imprisoned by death instincts, emerging as self-destruction and constant despair, while life instincts, hope, sanity, or the desire for progress, are constantly projected into the analyst. In such cases there is little in the patient to balance the pull of the self-destruction, and the patient becomes enthralled and captivated by the exciting self-destructive part of the personality. The patient will unconsciously attempt constantly and actively to undermine the analyst's hope and drag him down into despair. It is very hard for mere understanding to be anything like as important for these patients as their awful and active masochistic pleasures.

When discussing one group of patients, who use projective identification a great deal to be understood and not understood, I spoke about our being fortunate in being given the opportunity to experience what is going on. And yet we know that the experience is by no means an unmixed blessing, and can be very disturbing or pressurizing or invasive. I shall return to this latter point in a moment. But, in any case, there is always a problem as to how to keep the transference uncontaminated—not, or minimally, contaminated by the analyst's acting out verbally, in tone or attitude. It is clear that we are demanding that the analyst should be able to feel and explore most carefully the whole range of disturbance and yet not act out and not masochistically suffer without verbalizing. To go back to our first example, the case of the child—the analyst knew he felt immobilized and disgusting; it was important not just to interpret as if the child were only trying to tie him up, but also to suffer, and verbalize to the child the child's own unverbalized and, then, unverbalizable suffering.

It is important to explore in detail the nature of the patient's fantasies, ideas, convictions, ourselves, rather than hurriedly to try to interpret them back into the patient as projections or mere history. With one patient it was possible to open up her feelings that I was antagonistic and controlling, that I did not want her to get on in life or in her career. As we looked at her feelings about my motivation it became clear that in her mind I felt threatened by her, and deeply envious of her as a young intelligent person with her life ahead of her. I would then wish to explore most carefully her picture of me, this old, supposedly lonely, rather embittered person, and her quiet conviction of what I was like, and only very slowly and over a long period, hope to explore how much of these ideas might be linked with actual observations of myself or the way I function, how much were projected parts of herself, and so on. This is, after all, in a large part what we mean when we talk about "containing." To assume that all these ideas were projections from the beginning would almost certainly be inaccurate, would numb one's sensitivity as to what was going on and prevent one from seeing what else was being talked about or why it came up at that moment.

To return, then, to the issue of invasiveness: the types of projective identification that help us to experience and to understand our patients better are often, as I have tried to indicate, quite subtle and fine. But sometimes they are so powerful that the analyst has difficulty in not being drawn into acting out in one way or another. With a certain group of such patients, who are not interested in real understanding but demand understanding on their own terms, one's personality, one's body, and mind is being assaulted. These patients are observant in certain directions, but quite blind in others. They are convinced that they know what is going on, and that their theories are correct—as the woman I have just quoted, who was certain of my subtly envious attitude to her and some of the reasons for my attitude.

In these cases there is a very deeply encroaching type of relating, when the patient unconsciously in fantasy projects his mind and his eyes into the analyst and knows everything that is going on, and since he is living so omnipotently he has no awareness of wanting to know, he has no curiosity, all this is avoided and real relating is obviated. "Knowing" and "psychoanalytic knowledge" is put in its place. Such patients are often convinced that they should be psychotherapists or analysts, and from an external point of view may, or may not, convince people around them that they are very insightful. But in analysis one can see that the insight is based on a subtle getting in and taking over which will sometimes emerge grossly in dreams, then more subtly in their ways of dealing with sessions and actual interpretations.

In many ways this omnipotent balance is similar to what I described in A, the patient who conveyed a sense of tragic falseness. But the very invasive patients bring an additional, potentially disturbing quality into the analysis which one can experience vividly in the countertransference. With one such patient, as I interpreted, either she did not hear—though this was not obvious because she continued to talk with apparent relevance—or she slightly distorted and altered my interpretations and repeated them in a slightly different form already known to her; or the whole thing became textbook or tied up in some old interpretations, so that the newness, freshness, or unexpected part was lost. But what she said sounded *nearly* all right—and wasn't. This was a young woman who had experienced anorexic difficulties when young and to some extent even as an adult.

I have raised this difficulty because in a sense the omnipotence and the extreme invasiveness and the sense of conviction and knowledge that these patients have make the problem look obvious—but they are difficult to help and to give real understanding because they depend so deeply on their rigidly held omnipotent and omniscient balance. And there is another technical problem; these patients often appear so narcissistic, so arrogant, and disturbing that they ask to be badly treated or humiliated, and if they can get it, by a clumsy or unkind interpretation, they can slip into a, to them, very welcome sadomasochistic transference and insight will be further lost. After all, omnipotence is the hallmark of early defenses, and one which we can easily underestimate. Our patients who in fantasy get into our bodies, our houses, and our minds know and are not curious. In fantasy they live in our minds and therefore can talk about missing and gaps and weekends without having the trouble of experiencing them. We as their analysts have to recognize the omnipotence of omnipotence, and not, I believe, try to interpret their material as if these patients wanted it understood.

I have tried, in this paper, to raise some technical problems presented by patients locked in the paranoid–schizoid position where understanding is difficult to achieve if our attention remains focused on what they are actually saying. I have tried to show how the analyst, in order to understand, has to tune in to the patient's wavelength, which is a wavelength of action rather than words, though words may be used. All these patients are, to a great extent, using projective identification, either as a method of communication to achieve understanding on a deep nonverbal level, or to maintain their balance, in which case they are not interested in, or are inimical to, understanding as we understand it. If we approach such patients with the notion that they want us to give them real insight, we lose touch with the patient as such, and in any case much that these patients are conveying and projecting will still be beyond our understanding.

I have attempted, in this paper, to show something of the value, the richness, and the depth of Melanie Klein's work on these early processes, and how the implications of her work have increased our sensitivity to what is going on both in our patients and ourselves, and thus have helped to make more comprehensible that which was previously relatively incomprehensible.

SUMMARY

This paper discusses some technical problems arising from the diverse ways our patients have of making themselves understood or not understood. It shows how patients who have reached the depressive position are able to use understanding in a way that is very different from those in the paranoid–schizoid position. It describes particular methods that the latter patients have of avoiding understanding by splitting and projection and attempting unconsciously to draw the analyst into a type of acting out in the transference. It stresses the importance for the analyst, of listening to the patient in terms of the position from which he is operating, so that contact can be achieved and with it real understanding, as opposed to subtle acting out and pseudo-understanding.

REFERENCES

Bion, W. R. (1962), *Learning From Experience.* London: Heinemann.
———— (1963), *Elements of Psycho-Analysis.* London: Heinemann.
Klein, M. (1946), Notes on some schizoid mechanisms. In: *Writings*, Vol. 3. London: Hogarth Press, 1975, pp. 1–24.

EDITOR'S INTRODUCTION TO
THE DYNAMICS OF REASSURANCE

Traditionally, analysts have been sparing in their use of reassurance when they respond to patients' presentations of painful situations and experiences. They have shown the same restraint
when patients express concern about their prospects in treatment or their analyst's interest in them. They consider it essential to stay within the psychoanalytic frame of interpretation. To
this end, it is particularly important to maintain a steady focus
on conflict in the transference. Therefore, to offer reassurance
is too likely to provide gratification in the transference by taking sides in the patient's underlying conflicts. Taking sides only
makes it more difficult to further the analysis of conflictual transference. Judicious restraint, it has been held, affirms the analyst's
relative abstinence, maintaining equidistance from conflict,
neutrality, and management of his or her own countertransference.

This tradition has not lacked for critics. Analysts who adopt
this cautious position wholeheartedly have been looked at skep-
tically, if not disparagingly, throughout the history of psychoanalysis. Sometimes this criticism has emphasized Freud's own
inconsistencies in practice and has recommended doing as he
did and not as he said. Sometimes, it has emphasized the negative effect of undue deprivation on the patient's readiness to ana-
lyze. Freud himself, it has been pointed out, advised against too
much deprivation. It has also been pointed out repeatedly that,
anyway, various reassurances are built into the process, so that
a puristic attitude makes no sense; for example, there is the

analyst's steady attention to the analytic material, his or her accepting or nonjudgmental attitude, and the regularity of appointments. Those critics who have simply emphasized egalitarian values in human relationships have scorned the classical analyst's allegedly taking a "lofty" or ostrichlike attitude in this regard.

What all these criticisms lack is an even-handed examination of the finer aspects of the dynamics of reassurance in whatever way it is offered or experienced, and this lack is precisely what Dr. Feldman attempts to remedy in this technically valuable essay. Because it is, I believe, important to hold the line against the ever more popular attitude that it is best to be very "human" (whatever that means in the analytic framework), I shall summarize here the gist of Feldman's argument in more detail than I usually do in my introductory comments. I hope thereby to add to this essay's persuasiveness.

In his review of two detailed clinical examples, one of which is taken from a report by Melanie Klein (1961), Feldman applies the now familiar broad conceptions of transference-countertransference and enactment. Following the lead of Melanie Klein, he uses this material to show how reassurance, rather than having any kind of uncomplicated soothing effect, contributed significantly to a patient's conflict within the transference. He views patients as most likely to possess at least some understanding that analysts at work are required to do their best to remain personally integrated and in possession of their own minds. Only in this way will they retain their ability to think for themselves about their patients, draw on their understanding and expertise, and find ways to be helpful. From this understanding, the patients derive some sense of security. At the same time, they do yearn for some form of reassurance by the analyst; if nothing else, it relieves some anxiety that precious defenses will be questioned. Consequently, they cannot avoid feeling some anxiety and hostility in relation to the impartially interpretive analyst. As patients, they fear and hate the very person they depend on to gain much needed understanding and self-mastery.

Analysts may offer conflict-inducing reassurance in numerous ways other than simply uttering comforting words. They may do so simply by slanting interpretations in a particular direction; they may abstain from intervention, answer questions unreflectively, fill in blanks supportively, and so on. As already indicated, patients must experience these ruptures of the analytic frame ambivalently: on the one hand, gratified; on the other, threatened by what may be a sign of the analyst's own insecurity, vulnerability, weakness, or insincerity. At least, phantasies to that effect will be stimulated, and inevitably they will be linked to, and reinforced by, transference images of parental fragility and untrustworthiness.

Additionally, the analysts' attempts to be reassuring may well support patients' phantasies of their own omnipotent exercises of control; they will believe that they control their analysts by means of their projective identifications, especially those that foster enactments. Then, the reassuring analyst can be felt to confirm the existence of an exclusive dyadic relationship, the sort of relationship described in Ronald Britton's essay on the oedipal illusion in chapter 10. This phantasized achievement also induces anxiety and perhaps guilt as well; the patients fear their own power.

Thus, the analyst seems to be in a damned-if-you-do-damned-if-you-don't position. Michael Feldman's position is neither puristic nor judgmental. The analyst's balance is bound to be lost again and again, but it can be regained. He does, however, argue that it is best to try to maintain an independent interpretive role and not yield to the unconscious pressures toward delivering reassurances. In the individual case it is the dynamics of reassurance itself that must be analyzed, both in the transference and the countertransference. Only then can the analyst demonstrate that he or she has not been damaged by projections and, instead, has retained or regained the capacity to think independently as a separate, competent, integrated being. As in the classical tradition, though now for clearer and better reasons, the patient is thought to obtain deep reassurance, chiefly through the analyst's searching and accurate understanding and interpretation of reassurance itself, among many other things, of course.

Feldman does more: He further refines the analysis of splitting presented by him in chapter 5 and Betty Joseph in chapter 4. By viewing the patient as maintaining a number of versions of himself or herself that are kept apart by splitting, he understands the patient to be vulnerable to failures of integration in thinking and other aspects of being. Each version serves an important function, and the functions may clash with one another. Reassurance may only reinforce the patient's barriers against integration. Also, when analysts are being unduly reassuring, their patients sense that they, too, are demonstrating some degree of failure of personal integration—and in this the patients may be correctly diagnosing the structure of countertransference enactments. In these enactments, the analysts may be trying to reassure themselves against whatever anxieties they experience in maintaining the clinical stance with which they are both familiar and comfortable.

14
THE DYNAMICS OF REASSURANCE

MICHAEL FELDMAN

In an analytic session a patient spoke about an incident from his childhood. On the occasion of his mother's birthday, he had bought her a tub of ice cream, choosing his favorite kind. When he offered it to her, she said she supposed he expected her to give him some of it. The patient reported that he had felt deeply wounded by her response. He saw it as an example of the way she never wholeheartedly welcomed what he did for her, and always distrusted his motives.

This story, or some variation of it, had come up a number of times in the analysis. As on these other occasions, my patient portrayed himself as simply offering something good to his mother—the variety of ice cream that he liked best—only to have his motives suspected by someone who was critical and distrustful. It was understandable that he was wounded by the incident, one of many similar ones. Listening to his description of this episode from the past, I thought it also carried a reference to the situation between the two of us: he wanted to make the point that he often felt similarly misjudged and hurt in the analysis, confronted by my equally inappropriate suspicions of his motives.

321

In the particular session to which I am referring, I commented that he was not only describing an upsetting episode that had taken place, but also needed to emphasize how hurtful it was when his benign motives were mistrusted and misjudged by his mother in the past, and by myself in the analysis. He responded to my comment as if it had merely confirmed for him that I too was unsympathetic, distrustful, and not on his side. He protested in a hurt and angry way, and then withdrew into silence. This response was familiar, and I had a strong impression that it had a curiously comforting quality for the patient. It seemed to me that he now felt under no pressure to think, or to examine what his role as well as mine had been. He had settled instead into adopting a picture of himself as a child who had been mistreated by a parent or analyst who ought to feel clumsy and guilty.

In this paper I wish to focus on the value of attending to the way the patient tells a story, the extent to which this serves the function of influencing the way the analyst thinks and responds, and how this forms part of a defensive system against more severe anxieties.

It will perhaps be evident that we are dealing with more than one version of the patient, his object, and the relationship between them.[1] I wish to draw attention in particular to the way the patient used this story. The way he brought it into the session, and his interaction with the analyst served as a means of *enacting* one or other of the versions of his relationship with his mother, in the transference. I will argue that the patient sought to use these procedures to gain reassurance, to reestablish his psychic equilibrium, that I assume had been disturbed in some way that he may or may not have been aware of.

---

[1]Schafer has referred to different "versions" of reality, different "versions" of the present and of the history, that are dependent on the analytic context in which they are established, and which will change as the context changes (1983).

I am particularly concerned with the *function* which different versions of the patient's relationship with his object serve for him, the way he invokes one or other version intrapsychically, and seeks to recreate it in a living way in his relationship with the analyst. I will try to discuss some of the reasons why the achievement of these aims might be reassuring.

In the session that I described, the first version that is present as a potentially desirable scenario involved the patient's mother recognizing his generous and affectionate motives, and responding to him warmly and appreciatively. In the session, he felt entitled to expect that I would listen sympathetically to the episode he reported, understand his benign intentions, and realize how hurt he must have felt.

In the second version, the patient is misjudged by his mother who behaves in a typically suspicious, unfair, and damaging fashion toward him. The patient complained that my response carried a similar implication, and the scene with his mother was partially recreated in the consulting room. Both versions imply that the patient and his object are intensely involved with one another to the exclusion of anyone else.

There is, however, a third version, which I think my patient found most threatening. Here his mother, rather than immediately accepting the ice cream in the way he wished, observed the situation and suggested that his motives were not entirely straightforward. She may have recognized this correctly, and her comment could have been a tolerant and amused one, or she may have responded in a way that was harsh and critical; I am not sure about this. The patient implied that his mother habitually responded in this way, *for her own reasons*, making unfair and unfavorable assumptions about him, *without thinking, and without giving any space to what he himself was thinking or feeling*. However, what has gradually emerged in the analysis suggests to me that what he actually found most difficult was the possibility that she had made her own observations, and had her own

thoughts about what he was doing. She had not been immediately pushed or pulled into one of the roles that the patient
had, in fantasy, assigned to her in relation to him.

It was as if this third version represented the possibility that
his mother was neither fully occupied with him and his gift in a
gratifying way, nor totally preoccupied with something else in a
way that barred any access. Instead, he was confronted with someone who had space and time to think about him *in her own way*.
As I suggest later, I believe this always implies the presence of a
third figure in the mother's mind, with whom she has a relationship, and I think it was this that the patient found unbearable.

In the analysis the patient has sometimes been able to acknowledge how much he hates being aware that I am thinking
for myself. Of course this raises the possibility that I might mis-
understand him as a result of my own prejudices and preconceptions, again demonstrating that I have no room for him, his
thoughts, and feelings. There are, however, other aspects of this
situation that I think he finds even more disturbing. First, if I
am able to think for myself, I might call into question the familiar and reassuring ways he has evolved of seeing himself and his
objects that defend him against too much anxiety or pain. Second, as I have mentioned, my capacity to think for myself implies that he does not have an exclusive hold on me and my
mind, but I have an internal relationship with my own observations, theories, my own dialogue with internal figures from
which he is partially excluded.

In the fragment of a session I have described, I think the patient felt threatened by the approach I adopted, which I believe
was neither to fit in with him immediately, nor to react critically.
It was evident to him that I was observing him closely, and had
some thoughts of my own about what he was doing in the session, why he was repeating the anecdote with the particular
emphasis he gave it, and what function this was meant to serve.
As I have suggested, this implied that I was not exclusively involved

with him in a way he could control, but engaged in a dialogue within my own mind, thinking about the situation in a way that left him feeling isolated and vulnerable.

I was not unaffected by the subtle but powerful pressure and invitation either to enact the benign tolerant relationship on the one hand, or a suspicious and critical one on the other. I had often responded in one way or another without quite recognizing the nature of the pressure, and was sometimes able to think about it only after we had become involved in a repetitive and unhelpful interaction. I am suggesting that it was the fact that on this occasion I had not been driven to enact one of these roles, but had managed to preserve the capacity to observe and think, that the patient found so threatening.

The patient dealt with the anxieties associated with this situation in a familiar way: he insisted that I was in fact the same kind of suspicious and critical figure he constantly encountered in his mother. By fitting me into this representation of a familiar version of his object relationships, he was, paradoxically, able to reassure himself. I suspect, however, that this method of allaying such anxieties was only partially successful, since he both believed, and did not quite believe, that I actually had the characteristics he so forcefully attributed to me.

The analyst also experiences his role vis-à-vis his patient in a variety of ways. Each version is associated with a different degree of anxiety or discomfort. He may feel he is being too naive or too collusive on the one hand, or too critical and persecutory on the other. Such responses are structured by the analyst's training and theoretical background, the values of his professional peer group, his own psychopathology, and his previous experience with this patient or other patients. Part of the analyst's way of reassuring himself is to strive to function in a way that is consistent with a particular "version" with which he is relatively comfortable, and this will depend (to some degree) on the fantasy of being actively supported by an important element of the reference group to which he turns. This, of course, closely parallels the way my patient might have turned to one parent to support him in his dealings with the other, or the way he turned to me, apparently hoping that I would support him when he reported the story of his mother's response to the ice cream.

There may be a "fit" that is reassuring both to the patient and the analyst, which may reflect a healthy and constructive interaction on the one hand, or a collusive one on the other. Conversely, the version of his own role that the analyst finds reassuring may put pressure on the patient to accept a view of himself that he finds intolerable, and the patient is then driven to redress the situation, as in the case of the patient I have been describing. He may exert pressure on the analyst to function in ways with which the analyst is uncomfortable. If the analyst resists this pressure, an impasse may result.

I will return to consider this clinical situation later, but should first like to consider a few of the psychological mechanisms that underlie the clinical phenomena I have described.

The Concept of Splitting

Through the defensive mechanism of intrapsychic splitting, the individual builds up a set of fantasies or "versions" of himself, his objects, and their interactions. These different versions are, of course, closely related to, and dependent on each other. At any given time, one version usually predominates. Each version serves a different function in the person's psychic organization, has a different emotional connotation, and is associated with different degrees of anxiety. When, for any internal or external reason, a version associated with a degree of anxiety that the individual finds difficult to bear becomes more central, the consequent disturbance in his psychic equilibrium brings into play intrapsychic or interpersonal mechanisms designed to restore the equilibrium.

In *An Outline of Psycho-Analysis* (1940), Freud referred to the psychical splitting that he concluded existed not only in the psychoses, but in the neuroses as well.

> The ego often enough finds itself in the position of fending off some demand from the external world which it feels distressing and that this is effected by means of a *disavowal* of the perceptions which bring to knowledge this demand from reality. . . . The disavowal is always supplemented by an acknowledgment; two contrary and independent attitudes always arise and result in the situation of there being a splitting of the ego . . . [pp. 203–204].

Klein developed these ideas further, exploring various types of intrapsychic splitting. In her earliest published paper (1921), she reports a session with a child in which he spoke of a fairytale where a witch offers a man poisoned food. The man gives the food to his horse who dies of the poison. In the session the child said he was afraid of witches, and then went on to say: "There are queens also who are beautiful and yet who are witches too, and he would very much like to know what poison looks like, whether it is solid or fluid" (p. 41). Klein saw this material as an expression of the child's conflicts and anxieties in relation to his mother, and asked him why he was afraid of anything so bad from his mother, what had he done to her or wished about her. He admitted that when he was angry he had wished that she as well as his papa might die and that he had on occasion thought to himself "dirty mamma."

She comments, "The witch in the last-mentioned fantasy only introduces a figure . . . that he had . . . obtained by division of the mother-imago. . . . This second female imago [has been] split off from his beloved mother, in order to maintain her as she is . . ." (p. 42).

In this example we are not dealing simply with the acknowledgment and disavowal of an aspect of reality, but two different versions of the patient's mother and his relationship to her that alternate with each other.

In a later paper (1935) she writes: "In the very young child there exist, side by side with its relations to real objects—but on a different plane, as it were—relations to its unreal imagos, both as excessively good and excessively bad figures, and that these two kinds of object-relations intermingle and color each other to an ever-increasing degree in the course of development" (p. 306). She goes on:

> In the earliest phase the persecuting and the good objects . . . are kept wide apart in the child's mind. When, along with the introjection of the whole and real object, they come closer together, the ego has over and over again recourse to that mechanism—so important for the development of the relations to objects—namely, a splitting of its imagos into loved and hated, that is to say, into good and dangerous ones.

> At this stage of development, the unification of the external and internal, loved and hated, real and imaginary objects is carried out in such a way that each step in the unification leads again to a renewed splitting of the imagos [p. 308].

In her seminal paper of 1946 on schizoid mechanisms, Klein links this splitting of the object representation, and the ego's relation to it, to the type of ego splitting which Freud referred to. She postulates that the early ego is capable of active splitting of the object and its relation to it. Klein then makes the important suggestion that this may imply an active splitting of the ego itself. She goes on to say, "I believe that the ego is incapable of splitting the object—internal and external—without a corresponding splitting taking place within the ego. Therefore the fantasies and feelings about the state of the internal object vitally influence the structure of the ego" (p. 6).

Klein's theory refers to a split between good and bad figures, and good and bad aspects of the ego. It seems likely, however, that in the course of development the splitting that takes place on a number of planes results in the evolution of a set of "versions" of the primary objects and their relationship to the individual. I believe there are probably a limited number of such fantasies or "versions" of self, object, and the interaction or relation between them. Some are associated with a high level of anxiety or excitement, others with comfort and security.

CLINICAL EXAMPLE—RICHARD AND MELANIE KLEIN

In the *Narrative of a Child Psycho-Analysis* (1961), Klein gives a subtle and illuminating example of the reasons for, and the consequences of the use of "reassurance." She describes a session in which her 10-year-old patient Richard was anxious, depressed, and guilty, at a time when his father was seriously ill. In the next session he began by telling the analyst that he was leaving the hotel where he had been living, that day, and talked about parting. He then asked the analyst to tighten his shoelaces so that they would last for the whole day. Shortly afterwards he noticed that his drawings were in a new envelope; he said he was sorry about this and asked what had happened to the old one.

He was told that it had become soaked in the previous day's rain. The patient said he had liked the old envelope, and he asked the analyst whether she had burnt it. She said no, she had salvaged it.

The patient had obviously hoped for this answer: his face brightened and he said he was glad that Mrs. Klein was patriotic (this being wartime). Looking out of the window, he next said, about a girl with curly hair who was passing by, that she was like the monster in his book.

Taking Klein's own notes and comments into account, we can see, first, that she tells us that she knew that the old envelope had acquired a particular importance for the patient, being closely linked in his mind both with the analyst and with a lonely and deserted picture he had of his mother, to whom he was very attached. She points out that while she sometimes answered her patient's questions, which had the effect of reassuring him, in this session she had not only answered a question (about the envelope) but had given a very direct reassurance. She makes it clear that it was very unusual for her to do so, but her response in this case arose out of several things. First, her awareness of the child's fears about the real prospect of the ending of his analysis, and his parting from her. Second, her feelings of concern for him, arising out of her knowledge of his father's serious illness. Both these sessions are pervaded by a very moving sense of sadness and impending loss. She says this "no doubt had an influence on my countertransference."

We can see the consequences of her reassurance clearly illustrated. First, his saying with pleasure that she was patriotic (a very good object), indicating that at that moment she had increased the positive transference. However, his very next remark referred to the girl on the road who, although of quite harmless appearance, appeared to him like a monster. "That is to say, idealization of the analyst—the patriotic and not foreign and suspect Mrs. Klein—had not resolved his doubt in her; but this doubt was deflected and transferred to the girl passing by."

She continues:

> The only way to diminish such suspicions would have been to interpret them. The very fact that instead of giving an appropriate interpretation I had given him a reassurance, which he quite well understood was outside the psycho-analytical procedure, increased his doubts on another level—his doubts in my honesty and sincerity. We find again and again that mistakes of this kind are unconsciously—and with adults sometimes consciously—resented and criticized, and this is true in spite of patients longing to be loved and reassured [1961].

This example suggests that what the patient would *actually* have found reassuring would have been to encounter an analyst who was able to understand and to bear the patient's and her own anxiety and pain without trying to give an apparent reassurance to her young patient or to herself that deviated in a significant way from her usual mode of functioning. If, instead, she had interpreted his anxiety about the damage or loss of the envelope, and all it represented, and her part in this process, she would have conveyed that, while she might well be feeling anxious and distressed, she could still continue to function analytically. She would not have been demonstrating such concern to be a good object for Richard, but her capacity to tolerate him experiencing her as more mixed, and more real. When, as a result of her intervention, Richard felt confronted not only with a version of his analyst as good and kind, but also the doubtful, or "monstrous" version of her as someone who could damage or destroy what was precious to him, and was unable to face this with him, the situation was quickly dealt with by projection of the "monstrous" analyst onto the girl passing outside.

THE CONCEPT OF REASSURANCE

While the concept of reassurance is employed a good deal in analytic and psychotherapeutic work, it has not been studied, or written about to any great extent. Indeed, as the example from Klein's work illustrates, we often intervene in a way that we *intend* or *hope* will be reassuring to the patient, but where the effect is complex, and may even serve to increase the patient's anxiety.

There are several definitions of reassurance provided by the *Oxford English Dictionary*, that generally involve the reestablishment or confirmation of something, or the confirming again or restoring of something that had been lost, as in the example from 1637, "[They] were restored to their former dignities, and reassured their former honors."

The other, slightly different definition of reassurance is as a means of restoring (a person, the mind, etc.) to confidence, as in the following example, "I endeavored to reassure him and the rest from the fear which made him speak so."

Finally, there is the example taken from an authoritative work on marine insurance in 1787, "Reassurance may be said to be a contract, which the first insurer enters into, in order to relieve himself from those risks which he has incautiously undertaken, by throwing them upon other underwriters, who are called reassurers."

The Dynamics of Reassurance

When the patient has allowed some intrapsychic or external event to shift the equilibrium so that an anxiety-provoking representation of himself or his object becomes more central, he tends to use a variety of psychic maneuvers to restore the balance. Some of these mechanisms, the most important and complex of which is projective identification, are essentially intrapsychic, while others involve a dynamic interaction with another person. In the analytic situation, he may exert pressure on the analyst to enact particular roles, which serve to relieve the patient of "those risks which he has incautiously undertaken, by throwing them upon other underwriters, who are called reassurers."

I now want to return to the clinical fragment with which I began. I am suggesting that the patient had built up a set of versions of himself, the important figures in his life, and the relationships between them. One such version, which was potentially reassuring, was the fantasy of his mother responding warmly, gratefully, and unquestioningly to his gift. In the transference relationship, there is a corresponding fantasy of his analyst responding warmly to what he brings as a gift at the start of the session. If such a fantasy was actualized, we might assume that the patient would feel gratified, and relatively free of anxiety or distress. He might feel reassured about his benign and generous motives, and reassured about the exclusive nature of the link with his object, and his hold over the object's mind.

My actual response, which did not correspond with this fantasy, threatened to disturb him. As I have suggested, I thought my response evoked an anxiety that I was observing him and questioning what he was doing, so that he felt he did not control my mind; he felt I was thinking for myself, and I believe this was unconsciously associated with a threat to a defensive bond between us, upon which he felt his safety depended. I would be free instead to engage, in my mind, in an alliance with a figure other than himself. He was threatened by this representation of the parental intercourse, which manifested itself in what he referred to as my "thinking for myself," from within which he might be viewed, and which he did not directly participate in or control. He was not only excluded from this in a painful and disturbing way, but feared I might also recognize impulses and activities in him that aroused his anxiety and guilt.

I thought he reassured himself instead by evoking the familiar version of a critical and unsupportive parental figure that he then projected in fantasy into his representation of his analyst. While we might think this created a painful and difficult situation for the patient, his actual response in the session seemed actually to make him feel comfortable, by restoring a version of an object relationship that was familiar, and over which he felt he had control. In addition to his frustration and distress, there was a sense of grievance and blame, with the patient adopting the role of a well-meaning and innocent figure who was being abused. There was apparently no understanding of my actions or curiosity about my motives or his own, nor indeed any evidence of a wish to gain such understanding. Further, this version of our interaction in the session isolated the two of us in a sadomasochistic relationship, with no reference to the possibility of another perspective. His momentary awareness of my threatening capacity to think for myself had been dissipated.

I should like to look at two further elements of this situation. First, the extremely interesting phenomenon that analysts have become increasingly alerted to, namely, the pressure that the patient puts on the analyst to accept a particular version of himself and the nature of the relationship between them. This pressure does not, however, simply involve the analyst entertaining certain thoughts, images, or fantasies in his mind, but often gives rise to a propensity to enact elements of the relationship that have been projected. This is, of course, an aspect of countertransference, that has been usefully described by Sandler as "role actualization," and has been studied in some detail by Joseph who has clarified the way in which the subtle, often unconscious pressures and invitations to which the analyst is subjected can inform us about the dynamics of the patient's early object relationships.

One way of considering the pressure on the analyst to become involved in the enactment of a particular fantasy is as the patient's attempt at wish-fulfillment. Sandler and Sandler (1978) have made the interesting point that, "The gratification of a wish does not take place through the discharge of energy but through the achievement of what Freud referred to in *The Interpretation of Dreams* [1900] as an 'identity of perception.'"

They refer to the "attempt at actualization, the effort to make the perception of reality correspond to that which is wished for," as a means of obtaining wish fulfillment.

> To the extent that the interaction between self and object representations is reflected in the ideational content of the wish, so the attempt at actualization will often bring into play unconscious and subtle attempts to involve other persons to play the wish-fulfilling role. Nowhere is this more clearly seen than in the transference and as elements of the countertransference. . . . The patient in the analytic situation attempts to impose on the situation a role relationship with the analyst, and . . . this form of externalization of an internal role relationship represents an

integral part of the transference, just as it represents an integral part of object relationships in general [Sandler, 1988, pp. 868–869].

Joseph (1987) has explored some of these processes in detail. She is particularly interested in the way in which projective identification is used, for example, to maintain the patient's narcissistic omnipotent balance. It avoids the relationship between patient and analyst that involves the experience of dependency, anxiety about loss, the awareness of envy, or guilt.

Thus, in Sandler's terms, the patient attempts to effect the external situation in such a way that he achieves the identity of perception between his view of the object, and the wishful fantasy content. In Joseph's terms, the patient uses projective identification unconsciously to act upon the external world, to protect an equilibrium state. A slightly different way of expressing this would be that this state would be threatened if the patient were to experience a version of himself in relation to the analyst that involved feelings such as dependency or guilt.

If we return briefly to consider the analyst's role in this, I believe that the analyst's tendency toward enactment is a response to the anxiety and discomfort associated with a particular fantasy of himself in relation to the patient that has been induced in him. He may, for example, be disturbed by the fantasy of being an unsympathetic or cruel figure in relation to the patient. For the analyst too, the unconscious response to this is to function in a way that will redress the situation, so that a less anxiety-provoking version becomes central, thus restoring the analyst's equilibrium.

The analyst may unconsciously share the patient's fantasy of an exclusive relationship between the patient and himself— whether of a mutually affectionate and supportive kind, or a sadomasochistic kind, for example. For the analyst too the impulse to realize such fantasies or versions of himself vis-à-vis his patient involves splitting and the denial of psychic reality.

It requires internal work for the analyst to become able to recognize the extent to which he and the patient have embraced a complementary set of fantasies and beliefs of which he was partially unconscious, and within which the two of them have been functioning. Joseph (1985) illustrates, for example, how the analyst may become aware that he has been feeling rather comfortable and gratified in the analysis. It may become apparent that the patient, in turn, has been able to accept the analyst's interpretations without being particularly unsettled or disturbed by them, since the underlying unconscious assumption seems to be that he occupies some special place, or that there is some special symmetry between himself and the analyst. Neither patient nor analyst had any conviction that any real progress was possible, but both were curiously untroubled by this. They shared the belief that the situation was hopeless, but any real concern, that might have disturbed the equilibrium, was split off and projected.

The analyst's awareness of the nature of the fantasy underlying the relationship between himself and his patient (or the version of their relationship which is central) at a given moment, involves relinquishing the safety and reassurance associated with such omnipotent fantasies. This in turn involves partially reversing the splitting and projective processes upon which such fantasies depend. Segal (1978) has pointed out how thinking puts a limit on the omnipotence of fantasy and is therefore hated and attacked because of the individual's longing for such omnipotence, but she also emphasizes the freedom and relief offered by the recovery of those functions that were split off and projected. The analyst may become aware of his own resistance to, and hatred of, the *awareness* of these fantasies (both in himself and the patient), and the consequences that flow from having to *think about them*, rather than living them out.

If the analyst is able to tolerate some of the anxiety and uncertainty that arise when he begins to recognize and think about
the nature of his relationship with the patient, and the complexity of his own motives and fantasies, he may achieve a more substantial experience of reassurance. This depends on the recovery
of the links between different aspects of himself and his objects,
and the sense that these objects can be allowed the freedom to
engage with each other. If the analyst can retain the belief that
the outcome of this intercourse will, on balance, be a constructive one, this offers him some freedom from the tyranny of the
demand for exclusive attachments to particular internal objects,
as a means of avoiding anxiety and guilt.

While at one level, with my patient, the enactment of a benign
and unquestioning parent would have reassured, comforted, and
gratified him, the clinical illustration of Melanie Klein and Richard, that I quoted earlier, enables us to appreciate more fully
the possible consequences of this. When she responded un-
characteristically to just this type of pressure to be the benign and
reassuring analyst, there was a temporary experience of reassurance, not only for the patient, but also for the analyst. She makes
the point, however, that the temporary increase in the positive
transference was achieved at the expense of the splitting off and
projection of the more hostile and suspicious elements of the
transference onto the passing girl, whom, he said, looked like a
monster. Klein makes the important point that her own need, in
that particular session, to give an apparently reassuring reply to
her young patient actually served to increase his doubts about
her. I think patients often recognize such actions, that we all
engage in, as expressions of the analyst's own anxieties and wishes,
and they similarly increase the patient's uneasiness about the
analyst's strength and capacity to contain his projections.

In exploring the question of the patient's representation of
his analyst, we encounter problems with the notion of different versions of the object. The value of referring to Richard's

different versions of Melanie Klein (in the example quoted) will depend on our view of the degree of splitting in operation at a given time, and the question of the links that remain between the different elements that have been split and projected. If we are dealing with a situation where there is intense anxiety, and the degree of splitting is severe, it seems to me to be useful to speak of different versions of the object as if they were mutually exclusive. This is, of course, one of the characteristics of the paranoid–schizoid position described by Klein. If there is a greater degree of integration, however, it may be more useful to think in terms of a single version or representation of the analyst, that includes as its elements, for example, the good Mrs. Klein, the monster, the patient's recognition of her temporary weakness and anxiety, and her inability properly to tolerate the pain and guilt to which she was exposed, with each of these elements having an organic link with the others.

Thus, while it is undoubtedly true that my patient sought the comfort and gratification of an analyst responding in a benign, unquestioning, and appreciative way to what he had brought, I was not convinced that he either expected me simply to accept what he had brought without thinking, or that if I had done so it would have provided any more than a temporary and uneasy reassurance. I believe he would consciously or unconsciously have recognized that my enactment of the fantasy of the benign, affectionate mother would have been partly based on my own anxieties and needs; for example, on my need to split off and deny any connection between his rejecting mother and myself, and my wish to feel valued and loved by my patient.

Similarly, it was not merely that my patient turned for a particular type of reassurance to the fantasy in which he was with a cruel, even sadistic analyst. As the session unfolded he put increasing pressure on me to join in the enactment of this scenario by becoming impatient and frustrated with him, arguing with him, perhaps making some critical or sarcastic remark, or actually missing a helpful or illuminating contribution from him. While the enactment of this role (which I suspect we can rarely avoid completely) would have provided my patient with a degree of gratification, excitement, and triumph, this would have been achieved at the cost of the splitting off and projection of more benign, thoughtful aspects of his analyst. While this version of me as someone caught up in a sadomasochistic interaction with him might be accompanied by temporary gratification and reassurance, the success of this process has a disturbing and weakening effect on the patient. I suspect that there is always a conscious or unconscious recognition that such an enactment reveals anxieties and difficulties in the analyst, and gives the patient a sense of having drawn him away from a more creative method of functioning, which is ultimately neither strengthening nor reassuring for the patient.

I thought, at some level, my patient both expected and needed me to continue to function as someone who could receive and contain his projections (in Bion's sense), neither enacting something in response, nor being too disturbed by them.

CONCLUDING REMARKS

In this paper I have briefly described the way in which the process of splitting leads to the establishment of a set of "versions" of the self and the object, varying in the extent to which the connections between them remain active. I have suggested that the mechanism of reassurance is called into play when a particular anxiety-laden version becomes central, disturbing the individual's psychic equilibrium. The patient attempts to gain reassurance in order to reestablish the lost state of equilibrium. This seems often to involve the reestablishment of a familiar omnipotent, narcissistic object relationship.

I believe we can distinguish between two types of reassurance. The individual's equilibrium can be restored by making central a version of himself, his object, and their relationship that has

340   MICHAEL FELDMAN

been achieved through the splitting and projection of disturbing elements of the whole configuration. I think this mechanism
was vividly illustrated in the example from Melanie Klein. The
restoration of this equilibrium is achieved, however, at the cost
of the disavowal of important elements of the individual's psychic reality, including his perception of, and relation to, his
object as complex and integrated.

There are close parallels with the child's attempt to recruit one
parent into an exclusive relationship in which different facets of
that parent's personality, as well as his or her relationship to the
other parent, are denied. By this means the child may establish
what Britton (1989) has described as the "oedipal illusion." There
is no doubt that the realization of such a wishful fantasy can be
reassuring—confirming, for example, the version of the child as
someone able to gratify and fulfill all the parent's needs, excluding anyone else from the parent's mind or his or her life.

In the analytic situation, the analyst may feel under considerable conscious or unconscious pressure to participate in this.
The patient's projections often mobilize anxieties and conflicts
within him, and he may have his own reasons for wishing to dis-
own versions of himself as too harsh or sadistic, too seductive,
or ineffective. Thus, the patient's projections may recruit the
analyst's own difficulties in retaining an effective connection
with those elements in his personality, those thoughts or capacities, those versions of himself the patient may wish to banish
from the analyst's mind.

If the patient feels that the reassurance he seeks has been
achieved by drawing the analyst into the enactment of his wishes,
I suspect this always involves the fantasy of having separated
the analyst from those objects or functions that offer him balance and perspective. This confirms the patient's belief in his omnipotence, with the accompanying anxiety and guilt. More
importantly, perhaps, it confirms the presence (externally and
internally) of a weak and unsupported figure from whom he is

unable actually to gain reassurance. This may, of course, reinforce the need to go on using projective mechanisms, to defend
against the confrontation with a weak and divided parental
couple, or their representation in the analyst's mind.

The paradox we encounter in analytic work is that it is painful
and threatening for the patient that the analyst should be able
to think for himself; he engages in intercourse within his own
mind, whether with theories, colleagues, or his own previous experience, from all of which the patient is and has been excluded;
nonetheless, the patient relies on the analyst in all these ways. This
is, I think, connected with the reassurance derived from the
patient's belief that he has not been able to destroy either parent, or the parental couple in the original oedipal situation. He
then comes into contact with a version of the parent or analyst
who is able to struggle to maintain a capacity to "think for himself" that paradoxically involves a relationship with a third party.

I am thus suggesting that the creation of an illusion of an exclusive relationship between one parent and the child, or the
analyst and the patient, where vital but painful elements of psychic reality are split off and projected, cannot be the basis for a
genuinely reassuring experience. On the contrary, reassurance
must involve the survival or the restoration of an oedipal configuration in which both parents are allowed a relationship with one
another as well as with the child. The analyst is then allowed a
complex relationship with different parts of his own mind, and
different versions of the patient with whom he is dealing. The
internalization of this configuration enables the patient to achieve
a greater degree of integration between the different elements
of his own personality and, ultimately, a genuine experience of
reassurance.

SUMMARY

This paper describes the process of splitting that leads to the
establishment of a set of "versions" of the self and the object,

and the relationship between them. The author suggests that the mechanism of reassurance is called into play when a particular anxiety-laden version becomes central, disturbing the patient's psychic equilibrium. The patient then strives to restore the state that he has lost, either in fantasy, or by attempting to draw the analyst into a familiar enactment.

A brief description is given of a patient who felt most threatened by the prospect of the analyst being able to think for himself. This challenged more familiar and comforting versions of the two of them involved in the repetitive enactment of earlier object relationships. It is suggested that, paradoxically, the analyst's capacity to make his own observations and judgments invokes for the patient the presence of a third figure, with all the accompanying oedipal anxieties and threats. However, the patient's experience of true reassurance is ultimately derived from his belief that he has not succeeded in replacing the oedipal triangular relationship with one in which he and the analyst are exclusively involved with one another.

REFERENCES

Britton, R. (1989), The missing link: Parental sexuality in the Oedipus complex. In: *The Oedipus Complex Today; Clinical Implications*, ed. J. Steiner. London: Karnac Books, pp. 83–101.
Freud, S. (1900), The Interpretation of Dreams. *Standard Edition*, 4 & 5. London: Hogarth Press, 1953.
——— (1940), An outline of psychoanalysis. *Standard Edition*, 23:139–207. London: Hogarth Press, 1964.
Joseph, B. (1985), Transference: The total situation. In: *Psychic Equilibrium and Psychic Change*, ed. M. Feldman & E. Bott Spillius. London: Routledge, 1989, pp. 156–167.
——— (1987), Projective identification: Some clinical aspects. In: *Psychic Equilibrium and Psychic Change*, ed. M. Feldman & E. Bott Spillius. London: Routledge, 1989, pp. 168–180.
Klein, M. (1921), The development of a child. In: *Writings*, Vol. 1. London: Hogarth Press, 1975, pp. 1–53.

———— (1935), A contribution to the psychogenesis of manic-depressive states. In: *Writings*, Vol. 1. London: Hogarth Press, 1975, pp. 262–289.

———— (1946), Notes on some schizoid mechanisms. In: *Writings*, Vol. 3. London: Hogarth Press, 1975, pp. 1–24.

———— (1961), Narrative of a Child Psycho-Analysis. In: *Writings*, Vol. 4. London: Hogarth Press, 1975.

Sandler, J. (1988), On internal object relationships. *J. Amer. Psychoanal. Assn.*, 38:859–880, 1990.

———— Sandler, A.-M. (1978), On the development of object relationships and affects. *Internat. J. Psycho-Anal.*, 59:285–296.

Schafer, R. (1983), *The Analytic Attitude*. New York: Basic Books.

Segal, H. (1978), Psychoanalysis and freedom of thought. In: *The Work of Hanna Segal*. New York: Jason Aronson, pp. 217–227, 1981.

EDITOR'S INTRODUCTION TO
WORKING THROUGH
IN THE COUNTERTRANSFERENCE

In this essay, Irma Brenman Pick carefully teases apart the complex structure of countertransference analysis. She follows the lead of significant earlier contributors to the topic of countertransference. She emphasizes particularly Money-Kyrle's 1956 paper on countertransference which established the value of differentiating three principal factors: that which comes from the analyst's own personality and role in the analysis; that which the patient provokes by projective identifications into the analyst's specific personality vulnerabilities and role; and that which the patient feels in reaction to having influenced the analyst's countertransference. The second of these points, the patient's seeking out specific vulnerabilities for projective purposes, is especially worth noting because it is not often made as a principal point; usually, it is only what the projective identification can induce in the analyst. The patient's (usually unconscious) reality testing in this regard is not to be minimized.

Irma Brenman Pick goes on to articulate the ambivalence that pervades both the transference and countertransference: on the one hand, the set of loving, concerned, guilty, reparative intentions, and, on the other, the hateful, greedy, envious, destructive intentions. To varying degrees, both sets enter into the giving of interpretations as well as their reception. She also differentiates what may be inherent in the act of interpreting itself from the use of interpretation by the analyst to act out hostile or nurturant phantasies. In the latter regard, the acting out may be facilitated by the analyst's idealizing his or her own way of working as utterly invulnerable, unambivalent, conflict-free, or neutral.

The analyst's protection against this self-idealization is evident in his or her readiness to note countertransferential response tendencies, regress into them inwardly in order to experience them emotionally, sort out their constituents (as described above), and return with them to the integrative orientation that underlies the analyst's optimal performance. Then the analyst is in the best position to frame an interpretation that implies genuine experience of the analytic moment and to do so without being explicitly confessional or exhibitionistic. One is reminded here of Ernst Kris's (1952) essay on regression in the service of the ego and the applications of that idea to the analyst's functioning in the clinical situation.

Brenman Pick gives a number of instructive clinical examples, three from the same patient. Although some of these countertransferences had not been adequately analyzed then and there in the clinical interaction, each of them is presented here in thoroughly analyzed form. With these examples, Brenman Pick demonstrates both senses of "working through" in her title: (1) mastering countertransference conflict by analyzing it, and (2) using that countertransference calmly and effectively on the strength of firsthand experience. Only then will the patient feel safe and as available as possible at that time to receive an interpretation and perhaps begin to try to integrate it.

In her fourth case example, which concerns a patient hospitalized in a psychotic state, Brenman Pick encounters issues of management as well as interpretation, a full discussion of which would range beyond the scope of this book. The three preceding examples do extend at times deeply into the mother–infant experience in a manner reminiscent at times of Melanie Klein's interpretations and, to a lesser extent, Hanna Segal's (in which regard see chapters 3 and 12). Nevertheless, they also fit in well with the contemporary emphasis on moment-to-moment vicissitudes of transference–countertransference engagement and do not revert prematurely or evasively to reconstructions of the distant past. Most of the essays that make up this book contain specific clinical examples of the analysis and uses of countertransference that Brenman Pick approaches here as her main subject matter. At this point in the series of essays, further study of all these examples could solidify the reader's understanding of many of the essentials of contemporary Kleinian analysis.

15
WORKING THROUGH
IN THE COUNTERTRANSFERENCE

IRMA BRENMAN PICK

In this paper I hope to explore something about the complex interaction that takes place between analyst and analysand in our everyday work. Bion made the succinct remark that when two people get together they make a relationship whether they like it or not; this applies to all encounters including psychoanalysis.

Strachey (1934), in his now classic paper, spoke of a true transference interpretation being that which the analyst most feared and most wished to avoid. Yet later he went on to say that in receiving a transference interpretation, the patient has the experience of expressing murderous impulses toward the analyst and of the analyst interpreting these without anxiety or fear. Strachey is clearly implying that the full or deep transference experience is disturbing to the analyst; that which the analyst most fears and most wishes to avoid. He also says that conveying an interpretation in a calm way to the patient is necessary. The area I wish to address is this ambiguous problem, this walking the tightrope between experiencing disturbance and responding with interpretation that does not convey disturbing anxiety.

This is a revised version of a paper first published in 1985 in the *International Journal of Psycho-Analysis*, 66:157–66.

While earlier understanding regarded countertransference as something extraneous rather than integral, Heimann (1950) showed the use of the countertransference as an important tool for psychoanalysis and differentiated this from the pathological countertransference response. While this differentiation is an essential part of our psychoanalytic endeavor, I wish to show how problematic the clinical reality is. For there is no such absolute separation, only a relative movement within that orbit.

It was Money-Kyrle (1956) who considerably furthered our understanding of this issue by showing how closely the analyst's experience of the patient's projections may be linked with the analyst's own internal reactions to the material. For example, he showed that in a difficult phase of an analysis the projection by the patient into the analyst of his incompetent self became mixed up with the analyst's own feelings of professional incompetence in not understanding the material quickly enough, and these issues had to be disentangled.

Money-Kyrle, investigating this problem in its more ordinary manifestations, said:

> If the analyst is in fact disturbed [and here it is implied that the analyst is inevitably disturbed in the sense of affected], it is also likely that the patient has unconsciously contributed to this result, and is in turn disturbed by this. So we have three factors to consider: first, the analyst's emotional disturbance, for he may have to deal with this silently in himself before he can disengage himself sufficiently to understand the other two; then the patient's part in bringing it about; and finally, its effect on him. Of course, all three factors may be sorted out in a matter of seconds, and then indeed the counter-transference is functioning as a delicate receiving apparatus [p. 361].

Indeed, insofar as we take in the experience of the patient, we cannot do so without also having an experience. If there is a mouth that seeks a breast as an inborn potential, there is, I believe, a psychological equivalent; that is, a state of mind which seeks another state of mind.

The child's or patient's projective identifications are actions in part intended to produce reactions; the first thing that happens inside a living object into whom a projection takes place is a reaction. The analyst may deal with this so quickly as not to become aware of it: yet it is a crucial factor. The encounter is an interaction and, indeed, if it is being dealt with that quickly, we may have to ask whether the deeper experience is in fact being avoided.

A patient reported the following: when she was born, mother was advised to send away her 18-month-old brother, in the event, to relatives far distant, so that mother would be free to take proper care of the new baby. When the boy returned home six weeks later, mother was horrified to find that he did not recognize his parents, and mother said that after that "wild horses would not keep them apart."

I am struck by the metaphor and its relation to psychoanalytic practice. I think that the advice contained in Freud's metaphor of the mirror, or the analyst as surgeon, implicitly suggests that in order to take proper care of the patient's unconscious, the analyst's emotionality should be sent as far away as possible. The consequences of this attitude do result in the nonrecognition of essential areas and the danger that when the split-off emotionality returns, "wild horses won't keep it apart"—with all the dangers of acting out. To imagine that this split-off emotionality won't return is contrary to the very theories we hold in relation to mental life.

Unless we are to say that psychoanalytic function takes place in a conflict-free autonomous zone of the ego, we have to allow for the problems involved not only in digesting the patient's projections, but also in assimilating our own responses so that they can be subjected to scrutiny. The analyst, like the patient, desires to eliminate discomfort as well as to communicate and share experience; ordinary human reactions. In part, the patient seeks an enacting response, and in part, the analyst has an impulse to enact, and some of this will be expressed in the interpretation. This may range from an implicit indulgence, caressing the patient with words, to responses so hostile or distant or frozen that they seem to imply that the deprivation of the experience the patient yearns for is of no matter; a contention that a part object mechanical experience is all that is necessary.

Yet an interpretation, and the act of giving an interpretation, is not a part object selection of a number of words, but an integrative, creative act on the part of the analyst. It will include unspoken, and in part unconscious communication about what has been taken in, and how it has been taken in, as well as information about what has not been taken in.

The patient receiving an interpretation will "hear" not only words or their consciously intended meaning. Some patients indeed only listen to the "mood" and do not seem to hear the words at all. Joseph (1975) has shown vividly that we may be misled by the patient's words; the mood and atmosphere of the communication may be more important. The patient may operate with the same accent, listen to the analyst's speech in the same manner. His perceptions may be considerably dominated by his internal configurations and fantasies, but, I believe, following Klein's account in 1952, that: "In the young infant's mind every external experience is interwoven with his fantasies and . . . every fantasy contains elements of actual experience, and it is only by analyzing the transference situation to its depth that we are able to discover the past both in its realistic and fantastic aspects" (p. 437).

Inevitably, the patient too will take in, consciously and unconsciously, some idea of the analyst as a real person. When we speak of a mother giving the baby the nipple, we do not consider a simple nipple–mouth relationship; we recognize that the baby takes in a penumbra of experience. There is always something in excess of the actual process. We see reported: "The patient said . . . and the analyst interpreted," yet the complexities are enormous. To address the question of how the analyst features in the internal world of the patient, we need not only to move into the paranoid–schizoid internal world of the patient; we also require some flexibility in tolerating and working through the tensions between our own conscious and unconscious impulses and feelings toward the patient.

Constant projecting by the patient into the analyst is the essence of analysis; every interpretation aims at a move from the paranoid–schizoid to the depressive position. This is true not only for the patient, but for the analyst who needs again and again to regress and work through. I wonder whether the real issue of truly deep versus superficial interpretation resides not so much in terms of which level has been addressed but to what extent the analyst has worked the process through internally in the act of giving the interpretation.

A patient, Mr. A, had recently come to live in London (his first analysis had taken place abroad). He arrived for his session a few hours after having been involved in a car accident in which his stationary car was hit and badly damaged; he himself just missed being severely injured. He was clearly still in a state of some shock, yet he did not speak of shock or fear. Instead he explained with excessive care what had taken place, and the correct steps taken by him before and after the collision. He went on to say that by chance his mother (who lives in the same country as the previous analyst) phoned soon after the accident, and when told about the accident responded with: "I wouldn't have phoned if I'd known you'd have such awful news. I don't want to hear about it." He said that thanks to his previous analysis, he knew that he needed to understand that his mother could not do otherwise, and he accepted that. He was, however, very angry with the other driver, and was belligerent in his contention that he would pursue, if necessary to court, his conviction that the other driver would have to pay for the damage.

I believe that he conveyed very vividly his belief that he would have to bear alone or be above the immediate shock, fear, and rage generated both by the accident and the mother's response to it. Not only did he believe that his mother did not want to hear the awful news, but that the analyst did not want to hear the awful news of there being a mother-analyst who does not listen to or share pain with him. Instead, he felt he had been taught to "understand" the mother or listen to the analyst with an angry underlying conviction that the mother-analyst will not listen to his distress. He went along with this, pulled himself together, made a display of behaving correctly, became a so-called "understanding" person. He replaced the distress of bearing pain with competence in doing the right thing, but let us know that unconsciously he will pursue his grievances to the bitter end.

Although he moved quickly from vulnerable victim to perpetrator of competent cruelty (consciously against the other driver, unconsciously against the mother and previous, and current, analyst), I also experienced an atmosphere that led me to believe that there was space for a more genuinely creative relationship to develop. In the countertransference I felt that what I was asked to bear was not excessive, and that while there was a patient who does not want to know, I might also rely on there being a patient who shared wanting to know with me.

Now let us consider what took place in the session. The patient made an impact in his "competent" way of dealing with his feelings, yet he also conveyed a wish for there to be an analyst-mother who would take in his fear and his rage. I interpreted the yearning for someone who will not put down the phone, but instead will take in and understand what this unexpected impact feels like; this supposes the transference onto the analyst of a more understanding maternal figure. I believe, though, that this "mates" with some part of the analyst that may wish to "mother" the patient in such a situation. If we cannot take in and think about such a reaction in ourselves, we either act out by indulging the patient with actual mothering (this may be done in verbal or other sympathetic gestures) or we may become so frightened of doing this, that we freeze and do not reach the patient's wish to be mothered.

Yet already I had been lured into either admiring the sensible, competent approach, or appearing to condemn it. I found that I was having the experience of feeling superior to and judging the mother, previous analyst, and his own "competence." Was I being party to taking them all to court? I then needed to reflect about the parts of himself and his internal objects that did not want to know. These too were projected into the analyst, and also, in my view, "mated" with parts of the analyst that might not wish to know about human vulnerability (ultimately death) either in external reality, or currently in feeling "tossed about" by the patient in the session.

I then needed to show him that he believed that in presenting me with such an awful picture of mother-analyst, he persuaded me to believe that I was different from and better than them. Yet he also believed (and that was how he had behaved toward me at the beginning of the session) that I too did not want to know about the fear engendered either by unexpected accidents or by the impact which he believed he had upon me.

If we feel at the mercy of an analytic superego that does not support us in knowing about these internal buffetings, we are, like the patient, in danger of "wrapping it all up" competently. We may act out by becoming excessively sympathetic to the patient, taking the others to court in a superior or angry way, or becoming excessively sympathetic to the others, taking the patient to court in a superior or angry way.

The process of meeting and working through our own experience of both wanting to know and fearing knowing (in Bion's

terms +K and –K) facilitates, I believe, a deeper and more empathic contact with these parts of the patient and his internal
objects. If we fail to take into account *in statu nascendi* our own
conflictual responses, we risk enacting that which we should be
interpreting, that is, the hijacking of all the good propensities
and the projection into the other "driver" of all the evil; we may
behave as though we could meet with accidents or the vicissitudes of life with impunity.

In taking the case to court, the patient's belief in the superiority of competently keeping out passions and ostensibly pursuing "pure" truth, needs to be examined. What looks like
truth-seeking is suffused with hatred. There is an underlying
menace that if I make a wrong move, my name will be blackened,
as he has already blackened the other driver, mother, and the
previous analyst. My experience leads me to believe in the
patient's terror that if he makes a wrong move, he will be taken
to court and judged by a merciless superego.

I think that this raises a question for the analyst. If we keep
emotions out, are we in danger of keeping out the love which
mitigates the hatred, thus allowing the so-called pursuit of truth
to be governed by hatred? What appears as dispassionate, may
contain the murder of love and concern.

Bion (1962), referring to psychotically disturbed patients,
writes: "The attempts to evade experience with *live objects* by
destroying alpha function leaves the personality unable to have
a relationship with any aspect of itself that does not resemble
an automaton" (p. 13, emphasis added). Later he says: "The
scientist whose investigations include the stuff of life itself finds
himself in a situation that has a parallel in that of the patients . . . Confronted with the complexities of the human
mind the analyst must be circumspect in following even accepted scientific method; its weakness may be closer to the
weakness of psychotic thinking than superficial scrutiny would
admit" (p. 14).

356 IRMA BRENMAN PICK

One great difficulty in our work is in this dual area of remaining in contact with the importance of our own experience as well as our allegiance to the profound value of our technique; this forms part of the impossibility and the value of our endeavors. I think that this problem applies, for instance, to the controversial issue of interpretation versus response; in a way a false argument and in a way a very real one. Yet the issue becomes polarized, as though one was all good, the other all bad. Consider a patient bringing particularly good or particularly bad news; say, the birth of a new baby or a death in the family. While such an event may raise complex issues requiring careful analysis, in the first instance the patient may not want an interpretation, but a response; the sharing of pleasure or of grief. And this may be what the analyst intuitively wishes for too. Unless we can properly acknowledge this *in* our interpretation, interpretation itself either becomes a frozen rejection, or is abandoned and we feel compelled to act noninterpretively and be "human." We then do not help the patient to share with the analyst the experience that interpretation itself is not an ideal object, that is, a depressive position sharing within the analytic framework, rather than a frozen response or noninterpretive aside.

On a later occasion, this hitherto rather propitiating patient began a session the day before a General Election, telling me with pleasure and excitement that he was thrilled at the prospect of the Tory victory. It then emerged that he had picked up either from my careful inquiry or from previous knowledge that I was probably a Labour supporter. I interpreted that I thought he was anticipating with triumphant excitement watching whether in the heat of the moment I would address myself to his reactions or mine.

He associated to a visit to a cousin with a new baby, and the story of his own mother's labor with him. (He was not aware of the link labor/Labour Party.) As she was going into labor, she first offered to do all the family washing.

The patient not only reported a past family myth, but relived in the transference this relationship with an internal mother. My countertransference problem was that either I was programmed to react angrily at this assault in the negation of my "labor" pains, or to be a saintly mother who would selflessly deal with his "dirty washing" without a thought for my disturbance.

But beyond that I believe the patient mocked me as a mother whom he believed was above all concerned to keep her hands clean. Was I getting caught up with being technically correct, because I could not bear to take in how awful it feels to be a loser, and to be filled with hatred when someone else flaunts his or her success—the cousin with the new baby?

Like the young child, the patient, I believe, is consciously and unconsciously acutely sensitive to the way we interpret his difficulties in confronting the important issues; his labor in getting in touch with his infantile self—his propensities to become sadistic when he feels neglected or jealous or envious, when he feels mother-analyst is engaged with a new baby, and he feels himself to be the unwanted party. The patient raises very deep issues of rivalry between mother and child as to which "party" is best equipped to deal with the issues, all of which may stir up reactions or excessive defensiveness on the part of analyst as well as patient. It is our professional task to subject these reactions to scrutiny. I think that the extent to which we succeed or fail in this task will be reflected not only in the words we choose, but in our voice and other demeanor in the act of giving an interpretation. This will include the whole spectrum from frank self-righteous sadism to impeccable masochistic or hypocritical "patience" in enduring the cruelties to which patients subject us. The point is that we have to cope with feelings, and subject them to thought; as Segal (1977) stresses, we are not neutral in the sense of having no reaction.

Money-Kyrle (1956), in speaking of the analytic function, stresses not only sublimated curiosity on the part of the analyst, but the analyst's reparative and parental function. In his view, in the moment of the projective phase of the interpretation, the analyst is also taking care of an immature part of the self, which needs to be protected from the sadistic part. When we show the patient that he becomes sadistic when he feels neglected or that he identifies himself with the neglecting object and fails to take note of the needy infantile self, I think whether we know it or not, the interpretation will contain some projection of our own wish to protect the baby from the sadistic part. The maintenance of a careful setting is in some way a demonstration of this care.

In developmental terms the infant who is able to begin more genuinely to feel for the mother's hurt and wishes to protect her from it, is an infant who has taken in and identified with a mother who feels for his hurt and wishes to protect him from unnecessary hurt, as well as supporting him to bear pain. This experience does not come from a saintly mother, but a flesh and blood mother who knows about her own wishes to be rid of troublesome problems.

I have been trying to show that the issue is not a simple one; the patient does not just project into an analyst, but instead patients are quite skilled at projecting into particular aspects of the analyst. Thus, I have tried to show, for example, that the patient projects into the analyst's wish to be a mother, the wish to be all-knowing, or to deny unpleasant knowledge, into the analyst's instinctual sadism, or into his defenses against it. And above all, he projects into the analyst's guilt, or into the analyst's internal objects.

Thus, patients touch off in the analyst deep issues and anxieties related to the need to be loved and the fear of catastrophic consequence in the face of defects, that is, primitive persecutory or superego anxiety. I shall try to show this with a final example from this patient.

This patient began a Friday session, a week before the holidays, announcing that he felt ill. He did not know what it was;

he had the same symptoms as his little girl. But, said fiercely, "I was determined to come, even if that risks you [the analyst] getting my illness."

He was clearly frightened by illness and its potential threat. In the counter-transference I found I was worrying about being infected and becoming unable to cope with work next week (i.e., having his symptoms). I interpreted his fear and referred to the part of him that wished me to "catch the illness" of that fear.

He then told me about his small child's school play the day before. His wife had had a pressing work commitment and could not attend. He had given up his session to be there. He described the delight of watching the children; they would recognize parents and relatives and interrupt the performance to call, "Hello Mommy." He was hurt and angry that his wife was not present: it was plain that he felt lonely, unsupported by a family. I interpreted the loneliness; the wish for me to have been there as a "family." I related this to anger with *my* work commitments (I had not been able to change his hour), as well as my weekend and holiday commitments.

He acknowledged this, then remembered an occasion when he had seen me at a public lecture where psychoanalysis was under attack for not providing patients with sufficient support. He said that he had observed how well I had dealt with this.

I felt flattered and then needed to think about this. I interpreted that I was being flattered into a belief about how well I coped with this charge, while in fact I was being watched to see how I manage when I feel alone, unsupported and assailed by persecutors, external or internal.

He said he had woken in the night with a fear that he could die; previously with such a feeling he had experienced utter panic; now it was more with a feeling of terrible sadness to take in that one day he just won't be there. He had had a dream.

In the dream Freud was undergoing an operation for shoulder lesions. There was a worry that the operation was not fully successful; when Freud tried to lift his arm he could not do so. A group of people, including the patient, were trying to protect Freud in various ways, including sedation, so that he would not have to bear the pain.

He told me that I, and indeed Freud, the father of all psychoanalysts, needed group support; part of this support lies in sedation. While he claimed to be part of a group supporting Freud, he had also said at the beginning of the session, that he needed my help even if that meant not protecting me.

There was a seductive, spurious quality to the sedative support. I thought of the operations on Freud, not for shoulder lesions, but for cancer associated with smoking. My patient had seen me smoking at that meeting. I felt a strong urge to avoid this area.

I pointed out that he seemed to be protecting me from this issue; as though that would be too much to put on my shoulders. He admitted this and now said that in the dream the lesions seemed to be a consequence of cancer. He spoke of his aged father and the fear of his death. Now he protected me by placing the problem with an aged father.

We could say that the patient projects into the analyst parts of himself and his internal objects, as indeed he does. He presents two models; the one copes impeccably, the other is broken down. In the course of such projection, he affects me. In the session I found that I was lured into having experiences in both directions ("I'm terrific" or "I'm awful"). I have to remind myself that I was neither. In part, I do share, or am infected, by the child's symptoms, idealization, or persecutory fear, in which the depressive position mother gets lost. This has to be recovered so that I and also the patient can be helped to realize that in assailing the mother or father with these pressures, including guilt (putting it all on Freud's shoulders), the child's need to be protected and cared for gets lost. In part the patient projects anxieties about, and rivalrous triumph over, unable parents; he also fears an analyst triumphant over a patient unable to cope with feeling ill or abandoned.

I believe that there is evidence of movement in the patient from the impeccable coping after the accident (as reported earlier) to something that feels more hopeful about anxieties about not coping (more feelings of sadness, rather than feeling overwhelmed by panic). While there is pain and rage about missing parents, or what was missing in the parents, this is interrupted now by child parts delighted to recognize good aspects of parental and analytic support. The need for an impeccable performance has given way to the possibility of more spontaneous interaction.

My stress is that, within the analyst as well, spontaneous emotional interaction with the patient's projections takes place, and that if we fully respect this and are not too dominated by the demand for impeccable neutrality, we can make better use of the experience for interpretation.

The patient's projection of his experience into the analyst may be felt by both as an unwarranted intrusion and touches on issues in mental life where boundaries between internal and external, fantasy and reality, self and object become problematic in various ways. I shall give a brief illustration.

A young married woman had been exposed to a series of unpleasant burglaries. Now their apartment is secured like a fortress. She arrives on a Monday saying that the weekend has been awful, taken over by an event on the Friday night, a burglary, not to their apartment (which is now so well secured), but to the apartment above where the people are always away. "We were just going to sleep. We could hear the footsteps because the partitions are so thin. We called the police but by the time they got there, the bastards had got away." Meanwhile they tried to reach the owners at their country house. First they got the answering machine, and when eventually they reached them, the owners explained they'd been in the garden clearing up the aftermath of a huge party—"the discrepancy of our experience and theirs seemed crazy." The rest of the weekend she felt depressed, upset, exposed, and vulnerable, and in no state to look after her baby.

The patient reports an actual event at the weekend; an intrusion into her home. In the transference there are already hints linking the "upstairs owners" with me (I have an answering machine; I work in an upstairs room in a tall house, and I am also "always unavailable" on the weekend). She tells me that the discrepancy between the experience of those people who are away having a party and her experience is enormous, implying that I will be distanced from taking in her experience. But am I? On the contrary, as she continues to describe the detail of how the burglars climbed up the drainpipe to the third floor, and says that what was so specially disturbing is that "We really thought we had got the apartment secured; while it's happening, it feels so sinister." I find that my thoughts have turned, naturally enough, to my house, to thinking with some anxiety—"a burglary like this could happen to me; I'm not so secure either."

The patient continues: "In fact, when the police arrived, they came with vicious sniffer dogs—as I opened the door—the dogs, although held on a tight rein, jumped! I felt terrified and for a moment I felt sorry for the burglar."

In my view this patient was not only describing the events of the weekend; she was also engaged in intruding into me certain sinister fears, both of being intruded into in reality, but also about being "sniffed out" and "jumped on." She alerts me to her fear of being intruded into and sniffed out and jumped on (suggesting also certain sexual anxieties in the face of a frightening superego). But I would suggest that I am also being sniffed out as to how I take in her experience, and that secretly she will be ready to "jump on" me.

I would suggest that one view she holds of me as the mother in the transference, is that I so fear being intruded into by a

burglar-husband or by the patient–child's projections that I secure or defend myself as though I were living in an analytic fortress. In that way I would be impenetrable by a partner at the
weekend, but would also then be impenetrable to the patient's
experience. An interpretation of the patient's experience of rob-
bery at the weekend, or the internal experience of feeling robbed
of the analyst-mother by the intrusive "bastard" of a father would
be experienced as given by impenetrable or unreachable parents—those parents whose experience is so discrepant from hers,
engaged as they are in clearing up the aftermath of their sexual
party.

Yet the patient has also intruded into me a wish not to be
distanced in that way. On the contrary, I believe that I was invited to feel that I was in the same "boat" or the same exposed
house as the patient. Thus I am invited to feel that the "partitions are so thin" that there is no separateness. Then she is
the sniffer dog, not only sniffing the parents out at the weekend, but entering my mind as though we were "one." What I
wish to convey is that the "partition" between what we tend to
call normal projective identification (or empathic sharing) and
intrusion is very fine.

In the countertransference in such situations we may find that
we either become "lulled" into such states of mind by the patient, or so sensitized to that danger that we behave like an im-
personation of the police sniffer dogs, ready to pounce the
moment the door is opened.

Thus one gains access to the patient's view of her internal objects, felt to be either overidentified with her or so distant and
harsh that they are not able to take in her experience.

These issues are very real and we may become particularly vulnerable to them in these areas where the patient touches on our
"shared" external or internal world. Making space to work
through these issues internally will much affect the way in which
we give our interpretations in both taking care of the exposed

baby in the patient, and "sniffing out" and dealing with the nasty intrusive parts as well.

These issues I have been trying to illustrate become more rather than less problematic when we are dealing with borderline and psychotic patients. These patients may become more or less impervious to ordinary analytic cooperation and may act out in ways that present the analyst with serious management problems. They may make demands, say for an extra session at the weekend, where, for the analyst to acquiesce, may be to feed and reinforce tyrannical narcissistic parts of the patient; to refuse may be to indulge and reinforce sometimes profound grievances. In cases of suicidal patients, anorexia, or malignant hysterics, for example, such management issues may carry life and death implications.

Of course in these situations the patient massively projects parts of the self and internal objects into the analyst; such patients also arouse in the analyst feelings of being helpless and at the mercy of vengeful exploitative behavior while the patient indulges in imperviousness to the analyst's needs. The task of experiencing and bearing these feelings while at the same time not becoming alienated from those parts of the patient that are genuinely defective and in need of support, is a considerable one. In those cases where the situation becomes unmanageable it is easy to feel that the patient is "unanalyzable" (and sometimes this may be so). The very intensity of how unmanageable the situation becomes, may be the evidence of how unmanageable the internal dilemma is for the patient. In these cases the patient actually makes the analyst feel helpless and at the mercy of a ruthless persecuting object that goes on relentlessly and will not be modified by human understanding—the archetypal primitive superego.

I wish to emphasize that faced with such serious managerial problems, the analyst is also involved in a massive effort not only to contain the patient's projections but to manage his or her own feelings, subjected as they are to such intense pressure. And even in the case of, or perhaps most especially in the case of, such disturbed patients, the patient, either consciously or unconsciously, makes inquiry into the question of how the analyst deals with such feelings.

When analysis proceeds well, the analyst has the luxury of being able to manage the combination of some involvement and some distance. In the case of these very ill patients the power of the patient's predicament, and the capacity to intrude into the analyst's mind and disturb him, may put the analyst in the position, at least for some time, of being taken over and unable to function as a separate thinking person.

The analyst needs to work through the experience of feeling like an overwhelmed mother threatened with disintegration by an interaction with the overwhelmed baby. The analyst may need to be able to turn to an outside person, a "father" to provide support; for example, a hospital or colleague may be needed for support not only in the management of such a case, but also to encourage the analyst to have the strength to hold the feelings of hatred for the impervious, exploitative, parasitic patient-baby together with the love and concern for the needy or defective baby in the patient. This, in my view, enables the analyst to help the patient to feel that these intense, contradictory feelings can be endured, so that the patient may be helped to begin to meet the issues in relation to parts of the self and internal objects.

While these patients intrude problems relating to actual management, my contention is that these problems form an essential part of the management of any analysis; were it not so, working through would be a smooth, uninterrupted process. It never is for the patient, and my emphasis is that it cannot be so for the analyst either. Analytic thinking must then include a recognition of, and a struggle with, our desire to enact, in order to be able to think about and decide what to do in the circumstances.

I have tried to show that the experience for the analyst is a powerful one. To suggest that we are not affected by the

destructiveness of the patient or by the patient's painful efforts
to reach us would represent not neutrality but falseness or imperviousness. It is the issue of how the analyst allows himself to
have the experience, digest it, formulate it, and communicate
it as an interpretation that I address.

Summary

This paper is intended as a development of Strachey's classic
paper, "The Nature of the Therapeutic Action of Psychoanalysis"
(1934). Strachey states that the full or deep transference experience is disturbing to the analyst; that which the analyst most fears
and most wishes to avoid. He also stresses that conveying an interpretation in a calm way is necessary. The area addressed is the
task of coping with these strong countertransference experiences
and maintaining the analytic technique of interpretation. The
clinical illustrations attempt to show something of the process of
transformation or working through in the analyst, as well as showing that the patient is consciously or unconsciously mindful as
to whether the analyst evades or meets the issues.

The contention that the analyst is not affected by these experiences is both false and would convey to the patient that his
plight, pain, and behavior are emotionally ignored by the analyst. It is suggested that if we keep emotions out, we are in danger of keeping out the love which mitigates the hatred, allowing
the so-called pursuit of truth to be governed by hatred. What
appears as dispassionate may contain the murder of love and
concern. How the analyst allows himself to have the experiences,
work through and transform them into a useful interpretation
is the issue studied in this paper.

References

Bion, W. R. (1962), *Learning from Experience.* London: Heinemann.
Heimann, P. (1950), On counter-transference. *Internat. J. Psycho-Anal.,*
31:81–84.

Joseph, B. (1975), "The patient who is difficult to reach." In: *Tactics and Techniques in Psychoanalytic Therapy*, Vol. 2: ed. P. Giovacchini. New York: Jason Aronson, pp. 205–216.

Klein, M. (1952), The origin of transference. In: *Writings*, Vol. 3. London: Hogarth Press, 1975, pp. 48–56.

Kris, E. (1952), *Psychoanalytic Explorations in Art*. New York: International Universities Press.

Money-Kyrle, R. (1956), Normal counter-transference and some of its deviations. In: *The Collected Papers of Roger Money-Kyrle*, ed. D. Meltzer with E. O'Shaughnessy. Strathtay, Perthshire: Clunie Press, 1978, pp. 330–342.

Segal, H. (1977), Countertransference. In: *The Work of Hanna Segal*. New York: Jason Aronson, 1981, pp. 81–87.

Strachey, J. (1934), The nature of the therapeutic action of psychoanalysis. *Internat. J. Psycho-Anal.*, 15:275–293.

EDITOR'S INTRODUCTION TO
PROBLEMS OF PSYCHOANALYTIC TECHNIQUE:
PATIENT-CENTERED AND ANALYST-CENTERED
INTERPRETATIONS

Continuing his study of pathological organizations or "psychic retreats" (chapter 8, above), John Steiner focuses on the differential effectiveness of two types of interpretation in the context of these organizations. His clinical illustrations show concretely how one may frame interpretations in a way that will have better prospects of being tolerable to patients who are locked into pathological organizations. It is, of course, the tolerable intervention that may free patients to inch forward toward the depressive position instead of pushing them back toward the dreaded paranoid–schizoid position or compelling them to ignore the analyst altogether. In particular, it is the analyst-centered interpretation, one that addresses the patient's experience of the analyst, that often has the greater potential of being heard, responded to, and used constructively.

There are gradations between these two types of interpretation. It is the analyst-centered interpretation that has a better chance of presenting the analyst as standing not too far outside the patient's world and as seemingly intent only on objectifying it. Better that the analyst seem to be genuinely striving to understand what he or she must be like in the inner experience with which the patient is concerned at that moment. Although it is true that analyst-centered interpretations continue to refer to the patient's psychic processes, they are not so much explanatory as they are immediate, inquiring, and phenomenological-experiential. Thus they may get across a quality of tentatively reaching out, perhaps clearing the air, perhaps simply maintaining contact by joining the patient wherever he or she is or seems to be. It is important to keep in mind that, in that place, the patient may be concerned mainly with being understood rather than understanding, a matter that is discussed more fully in chapter 13, above.

It is my impression that the utility of analyst-centered interpretations extends far beyond gaining access to psychic retreats, the realm on which Steiner concentrates. There are many other types of patients for whom patient-centered interpretations may be too threatening or painfully alienating. When analysts speak in a way that seems to lay emphasis on one detached person's objectifying the other, they implicitly set up a hierarchy of observer standing over observed and in that way they are more likely to be experienced as threatening or seductive or both. Then the clinical moment may smack too much of being approached by a cold parent or a cruel authority. Consequently, many patients find it far more engaging and become more productive when their analysts (and their psychotherapists) speak to them in the manner of a knowledgeable guide who is interested in the problems each patient has in working with a helpful guide.

Helpfulness is not to be taken for granted; quite often it is a special issue to be worked through. In the long run trust and feelings of safety are more likely to be engendered by analyst-centered interpretations than by noninterpretive interventions such as reassurance or free acknowledgment of countertransference response.

In characteristically contemporary Kleinian fashion, Steiner issues no demand to avoid countertransferences if at all possible. As always, the job is to show the many ways in which the analyst, after sorting out unavoidable and disruptive personal intrusions, may draw on induced countertransferences to frame interventions beneficially. The noteworthy candor of the analyst's clinical material helps bring out clearly those instances in which his interpretations were not well attuned to the patient's momentary state and needs and also how his analysis of these occurrences helped him to better his understanding of the analytic situation and reestablish a more productive atmosphere.

16
PROBLEMS OF PSYCHOANALYTIC TECHNIQUE: PATIENT-CENTERED AND ANALYST-CENTERED INTERPRETATIONS

JOHN STEINER

The treatment of psychotic and borderline patients presents formidable technical problems for the psychoanalyst, and many of these arise from the uncomfortable countertransference feelings these patients evoke. They are usually aware of the disturbance around them and to which they react, but, they are unable to recognize their role in the creation of the situation and are unaware or unconcerned with their own internal problems. In analysis, the patient in this state of mind is not interested in discovering things about himself, and uses the analysis for a variety of purposes other than that of gaining insight into his problems.

Joseph (1983), who pointed out that many such patients are not interested in understanding, saw this as related to the fact that they are functioning at a paranoid–schizoid level. In these circumstances the patient's main concern is to obtain relief and

This chapter is based on chapter 11 of the author's book, *Psychic Retreats: Pathological Organizations in Psychotic, Neurotic and Borderline Patients*. London: Routledge, 1993.

security by establishing a mental equilibrium, and consequently he is unable to direct his interest toward understanding. The priority for the patient is to get rid of unwanted mental contents, which he projects into the analyst. In these states he is able to take very little back into his mind. He does not have the time or the space to think, and he is afraid to examine his own mental processes. Words are used, not primarily to convey information, but to have an effect on the analyst, and the analyst's words are likewise felt as actions indicating something about the analyst's state of mind rather than offering insight to the patient.

It is important to remember, however, that although he may not be interested in acquiring understanding, that is self-understanding, the patient does have a pressing need to be understood by the analyst. Sometimes this is consciously experienced as a wish to be understood and sometimes it is unconsciously communicated. A few patients appear to hate the whole idea of being understood and try to disavow it and get rid of all meaningful contact. Even this kind of patient, however, needs the analyst to register what is happening and to have his situation and predicament recognized.

The transference is often loaded with anxiety, which the patient is unable to contend with, but which has to be contained in the analytic situation. Such containment depends on the analyst's capacity to recognize and cope with what the patient has projected and with his own countertransference reactions to it. Experience suggests that such containment is weakened if the analyst perseveres in interpreting or explaining to the patient what he is thinking, feeling, or doing. The patient experiences such interpretations as a lack of containment and feels that the analyst is pushing the projected elements back into him. The patient has projected these precisely because he could not cope with them, and his immediate need is for them to continue to reside in the analyst and to be understood in their projected state.

Some analysts, in these circumstances, tend to phrase their interpretations in a form that recognizes that the patient is more interested in what is going on in the analyst's mind than in his own. At these times the patient's most immediate concern is his experience of the analyst, and this can be addressed by saying something like, "You experience me as . . ." or, "You are afraid that I . . ." or, "You were relieved when I . . ." or, "You became anxious a moment ago when I. . . ." I think of such interpretations as analyst centered and differentiate them from patient-centered interpretations, which are of the classical kind in which something the patient is doing, thinking, or wishing is interpreted, often together with the motive and the anxiety associated with it.

Of course, the distinction between the two types of transference interpretation is schematic, and in a deeper sense all interpretations are centered on the patient and reflect the analyst's attempt to understand the patient's experience. The problem is to recognize where the patient's anxieties and preoccupations are focused. In practice most interpretations take into account both what the patient feels and what the patient thinks the analyst feels, and include a reference to both patient and analyst. When we say, "You experience me as . . ." or "You are afraid that I . . ." a patient-centered element is present because we are talking about the patient's experience and fear. Moreover, it is clear that the distinction depends more on the analyst's attitude and state of mind than on his or her wording. If the analyst says, "You see me as . . ." and implies that the patient's view is one that is in error, or hurtful, or in some other way undesirable, then the emphasis is on what is going on in the patient and the interpretation is primarily patient-centered. To be analyst-centered, in the sense which I intend to use it, the analyst has to have an open mind, be willing to consider the patient's view, and try to understand what the patient means in a spirit of inquiry. Although these considerations complicate the distinction between the two types of interpretation and suggest gradations between them, I will consider them to be distinct for the sake of clarity. Both types of interpretation are necessary for the patient's total situation to be understood, and both types have dangers attached to them if they are used excessively and without due attention to the feedback the patient gives in reaction to them.

Sometimes the patient-centered element is elaborated further, and we may say something like, "You are trying to get me to feel . . . such and such," or, "Your attack on me just now gave rise to such and such a result." The interpretation then involves a link between what the patient does, thinks, or wishes, and the state of the analyst. Sometimes these links take the form of a *because* clause that is added to an analyst-centered interpretation. We may say, "You are afraid that I am upset because of the fact that you did such and such." Such links are the essence of deep analytic work but are particularly difficult for the patient who is operating at a paranoid–schizoid level. They imply that he is not only capable of taking an interest in his own actions but able to accept responsibility for them as well. Especially in the early stages of an analysis and particularly with schizoid, borderline, and psychotic patients, it is necessary to recognize the problems that ensue from both types of interpretation and from the links that arise between them.

CLINICAL MATERIAL

I believe that the distinction between these two types of transference interpretation can help the analyst to examine the technical problems he has been struggling with and may allow him to shift from one type of interpretation to the other when it appears to be appropriate. To examine these issues I will first briefly look at some material from a psychotic patient whose case I have discussed in a previous article (Steiner, 1991).

This patient had recently recovered from a major breakdown, and although just able to return to work was still very paranoid and concrete in his thinking. He began a session by voicing bitter complaints against his employers, who had been unfair to him, and then against his analyst, who did nothing to rectify this unfairness. He next described a breast infection that his mother had when he was a baby, and moved on to speak with triumph about his ability to hurt the analyst. He then announced his intention to change his job; since this would necessitate a move to another city, it meant the end of his analysis.

The analyst felt sad at the idea of losing his patient and interpreted that the patient wanted to get rid of his own sadness and wanted him, the analyst, to feel the pain of separation and loss. The patient said, "Yes, I can do to you what you do to me. You are in my hands. There is an equalization." A moment later he started to complain that he was being poisoned and he began to discuss government policies of nuclear deterrence. He argued these were stupid because they involved total annihilation, but the policies of nuclear disarmament were no better because you could not neutralize existing armaments. He then complained of gastric troubles and diarrhea and said he had been going to the toilet after each session recently. He explained that he had to shit out every word the analyst gave him in order not to be contaminated by infected milk.

In his response to the analyst's interpretation the patient at first appeared to agree that he wanted the analyst to feel the pain of separation and loss in order to effect an "equalization," but a moment later he complained of being poisoned. I believe that he found this interpretation correct but threatening because it exposed him to experiences such as grief, anxiety, and guilt, which were associated with the loss of his analyst. He felt that the analyst had forced him to take these feelings back into himself and he experienced them concretely as poison and tried to evacuate them in his feces. The patient indicated the catastrophic nature of his anxiety by talking about nuclear disaster. His insistence that no defense was possible against a nuclear attack may have had its roots in his conviction that his defenses could not protect him against his analyst's words. He needed the analyst to recognize that he could maintain a relationship with him only if the analyst agreed to hold the experiences associated with loss in his own mind and to refrain from trying to return these prematurely to the patient. After a transient contact with the experience of loss, the psychotic process reasserted itself in the patient's assertion that he would shit out every word the analyst said.

This is a situation where the interpretation may be unbearable even when it is correct. The psychotic process has made experience so concrete that insight is poison and has to be evacuated in feces. When the analyst suggested that the patient wanted to get rid of his sadness and wanted the analyst to feel the pain of separation and loss, he was making a link between the patient's wishes and the analyst's state of mind. The patient felt the analyst disapproved of these wishes and was himself pushing the distressed feelings back onto the patient.

A different situation is seen when the patient is not psychotic and has a greater capacity to tolerate understanding and insight. This was the case in the material I will next discuss, taken from the analysis of a 40-year-old academic woman some two years after her analysis began. As a child she habitually withdrew to a fantasy world in which she joined figures from books or television to escape from the distress and anxiety going on in the family around her. The history contained many reports of extremely disturbed, wild, and even violent behavior, and she often found herself in situations where she seemed to invite exploitation, mistreatment, and even danger. This was particularly true in her adolescence and was now being repeated by her 14-year-old son, who created enormous problems for her.

After missing a Monday session she began on Tuesday by saying:

I wondered if you would get the message. I spoke to a girl who said that she would put it in your drawer. I know what happens to messages like that. On Sunday I had wondered about ringing you at home.

On the train I imagined meeting someone I know who would ask, "How are you?" I would reply, "Fine. Only my department is collapsing, my son has run off, and I don't know where he is, my husband is fed up and helpless, and otherwise I am fine."

She continued by explaining that she had missed Monday because of an important meeting with the University Bursar to discuss finance, that she decided she had to attend. She knew about this on the weekend and had wondered if she should phone to see if I could offer a different time. Instead she phoned my secretary early on Monday morning, and, suspecting that the message would not reach me, had phoned again during her session time to explain that she was not coming. In fact it turned out that just before going into the meeting, she was told it would be better if she did not attend, and she said that they implied that she would be a liability. She added that there was something theatrical about the way her colleagues were behaving and that, as a result, the negotiation with the Bursar was not straightforward.

It is clear that we already have a complex communication and enactment between patient and analyst. There is a patient who wants to get a message through to her analyst and various obstacles come in the way. There is a woman who tells a friend that everything is fine but makes sure that the friend knows there are disasters all around. Finally, there is a professor who tries to attend an important meeting but is told she is not wanted because she is a liability. These stories all have powerful transference implications, which I believe center on the patient's need to get through to the analyst that there is something very seriously wrong that needs attention. This need to get a message through is central to the interactions in the session, but it is complicated by other motives. For example, it was possible to recognize a perverse side of her, which hated being understood and which hindered or sabotaged communication, making everything far from straightforward. The imagined comment to the friend on the train was not simply a message indicating how she felt, but was likely to make the person hearing it very uneasy, guilty, and confused.

In this situation I believe it is possible to concentrate our attention on either the patient's or the analyst's state of mind, mental mechanisms, and behavior. Ultimately the aim of an analysis is to help the patient gain an understanding of herself, and even with this material, interpretations could have been used to explore the way she reacted and behaved. However, in this instance, I believe the patient was primarily concerned with the way her objects behaved. She felt that I did not make it easy for her to make contact with me on the weekend, and she had to overcome a feeling that she was a liability and unwanted if she intruded. Consciously she felt that she did her best and tried to get through to my secretary, but she knew what happened to messages which are supposed to be left. When she imagined saying everything was fine she was partly being ironic, and partly trying to make me uncomfortable. Moreover, she left open the possibility that she was being theatrical, so that it was not clear what her inner reality was. I thought there were elements of despair and helplessness in the way she felt obliged to say she was fine and to go on coping somehow. The statement, although clearly a negation of feeling fine, left it open to me to choose to ignore the irony and against all the evidence to hear her to mean that she *was* actually fine. She herself was sometimes convinced that this was the case and that it was other people who were making an unnecessary fuss. These thoughts led me to feel that despite the fact that she was not always able to carry out a straightforward negotiation, she needed me to recognize her desperation and she feared that I would prefer to agree that everything was fine even though I knew very well that the contrary was true.

If I made patient-centered interpretations, I thought she would experience this as an attempt to make her responsible for her failure to get through to me, and that it would indicate my reluctance to accept responsibility for my contribution to the obstacles that stood in her way. In fact it was probably true that her passivity and inability to fight for her needs helped to achieve the projection into me of guilt, pain, and responsibility. If so she would, in principle, benefit from an understanding of these mechanisms, which no doubt contributed to her difficulties, but I feared that she was in no state to be interested in understanding issues such as this. What she wanted was that I recognize that something was terribly wrong with her, and that I accept the feelings this aroused in me and refrain from projecting them back into her. She was afraid that I was not going to be able to cope with these feelings because they would disturb *my* mental equilibrium.

I interpreted that she feared I was not able to create a setting where messages would get through to me, and I drew her attention to the atmosphere of the current session, where she seemed relatively composed. I thought that she hoped that I would see that beneath this composure things were very far from fine. However, I found myself adding that she also hinted that something theatrical was going on, and I wondered if this was expressed in the way she tried to make contact. I thought that this left her unsure if I could see through the theatricality to what she really felt.

After I had spoken I realized that this additional comment had a somewhat critical tone to it, which I suspected arose from my difficulty in containing feelings, including those of anxiety about her, and possibly my annoyance that she made me feel responsible, guilty, and helpless. I also knew from past experience that a critical comment could lead to the enactment of a sadomasochistic relationship in which she would feel the victim of an unfair attack.

She was silent for a while and then spoke about her fraught relationship with her son. She described the way he wound everyone up, and how he had screamed that he could not bear to live with her, and had stormed out. At first he said it was for good, but later he phoned and said he would be back for school on Monday. In fact he failed to turn up, and she had to ring the school and explain because they were also at the end of their tether with him and threatened expulsion. She told them she knew it was terrible, but what could she do?

I considered this to be a comment on the interaction that had just taken place and a reaction to the interpretation I had made. At one level I thought she felt I had been critical, and like her son she had the impulse to withdraw in anger. It was difficult to know how to respond, but I thought it was probably better to refrain from emphasizing this side of the relationship. I did not think she would be able to take responsibility for her contribution to the difficulties in communication between us, and that interpreting them would probably feed a view of herself as an abused victim. I thought she disowned these feelings in the session and identified with me as a parent who could not cope.

It was thoughts like these that made me interpret that she needed me to accept the sense of helplessness when my patient disappears which may be something like her feeling when her son disappears. She needed me to cope with the anxiety associated with her not coming to her session and not being able to get in touch with me. She felt I blamed her for this just as she now feared I was too critical and defensive to understand her anger and disappointment with me, and to recognize that she also wanted to make contact, and did try to reach me and get through to me.

After a silence she continued with more material about her son and the dangerous company of older criminal youths he was associating with. She described how she had tried to trace him by phoning his friends and their parents, and that when he had discovered this he was furious, abusing her, and accusing her of spying on him and controlling him. She had also tried to get her ex-husband, his adoptive father, to go and bring him home, but he said he was busy and had no car. He thought the boy should be allowed to find his own way back in his own time.

This made a direct connection with my own experience of her behavior in the session. I thought that she was identified with her role as a helpless mother but that the angry disturbed patient who was furious with me, who could not bear to be with me, and who had such difficulties in getting through to me was not directly available. This was a familiar problem and left me uncertain whether I should try to pursue her or wait for her to return.

I interpreted that she saw me as helpless when she withdrew and that I left it to her to find her way back to the session. This made her fear that I did not take the danger she was in seriously. However, she also made it clear that when she felt disturbed, violent, and out of control, she would be angry and feel intruded on and controlled if I tried to reach her with interpretations.

The remainder of the session continued in a similar vein. She described how her colleagues had to put on an act with the Bursar to persuade him that the department was in a terrible state, but that with applicants and colleagues from other universities the problem was exactly the opposite—they had to be convinced that the department was viable. There were references to the real possibility of being closed down and to the necessity of staff cutbacks to avoid this. I had a strong impression of her insecurity, and because of numerous recent hints that she may not be able to continue her analysis, of my own possible redundancy.

This session was fairly typical in terms of the anxiety she generated and also showed both the problems she had in staying in touch with it and the problems she generated in me. If I tried to make contact with a very disturbed patient who found it difficult to come to the session, she felt that I pursued her, and she made it clear that she would not tolerate that. If, on the other hand, I was too passive, if I seemed to throw up my hands as she did and claim that there was nothing more I could do, she was afraid that I would give up and see the analysis as bankrupt and hopeless. If I made *patient-centered* interpretations, she felt intruded upon and experienced it as my failure to cope with the anxiety, which led to me blaming her and pushing the anxiety back onto her. I thought she tolerated *analyst-centered* interpretations better, but she sometimes saw them as a confession that I was not coping and as an admission that I was afraid to tackle her difficulties and face the consequences.

Discussion

Technical problems such as those I encountered in this material can be thought of as expressions of the patient's resistance on one hand, and of the analyst's countertransference difficulties on the other. Our understanding of both of these has been enhanced as we have learned more about the mechanism of projective identification (Klein, 1946; Rosenfeld, 1971), and about containment (Bion, 1959, 1962, 1963), and countertransference (Heimann, 1950, 1960; Money-Kyrle, 1956; Racker, 1957; Sandler, 1976), which are closely related to it.

Both Sandler (1976) and Joseph (1981) have recognized the way patients nudge and prod the analyst in order to create a particular situation in the transference. Sandler describes how an internal relationship between the self and an object becomes "actualized" in the relationship with the analyst, who is led to enact an "infantile role-relationship." As a counterpart to Freud's "free-floating attention," he points out, the analyst has to have a "free-floating responsiveness," and that the analyst's reactions, as well as thoughts and feelings, contribute to the countertransference. Joseph shows how through such "enactments" the analyst is drawn into playing a role in the patient's fantasy and as a result is used as part of the patient's defensive system. The

patient may of course interpret such actualizations and infantile role relationships in a delusional way and come to believe
that they were achieved not by natural means, but by omnipotent fantasy.

We have come to use "countertransference" to refer to the
totality of the analyst's reactions in the relationship with the patient. The recognition of the importance of projective identification in creating these reactions led naturally to the idea that
countertransference is an important source of information
about the patient's state of mind. The analyst can try to observe
his own reactions to the patient and to the totality of the situation in the session and to use them to understand what the patient is projecting.

But countertransference also has its problems when we come
to try to use it in practice, perhaps most of all because the
analyst's introspection is complicated by his own defensive needs
so that many important countertransference reactions remain
unconscious. Self-deception and unconscious collusion with the
patient to evade reality makes countertransference unreliable
without additional corroboration. Here a third point of view can
help the analyst to recognize his blind spots and fortify his judgments (Britton, 1989; Segal, 1991). He may use colleagues and
supervisors between sessions and to some degree internalize
them. Most of all an analyst can use the help the patient gives,
sometimes through a direct criticism of his work, but more often
through reactions to interpretations he has given.

Because of the propensity to be nudged into enactments
with the patient, it is often impossible to understand exactly
what has been happening at the moment when it is taking
place. Sandler (1976) suggests that the analyst may catch a
countertransference reaction, within himself, particularly if it
is in the direction of being inappropriate, but he recognizes
that such self-awareness may only occur after the responses
have been carried over into action. In either case it is clear that

immediate countertransference reactions have to be reviewed a few minutes later when the patient's reaction is available, and this may have to be repeated as further understanding develops later in the session or in subsequent sessions. Using all the means available, including self-observation, the observation of his actions, the responses of the patient, and the overall atmosphere of the session, the analyst can arrive at some kind of understanding of his patient and of his interaction with him. If the analyst can stand the pressure, he can use this understanding to formulate an interpretation that allows the patient to feel understood and contained. When this is convincing the patient feels that the analyst can contain those elements the patient has projected into him, and as a result the projected elements become more bearable. The patient feels relief and is able to use the analyst's capacity to think, feel, and experience to help him cope.

If the analyst is unable to contain the projections and closes himself off or counterprojects, the patient feels attacked and misunderstood and is likely to become increasingly disturbed and to intensify the splitting and the projective mechanisms he has been using. On the other hand, successful containment leads to integration, and the experience of being understood may then provide a context where further development can take place.

Such further development is necessary for lasting psychic change to occur, and, in my view, it does not automatically follow containment but depends on the acquisition of insight and understanding by the patient. Successful containment, which is associated with being understood rather than with acquiring understanding, is a necessary but not a sufficient condition for these developments. Containment requires that the projected elements have been able to enter the analyst's mind, where they can be registered and given meaning that is convincing. It does not require that the patient himself is available or interested in achieving understanding. If the patient is to develop further he must make a fundamental shift and develop an interest in understanding, no matter how small or fleeting. This kind of shift, which reflects the beginning of a capacity to tolerate insight and mental pain, is associated with a move from the paranoid–schizoid to the depressive position. I will try to illustrate how such a development depends on the experience of separateness and loss.

A few months following the sessions already described, the patient was told that I was taking an extra week's break in midterm. She usually dealt with such disruptions in routine by missing a few sessions, partly in revenge, but mostly, I thought, to serve as a means of projecting the experience of being left onto me. This time she began a session by describing how she had walked to work as usual with her husband and passed a neighbor's house, where she saw that a light was on in an attic room. She knew that this room had been recently converted to house the family's new baby, and she imagined one of the parents attending to the baby as they passed. This made her wonder if it really was too late for her to have a baby with her present husband, and she shuddered as she thought of all the gynecological problems that would have to be overcome and that had led to so many complications and to endless painful investigations in her first pregnancy. They turned a corner and she passed the street where her colleague and chief rival lived. She had a very difficult relationship with this woman, whom she admired but also felt controlled by, and she described how, normally, when she passed she would look right into the house and would often see her colleague moving around choosing what she was going to wear that day. On this occasion, however, she could not see into the house clearly because tears were in her eyes.

I interpreted that while she reacted to my week off in various ways, she seemed today to associate this with the idea that I had other things to attend to—like a baby—and that this put her in touch with her grief and made her feel more separate and tearful. Her mood was quiet and thoughtful, and I was able to go on to interpret that she had previously dealt with separations by entering my mind just as she used to enter her colleague's house, her family, and her department.

Periods of contact like this were not frequent and were not sustained, but they did give rise to moments when she seemed genuinely interested in the way her mind worked and was consequently able to accept patient-centered interpretations. On this occasion the shift was associated with the patient's sadness when she feared that she no longer had the mental and physical capacity to have a baby of her own. She felt more separate from me and her tears enabled her to accept a momentary contact with a psychic reality. This small and transient shift to the depressive position allowed her to become interested in her own mind and her own mental processes.

Further Discussion

In psychotic and borderline patients, as well as others functioning at a paranoid–schizoid level, containment brings relief but does not necessarily lead to growth and development. One of the reasons for this is that the relief depends on the continuing presence of the containing object since, at this level of organization, true separateness from the object cannot be tolerated, and, as a result, the capacity to contain cannot yet be internalized. The threatened loss of the object leads to panic and to the deployment of omnipotent fantasy to create the illusion that the object is possessed and controlled. The patient internalizes an object containing the projected elements and does not truly face the experience of separateness. Sometimes such omnipotent fantasies are delusional and survive all evidence to the contrary, but in most cases contrary evidence is more subtly evaded and experiences such as the regular timing of sessions fuel the patient's illusion that the analyst is not free to act independently and unexpectedly.

This was illustrated by the way my patient ordinarily dealt with separations by projective identification, which she experienced as entering my mind and body, where she was able to control me but where she also saw herself as inside me and hence as my responsibility. In the first section of the clinical material I tried to show how difficult she was to contain when this happened. Her wild, dangerous, and aggressive behavior was subtly hidden behind her composure but was apparent when I had such trouble finding and reaching her. My worries about her were paralleled in the terrible worries she had about her son. When I was able to contain her anxiety about my ability to cope with such responsibility she seemed relieved. But this relief needed my presence to act as a container and could survive beyond the end of the session only through a denial of separateness. Such denial was associated with a possessive hold of her objects, which remained under her omnipotent control.

Inevitably, occasions arise when the analyst temporarily steps outside the patient's omnipotent control and a degree of separateness is achieved. This seemed to take place in the session I reported soon after I announced an unexpected break in the analysis, and was connected with a recognition that it was her neighbor and not herself who had the baby she so much wanted. My freedom to act was associated with a lessening of omnipotent control and led to an experience of loss that enabled her to feel more separate, and in the process to express some of her sadness and grief, which I think made up part of the work of mourning her lost objects and lost opportunities. I (Steiner, 1990, 1993) have argued elsewhere that it is through the work of mourning that the patient is able to regain those parts of herself that she previously got rid of through projective identification, and that with further work these projected fragments can be reintegrated into the ego.

It is at these times that the patient can take a true interest in her own mind and begin to differentiate what belongs to the analyst and what belongs to her. Such moves toward the depressive position are clearly more frequent in less disturbed patients and at later stages of an analysis, but they may occur at any time even if only for brief and isolated moments. They require a prior capacity on the part of the analyst to contain and integrate the projected elements, but I believe that they also demand that the analyst have the courage to take risks and, when appropriate, give a patient-centered interpretation even if this may lead to a persecuted patient.

SHIFTING BETWEEN THE TWO TYPES
OF INTERPRETATION

In the clinical material I presented I tried to be sensitive to the need to shift between the two types of interpretation, and I encountered problems with both. When I focused on the patient's behavior and, for example, interpreted her theatricality or her withdrawal into silence, she felt intruded upon and blamed for the failure to make contact with me. It was when patient-centered interpretations implied that she was responsible for what happened between us that she became most persecuted and tended to withdraw. It was particularly over the question of responsibility that she felt I sometimes adopted a righteous tone, which made her feel that I was refusing to examine my own contribution to the problem and unwilling to accept responsibility myself. In the countertransference this issue created serious problems for me since, when the patient projected feelings with such intensity, I often felt that I was being made responsible for the patient's problems as well as my own.

In such situations I believe it may be better to be sparing with the patient-centered elements in the interpretation, to concentrate on the patient's view of the analyst, and to avoid making premature links between the two. Of course this is not a formula that can be used to solve technical problems, and, as we have seen, analyst-centered interpretations have their own difficulties.

They too can fail to offer containment, sometimes because they are simply wrong and out of touch, and sometimes because the patient feels the analyst is interpreting to cover up the situation rather than to confront it. Too many analyst-centered interpretations make the patient feel that the analyst is preoccupied with himself and unable to observe and respond to the patient and his problems. Moreover, sometimes this view of the analyst is justified. The patient is always listening for information about the analyst's state of mind, and whatever form of interpretation the analyst uses, verbal and nonverbal clues give the patient information about him. The patient can use these to see if what the analyst says matches how he expresses himself, and this is important in the patient's view of the analyst's character and trustworthiness.

Sometimes, interpreting the patient's view of the analyst helps the patient recognize that he has projected an archaic internal figure onto the analyst and is expecting the analyst to behave, say, as his mother would have behaved. The interpretation may clarify this and enable the patient to see the analyst subsequently in a different light. Sometimes, however, the interpretation simply confirms the patient's fears. To be effective it must neither be a confession, which simply makes the patient anxious, nor a denial, which the patient sees as defensive and false.

The technical challenge is to find an appropriate balance of patient-centered and analyst-centered interpretations. Interpretations may temporarily have to emphasize containment, but ultimately must be concerned with helping the patient gain insight. An analyst who is perceived as reluctant to pursue this fundamental aim is not experienced as providing containment. Indeed, these two aspects of interpretation can be thought of as feminine and masculine symbols of the analyst's work. Both are required, and insight, which is so often disturbing, is only acceptable to the patient who is held in a containing setting. If the analyst remains sensitive to the patient's reaction to his interpretation and listens to the next piece of material partly as a comment on what has preceded it, then it is possible to shift from one type an interpretation to the other sensitively, flexibly. As development proceeds, the distinction becomes less important, and many interpretations of an intermediate kind become possible, often showing the links between the activity of the patient and the resultant view of the analyst. Such links are impossible to make when the patient is functioning at a more primitive level where containment and being understood take priority over understanding.

REFERENCES

Bion, W. R. (1959), Attacks on linking. In: *Second Thoughts*. London: Heinemann, 1967, pp. 93–109.
———— (1962), *Learning from Experience*. London: Heinemann.
———— (1963), *Elements of Psycho-analysis*. London: Heinemann.
Britton, R. S. (1989), The missing link: Parental sexuality in the Oedipus complex. In: *The Oedipus Complex Today*, R. S. Britton, M. Feldman, & E. O'Shaughnessy. London: Karnac, pp. 83–101.
Heimann, P. (1950), On countertransference. *Internat. J. Psycho-Anal.*, 31:81–84.
———— (1960), Countertransference. *Brit. J. Med. Psychol.*, 33:9–15.
Joseph, B. (1981), Defence mechanisms and phantasy in the psycho-analytic process. In: *Psychic Equilibrium and Psychic Change*, ed. M. Feldman, & E. Bott Spillius. London: Routledge, 1989, pp. 116–126.
———— (1983), On understanding and not understanding: Some technical issues. In: *Psychic Equilibrium and Psychic Change*, ed. M. Feldman, & E. Bott Spillius. London: Routledge, 1989, pp. 139–150.
Klein, M. (1946), Notes on some schizoid mechanisms. In: *Writings*, Vol. 3. London: Hogarth Press, 1975, pp. 1–24.
Money-Kyrle, R. (1956), Normal countertransference and some of its deviations. In: *The Collected Papers of Roger Money-Kyrle*. Perthshire: Clunie Press, 1978, pp. 330–342.
Racker, H. (1957), The meaning and uses of countertransference. In: *Transference and Countertransference*. London: Hogarth Press, 1968, pp. 127–173.

Rosenfeld, H. A. (1971), Contributions to the psychopathology of psychotic patients: The importance of projective identification in the ego structure and object relations of the psychotic patient. In: *Melanie Klein Today,* Vol. 1, ed. E. Bott Spillius. London: Routledge, 1988.

Sandler, J. (1976), Countertransference and role-responsiveness. *Internat. Rev. Psycho-Anal.*, 3:43–47.

Segal, H. (1991), *Dream, Phantasy, and Art.* London: Routledge.

Steiner, J. (1990), Pathological organizations as obstacles to mourning: The role of unbearable guilt. *Internat. J. Psycho-Anal.*, 71:87–94.

——— (1991), A psychotic organization of the personality. *Internat. J. Psycho-Anal.*, 72:201–207.

——— (1993), *Psychic Retreats.* London: Routledge.

EDITOR'S INTRODUCTION TO
PSYCHIC CHANGE
AND THE PSYCHOANALYTIC PROCESS

Patients enter treatment because of dissatisfaction with the limiting and painful psychic equilibria they have achieved. Yet they
dread any change in their psychic balance, and they find it painful to confront these balances in a questioning way. Consequently, they defend them vigorously and avoid looking at them
squarely.

Inwardly, torn by these disparate goals, patients bring material into the transference that illustrates a complex network of
defenses. It is the analysis of that defensiveness that makes possible productive sorting out of the pathogenic issues and so-
lutions. At the same time, analysts try to identify the salient
features of the object relationships that make up their patients'
psychic realities. How the patients cope with these internal relationships is another valuable source of understanding; indeed,
its study cannot be distinguished from the analysis of defense.
The patient must be helped to stay with these painful internal
experiences long enough and with enough cognitive and emotional presence to take responsibility for the understanding
being developed in the analytic work. Only then can the patient's
anxieties about the consequences of change be worked through
effectively.

So Betty Joseph argues in this essay. It is perhaps this one that
epitomizes the insights and technical methods she presents
throughout her valuable collection of essays, *Psychic Equilibrium*

393

and Psychic Change (1989). Once termination is being considered or provided for, the analyst must continue to pay the closest attention to moment-to-moment changes of equilibria in each session, especially as these become manifest in the transference. Centering on long-range, global assessments of change at that time is likely to be counterproductive.

Both in her general discussion and in her clinical examples, one of which concerns a patient beginning to move toward termination, Joseph takes up the defenses of splitting, projective identification, introjective identification, and varieties of narcissistic phantasies of omnipotence. She shows how these defenses may be reasserted with special force as termination approaches and yet be relatively quickly reversible on the basis of previous working through.

REFERENCES

Joseph, B. (1989), *Psychic Equilibrium and Psychic Change*, ed. M. Feldman & E. Bott Spillius. London: Routledge.

17
PSYCHIC CHANGE
AND THE PSYCHOANALYTIC PROCESS

BETTY JOSEPH

There is some ambiguity about our use of the term psychic change. We sometimes use it to mean any kind of change in the mental state or functioning of our patients, sometimes we use it to mean a more long-term durable and desirable kind of change. In this paper I want to consider both uses of the term and their interrelationship.

One of the main points that I want to make here is that psychic change is not just an end, a final state, but is always going on in treatment, and that we as analysts need to be able to find and follow the moment-to-moment changes in our patients, without concerning ourselves as to whether they are positive, or signs of progress, or of retreat, but seeing them as our patients' own individual methods of dealing with their anxieties and relationships in their own unique way. Otherwise we cannot hope to help our patients to achieve real, long-term positive psychic change as a result of treatment. If we get caught up in preoccupations about whether the shifts show progress or not, and look for evidence to support this, we may become enthusiastic for

This paper was first presented as a Public Lecture of the British Psycho-Analytic Society in November 1986.

what we feel to be progress or disappointed when there is apparent regression. We shall find that we get thrown off course and unable to listen fully, or we may well bring unconscious pressure on our patients to fit in, to comply with our felt wishes, our needs; or our patients may just feel misunderstood.

Indeed, our capacity to listen fully and stay with our patients must help them increasingly to be able to observe, tolerate, and understand their own habitual ways of dealing with anxiety and relationships, and this is part of the process of changing these habitual ways and becoming what we could call psychically more healthy. However, although we need, I am suggesting, to be able to stay with and to follow our patients' own ways of dealing with their problems, we do have in our own minds ideas, theories, about desirable long-term psychic change, which I want to discuss in a moment.

First, it is important to look at our patients' attitude to change. Patients come into analysis because they are dissatisfied with the way things are and they want to alter, or want things to alter. There is a desire for change and pressure toward greater integration; without it analysis would fail. And yet there is a dread of change. Unconsciously they know that the change that they ask for involves an internal shifting of forces, a disturbance of an established mental and emotional equilibrium, a balance unconsciously established of feelings, impulses, defenses, and internal figures, which is mirrored in their behavior in the external world. This balance is maintained by very tightly and finely interlocked elements, and a disturbance in one part must reverberate throughout the personality. Our patients unconsciously sense this and tend therefore to feel the whole process of analysis as potentially threatening. This is, of course, essentially linked with Freud's ideas on resistance.

For example, a patient whose balance depends largely on maintaining a highly narcissistic structure will be unable to let us help properly or to take in our interpretations, and, for example, will tend to take them over or repeat them intellectually or alter them. When we are able to get through this momentarily we may see a sudden flash of anger, but this anger disturbs the balance and is therefore immediately intolerable to the patient and a new shift takes place and the balance is reestablished. Why such anger is so intolerable at this stage we cannot tell. Is it felt to be so cruel or does it cause so much guilt or humiliation and is this so unbearable, and, if so, why? These issues will have to be teased out over time.

Another patient's basic method of keeping his equilibrium may be more obviously phobic, with anxiety defended against by various avoidances, self-limitations, and related defenses. With some patients passivity and a kind of inertia in response to movement or change, may be more obvious. But what I am stressing here is not just the obvious point, that all our patients use different defense mechanisms, but that the interlocking of their defenses is so fine that shifts in one area must always cause disturbances in another, and that a major part of achieving psychic change lies in our trying to unravel within the analysis the various layers and interlockings so that they may be reexperienced and opened up within the transference. This opening up and reexperiencing within the transference, with all the shifting of balance that this implies, is part of psychic change (this changing is going on all the time within the analytic process), so that moment-to-moment shifts and change is what we are analyzing all the time, and is the stuff that we hope is eventually going to lead to long-term positive psychic change. I do not think that the latter long-term psychic change is ever an achieved absolute state but rather a better and more healthy balance of forces within the personality, always to some extent in a state of flux and movement and conflict.

To return now to the issue of what we are hoping to achieve in long-term psychic change—Freud in various places discussed the aims of analysis, which includes, of course, the question of

change. I am not attempting to consider his ideas, only to indicate that he put much stress on making the unconscious conscious, and on the idea that he expressed succinctly as, "Where
id was, there ego shall be." He implied in that statement not
only making impulses conscious, but making them available to
be used by, and under the control of, the ego. The notion of
greater integration between ego and impulses, love and hate,
superego and ego, runs through his work especially in the
middle and later years.

Melanie Klein, following on Freud's thinking, worked out in
great detail the problems that the individual meets with in his
attempt to achieve greater integration, and her ideas are fundamental to our understanding of psychic change today. She described what she called two positions, and by *positions* she meant
a configuration of impulses, defenses, anxieties, and relationships to objects which she called the paranoid–schizoid and the
depressive positions. In the paranoid–schizoid position she saw
that the individual, or infant, attempts to deal with anxiety
caused by painful or conflicting feelings and disturbing parts
of the self by splitting them off and projecting them into other
objects, people, and thus relieving himself of them. She stressed
how this is a normal mental state in a young infant and that it
colors what he feels about his objects, as it does in older children and adults who continue to operate in this way in later life.
Thus the individual who splits off his rage, for example, and unconsciously in phantasy projects it into his nearest object, will
feel that object as hostile, will tend to withdraw, or to fight it.
Further, the way that the infant experiences objects is, of course,
fundamental to the way he takes them into his inner world, to
the building up of his ego and his superego and the way he relates to people. It is only as the infant develops over the early
weeks and months and splitting and projection lessen, that he
begins to be increasingly aware that his impulses are his own and
he is then able to bear both his love and his hate at the same

time and toward the same person. His perception of human beings then becomes more real, more human, and they can be introjected and identified with as such. This step, or rather, minute series of steps, forward and backward, toward integrating love and hate, brings with it momentous changes within the personality. Guilt and concern emerge. Once the individual starts to recognize and take responsibility for his own impulses and for what he has done in fact or in phantasy to his object, then guilt for this is inevitable, but also there opens up the possibility of feeling for and repairing the object. With this there is also relief and a deepening of emotions.

I have naturally described these positions in a somewhat schematic way. I am trying to convey that the problem that every individual has in his own development, in relating to people as they really are, in coping with his own feelings and phantasies, and dealing with the pain of guilt that arises from them, all these problems will necessarily emerge again in the analytic treatment, and the analysis gives the individual the opportunity to rework them in a different way.

But it is more than that. There are shifts toward taking more responsibility for one's impulses, or away from it; the emerging of concern and guilt, and the wish to put things right, or going into flight from it. There is the awareness of part of the personality, the ego, feeling able to look at and struggle with what is going on and face anxiety, or starting to deny it. These movements are the very stuff that is inherent in our understanding of psychic change and will emerge being lived out minutely in the transference, if we are able to follow the shifts. This is, in fact, psychic change.

As part of this process we see changes in our patients' object relationships, in the way that they see, feel, anticipate, and remember people. If there were not changes in object relationships, both external and internal, there could be no real changes in the ego and vice versa. For example, a patient felt he had altered a lot in relation to his parents, things were much better since his previous therapy, which I am sure was so. Nevertheless, from the beginning of his treatment with me, I felt that there was a lack of real strength and masculinity. In the analysis, he would constantly, unconsciously, take back any doubt or criticism, reassure me that I was right, and behave in a way that was oversmooth and vaguely seductive in the broad sense of the word. At first it appeared as if he felt me unconsciously as someone unable to tolerate anger and criticism and needing reassurance, which was not his conscious picture of me. Later we learned that one picture he had of his mother was of a person who was especially fondly attached to him, subtly influencing him to agree with her and with her criticisms of the father. We have, therefore, a number of elements here that need to be teased out in order to achieve real psychic change. There seems to be a projective identification of his own fear of his aggression into the object, myself, so that I am felt to be a timid person, mother, who needs reassurance, and he introjects this object into himself. There seems to be a relationship to mother, who may well have been rather seductive with her son, although we do not know how much this picture is built up from projections, and with whom he is in collusion and has partially identified with. There seems to be a need to control me by agreeing with me, slightly seducing me, and becoming at times my favorite patient-child, at times my near equal, in our thinking.

All these elements and many more will need to be teased out as they recur and shift in different forms and with different motives, before he will really be able to relate to me as a more real object, and be able to introject and identify with a stronger and firmer object, which should help in the development of a more real masculinity. Thus, when we are talking about psychic change in relation to objects, we are considering the importance of our patients being able to withdraw their projections, take more responsibility for their own impulses, and, alongside this, their being able to face the separateness of their objects, and the state of their objects, in a sense, the reality of their objects, and the reality of their feelings toward them—their own psychic reality.

In order to look further at some of the problems that we have been talking about, change and antagonism to and fear of change, and the process of change, I shall bring some brief examples. I shall bring, first, material to show changes that took place during or between two sessions and how the picture of the analyst and the patient's self shifts, and then discuss something of the mechanisms involved. Then I shall try to discuss changes going on in the transference as a response to analytical interpretative work.

First I want to discuss a dream from a basically phobic man, C, who came to analysis with a great wish to change but who, as I discussed at the beginning, showed a very deep fear of inner disturbance and very rigid defenses. He had recently increasingly been able to become aware of problems going on in people around him, of their difficulties or their illnesses, and had even started to allow himself to enquire a little into them—even to become aware of his triumph over sufferers, so that the analysis seemed to be helping him to open his mind where he would previously have remained shut into his own world and closed off from other people. During the early part of the week with which we are concerned he had told me how disturbed and invaded he had felt by so many people around apparently being in a bad state— a colleague admitted to mental hospital, another man who had become suicidal, somebody else whose marriage was breaking down. Such things would somehow have passed over him before. The following day he came to a session and brought a dream.

In the dream C had gone to the doctor with a sore throat. The doctor examined him and said it was due to stones in the bladder. He understood by stones, minute ones like gravel. But the doctor said they could be operated on not by cutting but by the use of an endoscope which would apparently suck them out of the urethra. The patient asked would it be very painful. The doctor said yes, if they didn't use an anesthetic, but an anesthetic would be used. C thought he had better get a second opinion. The doctor then seemed to go mad. He came around his desk in a menacing way and started digging something into my patient's groin, saying it would hurt as much as that!

I shall give some associations rather briefly. C had had a slight sore throat the previous day. About the endoscope: his father when old had prostate trouble and was told that it could be dealt with, without surgery, in some way like in the dream. The father, however, had become very anxious, postponed the operation, and died before it actually became necessary. C then started to link the dream with his son's dental problems, the dentist had said that the boy needed to have two teeth removed for a brace to be fixed. C thought that this was excessive if it was just for cosmetic purposes, and that he himself should go and see the dentist and if necessary get a second opinion. There had been a mention of second opinions the day before concerning the colleague who had been admitted to a mental hospital.

I reminded C that his son had himself had three operations on his penis for a congenital deformity. (I had always felt that C very much denied the importance of this to the boy.) C was upset to realize that he had failed to connect this with the operation in the dream. What we also knew was that C had had a better education and gone further in his life than his parents, and his father had been in some ways dependent on him as he grew older. Indeed, when his father lost his job, C found him some rather lowly work in the firm in which he himself was employed in a comparatively senior capacity.

What I particularly want to show in this material is the change that we can see taking place during or between the two sessions, manifested in the dream; changes both in his way of facing, or not facing, impulses and anxieties, and in the nature of his objects, and how this latter takes place.

In the previous session C had been better able to open his mind, be curious and look at what was going on around him (and, I suspect, but am not discussing here, what was going on inside him as his balance shifted). He had been able to think about the various breakdowns, but felt invaded by them; and, as I suggested, had been able to tolerate up to a point feelings of triumph and excitement over the people who were breaking down. This meant that he had been able to put some trust in me, as we see at first in the doctor in the dream. Then there is a shift. He begins to think about a second opinion, as if turning with hostility against the trusted object. The doctor goes mad, as if he, the doctor, could not stand the doubts, and we see in this a projection of the patient's own inability to stand self-doubts and feelings of rejection, or stand pain after a certain point. Then there is the nature of the madness—I think that for C interest and curiosity are so much linked with crazy excitement and triumph that they have to be got rid of. They are projected into me, so that, instead of my remaining a dispassionate, helpful analyst, I become the doctor who does not just examine him, but becomes madly, excitedly invasive, digging hurtfully into his groin. Then there is the issue of how much pain near guilt, he can bear. I think C's triumph over his suffering colleagues has become linked with his old unconscious triumph over his own father and his current concern about his son. He can tolerate pain up to a point and then it becomes too much. Instead of tolerating it, he introjects his object, here the father-son, and suffers his operation, his pain. C's way of dealing with these various anxieties and parts of his mind is to fragment them into bits like gravel and evacuate them. In these various ways mental pain is avoided and he is anesthetized.

In C's case we can see a patient who consciously really wants to change, but is caught up in the paranoid–schizoid position with much splitting and projective identification. He makes brief sorties toward trying to make contact with his own feelings and parts of his self that he usually keeps split off, and then retreats again in the face of anxieties. But for brief moments now, a part of the ego can stand outside and actually help to investigate what is going on inside himself. In terms of psychic change I think it is most important that the analyst should search out the part of the ego that is able from moment to moment to take responsibility for the patient's own insight into his impulses, even though that part may quickly be lost again. For long-term psychic change, and for thinking about the ending of an analysis, the strengthening of this part of the personality is, I am sure, fundamental, and is, I think, based on a healthy and comfortable identification with the analyst and the analytical process. It is quite different from a constant self-conscious self-questioning which may have more masochistic roots, or a constant need to have theoretical analytical ideas about self and others, which may be more associated with narcissistic and omniscient attitudes.

I have now discussed something of the nature of psychic change and have given brief examples of change talking place, within and between sessions in C, leading to some regression. Now I would like to look briefly at change taking place within a session from moment to moment. It would, of course, only be possible to consider this convincingly if we could follow the session in much greater detail than is possible in a brief paper like this. So I intend just to look at a small piece of one session.

I am stressing that changes in a session mirror the changes that are taking place within the patient constantly in his everyday living as anxieties emerge, defenses are mobilized, the picture of the analyst shifts, and the inner world shifts accordingly. Interpretations, of course, play a very major part in stimulating this change, partly because they give understanding and insight, but not only this. They frequently stimulate change not in the way we intended, not the way we were thinking. What we say may arouse anxiety, or ease anxiety; our speaking may reassure our patient that we understand or concern ourselves with him; our interpretations may be right but arouse rivalry; or wrong and then reassure him for the wrong reason. Our words may cease to have the meaning that they have to us and become like a tune that the patient can lull himself with or a gloomy bog into which he can sink. All this becomes part of the movement that is going on in the session as we are trying to understand our patients.

I am going to bring shortened material from a session of a patient at a time when the ending of the analysis was under discussion. The result of treatment, so far, in view of the nature of the patient, seemed quite encouraging, though far from perfect. He had come as a very schizoid, passive man, who, by now, was happily married, positively enjoying life, and much more thoughtful and concerned and confident as a human being. Before actually giving the material, I should add a general point about it. Of course it is deeply influenced by our planning the ending of the treatment, and you will see how this was, almost certainly, in itself bringing up a great need to protest, to go backwards, and mobilize old defensive retreats. It needs to be kept in mind from this angle, as well as from the detailed movement in the session. But it is on the latter that I particularly want to concentrate here.

The session was on a Friday. My patient, N, arrived saying that he felt bad and anxious as if too much was going on. He and his wife were currently selling their house and there were important changes going on in his work. I clarified that it seemed that the anxiety was more focused round the issue of stopping the analysis. This he agreed but went on to describe in detail his feelings of discomfort, as if he were angry and resentful. I thought at that point, and suggested that it was partly that he had not really been able to believe that I could let him go, but that now he was having to face this aspect of stopping. (This patient had for a very long time lived in the belief that he was the very special child of his mother, he was in fact the youngest of the family; and he believed that he was my very special patient, and from this angle alone the idea of stopping treatment had been very difficult to accept.)

My patient responded, however, to my remark by going back to discussing his difficulties, his resentment, his coldness. I thought, and showed him, that he was sinking into a kind of anger and misery, shown by his settling into and stressing all the difficulties and getting caught up into it, in order to avoid the specific feelings about actually leaving and what it really meant to him at that moment. In other words, I thought that he was sinking into a kind of bog of misery as a defense, so that the anger was part of the bog and was not anger in its own right.

N became silent—a pause—and then he said he had the thought "clever old bag." He explained he thought I was right and that he was aware when he made that remark that he resented my being right, so he went quiet. Now we could both agree about the misery, being used actively as a kind of masochistic defense, and he himself had clear insight into his resentment about my being right.

N went on to talk about this and how when I had first spoken about the defensiveness and he went quiet, he felt he was taking over what I was saying and, as he put it, "putting it into a box." I discussed with him the way he had not quite been able to acknowledge that I was right, and that he was grateful, and how this very awareness stimulated rivalry and envy. Clearly by now his mood had changed and he was talking freely. N went on to say that he had now gone off at a tangent. He was thinking about yesterday. They had been invited to the X's where the wife is a very poor cook, so his wife had a brilliant idea. She would offer to make a summer pudding, which the patient just adores, and they could take it with them to the supper. He would help his wife by topping and tailing the fruit. This was said in a very positive and warm way.

Here it was clear that N was describing a movement, that he had now got into contact with a good experience again, with a feeling that there was a good smell and a good taste about, and appreciation of what I had been able to see and what he really deeply knew about the analysis. Also there was awareness that he could help to get hold of these feelings and get the analysis consolidated, as is shown by his telling about helping his wife preparing the fruit.

I shall leave the description of the to-and-fro of the session at this point and only add that toward the end of the session N talked about a feeling that he had had about analysis, how he thought that not only he, but he believed, I, the analyst, must have some special feelings about his leaving and about our work together. I think that we can see the shift in my patient's feelings during the session. At the beginning he was largely sinking into a bog of mindless misery, by the end he was well in contact with very moving feelings of loss and contact with myself.

We can see here how this patient, though moving toward the ending of analysis, is not in a state of achieved change, but still in a state of psychic changing in which the positive gains and increased flexibility are now very clear. I want to look briefly at some of the shifts as see them in the session; we can see the movement, after interpretations, out of the bog of verbal misery, so that very soon insight is available. In the old days N would get caught up for sessions, dragged down by and almost wallowing in masochistic misery. Here with insight appreciation emerges, even though ambivalently so, and I become the "clever old bag," and he files away what I have said. At this point his envious resentment is obvious, but is limited. It indicates an important piece of integration since this awareness of naked envy came very late in the analysis and can now be felt by my patient quite clearly and not too strongly. The shift that is indicated by the "brilliant idea" of the summer pudding, with which he will help, shows not only appreciation again, but a capacity for sensual and emotional enjoyment, strikingly missing throughout much of this patient's analysis and life, also the enjoyment and appreciation is on a symbolical level (the good food with its lovely taste and smell); and the capacity to help make it is there in contrast with his old tendency to retreat into gloomy passivity.

It is also important to see the shift in this patient's notion of being special. Through much of N's analysis he had maintained an omnipotent superior picture of himself in relation to his mother, his place in the family and clearly in relation to myself. This slowly altered in the analysis and here we see a picture of myself as a person who must, after this long analysis, have some unique feelings about him and my work with him, as we could assume every healthy mother must have with each of her children. This sense of his being special and unique had a warmth and concern which was completely lacking in the old omnipotent narcissistic phantasies of being special.

I have brought this material to indicate very briefly the kind of moment-to-moment change that one sees going on in the ordinary analytic session as part of the analytic process. In this way we have the opportunity to see hopes, anxieties, defenses, phantasies, and relationships emerging in the transference and shifting according to the patient's own pathology, stimulated by the analytic situation and interpretative work. I think that one of the main aims in our therapy is to work with such shifts, to enable them to happen less blindly and automatically, to make them and their elements more conscious and more manageable to the ego in a more healthy, flexible, and realistic way, and thus to achieve a change in the balance. If we were to believe that we could eliminate them, we would really be encouraging splitting.

I have tried to indicate some of our aims when we are considering long-term psychic change, in terms of movement toward and into the depressive position; in terms of greater integration of the self and a more whole and realistic relation to objects. I have suggested that long-term psychic change is based on, and is a continuation of, the constant minute shifts and movements that we see from moment to moment in the transference, and like all manifestations of conflict it can never be ended.

EDITOR'S INTRODUCTION TO
THE CHILD IN THE ADULT:
THE CONTRIBUTION OF CHILD ANALYSIS
TO THE PSYCHOANALYSIS OF ADULTS

From Melanie Klein's groundbreaking work in the 1920s on the analysis of children there flowed many creative ideas that have remained basic guides to present-day Kleinian analysts. In their publications, these contemporary Kleinians sometimes feature examples of their refinements of Melanie Klein's work with children. Consequently, this book would be incomplete if it did not include some discussion of child analysis per se. The present essay provides an excellent albeit brief overview of the contemporary approach to child analysis, and it does include carefully and vividly described sessions drawn from the analysis of a 4-year-old boy (see also chapters 1, 4, 13, and 14 for other examples drawn from child analysis).

Robin Anderson's discussion of his material ranges beyond just this overview and clinical example. He goes on to develop an enlightening comparison of child and adult analysis. In that comparison he shows how the child's play sessions are paralleled by the adult's largely verbal, though also gestural and attitudinal productions. He argues that, because each adult brings an internal world to the consulting room, he or she will enact the internal child through the verbal and other means of communication used in the sessions. Analysts familiar with child analysis are bound to see a more subtle and perhaps less raw version of the child's inner world in the adult's productions. To bring this point home, Anderson also presents illustrative material

411

from the analysis of a man. His particular choice of this patient provides an added bonus for the reader in that it concerns the same male patient Anderson presented in chapter 9, above, only now we encounter some fresh material on this man and also enriched insight into him.

Robin Anderson's account of his two cases in this chapter is again graceful, graphic, and candid. Especially important, I would say, is his demonstration that by becoming able to put to use his countertransference responses to the destructive components of transference, he could arrive at analytically helpful interpretations. His interventions showed the patients that he had kept possession of his mind and that he could stand fast against their onslaughts. The effect was to help these patients experience the analyst as hopeful as well as safe. In this way, he broke into their vicious circles of violence giving rise to guilt which in turn gives rise to further violence as a defense against unconscious phantasies of guilt and persecution.

Although his essay does not highlight the concepts of projective and introjective identification, containment, and depressive reactions to loss, his exposition makes it plain that these contributed significantly to the armatures around which he shaped a number of his effective and empathic analytic interventions. Here again the reader may find it a helpful learning experience to review Anderson's material to tease out the indications of the important roles played by these various dynamic features.

Anderson brings home to the reader a truth that too often can get lost in encounters with the complex subterfuges and manipulations worked out by adult ego functioning; for there is a child in the room always, no matter whether the patient's chronological age is that of a child or an adult. Interpretation should somehow reflect the analyst's knowledge that that is so. I would add that, in view of the typical Kleinian careful attention to countertransference, note must also be taken of a second child in the room: the child in the analyst, still alive in unconscious phantasy even though, under good conditions, not nearly as desperate and dominant as the child in the adult patient. The child in the analyst is, in the end, a source of useful understanding of shifts in the emotional atmosphere of the analytic relationship.

18

THE CHILD IN THE ADULT: THE CONTRIBUTION OF CHILD ANALYSIS TO THE PSYCHOANALYSIS OF ADULTS

ROBIN ANDERSON

I would like to begin this discussion with some brief comments on the nature of child analysis in comparison with adult analysis. I, like many child analysts, hold the view that analysis of children *is* psychoanalysis in the fullest sense, and it is simply that the setting is modified to take account of the child's need to communicate through the medium of play. However, analyzing children places many demands on the analyst which are more extreme and severe than work with most adult patients. It is often necessary to be able to process complex material quickly—to be able to "interpret under fire," as Bion described it. To do this, the analyst is required, often very rapidly, to observe manifest behavior, to consider personal feelings and their possible relevance to the child's behavior, to come to a view about the underlying meaning of this in the child, and to respond by interpretation, sometimes simultaneously with some physical restraint of the child. Melanie Klein's contribution to psychoanalysis was very profoundly influenced by her work with children. In her paper on the play technique (1955), she says:

My contribution to psychoanalytic theory as a whole derives ultimately from the play technique evolved with young children. I
do not mean by this that my later work was a direct application
of the play technique; but the insight I gained into early development, into unconscious processes and into the nature of the
interpretation by which the unconscious can be approached, has
been a far-reaching influence on the work I have done with older
children and with *adults* [p. 122, emphasis added].

I have always been impressed by the accessibility of child analytic material to nonchild analysts, and yet the superficial characteristics of the setting are so different. But once we see adult
material as consisting of a constant process of action through
words, that it is not so much that children are like little adults
in their analyses, but rather that adults in analysis continue to
be children, then it is not so mysterious. There is a sense in child-
analytic material that a veneer of adult respectability, civilization,
is not present; and although it often makes for a very uncomfortable time, I think it is useful psychoanalytically to be that
much nearer to the unconscious. I think that this sense of raw-
ness allows the gestalt of the underlying object relations to become more visible as it allows the transference to stand out in
relief.

We try to be sensitive to the moment-to-moment shifts during the session in all our patients, and to see what the patient is
doing to us, or attempting to do to us, in the session.

The analyst, therefore, now takes a view of the patient's
material from many different perspectives, often using the
countertransference as a guide. It may be that there is a sense
of a patient who is bringing material and wanting an interpretation in the ordinary sense. But it may be that in the name of
free association the patient is throwing water at us, getting us
to chase round the room after him, and attempting to discon-
nect our thoughts and confuse us. If one has found oneself
doing these things literally, concretely, in child analysis, and

has had to think about what is going on, it becomes easier to see this kind of acting in in our adult patients. It is not that such activity by patients is an interference in our work, any more than the classical resistance was an interference in classical analysis as Freud originally thought it was. Rather, it is in this way that the patient's internal world becomes visible to us. For some borderline and narcissistic patients, it is the *only* way they can relate to the analyst. It is by seeing how we are pulled and stirred up, left with unwanted feelings, that we see in an alive way the patient's object relationships as they are now, in the session with us, and to some extent, how they were perceived by the patient in his relationship to his original objects.

I would like to present two episodes in the analyses of two patients, one a man of 30 and the other a boy of 9.

Of course they are different, and their analyses took very different courses, but as I was working with the adult I was reminded very often of child analytic experience, not only the ones that I am presenting here. I felt that the possibility of understanding the adult patient owed much to my experience as a child analyst.

First the adult patient.

He was a very difficult patient, withdrawn, socially isolated, sexually inhibited, and rather paranoid. He often seemed to prefer to nurse grievances rather than try to resolve his difficulties. He described his childhood with a weak, depressed father and a rather cold mother who preferred his younger brother to him. But his descriptions were very incomplete and I never felt I could be certain what the real situation had been. He had made some progress in his analysis and his career had become more successful, but he still felt very isolated and bitter that he had no girl friend.

In working with him, I became increasingly aware of an atmosphere created by his way of relating to me which had a powerful effect on me, and on himself too. I would like to illustrate this by bringing some fairly typical material.

He arrived a few minutes late for a Monday session, looking rather gray and unsmiling. He began:

> The weekend was awful. What could anyone expect, as I have no girl friend. Without a girl friend there isn't really any point to anything. I did almost nothing—all the things I had intended to do, like studying, producing food for the party, cleaning my flat—none of them. I haven't seen anyone except my parents . . . how devastating to be in my thirties and only have my parents to go and see . . . they have so much to answer for—to have been treated so terribly as a child and with such a cold mother. Then my father spoke about the homosexuals at his hairdresser, and I knew by the way he spoke that he just can't cope with homosexuality. . . . Anyway, what's the point in coming here. You can't deal with my problems. I think you're not up to it. In fact, if it wasn't for the fact that I know you give lectures I would be absolutely convinced that you aren't capable of working with me. I don't know whether I'm too much for you, or my case is just too difficult. . . .

And so it went on, in an all-too-familiar unfolding of a kind of commentary which I would try to relate to, to work with, and think about the ideas. Yet I knew from experience that this did not really arise from someone who wanted the situation to be any different, or indeed had any idea that it could be. And yet the notion that he was feeling hopeless and wanted to be understood did not seem right either. The sense that he wished to nurse this aggrieved state felt nearer the mark and aroused some counterindignation in me. And yet I knew too that such an interpretation would not change the situation and would be likely to lead to a sense of two people complaining, an aggrieved patient and an aggrieved analyst.

His way of relating conveyed a sense of lifelessness, a feeling that any goodness was absent and had never been present. But much more importantly, it aroused and created this sense of lifelessness in the room, and this was most disturbing. What was sometimes possible to observe was that what motivated this material was not a wish to convey what was true, but a desire to induce feelings in the object (and, I felt, in himself too) of despair and paralysis. But this was done with such conviction and forcefulness that they became *the* reality for him, and frequently for me too, despite my attempts to resist the pressure. I was at times aware of a kind of relish which this hold over reality gave him, and this provided some evidence of the underlying sadism and violence taking place.

By this activity he locked himself into the object, creating an inseparable couple, united in a kind of loveless sadistic marriage. Listening to his material at such times, did not result in a sense of a patient willing to listen. There was no sense of two people talking and listening to each other. Instead, the analyst was trapped and able only to endure, with no prospect of escape. This kind of experience, an extremely unpleasant one, has occurred to me in a way that felt very similar in the analysis of a child.

John was 4 when he came into analysis with me, having turned his back on his previous development when his older brother was struck down with a chronic, life-threatening illness. Sessions with him had consisted of an endless barrage of attacks against me and against anything that could have any emotional meaning for him. He would literally obliterate all his toys, when possible trying to push the fragments down the sink. After a period of improvement, all sense of progress in his development and in the analysis seemed to be lost. He became consistently hostile, and at times violent, alternating with many occasions of sleeping throughout the session. I began to notice how inhabited by feelings of despair I was, how my interpretations lacked conviction, how it seemed that he and I were trapped in a horrible and hopeless process from which there seemed little prospect of escape. I noticed that I was holding back from attempting to interpret his material for long periods, or doing so in a too diffident way. Looking back over this period, I noted how I had not really noticed the extent of the cruelty toward me, and had suffered it (colluded) rather than face him with it. Once I could become aware of this, and I could come to his sessions in a different state of mind, then his analysis once more began to come to life, as I think is illustrated in the following material.

A SESSION

As usual recently, John is pressing the buzzer continuously, the noise reverberating through the whole house. As I open the door, he is looking up triumphantly at his au pair who has brought him, and she is laughing, but in an embarrassed way. He says (to her), "Oh, sorry, I forgot," but quite insincerely. I remove his hand from the buzzer quite gently, but firmly, and say, "Hello John." At the door of the playroom he asks if I will please wait outside as he has a surprise for me. I agree, somewhat against my inclination. I hear noise that could possibly be striking matches and I open the door. He is not striking matches, and although I cannot see what he is doing I wait before entering the room. When I do go in after about a minute, he has arranged some sheets of drawing-paper on the floor and there is obviously something underneath them. He treads on the paper and then shows me that he has "secretly" crushed some peanut-shells all over the floor. He says nothing to my enquiry as to what the purpose of this is, though I assume I was intended to walk over the paper and make the mess myself as I walked into the room. I am now sitting in my chair and he picks up his own small chair and spins it round fast; then throws it at me with an excited expression on his face. I catch it.

Analyst: I think you want me to feel crushed now. I think I am supposed to feel a real fool for trusting you when we probably both knew that you would play a trick on me. That made you feel you had weakened me and then you feel excited and everything spins out of control.

John: By the way, I'm not coming tomorrow, am I? Well, I can't come on Saturday. [I had had to cancel the session for the following day and had arranged an extra one for the following Saturday.] My mother says she can't manage to bring me then as she is going out. So I'm sorry about that.

I do not know if he is telling the truth or not. He sounds sincere, but the mood of the session is so against this that I rather suspect this is another trick.

John then takes a piece of string and gets me to hold one end, while he holds the other.

Analyst: I think you want me to hold onto that story whether it's true or not.

John then holds the string tight and plucks a note on it, wanting me to listen. Then he asks me to do the same, which I do. Then he speaks down the string, getting me to do the same. He expresses disappointment that words don't travel down the string.

Analyst: You are showing me that you would like to be able to be in contact with me but it seems that it can't be in words; they don't seem to get through. I think you are saying it only seems that we are really in contact when you have an effect on me, say by tricking me and seeing how I react to that.

John gets down, takes the string, makes a loop on the end with which he tries to lasso me. Then he gets onto a chair.

John: It was a trick. I can come on Saturday really. . . . This is a boat and I'm looking for a firm post to hook onto so I can pull myself in.

Analyst: I think you feel that when I take a firmer hand with you I seem stronger to you. That makes you feel more hopeful about being rescued and you can speak straightforwardly to me. And you can allow there to be a Saturday session.

John was communicating with me from the beginning of the session, but there was a change. At the beginning of the session he was intent on doing something *to* me: to fill me with irritation at his use of the buzzer; to make me feel tricked by agreeing to trust him by waiting outside the room, and have the messing up of the room. When I could interpret his wish to demoralize me, and by doing so show him that I was still able to feel hopeful about my work, I believe he could then recover and manage to engage in a more constructive way, in which the analysis is used for communication; and his wish to trick me lessens, as in his telling me that he can come on Saturday.

> John hitches the boat up to one of the taps and pulls the chair up to the sink. Then he gets down and ties the other end to the arm of my chair. He then climbs onto the string, saying he is going to walk the tightrope. Do I think this will be possible? I don't say anything, and he climbs on the string, which then breaks. The atmosphere changes immediately. He starts to fill the sink up with water and then turns his back on it as it threatens to overflow. As I get up to turn off the taps he says, condescendingly, "Will you turn it off please."

Analyst: You knew the string would break under your weight. When you felt something better was happening, something in you that only wants to be the tightrope star hated that and wanted to break us apart.

John seems quite oblivious of what I am saying, reminding me of the string telephone that won't carry words. He is busy on his own and says, half to himself:

John: What I need is a weight . . . Ah, this will do. (He picks up the small padlock from his toybox and attaches it to one end of the broken string. He whirls it around his head and lets go, seemingly allowing it to fly off at random. In fact it hits me on the shin quite hard. It hurt me and frightened me a little.) "I'm sorry."

He seems to mean this, and yet picks it up; and before I can stop him, lets it fly off again; it hits the wall. I get up to take it from him, but he dashes across the room, grabs it and lies down with it underneath him on the couch. I decide not to grapple with him, but simply to be watchful. I go back and sit down.

Analyst: When you broke the string you lost the feeling that you want me to help you, and I think you're then afraid that I'm not strong enough to stop you and the side of you that gets so excited by battering me and the room.

John looks white and says:

John: I'm tired and I'm going to sleep.

I think it is clear that the moment the contact with me had broken, John's aim was once more to affect me, to have me take responsibility for my own and the room's protection—but utterly despising me for doing that (e.g., his condescendingly telling me to turn off the taps). I understood the whirling padlock on the string as his excitement at relinquishing any responsibility for his own destructiveness and his freedom to despise *me* for doing so. In doing this he was not only attacking his objects, but also that part of *himself* that could, and earlier in the session did, take some responsibility for his destructiveness and wished to be in contact with his object. I believe, though I did not interpret this to him, that the breaking of the string reminded him suddenly of the fragility of his objects and the power of his own destructiveness, and led quickly to a wave of depressive anxiety which was unbearable for him and from which he fled to this defensive denial of concern for himself or his objects. Which, of course, is deeply affected by the actual situation with his brother.

This process of breaking down or breaking off communication and reestablishing it continued for the remainder of the session.

What I am struck with when I compare child and adult material is this sense of vividness which I referred to earlier and which, when one is working with adults with this experience in mind, can be helpful in trying to decipher some of the otherwise obscure phenomena which we encounter in all analytic work.

To return now to my adult patient.

I had found that when I could begin to study the situation I could become aware of an active process at work not unlike what happened with John. This was not only a powerful pressure to control and flatten the analyst, but it seemed to be related to a sense of a damaged object which had to be prevented from having significance for him, because to do so would have stirred up unbearable persecution. Thus I noticed that when I could interpret, firmly but without violence or retribution, he would be very relieved and the atmosphere of the session could change abruptly and profoundly. It seemed as though his tyranny obliterated the possibility of any inquiry into the state of the object, or even any knowledge of it, and in this way operated as a powerful defense against depressive anxiety. But it also produced such additional damage to the object that the resulting guilt induced even greater persecution, so that any real facing of the state of the object and the associated guilt remained an almost insuperable task.

This more overtly violent reaction to a damaged object was illustrated in some later material.

It was the first day back after a Bank Holiday, and I had forgotten to unlock the entry door to my rooms. As a result, the door failed to open when I pressed the lock release, so that the patient was denied his usual "automatic entry," and had to wait until I unlocked the door. I knew that this was likely to cause a reaction—perhaps for several weeks—and in a slightly flustered way I accidentally set off my watch alarm at the end of the session. He seemed somewhat less upset than I had expected, and the next day he brought a dream in which a bumble-bee had got into his home. He had mixed feelings about this bee: on the one hand he hated it and feared it would sting him and should be killed; on the other, that it was trapped and only wanted to be able to follow its natural instincts to get out and pollinate flowers, collect nectar, and breed.

He began to kill it by hitting it repeatedly, but after five or six blows he was surprised to notice that it was more resilient than he had expected. (He described it as "tougher" and therefore less squashable than he had thought.) And he wished he had not started to kill it. But now he had started, he felt he had to continue, because otherwise it would be left injured and he could not let that happen.

The dream seemed to demonstrate how he could not stop his violent, damaging activity, not only because of his sadistic gratification, but just as importantly because he would have to stop and face what he had done; and so he went on with the killing. It may be that what could initiate this process was some sense of an already damaged object, as manifest in this material, by my forgetful and bumbling behavior on that day. Equally, the perception of a more resilient and less squashable object enabled him to bring a dream about the incident and to recover from the episode more quickly than usual.

I think the fact that he could bring a dream about the incident was in itself an indication of some development of a more resilient, and therefore less persecutory, internal object; and this had (to his surprise) survived better over that holiday weekend. At the same time, it revealed his despair at what he felt caught up in and unable to stop. He was confronted by his violent defense against depressive anxiety, the awareness of which pained him and made him have to engage further in this defense. This kind of unstoppable violence is something which I have been very familiar with in child material, including John, and it seems comparable to the situation where a child cannot stop trying to destroy the toys or the room. As soon as he stops the frantic destructive activity he is forced to see what he is doing, the original guilt now being compounded by the additional damage, and so the violent activity designed to obliterate thinking is returned to with renewed vigor. I think that the way in which this is manifest in the bumble-bee material represents an entirely similar process.

Space does not permit me to take this comparison of two cases further, but I hope that what I have presented gives some sense how, amongst the many contributions child analysis makes to adult analysis, the one which I feel cannot really be obtained in any other way is the manner in which the inner world unfolds in such powerful and dynamic ways with children. The sensations are more powerful because children have not yet managed to apply the bandages that adults protect themselves with— "adulthood," "intellectualization," "cooperation," "being a good patient." It is not that work with children is not very difficult, it is just that if we can hold onto our analytic attitude it is more vivid and can help us see similar processes in adults which are more subtle and less raw.

As I work with adult patients, I try to observe the movement between one object and another—to build up a three-dimensional experience of objects relating to each other. I use my observation, and especially my countertransference, to do this. Sometimes I am aware of direct links with child-analytic experience, sometimes more general ones. What is always there as a background experience is a child in a playroom constantly on the move, now playing, now with toys, now role-playing, now trying to get me to act, now talking thoughtfully to me. In this way, child psychoanalysis forms one of the pillars on which my work rests.

REFERENCES

Klein, M. (1955), The psychoanalytic play technique: Its history and significance. In: *Writings*, Vol. 3:122–140. London: Routledge, 1975.

EPILOGUE

I began to pursue my interest in Kleinian psychoanalysis in the late 1950s. A number of circumstances combined to lead me to become aware of numerous biases and idealizations that I had either consolidated or freshly incorporated in the course of studying the extant ego psychological literature. All this took place under the guidance of some strongly influential teachers. I was being indoctrinated to consider Kleinian analysis a wildly speculative system basing itself on inadequate evidence and giving rise to unverifiable interpretations; also, as a mythology or demonology that was taking Freud's already discredited death instinct speculations too seriously and literally. Dutifully, I went even further and concluded that it was a system designed to exonerate mothers from any "real" responsibility for the trials and tribulations of their children, because, as it then seemed to me, the "real" environment didn't really count for much in Kleinian thought; all was instinct-driven phantasy. Furthermore, the early, so-called preoedipal mental activity that the Kleinians emphasized had to be inaccessible to the psychoanalytic method.

I was impelled to reopen all these closed questions partly by my clinical experiences at the Austen Riggs Center and then at the Yale University School of Medicine, Department of Psychiatry. These experiences kept directing my attention to primitive, violent fantasy, and acting out, fears of dependency, extreme uses of projection and introjection, ruthlessly implemented narcissistic needs for omnipotence and guiltlessness, and persuasive transferences and induced countertransference responses. These were the very phenomena that were already well established in Kleinian analytic interpretation. Also, I was increasingly stimulated to question my prejudices and idealizations by the increasing flow of new ideas in the post-World War II Kleinian literature about human relatedness, psychopathology, and clinical technique.

Some of my change began to crystallize in my 1968 book, *Aspects of Internalization*, not, however, without my ambivalence showing. When I moved on to develop my thoroughgoing critique of Freud's metapsychology as establishing an inappropriate language for psychoanalytic discourse and to work out an alternative "action language" in my 1976 book, *A New Language for Psychoanalysis*, and in my 1978 book, *Language and Insight*, I began to see that much of the Kleinian writing on unconscious phantasy about part and whole object relations was couched in the terms of action: self and others doing things to one another and themselves. Or at least, if not that, couched in terms compatible with action language. Although I remained aware of important differences and did not idealize the similarities, my sense of comfort in studying Kleinian clinical work increased greatly.

My change was capped off once I had recognized that action language was easily integrated into an overarching employment of narrational concepts. This narrative-oriented integration seemed to apply both to psychoanalytic theories (as different metanarratives) and to psychoanalytic interpretations (as retelling the patients' accounts of themselves along psychoanalytically regulated narrative lines). Kleinian unconscious phantasy and my "narrations of action" had become, for me, members of the same family of thought. I wrote about some of this change in my *The Analytic Attitude* of 1983 and my *Retelling a Life* of 1992, and I have been going even further in recent writings, some of which appear in *Tradition and Change in Psychoanalysis* (1997).

With my wife, Dr. Rita Frankiel, also an enthusiastic student of contemporary Kleinian work, I have organized some private, clinically oriented study groups in which the two of us and all the other participants could together develop some experience in rethinking case presentations in Kleinian terms. And now this book. We have been encouraging an open-minded approach both to the work of Klein's modern followers and to that of Klein, Bion, and others who laid the foundations of this modern work. Our intentions are not those of missionaries striving for conversions; they are to reopen closed eyes and ears not only to a valuable body of analytic contributions but also to the rich, primitive world of object relational phantasy that so many of our patients seem to require us to attend to and that doctrinaire ego psychological work so often encourages us to ignore. "Conversion" is not at all called for, because the Kleinians are right when they emphasize that they, too, are Freudian analysts, only that they have *also* been developing a number of other major potentials of Freud's basic contributions, appreciation of which they trace particularly to Melanie Klein's insights, and that in some respects they give these insights pride of place.

References

Schafer, R. (1968), *Aspects of Internalization.* New York: International Universities Press.

———— (1976), *A New Language for Psychoanalysis.* New Haven and London: Yale University Press.

———— (1978), *Language and Insight: The Sigmund Freud Memorial Lectures, University College London, 1975–1976.* New Haven and London: Yale University Press.

———— (1983), *The Analytic Attitude.* New York: Basic Books.

———— (1992), *Retelling a Life: Dialogue and Narration in Psychoanalysis.* New York: Basic Books.

———— (1996), *Tradition and Change in Psychoanalysis.* New York: International Universities Press.

NAME INDEX

431

SUBJECT INDEX

Note to readers: The authors of the papers collected herein utilize a number of core concepts frequently and often implicitly and in equivalent terms, sometimes defining them, sometimes illustrating them with clinical examples, and sometimes in generalizing statements. Consequently, to index all these uses would make this subject index unwieldy. They have, therefore, been indexed selectively. Outstanding among these concepts are: Aggression, Ambivalence, Anxiety, Concrete Thinking, Conflict, Containing, Countertransference, Defense, Depressive Position, Destructiveness, Enactment, Guilt, Interpretation, Mourning, Object Relations, Omnipotence, Paranoid-Schizoid Position, Phantasy, Projective Identification, Reality, Splitting, Superego, and Transference.

433